COMICS OF THE ANTHROPOCENE

COMICS OF THE ANTHROPOCENE
GRAPHIC NARRATIVE AT THE END OF NATURE

JOSÉ ALANIZ

UNIVERSITY PRESS OF MISSISSIPPI / JACKSON

The University Press of Mississippi is the scholarly publishing agency of
the Mississippi Institutions of Higher Learning: Alcorn State University,
Delta State University, Jackson State University, Mississippi State University,
Mississippi University for Women, Mississippi Valley State University,
University of Mississippi, and University of Southern Mississippi.

www.upress.state.ms.us

The University Press of Mississippi is a member
of the Association of University Presses.

Any discriminatory or derogatory language or hate speech regarding race, ethnicity, religion, sex, gender, class, national origin, age, or disability that has been retained or appears in elided form is in no way an endorsement of the use of such language outside a scholarly context.

Copyright © 2025 by University Press of Mississippi
All rights reserved
Manufactured in the United States of America

∞

Publisher: University Press of Mississippi, Jackson, USA
Authorised GPSR Safety Representative: Easy Access System Europe - Mustamäe tee 50, 10621 Tallinn, Estonia, *gpsr.requests@easproject.com*

Library of Congress Cataloging-in-Publication Data

Names: Alaniz, José, author
Title: Comics of the anthropocene : graphic narrative at the end of nature / José Alaniz.
Description: Jackson : University Press of Mississippi, 2025. | Includes bibliographical references and index.
Identifiers: LCCN 2025004086 (print) | LCCN 2025004087 (ebook) | ISBN 9781496857743 hardback | ISBN 9781496857736 trade paperback | ISBN 9781496857750 epub | ISBN 9781496857767 epub | ISBN 9781496857774 pdf | ISBN 9781496857781 pdf
Subjects: LCSH: Comic books, strips, etc.—United States—History and criticism | Human ecology in comics | Nature—Effect of human beings on | LCGFT: Comics criticism Classification: LCC PN6725 .A35 2025 (print) | LCC PN6725 (ebook) | DDC 741.5/36—dc23/eng/20250508
LC record available at https://lccn.loc.gov/2025004086
LC ebook record available at https://lccn.loc.gov/2025004087

British Library Cataloging-in-Publication Data available

TO THE MEMORY OF MABEL (2016-2024)
AND
FOR THE YOUNGLINGS:
ALLISON, AMY, CAMERON, JULIA, KALINA,
ROBERTO ROMAN, XENA
DISCÚLPENOS

CONTENTS

Acknowledgments ix
Introduction: "We Are the Asteroid":
   Comics and the "End of Nature" 3

PART I
1. Art, Affect, and the Anthropocene. 21
2. Nature, Comics, and the Mega-Image. 41
3. Comics as Ecological Objects 81

PART II
4. How Many Trees Had to Be *Cut Down* for This Chapter?
   R. Crumb as Ironic Eco-Elegist. 113
5. "Winner Take All!": Children, Animals, and Mourning in
   Kirby's *Kamandi* 139
6. Wakanda Speaks: Animals and Animacy in "Panther's Rage" . . . 159
7. "Death Drive" to Los Alamos:
   Puma Blues as Eco-Male-ancholia. 185
Conclusion: The Pacific Northwest in Words and Pictures 214

Notes 257
Bibliography 291
Index 319

ACKNOWLEDGMENTS

This book burst out of me, displacing other projects for the last five or so years. I hope that urgency comes through in some of the writing.

I want to especially thank Daniel Stein, Eliot Borenstein, and Charles Hatfield for their unwavering support. Theirs are the scholar/*Homo sapiens* examples I try to live up to.

My participation in the inaugural Colby Summer Institute in Environmental Humanities in August 2019 proved catalytic, and I'm forever grateful to the organizers and speakers, especially Stephanie LeMenager.

Also much thanks to my editor at University Press of Mississippi, Lisa McMurtray, and to the stalwart David Lasky for his technical help.

All comics emphases are in the original unless otherwise indicated.

Our beloved first-generation hen Mabel was passing on from this life as the book was in the latter stages of production. I hope my love for her and for all our multispecies family shows through as well.

And finally, like always and forever, I am unworthy of Kristin.

ACKNOWLEDGMENTS

This book burst out of me, displacing other projects for the last five or so years. I hope that urgency comes through in some of the writing.

I want to especially thank Daniel Stein, Eliot Borenstein, and Charles Hatfield for their unwavering support. Theirs are the scholar/*Homo sapiens* examples I try to live up to.

My participation in the inaugural Colby Summer Institute in Environmental Humanities in August 2019 proved catalytic, and I'm forever grateful to the organizers and speakers, especially Stephanie LeMenager.

Also much thanks to my editor at University Press of Mississippi, Lisa McMurtray, and to the stalwart David Lasky for his technical help.

All comics emphases are in the original unless otherwise indicated.

Our beloved first-generation hen Mabel was passing on from this life as the book was in the latter stages of production. I hope my love for her and for all our multispecies family shows through as well.

And finally, like always and forever, I am unworthy of Kristin.

COMICS OF THE ANTHROPOCENE

Introduction

"WE ARE THE ASTEROID"

COMICS AND THE "END OF NATURE"

> Parallel to climate science's tracking of the stresses placed on the environment
> by industrialization, film and media texts trace a cultural history of the
> Anthropocene, charting the ways of living and thinking that have led to this crisis.
> —PETERSON AND UHLIN 144

1982 saw an average global temperature of 0.25 degrees Celsius above historical patterns.[1] Early that year, I picked up from the stands a copy of *Fantastic Four* vol. 1 #240 (Mar. 1982), the latest issue of the storied comics series published by Marvel. It contained "Exodus!" a twenty-two-page epic written and drawn by fan favorite John Byrne (who had recently left Marvel's landmark series *The Uncanny X-Men*). Though my fourteen-year-old self did not think of it in these terms at the time, "Exodus!" was an eco-parable about climate refugees.

The issue opens on a dramatic note, with Quicksilver/Pietro Maximoff, a mutant speedster, come to New York to seek the aid of the Fantastic Four. Distant Attilan, secret homeland of the Inhumans in the Himalayan mountains, is suffering the twin calamities of war and a "mysterious malady" that has felled the Inhumans "by the thousands" (7). Quicksilver, who is not an Inhuman (though he is married to a member of their royal family), seems untouched by the disease, so he has come for help.

The quartet of heroes—Mister Fantastic/Reed Richards, the Invisible Girl/Sue Richards, the Human Torch/Johnny Storm, and the Thing/Ben Grimm—journey back with Quicksilver to the hidden land, to find widescale devastation. Though the war has ended with victory, the Great Hall of Attilan has been converted to a hospital for thousands of ailing Inhumans (11). Reed Richards, one of the world's most brilliant scientists, soon discovers the cause. As he grimly informs Black Bolt, the Inhumans' ruler, the Attilans have "no immunity to the pollutants in the air beyond the Himalayas. But there is no longer anywhere on Earth where the air is truly clean" (12). Or as Mel Chen puts it, environmental toxicity is "already 'here,' already a truth of nearly every body" (218).

However, the Fantastic Four and Inhumans together come up with a solution: They will move the Great Refuge in its entirety to the moon. (A necessary explanation for those unfamiliar with Marvel continuity: Attilan had changed locations through antigravity technology before, and the moon has a "Blue Area" that contains a pristine, breathable atmosphere.[2]) And so, braving "grave risk" and "great hardships" (13), the royal family and the FF prepare the city for its flight: Grimm and Sue Richards plot out the course, the Inhumans Gorgon and Karnak start the process of severing the city from its foundations with powerful blows, and their ruler Black Bolt completes the task with his extraordinarily powerful voice. (In hallowed Marvel fashion, the accompanying text box inserts a facetious editorial commentary: "We're not going to insult your intelligence by placing a *sound effect* in this panel. Believe us, no mere words could convey the awesome noise of *Black Bolt's* single syllable!" [16].[3])

"Like some great winged insect," the city rises higher and higher until it breaks Earth's orbit—a fact not unnoted by other denizens of the Marvel Universe: S.H.I.E.L.D.[4] director Nick Fury puts his satellite on red alert in response to the unidentified object (18), while the ancient alien Uatu the Watcher gazes from afar at his new "neighbors" on the moon (19).

Safely landed in the Blue Area, the refugees disembark: "From every doorway in vast Attilan flows a flood of *life!*" as "*the Inhumans come forth to greet their new world!*" (21). As it happens, the Inhumans' emigration from Earth coincides with the birth of Quicksilver and his wife Crystal's baby (later named Luna). Due to a quirk of genetics, the mutant and the Inhuman's child is born *Homo sapiens*, prompting Richards to quip, "It somehow seems fitting that the first child born on the moon should be so . . . *human!*" A text box that concludes the story chimes in: "*Amen* to that!" (22).

Along with its biblical references to Noah's ark, the flood, and Exodus,[5] this issue of *Fantastic Four* bears troubling implications: Richards's determination of the Inhumans' destiny links it to a long history of "white savior" narratives, while Attilan's unceremonious landing onto the ruins of an ancient civilization brings up problematic notions of colonization and the extirpation of nature (since the colonizers never bother to check whether anything is already living in the Blue Area, and if so, how it might be affected by a huge city-state dropping onto it). Nonetheless, Byrne's narrative reflects Reagan-era concerns about air quality, environmental justice, and the vulnerable position of Indigenous populations on a changing planet. In fact, a realization, similar to one articulated by Bill McKibben later in the decade in *The End of Nature*, that humanity has left no inch of the planet untouched, unaffected, or in some way unpoisoned, drives the plot of "Exodus!":

> Now that we have changed the most basic forces around us, the noise of the chain saw will always be in the woods. We have changed the atmosphere, and that will change the weather. The temperature and rainfall are no longer to be entirely the work of some separate, uncivilizable force, but instead in part a product of our habits, our economies, our ways of life. Even in the most remote wilderness, where the strictest laws forbid the felling of a single tree, the sound of that saw will be clear, and a walk in the woods will be changed—tainted—by its whine. (40)

That a popular mass form like the mainstream superhero comic book would engage with such urgent global concerns, making them thinkable and actionable for young readers in the early 1980s, is only part of why I chose "Exodus!" to inaugurate a study on comics in/of the Anthropocene. Byrne's eco-parable was in fact continuing a trend in the genre exploring environmentalist themes going back at least a decade, while—as I discuss in the next several pages—graphic narrative had long contended with issues of pollution, a changing natural environment, the effects on nonhuman life, and the ecological crisis writ large.

Further, "Exodus!" succinctly demonstrates the unique tools comic art brings to the challenge of depicting the Anthropocene. The immediate hurdle: how to represent the unrepresentable.

The Anthropocene (our current era of human-induced transformation of the environment, from mass extinctions to deforestation to ocean pollution to climate change) resists narration in prose or other text-based media, while visual renderings often risk leaving out crucial context. The subject, argues John Parham, calls "for human perspective to readjust to vast spatial, temporal and existential scales," perhaps lending itself better to graphs, statistics, computer projections, and the like (5–6). However, few nonspecialists will ever engage with such materials.

But look what Byrne does with the theme!

He presents a high-stakes drama of survival, allyship, and resilience in the face of apocalypse. He vividly illustrates how climate change disrupts borders and impacts even the most advanced societies, destabilizing them and compelling migrations and refugee flows on a global scale. No species, not even the biosphere itself, is safe when the environment undergoes radical change beyond our ability to adapt.

Yet the Anthropocene is no monolith, affecting everyone and everything in the same way. Here Byrne's drawings in "Exodus!" serve to convey that idea

The Inhumans, fleeing a polluted Earth, disembark on the moon in John Byrne's *Fantastic Four* vol. 1 #240 (Mar. 1982). © Marvel Comics.

through the astonishing diversity of a species in which individuals differ markedly in size, color, shape, and appearance. The penultimate splash page in which the Inhumans, in all their multifarious splendor, disembark en masse to explore their new lunar home (21) validates Ramzi Fawaz's insight that "the capacity to judge and develop substantive responses to differences is the signal feature of superhero storytelling, which produces countless fictional superhuman beings whose differences in origin, physiognomy, skill, identity, psychology, temperament, origin, and ethical philosophy become the basis for narrating heterogeneous engagements between, and eliciting identification with, aliens, mutants, freaks, and 'inhumans' variously construed" (33). Post–Silver Age superhero comics' utopian ethos of heterogeneity and collaboration helps crystallize the double-sided notion that the Anthropocene affects all collectively, though each individual experiences it in their own unique fashion; the Inhumans literally incarnate that message in "Exodus!" through their suffering, ill, and redeemed bodies—of which no two are alike.

Fantastic Four #240 reflects at least two other key concepts for a discussion of the Anthropocene in the environmental humanities: time and scale. On the one hand, the Inhumans' plight reflects Rob Nixon's ecological "slow violence," which "occurs gradually and out of sight" and whose "delayed destruction . . . is dispersed across time and space" (*Slow Violence* 2). The pollution that threatens Attilan is invisible and insidious, building up gradually, while its effects only come to light once the damage has been done. An environmental hazard that over a longue durée lays low most of a population poses a radical challenge to notions of conventional narrative, linearity, and cause and effect, which may be separated by decades or even centuries in the case of climate change. "Exodus!" makes Nixon's slow violence perceptible by couching it in standard Marvel continuity, which itself unfolds over decades in the real world and in millennia (or more) of story time. Devoted fans of the series would know, for example, that years earlier the Inhuman Crystal, former member of the Fantastic Four, had to leave the team when she herself could no longer tolerate the air pollution in New York City (where the quartet is based).[6] Byrne picks up that narrative strand and expands on it in plausible ways.

Second, "Exodus!" swings wildly between different scales of action. Since we're talking continuity-driven Marvel comics here, these include the interpersonal (the FF, Black Bolt, and the Inhuman royal family, along with their deep histories); the communal (Attilan, with its rather troubling social hierarchies, e.g., those who live in the city and those who dwell beneath, the so-called Alpha Primitives); the planetary (Fury, etc.); and the cosmic/multiversal (Uatu). A similar reorientation away from habitual human-scale concerns to those encompassing such dauntingly vast subjects as the global economy, Earth systems like climate, and other "hyperobjects" (in Timothy Morton's coinage)⁷ is crucial for dealing with the wide-ranging, long-term effects of the Anthropocene. As most famously argued by Amitav Ghosh in *The Great Derangement*, dominant literary modes—which emerged during the age of resource extraction and carbon-based economies—have largely fallen short of that vital task. Along those lines, Erin James has called for the "need to be able to think on two scales at once: on the one hand, thinking about humans as a collective with group agency, but on the other hand recognizing humans as a very nuanced and bifurcated or separated group" (James and Spengler, "(Life) Narrative" 246) so as to equitably address the Anthropocene's disproportionate impact on the poor and disadvantaged. As noted, through word and image, "Exodus!" models such multiscalar thinking, from the migration and survival of an ancient species to arrival of a tiny baby pointing the way to the future.⁸

Indeed, as more and more scholars contend,⁹ the multimodal affordances of comic art offer promising alternatives at an urgent moment when our narrative forms need reconsideration to better grapple with the challenges of the Anthropocene. In these discussions, let me add a word for superheroes.

If nothing else, works like "Exodus!" underscore how popular genres such as superhero comics can bring difficult-to-visualize abstractions (environmental illness, climate-driven migration) into sharper focus through fantastic scenarios and ludicrous solutions (with baggage of their own). In fact, it is precisely the genre's rigid formulae, "flashy" conventions, and tiresome clichés, forged over decades by diverse hands,¹⁰ that make it one of the most accessible on-ramps to discussions of difficult, high-stakes issues like the Anthropocene and how to respond to them. (At any rate, a May 2022 photo-comic supported by the Association for the Study of Literature and the Environment, *Against the Eco-Fascist Creep*, uses stills from Marvel Studio's Avengers films as a vehicle for just such a conversation.¹¹)

Said clichés and formulae are in turn altered by their encounter with a subject as complex as the Anthropocene, which redefines the parameters of superheroics; "Exodus!" has no clear supervillain, unless it's the emissions-spewing human race itself, represented by gawking bystanders as Quicksilver streaks through the New York streets. We only ever see the pollution's effects and symptoms—so there's nothing at which our heroes might direct a punch or a fireball. The threat is everywhere and nowhere, and experienced asymmetrically, depending on one's species. The FF and Inhumans in collaboration have to think their way out of this one, then put into action their risky plan to pilot an entire city to the moon.

Above all, "Exodus!" shows how overcoming a threat of this magnitude requires broad-based solutions, community ties, cross-border cooperation—and lots of privilege. After all, not everyone belongs to an elite hidden Great Refuge created through super-science, nor can most of us call up the Fantastic

Four to help us survive. That said, the story makes palpable (and fun!) the ways in which gradual change over time morphs into real existential threats, reminding readers that hope is not extinguished as long as we work together. As Daniel Stein (channeling Bruno Latour) avers: "Superhero comics are indeed a playground for what makes us all act" (277).

As noted, my fourteen-year-old self remained largely unaware of all this when I paid my sixty cents plus tax and brought this comic home from the Valley Mart in my hometown, Edinburg, Texas, in 1982. I was just enthralled by the story—one of many Byrne produced in his celebrated (and divisive) five-year run on *Fantastic Four*. To the extent I saw a moral, it was something like "friends in need are friends indeed." But something else about "Exodus!" did penetrate my complacent teen mind. There was real terror, I dimly registered, in the possibility that—unlike the Inhumans—we *Homo sapiens* could not easily leave Earth if the environment started killing us. Little did I know that such a fate was already unfolding for ourselves and our sad planet. I would learn soon enough, just as in due time I'd discover that *FF* #240 was far from the first example of comics addressing the death of nature.

In this book I have woven together insights primarily from the environmental humanities, critical animal studies, comics studies, and affect studies for an examination of the representation of animals, mass extinctions, and climate change of the era popularly known as the Anthropocene in (mostly) US comics, predominantly since 1970.

How have artists dealt with the human-caused destruction of the natural world in graphic narrative, how do these representations manifest in different genres (superheroes, autobiography, underground comix, dystopian sci-fi, journalism), and what resources unique to the comics medium do they bring to their tasks? How do these works resonate with the ethical and environmental issues raised by global conversations about our ongoing anthropogenic sixth mass extinction and climate change? How have comics mourned the death of nature over the last five decades? Animated by these questions, *Comics of the Anthropocene* aims to break new ground in confronting our greatest modern catastrophe, through an analysis of how graphic narrative has uniquely addressed the ecological crisis since the first Earth Day.

In part I, I discuss some of the ways the scientific community, the public, and the arts have responded to the Anthropocene, with particular focus on approaches derived from affect theory, before turning to how comics have historically treated the theme. I lay special emphasis on the representation of animals as special cases that situate us as nothing else does within the affective stakes of the problem. I conclude, through ideas introduced by the philosopher Timothy Morton, with a consideration of what makes comics themselves "ecological objects."

THE ANTHROPOCENE BLUES

In the words of one of my students: "The Anthropocene is the era when humans burn down forests with gender reveals."

They were alluding to incidents like one from Labor Day 2020, when a "smoke-generating pyrotechnic device" used during a gender reveal party sparked the El Dorado Fire, which scorched over twenty thousand acres, and one from 2017 in which a Tannerite explosion used to announce the gender of an expected child at another such gathering ended up consuming over forty-five thousand acres in what came to be known as the Sawmill Fire (Morales and Waller).

I do not know if my student meant their statement facetiously, but it does capture something central about Anthropocene discourses in the twenty-first century: a disconnect or lack of interest (here, in fire risk) coupled with obliviousness toward the environment, which brings to mind Richard Louv's "nature deficit disorder." The argument goes that the people who set off those fires regarded the natural settings of their unintended crimes as little more than pretty, Instagrammable backgrounds, a variation of what the anthropologist Heather Anne Swanson has termed the "banality of the Anthropocene."[12] My student's piquant turn of phrase seemed to capture the absurd, tragic zeitgeist all too well.

In 2000, atmospheric chemist Paul J. Crutzen and ecologist Eugene Stoermer proposed "Anthropocene" (from Greek *anthropos* [ἄνθρωπος], "human," and *cene* [καινός], "recent" or "new") as a new geological term for the current epoch of human-induced transformation of the environment, from mass species collapse to climate change, especially since the dawn of industrialization.[13] They intended the designation to draw attention to the degradation of the natural world as a result of *Homo sapiens*' exploitation of land and sea, overpopulation, resource extraction, industrial pollution, fossil fuel emissions, and other staples of modernity. According to these scientists, we had become a geological force, bringing about the planet's sixth mass extinction akin to the one some sixty-six million years ago that wiped out the dinosaurs. (As one scientist put it, "We are the asteroid."[14]) Or in the words of Jennifer Peterson and Graig Uhlin, the concept of the Anthropocene "puts an end to any separation of natural history from human history" (145).

Resistance to the term arose along a number of fronts and across disciplines. For one thing, Crutzen and Stoermer were not geologists, nor did they belong to the International Commission on Stratigraphy, the body responsible for the scientific classification of geological eras. This has strict criteria for the determination of what separates one era from another, chief among them the requirement that a clear trace appear in the geological record. Geologists, who work with far longer periods of time than most humanists, were dubious of the whole enterprise.[15] As Jesse Oak Taylor explains, "In attempting to date the Anthropocene, stratigraphers are looking for the 'signature' of human action, the mark of a single species operating as an agent at the level of planetary systems" (573).

Finding such a "signature" proved rather elusive, sparking another debate: When precisely did the Anthropocene begin? Was it really the Industrial Revolution? Or the emergence of agriculture eight thousand years before? Andreas Malm pins the date to somewhere around 1784, when James Watt patented his steam engine, laying the foundations of the fossil economy (16). Maybe it happened much more recently, in the postwar era, with the detonation of the first atomic bombs and the rise of a voracious consumer culture in the West? (Some dubbed this the Great Acceleration.[16])

Whatever the case, we remain officially in the Holocene epoch (Zhong).

What is also not in doubt—at least for those paying serious attention—is that human beings over the last 250 years or so have had a ruinous impact on species populations through deforestation, pollution of all sorts (air, land, water), and climate change, which has seen a steadily warming trend due to anthropogenic emissions of carbon, methane, and other greenhouse gases; these trap the sun's heat in the atmosphere. As Andrew M. Bauer and Mona Bahn insist, "There should be no doubt that the magnitude of human influence on earth's environmental systems has intensified alarmingly since the Industrial Revolution, and particularly since the 1950s" (33), however difficult it may be to make clear demarcations between periods. Though it remains unratified, the International Geological Congress has debated the term, which in 2019 was affirmed by 88 percent of the International Commission on Stratigraphy's Anthropocene Working Group (Parham 1).[17] Whatever the specialists' misgivings, in the third decade of our doomscrolling twenty-first century, we increasingly live in an era of the "public Anthropocene" (Nixon, "The Great Acceleration"), when the vast global environmental changes mentioned are getting harder and harder to ignore—with or without the involvement of gender reveals.

There's some good news. Westerners today are more keyed in to nature than ever. Environmentalism, first sparked in the Romantic era as a reaction to industrialization,[18] inaugurated in its modern phase by the publication of Rachel Carson's *Silent Spring* (1962) and codified in the US through such landmark Nixon-era legislation as the Clean Air Act (1970), the Clean Water Act (1972), and the Endangered Species Act (1973), as well as the formation of the Environmental Protection Agency (1970), has at least on paper made conservation of our natural resources a national value. (Today, even those who actively destroy nature have to at least pretend to care about it.[19])

More recent years have seen such hopeful trends as the public acceptance of the scientific consensus on human-caused climate change, despite a vocal denialist minority; the 2015 Paris Agreement, obligating its signatories to specific emissions cuts over the next several decades, though too little too late for many; the widespread on-ramping of green energy alternatives such as solar and wind, though fossil fuels remain the predominant norm for Western economies; and environmentalist protest movements demanding more and swifter action, such as Greta Thunberg's Fridays for Future[20] and the UK's Extinction Rebellion[21]—even if many still regard theirs as fringe, extremist views.[22] Even Pope Francis lent his authority to the issue, releasing his 2015 encyclical *Laudato si'* to call for greater care of the natural world; it ignited as much fury as acceptance (see Scammell; Federalist Editors).

Sure, there's good news, but the tortured phrasings of my last paragraph, with all their reservations and qualifications, speak to the fact that, in the final analysis, the industrialized developed world is not doing nearly enough to avert the worst of climate change, biodiversity loss, pollution, and the other evils of modern life. There is no "good Anthropocene," however "keyed in" Westerners may have become toward nature (a term much complicated below).

Trying to keep up as an informed citizen with this ongoing disaster, the major historical event in all our lives, makes for distressing reading. Try this 2020 *Smithsonian* headline on for size: "Humans Wiped Out Two-Thirds of the World's Wildlife in 50 Years."[23] Or how about this tidbit: "Researchers have pinpointed how years of civil war and poaching in Mozambique have led to a greater proportion of elephants that will never develop tusks," this after more than 90 percent of the elephants in that region's Gorongosa National Park were killed by both sides to raise funds to fight a civil war (AP, "Elephants"). Oh, look: pictures of a pregnant orangutan in Indonesia, clinging in terror to the last tree standing after her rainforest home was razed for a palm oil plantation. (Palm oil goes into your shampoo, cosmetics, and biofuel.[24])

And that's just land animals. Let's not get started on Pacific garbage gyres, severe overfishing, coral reef collapse, or rising ocean acidification, shall we? And how about our international community—how is it handling these serious calamities? Surely with all the alacrity and professionalism of characters from a Kim Stanley Robinson utopian novel? Let's check in on the results from COP26, the 2021 climate summit in Glasgow, which is effectively the sole mechanism to bring global warming under control:

> While some countries committed to more ambitious cuts to heat-trapping pollution, many nations did not agree to rein in emissions fast enough for the world to avoid the worst damage from climate-driven storms, heat waves and droughts . . .
>
> The agreement was built from compromises on many fronts, including a last minute effort by India to weaken efforts to phase-out coal. Still, it broke new ground in creating a worldwide consensus to transition away from fossil fuels and to speed up countries' ambitions to cut emissions faster.

As negotiators met in closed-door sessions, thousands of activists filled the streets to remind them the world has less than a decade to get greenhouse gases under control. Emissions need to fall around 45% by 2030 to give the world a chance of limiting warming to 1.5 degrees Celsius by 2100 (2.7 degrees Fahrenheit). Instead, they're expected to rise almost 14% over the next nine years. (Sommer)

This endlessly unfurling screed of gloom starts to resemble "The Fraying Weave," a depressing paratextual column on environmental collapse from the 1980s independent comics series *The Puma Blues* (addressed elsewhere in this book). Corporate greenwashing, liberal half measures, technophilic transhumanism, de-extinction programs, and right-wing demands to preserve the economy for the sake of our "Western way of life" all seem puny, laughable/cryable in their inadequacy as a response when one has read the umpteenth dispatch on, oh, how world bird populations have crashed by 50 percent since 1970 from habitat loss, pesticide use, insect decline, and housecats (doubtless adorable), which slaughter over one billion birds a year in the US (Strycker).

We are the asteroid.

And like that dinosaur-killing rock, we are taking ourselves out right along with everything else on Earth, our only home. As Elizabeth Kolbert sums it up in *Field Notes on a Catastrophe*: "It may seem impossible to imagine that a technologically advanced society could choose, in essence, to destroy itself, but that is what we are now in the process of doing" (189).

How did we get here?

While I don't consider *Comics of the Anthropocene* the ideal forum for deciding such questions, Lynn White Jr.'s controversial essay "The Historical Roots of Our Ecological Crisis" (1967) has influenced many:

> I personally doubt that disastrous ecologic backlash can be avoided simply by applying to our problems more science and more technology. Our science and technology have grown out of Christian attitudes toward man's relation to nature which are almost universally held not only by Christians and neo-Christians but also by those who fondly regard themselves as post-Christians. Despite Copernicus, all the cosmos rotates around our little globe. Despite Darwin, we are not, in our hearts, part of the natural process. We are superior to nature, contemptuous of it, willing to use it for our slightest whim. The newly elected Governor of California,[25] like myself a churchman but less troubled than I, spoke for the Christian tradition when he said (as is alleged), "when you've seen one redwood tree, you've seen them all." To a Christian a tree can be no more than a physical fact. The whole concept of the sacred grove is

alien to Christianity and to the ethos of the West. For nearly 2 millennia Christian missionaries have been chopping down sacred groves, which are idolatrous because they assume spirit in nature. (410)

While some vociferously objected to White's thesis,[26] I find useful how he locates the Western disconnect from nature—the primary culprit for environmental devastation in the Anthropocene—in unconscious ideological processes, a sort of religio-cultural mental inertia inherited from the past. Sadly, this only makes the attitudes fueling the environmental apocalypse all the harder to defuse; many will simply see complex phenomena like anthropogenic climate change and species extinctions as "just the way things are."

Maybe a different name would help?

In fact, scholars have offered alternative designations for this era, largely in the hope it might redress what they see as one of "Anthropocene's" main flaws: its tarring of all humanity with one broad brush of blame for the crisis. Surely in a world where the 85 richest people own as much as the 3.5 billion poorest,[27] we don't all bear equal responsibility? Just who is the "we" in "We are the asteroid," anyway?[28] Such reasoning led historian Andreas Malm to deride the Anthropocene as "an indefensible abstraction" (391).

Hence "Capitalocene," promoted by Malm and Jason W. Moore to highlight the starring role of colonialism and extractive capitalism since the eighteenth century; "Chthulucene," coined by cultural critic Donna Haraway to foreground a radical decentering of the human, interdependence, sym-chthonic, and sym-poetic multispecies stories (see Haraway, *Staying*); "Plantationocene," proposed by a group of environmental humanities scholars to further implicate structures of capitalism in abuses related to forced labor, slavery, and large-scale industrial farming;[29] and "Homogenocene," popularized by historian Charles Mann, which lays stress on the diminution of species diversity since Columbus's arrival in North America.[30] Françoise Vergès puts it most succinctly in their articulation of a "Racial Capitalocene": "Global warming and its consequences for the peoples of the South is a political question and must be understood outside of the limits of 'climate change' and in the context of the inequalities produced by racial capital" (74).

However, these and other alternatives to the standard term are rejected with characteristic contrarianism by philosopher Timothy Morton (the environmental humanities' most original thinker). They defend Anthropocene precisely *because* it "homogenizes" *Homo sapiens*, allowing us like nothing else does to glimpse it as a "species at Earth magnitude" (*Dark Ecology* 24).[31] The Anthropocene concept recognizes humans as a "hyperobject," what Morton calls "massive entities distributed in time and space, in such a way that we can only point to tiny slices of them at a time" (*All Art* 34–35). (Other examples include fossils, capitalism, the unconscious.) As they explain, "The Anthropocene is an antianthropocentric concept because it enables us to think the human species not as an ontically given thing I can point to, but as a hyperobject that is real yet inaccessible" (*Dark Ecology* 25). For Morton, such paradoxes are crucial for starting to understand the era we are living in, as well as our fundamental relationship with an environment we are annihilating as a matter of blithe routine:

> Humans have started mass extinction, but me, little Tim Morton, and little you, didn't do anything. Once again, nothing, nothing that you did, such as starting your car, has had a statistically meaningful effect. Yet billions of car startings and burstings of coal into flame and so on totally have had an effect. There is an uncanny gap between little me and me as a member of what is called *species*. The human species caused global warming, not the octopus species, let's be very clear about that. But species is exactly what we can't point to. I find that I am and I am not human, insofar as I did and did not contribute to global warming, depending on what scale you think I'm on. . . . (*All Art* 24)

The crux for Morton is that alternate terms like Capitalocene or Plantationocene, while useful for political critique, detract from what the Anthropocene foregrounds: the uncanniness of living in an age of profound natural degradation brought about by human beings *in the aggregate*. (In this regard humans are no different from the microbes that may have caused the global warming that led to the end-Permian extinction some 252 million years ago; see Wald). This is not to deny the outsized roles played in this process by petro-corporation executives and the Koch brothers, much less to lay undeserved blame at the feet of indigent laborers who cut down rainforests because they have families to feed. It is simply to underscore the crucial point that to be human today means—like it or not, fairly or not—to participate in a breathtakingly thorough biocide of planetary scope.[32] *We are the asteroid.*

The author Alice Walker, in a 1989 essay titled "Everything Is a Human Being," says something similar:

> The Earth holds us responsible for our crimes against it, not as individuals, but as a species—this was the message of the trees. I found it to be a terrifying thought. For I had assumed that the Earth, the spirit of the Earth, noticed exceptions—those who wantonly damage it and those who do not. But the Earth is wise. It has given itself into the keeping of all, and all are therefore accountable. (662)

The eco-terrorist Jake reminisces in Murphy and Zulli's *The Puma Blues* (1986–89/2015). © 2024 Stephen Murphy and the estate of Michael Zulli.

Our deep cross-border entanglements—ideological, logistical, economic, ethical—what Morton and Walker describe as our unavoidable collective *responsibility* for the Anthropocene, receive explicit attention in Stephen Murphy and Michael Zulli's independent comics series cum graphic novel *The Puma Blues*. I'm thinking specifically of page 93 in a chapter titled (appropriately enough) "Indistinctions," in which the eco-terrorist Jake hears the cry of a loon while snooping around the forested area of the Qabbin reservoir. The page in question shows six panels against a black background, in two loose tiers. The panels are laid out obliquely, with unevenly spaced gutters between them; some of them overlap. The unconventional design evokes what we come to realize is an experience of reverie.

The loon's call "was *very* beautiful, very *sad*," Jake recounts to his lover Ruth in a text box, "reminding me of this *other* bird-call I heard off in the forest once when boating up the Amazon." From one panel to another, we see the background shift from Jake's "real-time" New England woods to an Amazonian rainforest with palm trees. He goes on: "The Amazon, in turn, triggered this other memory, of an Indian felling a tree with a chainsaw." The third panel presents just that: a bare-chested logger with vaguely Indigenous features (partly obscured by a hard hat) slicing into a trunk. "As I stood there in the Qabbin," Jake concludes, "I actually thought I could hear *that* chainsaw devour *that* tree. / But then I realized that the sound was too unwavering . . . / . . . for a chainsaw, and that it was steadily getting louder." The sound effect *RRRR . . .* extends in two lines beneath both tiers, increasing in size as it breaks the bottom border line. The final panel shows the series' protagonist Gavia Immer driving a motorized raft on the reservoir, approaching Jake (Murphy and Zulli 93).

The page visually and thematically links the different actors of the Anthropocene across locales and time zones: the nameless South American peasant, doubtless doing the work of some agri-corporation; the eco-radical Jake, seeking to resist modern "progress" (but still with a carbon footprint); and Immer, the tragic everyman struggling to recover his moral compass in a dying world (and emitting carbon with his vessel's engine). Murphy and Zulli further convey how these figures bleed into each other and the natural setting through a morphing sound effect (loon to chainsaw to motor engine) that engages the reader's auditory as well as ocular sense and subverts distinctions between animal and machine.[33] Above all, this brief moment from *The Puma Blues* subtly evokes what Erin James calls the "conflated temporalities" of "our everyday, 'natural,' nonfictional reality in the Anthropocene" (James, "Narrative" 193). Across scales of time, space, class, race, etc., these men are all *implicated*.

In sum, as regards the utility of the term, the present study will follow Richard Kerridge's lead when he writes: "When it is considered in relation to [other] schools of theory, rather than on its own, the Anthropocene idea can serve as a provocation, challenging people *to accept as much responsibility as possible*, but also to see clearly the relationship between environmental responsibilities and the distribution of wealth and power" (xvi, my emphasis).[34]

It remains for us to acknowledge those who would have us accept *no responsibility*—i.e., the anthropocentrists, whose reactions range from outright denial to "I don't care." As the late columnist Charles Krauthammer rather sneeringly put it in 1991: "A sane environmentalism is entirely anthropocentric: it enjoins man to preserve nature, but on the grounds of self-preservation"—though even by that measure governments/markets have failed, given the very real deleterious effects climate change and pollution have on people. More recently, biological sciences professor Alexander Pyron caused a scandal when he extended Krauthammer's position in an op-ed with such pithy one-liners as "Extinction does not carry moral significance, even when we have caused it" and "Conservation is needed for ourselves and only ourselves."[35]

More worthy of our valuable time are those who do not dispute or minimize the damning evidence but like the "alternate term" contingent argue that our priorities are disproportionate. For example, author and birder Jonathan Franzen groused—to no small controversy—that the environmentalist movement had "fallen captive" to a trendy single issue, climate change, at the expense of others more immediately relevant to declining bird populations in the US, like habitat loss and outdoor cats (16).[36]

For her part, Jenny Price lambastes a primarily white, middle-class US environmentalist movement for failing to acknowledge its own stark failures in the arena of environmental justice:

> If you live in southeast LA, you contribute the least to creating the messes. You benefit least from how we change environments to create stuff and wealth. You suffer the worst of the ultra-toxic consequences where you live, work and play. You generally benefit least from the solutions. And you're castigated for not being virtuous enough.
>
> And environmentalists wonder why you might find environmentalism infuriating. (*Stop Saving the Planet!* 59–60)

Ecocritical and environmental humanities scholars such as Stephanie LeMenager, Stacy Alaimo, Erin James, Anna Lowenhaupt Tsing, Dipesh Chakrabarty, Amitav Ghosh, Kyle Whyte, Donna Haraway, and others continue to explore and debate both the Anthropocene and the cultural/artistic responses it provokes, through such critical frameworks as narratology, transcorporealism (the blurring of bodies and environments)[37] and other variants of new materialism and affect theory. My own study draws in part on these scholars and frameworks throughout.

We will next survey said cultural/artistic responses.

PART I

1

ART, AFFECT, AND THE ANTHROPOCENE

> Reading the news is never the task of a wholly disembodied mind.
> —BLADOW AND LADINO 2

In a very real sense, all culture since the advent of the industrial age is Anthropocene culture, all art Anthropocene art. With extractive technologies leading to widespread use of fossil fuels and their harmful emissions contributing to accelerated climate change; an unsustainable consumption-driven Western lifestyle whose very tempo is dictated by the internal combustion engine; industrial pollution of earth, air, and water on a global scale; mass deforestation, ocean acidification, and habitat loss producing steep declines in biodiversity; and myriad other such phenomena yada yada yada all forming the great backdrop to our existence, in ways direct and indirect, it appears that the wide-scale decimation/transformation of the planetary biosphere represents our central achievement as the dominant species. Congratulations.

If human life has any meaning—in fact, if it plays any discernible role at all in the cosmos—this seems to be it: the role of *Homo destructor*.

We are the asteroid.

Thus, in a variation on Fredric Jameson's political unconscious, that reality translates into art that carries the Anthropocene in its DNA. This in part is how I understand Astrid Bracke writing, in 2020, that climate fiction "can be seen to reflect, and engage in, the cultural discourse of environmental crisis over the past two decades" (169). What Stephanie LeMenager calls our "neoliberal feeling-state" or "everyday Anthropocene" ("Climate Change" 223) is in one way or another the structuring principle of modernity.[1]

Hence, as scholars and ecocritics our task is to expose, interpret, complicate, and critique this grandest of grand narratives, along with the bad faith and false consciousness that so often undergird it. So, in the highly selective arts/media overview below I follow Sidney Dobrin when he writes, in the first edited collection of scholarship devoted to comics representations of the environment:

> The fundamental work of ecocriticism is to make evident the ways in which particular texts have contributed to our understanding of the relationships between humans and the natural world. Those relationships, as well as the definitions of things like "texts," "human" and "natural world" are bound up in various, shifting cultural imaginaries, understood not as fixed in meaning or effect. Rather ecocriticism's value grows, in part, from its inquiry about how representations of nature influence cultural imaginaries and how those same cultural imaginaries influence representations of the natural world. Furthermore, ecocriticism considers how those representations affect human interaction with the natural world. ("Follow the Concrete Submersible" 80)

Several things stand out in this process. First, Anthropocenic readings upend traditional understandings/boundaries of genre (like the definitions of sci-fi, cli-fi,[2] the realist novel),[3] storytelling (exceeding human scales/subjectivity), narrative (cause and effect, deep time) and conventional historiography (e.g., racist colonial expansion, which the Anthropocene brings to its logical end).[4] Second, with each passing season, the human impact on nature (of which we are a part) grows harder and harder to deny, leading practitioners of econarratology (a term coined by Erin James) to stress the defamiliarizing power of climate fiction, how it "creates an uncomfortable sense of proximity, confronting readers with a crisis that is present and imminent rather than at a comfortable distance" (Bracke 166). We return to Morton's point that life in the Anthropocene is fundamentally uncanny.

With the foregoing in mind, we could certainly maintain that art made since, say, atmospheric scientist James Hansen's 1988 testimony before the US Senate (which brought the climate change issue into greater public consciousness) is "Anthropocene art." Though we need not adhere to such a strict chronology; since Classical times, people have been dreading the death of nature,[5] while even the Lascaux cave paintings depict large-scale hunting, including of now-extinct species like the auroch.

In any case, Alain Resnais's hauntingly beautiful documentary *Le Chant du Styrène* (France, 1959) celebrated the advent of modernity's addiction to plastic, likening it in the title to the song of the sirens. Deia Schlosberg's more conventional *The Story of Plastic* (USA, 2019) utilizes its own horrific "pollution sublime" to detail the production, consumption, and (non)disposal throughout the world of this ubiquitous (petroleum-derived) substance.

Art films like Lars von Trier's *Melancholia* (Denmark/US, 2011) and *Antichrist* (Denmark/US, 2009) take the end of the world as a given, either in the literal sense (the former) or in an epistemological sense (the latter).[6] Popular franchise movies like Yoshimitsu Banno's *Godzilla vs. the Smog Monster* (Japan, 1971) and the Russo Brothers' *Avengers: Infinity War* (USA, 2018), with its villain's brutal Malthusian "solution" to overtaxed cosmic resources, render the ecological crisis in more accessible terms. Ditto dystopian sci-fi films, from Douglas Trumbull's *Silent Running* (USA, 1972) to George Miller's *Mad Max: Fury Road* (2015).

In this regard, I fondly recall a movie I watched around the same time I was reading about the Inhumans fleeing to the moon: John Badham's *WarGames* (USA, 1983). A key scene first brought to my fifteen-year-old awareness the radical idea that maybe humanity wasn't even meant to last. As the disillusioned computer scientist Stephen Falken (John Wood) explains, "When we go, nature will start again. With the bees, probably. Nature knows when to give up, David." As the film and and, say, the Police's "Walking in Your Footsteps" (also 1983) foreground, anxieties over nuclear annihilation and environmentalist angst overlapped in the final phases of the Cold War (a strand I pick up elsewhere in this study).

A certified megahit seems to begin where Falken's gloomy vision leaves off. In fact, Andrew Stanton's *WALL-E* (USA, 2008) goes places most children's animated films never venture, presenting a detailed portrait of a ruined post-Anthropocene planet Earth centuries in the future. Only, this being a family-friendly Pixar movie (an acquaintance told me upon its release, "The world's ended, but we still have love!"), it's not the bees that start over, but humans along with their robot helpers. And though Stanton (who also wrote the film) said he did not intend to create an anti-consumerist fable, it's hard not to draw a connection between the habits of the humans aboard the space cruiser *Axiom* and the despoiled, trash-strewn home planet they left behind.

Nature and science series often take the opposite strategy, either leveraging the beauty of unknown worlds/habitats to spark wonder (e.g., David Attenborough's *Planet Earth II*)[7] or through devices like the Cosmic Calendar, a visualization that compresses the universe's fourteen-billion-year history into one Earth year, popularized by astronomer Carl Sagan in his TV show *Cosmos* (1980). I remember this as my twelve-year-old self's first exposure to the concept of deep time.

Television, especially broadcast news with its footage of wildfires and floods, capitalizes on what LeMenager calls "the charisma of crisis" ("Climate Change" 225), though such repetitive spectacle threatens to overwhelm the sentiments and shut down empathy. We can only handle so many forests burned down by gender reveals. Worse, such imagery deflects our attention from the everyday, here-and-now nature of the Anthropocene, how it pervades us to our core in this very moment.

Series like *Midnight Sun* (Sweden, 2016) do better by using familiar formulae such as the noir detective story to explore how present-day colonialist resource extraction affects Indigenous populations. The show's Arctic setting, meanwhile, defamiliarizes conventional understandings of night and day in ways that thematically resonate with some of the main figures' nonwhite identity. A similar strategy pays off brilliantly in a scene from season 2 of *Treme* (2011). The ne'er-do-well musician Sonny (Michiel Huisman), reduced to working on a shrimping boat trawling the Gulf of Mexico, comes across a startling vista. Far out in the "freedom" of the open water, Sonny encounters the most industrial of settings: mammoth oil-drilling installations. These floating rigs routinely leak, his Vietnamese boss tells him, impacting Louisiana's largely Vietnamese shrimping industry. The episode aired about a year after the 2010 Deepwater Horizon disaster, the largest marine oil spill ever documented, which occurred in the Gulf.

Like Resnais and Schlosberg, visual artists do not shy from depicting, even embracing, the maleficent beauty of the Anthropocene, whether in Steven Meisel's 2011 *Vogue* magazine spread posing models covered in what looks like oil and pollution (another response to Deepwater Horizon), or *Petrochemical America* (2012), in which photographer Richard Misrach and landscape architect Kate Orff document Louisiana's "Cancer Alley" oil industry region through photographs and an "ecological atlas." In effect, we all live in the age of an Anthropocene sublime, when we admire a sunset altered by industrial particulates in the air; gaze from 35,000 feet on a "rationalized" US land mass (I'm often reminded of Mondrian or Klee); or as happens not uncommonly for us in the logging-happy Pacific Northwest, when we stumble upon an acres-spanning clear-cut.[8]

In theater, meanwhile, Karen Malpede's plays *Extreme Whether* (2014) and *Other Than We* (2019) deploy family drama tropes and dystopia, respectively, to discuss environmental justice and the societal response to cataclysmic climate change.

Fiction has long explored "nature under threat" themes. Sticking just to the last hundred years or so, Ernest Hemingway's post-WWI short story "Big Two-Hearted River I & II" (1925) springs to mind, as does Ray Bradbury's sci-fi piece "The Townbee Convector" (1984), credited by some as the first literary response to climate change. Narrative may hold a particular potency in communicating the reality and urgency of the Anthropocene; as Adam, a student of psychology puts it in Richard Powers's 2018 novel *The Overstory*: "The best arguments in the world won't change a person's mind. The only thing that can do that is a good story" (336).

An emergent genre in the twenty-first century, cli-fi as noted has its immediate ancestor in Cold War–era literature about atomic disaster, like Nevil Shute's *On the Beach* (1957). Definitions of cli-fi remain somewhat in flux (see Bracke), though most scholars trace it to the late Octavia Butler's unfinished "parable" trilogy, comprising *The Parable of the Sower* (1993) and *The Parable of the Talents* (1998). The genre addresses real historical disasters such as 2005's Hurricane Katrina in Jesmyn Ward's *Salvage the Bones* (2011) (see Bares) or the near-future utopia of Kim Stanley Robinson's *The Ministry for the Future* (2020). It's crucial to point out, though, that Robinson himself told an interviewer that at this moment in history, "I have to set a pretty low bar for 'utopia.' If we dodge a mass-extinction event in this century, that's utopian writing" ("Kim Stanley Robinson"). Spoiler alert: We're not dodging it.

Be that as it may, the nature writers have been there perhaps longer than anyone, from John Muir to Henry David Thoreau to Aldo Leopold, who in his seminal *A Sand County Almanac: And Sketches Here and There* (1949) expounds on tree temporality with a famous account of cutting through an oak, revealing growth rings that mark different eras of its life and that he relates to human events (see the chapter titled "February"). Leopold's vision here is both sympathetic and clinical; the episode contrasts sharply with Leo Tolstoy's more sentimental 1859 short story "Three Deaths" (one of the deaths is a tree).

Perhaps no one has written in this vein more powerfully and persuasively than Rachel Carson, whose aforementioned *Silent Spring* (1962) did much to ignite the modern US environmentalist movement. Yet long before that landmark work, Carson was bringing to vivid life on the page such natural marvels as the migration of Atlantic eels, as seen in *Under the Sea-Wind* (1941).[9] Those combining nonfiction, science writing, and the humanities in newer media today, on platforms like the Dark Mountain Project and Edge Effects, owe Carson perhaps the largest debt.

In examining these and innumerable other cultural productions of the Anthropocene era—especially comics—I feel an urgency to, in the words of Peterson and Uhlin, "remai[n] attentive to how media forms both perpetuate and critique the ideologies that underwrite the Great Acceleration" (145). We turn in the next section to a prominent mode employed by these media forms in their engagement with the Anthropocene.

AFFECT

Most if not all of the examples cited above, whether from film, literature, or other media, appeal to the senses and in particular the emotions to move the consumer to somber reflection, pathos, action, etc. In other words, they function along affective axes to produce their effects.

Affect refers to the ways in which environmental factors (including ideas, ideology, and the natural world) influence bodies, as expressed through emotions, physiological responses, and subjective states. Since the 2000s, scholars in the humanities have taken up this critical approach to interpret literature, political speech, and other cultural expressions in what came to be called the Affective Turn.[10]

Despite an irreducible subjectivity, affect has very real effects in the concrete world. As one of the method's pioneers put it,

> I do not assume there is something called affect that stands apart or has autonomy, as if it corresponds to an object in the world, or even that there is something called affect that can be shared as an object of study. Instead, I would begin with the messiness of the experiential, the unfolding of bodies into worlds, and the drama of contingency, how we are touched by what we are near. (S. Ahmed 30)

Calling affect "ecological 'by nature,' since it operates at the confluence of environments, texts, and bodies—including nonhuman and inanimate bodies," Kyle Bladow and Jennifer Ladino find most valuable affect theory's capacity to "disrup[t] both discrete notions of embodied selfhood and static notions of environment, encouraging us to trace the trajectories of transcorporeal encounters that are intricate and dynamic" (8).[11]

We are the asteroid, but we are also the thing the asteroid is crashing into—and we can feel it.

Scholarly discussions of affect in the Anthropocene have tended toward such emotions as anxiety, terror, rage,[12] and—as explored more thoroughly in the next section—grief. Later developments have brought more irreverent approaches drawing on popular culture studies and queer studies, such as Nicole Seymour's "bad environmentalism,"[13] which resists environmentalist discourse's "prevailing moralism accompanied by rigid affective norms" (*Bad Environmentalism* 79).[14] (I turn to Seymour's work in chapter 4's discussion of Robert Crumb.)

"Rigid affective norms" in the guise of pain and melancholy most often manifest in response to environmental loss. Let this passage from Helen Keller's *The Story of My Life* (1903) stand in for innumerable others:

The other day I went to walk toward a familiar wood. Suddenly a disturbing odor made me pause in dismay. Then followed a peculiar, measured jar, followed by dull, heavy thunder. I understood the odor and the jar only too well. The trees were being cut down . . . to-day an unfamiliar rush of air and an unwonted outburst of sun told me that my tree friends were gone. The place was empty, like a deserted dwelling. I stretched out my hand. Where once stood the steadfast pines, great, beautiful, sweet, my hand touched raw, moist stumps. (quoted in Kleege 24–25)

"My tree friends were gone": In endless variations, this scenario or its threat plays out through the decades in TV public service announcements[15] such as "People Start Pollution, People Can Stop It" (popularly known as "Crying Indian"), televised starting on Earth Day in 1971;[16] nature writing like Barry Lopez's 1988 essay "Apologia"; Juliana Spahr's wrenching 2005 poem "Gentle Now, Don't Add to Heartache" on the gradual pollution of a beloved stream; Arjan Brentjes's animated short film *Sad Beauty* (Netherlands, 2020), whose "hopeful" ending is premised on human beings dying off; and Greta Thunberg's speeches, which some have mocked as too "emotional."[17]

This despite the fact that activists at least since Muir and Thoreau have made affective appeals to safeguard nature. The presumed power of such appeals also motivates much environmental humanities research and writing. As Alexa Weik von Mossner puts it, "Ecocriticism has placed great trust in the ability of environmental narratives to have lasting effects on the attitudes and behaviors of their readers" (8).[18] If *The Overstory*'s Adam is right that only a good story will change a person's mind about the state of the natural world, then a good story is one that grips the reader/auditor on a deep emotional level. Some of these appeals are frantic, panic-fueled; see for example the suicidal Michael (Philip Ettinger) in Paul Schrader's *First Reformed* (2018), who imagines his daughter growing up and confronting him with his inaction on climate change when he might have made a difference—he asks his priest, "What're you supposed to say then?"

Satire offers another route to access and express difficult affective states. One may go over the top, as in Adam McKay's *Don't Look Up* (USA, 2021),[19] though I found Jenny Offill's 2020 novel *Weather* more relatable through its low-key, nuanced, in some parts anhedonic narrative about Lizzie, a middle-class white woman navigating the fluctuating emotional "weather" of twenty-first-century life in the Anthropocene—even though she herself has yet to experience any of its direct effects. *Weather* is also very funny. Offill manages to make humor out of the ways contemporary Westerners think, feel, and especially distract themselves about things like mass extinctions, climate change, and the pollution crisis by retreating into their own thoughts and entertainments. It might even be necessary to do so, Offill hints, for their mental health.

The complicated ethics (interpersonal versus environmentalist) involved come to the fore when Lizzie feels sorry for "Mr. Jimmy" (she only knows him by the name on his business card) and goes out of her way to support his floundering taxi business—despite the avoidable carbon emissions it spews: "I used to take a car service only if I was going to be late, but now I find I am building in double the amount of travel time. A bus would be the same or faster. Also, I could afford it. But what if I am the only customer he has left?" (20).

Lizzie's is an act of kindness and fellow feeling, but as Morton reminds, scale this scene up to ten million "Mr. Jimmys" and that's a big part of the reason why we have a greenhouse effect.[20] Clare Fisher puts it like this in her review of the novel:

> Our individualistic, anthropocentric stories create notions of cause and effect which elide the complexity of the crisis, as well as our collective responsibility for it. [Offill's] novel, written in gnomic fragments, stages the contemporary Western subject's centring on its own trivialities as paradoxically necessary to survival on an individual scale, yet also as threat to the survival of the planet. . . . The text prises open a space of dissonance between the affective knowledge of climate change as it appears in our everyday lives (trivial, innocent, diffuse) and the intellectual knowledge that the broader situation is immense, terrifying and very serious.

To say nothing of the constant psychic work to keep such anxieties suppressed—though as noted it's another fact about the Anthropocene that one can't, not really. Not without shutting out reality itself. An autobiographical passage in a 2020 article by Alden Wicker on "zero waste" practices captures these affectual stakes through shock and eruptive horror. The author describes his stroll on one of the "idyllic islands of white sand" off the coast of Panama, home to the indigenous Guna people:

> The side of the island with the hostel was almost pristine, but one morning I set off down the beach picking up little bits of litter and putting them in my resusable bag, feeling quite good about myself. When I rounded the end to the other side of the island, where the villagers lived, I was confronted with a dump truck's worth of plastic trash piling up on the sand. More plastic bags and jugs were floating in on the waves, like product zombies. Ten feet away, an elderly woman dressed in a hand-embroidered mola blouse and sarong sat in the door of a thatch-roof home, regarding me impassively. I wanted to tell her I was sorry, lo siento, but in that moment, everything—my poor Spanish, my little beach clean-up, my zero-waste travel kit—struck me as inadequate and embarrassing. (32)

Aside from the self-lacerating Godzilla versus Bambi quality of this discourse, the *anagnorisis*-like moment when the cheery complacent Westerner (naïvely trying to curb pollution on an individual level) slams into the true systemic state of affairs, I find riveting how Wicker stands figuratively naked before the woman. He seems unprepared not only for what confronts him on the beach, but also for how to feel about it. Yet feel he does: inadequate, embarrassed, *exposed*. It's also notable that (as in Offill's novel), even in such authentic encounters with the Real, evocative as they are of our collapsing ecosystems, the Western subject still manages to make it all about himself. Which only makes it both more pathetic and tragic.

Perhaps the pop culture example *par excellence* of making it all about yourself is that of Tony Soprano. Early in *The Sopranos* (1999–2007), suburban mobster Tony (James Gandolfini) feels forlorn and experiences other mental stress when some wild ducks he's been feeding by his backyard swimming pool take wing and fly away. Later, in reluctant therapy with Dr. Jennifer Melfi (Lorraine Bracco), Tony comes to understand that the ducks represent his family (in the dual sense of biological and mafia), which he's terrified of losing. In other words, those flesh-and-blood creatures that flew away to an uncertain fate serve only as a metaphor, a symbol for Tony's paternal/gangster insecurities. "That's the link," he says. "The connection."

But I can't help thinking about those ducks as ducks. In particular, I think of the 2008 incident in which hundreds of these migratory birds died when they landed in an Alberta toxic pond run by Syncrude Canada, an oil sands project firm. Kate Beaton would commemorate the event in her 2022 graphic memoir, *Ducks: Two Years in the Oil Sands*.

At one point in the series Tony even muses about his duck guests: "They're from Canada or someplace."

ECO-GRIEF

Beaton's ducks, Tony's tears, and Wicker's unresolved "I'm sorry, lo siento" speak to the ineffectuality and felt helplessness of the many so-called "bad" affects (Sianne Ngai calls them "non-cathartic emotions") of the Anthropocene. These include despair, resignation, disappointment, anxiety, rage—all that "environmentalist killjoy" stuff (Bladow and Ladino 11). Want to bring a fun party conversation to a grinding halt? Bring up how if we don't cut carbon emissions by 50 percent before 2030 we're going to burn the whole furshlugginer planet down.

Hence, the species of grief that attaches to existential dread and apocalyptic collapse has received outsize attention in the environmental humanities. In this brief excursus through the literature, I will focus on some key themes, including the stressors placed on bodyminds in the Anthropocene; the struggle to create a language in the new era; and what a path forward might mean.

Mental Health and Our Changing Climate: Impacts, Implications, and Guidance, a report issued by the American Psychological Association in 2017,[21] described the effects of such proliferating phenomena as wildfires, floods, and environmental transformation:

> Major chronic mental health impacts include higher rates of aggression and violence, more mental health emergencies, an increased sense of helplessness, hopelessness, or fatalism, and intense feelings of loss. These feelings of loss may be due to profound changes in a personally important place (such as one's home) and/or a sense that one has lost control over events in one's life due to disturbances from climate change. Additionally, a sense of loss regarding one's personal or occupational identity can arise when treasured objects are destroyed by a disaster or place-based occupations are disrupted by climate change. (7)

The report did not leave it at dramatic, immediate events like disasters, noting that "gradual, long-term changes in climate can also surface a number of different emotions, including fear, anger, feelings of powerlessness, or exhaustion" (Clayton 27). The burden weighs us down even further when we accept our own complicity in this planetary ecocide, be we consumers, carbon emitters, meat-eaters, bitcoin miners, and the like (see Cunsolo and Landman 16).

Such persistent feelings of insecurity and guilt take a grisly toll, leading in many cases to what the gerontologist Ken Doka terms "disenfranchised grief." Disenfranchised because the developed West (whose industrialized economies ignited the crisis) lacks the sophisticated vocabulary and social rituals to acknowledge or discuss, much less mourn, the enormous losses it can no longer ignore. Headlines like "Scientists 'Must Be Allowed to Cry' About Destruction of Nature" and "It's the End of the World as They Know It" bespeak the especially heavy toll on those at the front lines of the great planetary transformation, who understand it the best.

Renee Lertzman, in a not uncommon rhetorical move for those who write on this subject, channels her own grief in elaborating the mental challenges involved:

> This project arose out of my sense of powerlessness as I contemplated my own complicity and inadequate response to our ecological crises. It was born out of my environmental subjectivity as anxious, sad and concerned. However, I was simultaneously experiencing an inchoate, mute sadness in the face of rampant industrial development. Inchoate because such losses

exceed the language needed to express them and mute because of the lack of socially sanctioned forms for sharing emotional responses about ecological issues. Mourning is a social process, and in the absence of sharing it, we remain stuck and our mourning in stasis. (73)

Today it is largely climate scientists, poets, humanists, psychologists, and climate activists—not society as a whole—who speaks in such terms, due to the real risk of being labeled alarmist, fatalistic, even unpatriotic. The hyperpoliticization of the climate change issue, which sees it as a zero-sum struggle between capitalism and "climate change idiocy" (see for example Kudlow), hardly helps.[22] As a denizen of Canada's oil-extraction heartland (where Beaton's ducks went to die) put it, "If I say I'm experiencing eco-grief, what [people assume] I'm really saying is that I am not supportive of the industries that gave me my high quality-of-life" (Llana).

And yet, as Chris Jordan, director of the devastating documentary *Albatross* (2017), puts it, grief is a doorway to love and as such a crucial aspect on the road to a substantive engagement—to say nothing of vital to mental health (Craps and Olsen 115). We saw this during the AIDS crisis of the 1980s and beyond: Grief and activism need not exclude each other. Donna Haraway's *Staying with the Trouble*, in fact, is largely a call to active mourning for a damaged and dying world. "Rigid affective norms" are not all bad.

But as noted, we need words to speak our grief in all its gradations. To that end, and building on work dating back to the 1960s in ecopsychology, deep ecology and death and dying, social scientists and others have advanced such terms as "climate grief," "environment grief," "eco-anxiety," "reef grief," "snow anxiety," "winter grief," "eco-anger," "climate rage," "terrafurie" (inordinate wrath at the wanton destruction of the natural world), and "eco-irritation."[23]

In 2013, Australian philosopher Glenn Albrecht contributed "solastalgia," for "psychoterratic distress connected to negatively perceived and felt changes to a home environment, changes that one is powerless to prevent." More colloquially, he describes it as "the homesickness you have when you are still at home" in the Anthropocene (299). Such a lexicon-in-progress, notes grief researcher Thomas Attic, helps mourners in their great task: the adjustment to a new environment (in this case, literally), to "relear[n] the world" (quoted in Pikhala).

Along with the new vocabulary, there have formed communities and eco-grief support circles, large and small, among them the Calgary-based Refugia Retreats, the Climate Psychology Alliance of North America, the Good Grief Network, Jennifer Atkinson's podcast/forum *Facing It*, and the youth-aimed Uplift Climate. At these gatherings, participants may feel listened to as they discuss, for example, the ethical complexities of having children knowing what they know. Notably, one participant compared her group to a wake (Llana).[24]

As for the road ahead, Iraq war veteran Roy Scranton did much to jumpstart that conversation with a 2013 *New York Times* op-ed, "Learning to Die in the Anthropocene." In that and the 2015 book in which he expanded on his ideas, Scranton argues for coming to terms with the end of Western civilization as we have known it, the better to adjust to a new, much-diminished environment. "The reality of global climate change," he warned, "is going to keep intruding on our fantasies of perpetual growth, permanent innovation and endless energy, just as the reality of mortality shocks our casual faith in permanence" (22–23). Lesley Head meanwhile suggests that "Anthropoceneans need to be able to live in uncertainty," in multiple temporalities, with nonlinear conceptualizations of progress and causation, and as inescapably biological, terran subjects (168).

LeMenager stresses that the new era also signals a reckoning with—among other things—the racial ideologies that brought us to this turn:

> Climate change presents a radical challenge to ways of living once seen as unencumbered by material constraint—for example, living as white, living as hypermobile in a culture of speed, living as a top consumer in an age of credit. Learning to die, as a theme of cli-fi, is always in part the problem of coming back to oneself and one's defining conditions as problems of recalcitrant matter. "Letting go" is losing any trappings of social transcendence—whether these are understood as whiteness, wealth, heteronormativity, or national belonging. ("Climate Change" 229)

In the middle of it all, we must grieve and bear witness. As Jordan urges, describing the birds he saw on Midway Island choking to death on discarded plastic: "The only thing there is left to do is to stay there, in that crucible, and *not turn away*" (Craps and Olsen 115). *Stay with the trouble*. It's true that the anguish of dealing with such material—of a lot of material in the Anthropocene—drives some to anger and frustration over the need for more "solution-oriented" visions. But grief has no "solution." Works like *Albatross* are first and foremost about grief, not "answers" to a particular crisis. (Don't get me started on "de-extinction" . . .[25])

In *The Moth Snowstorm: Nature and Joy* (2015), Michael McCarthy manages to congeal the sadness of the Anthropocene into a potent image, one achingly familiar to those of a certain age, less so to the young:

> The headlight beams of a speeding car on a muggy summer's night in the countryside, turning the moths into snowflakes and crowding them together the faster you went, in the manner of a telephoto lens, meant that the true startling scale of their numbers was suddenly apparent, not least as they plastered the headlights and the windscreen until driving

became impossible, and you had to stop the car to wipe the glass surfaces clean. . . . Of all the myriad displays of abundance in the natural world in Britain, the moth snowstorm was the most extraordinary, as it only became perceptible in the age of the internal combustion engine. Yet now, after but a short century of existence, it has gone.

In recent years I have often talked to people about it, and I am surprised, not just at how many of those over fifty (and especially over sixty) remember it, but at how animated they become once the memory is triggered. It's as if it were locked away in a corner of their minds, and in recalling it and realizing that it has disappeared, they can recognize what an exceptional phenomenon it was, whereas at the time, it just seemed part of the way things were. (102)

Such emotion-pictures brilliantly evoke what Aldo Leopold meant in his most-oft-cited quote, "One of the penalties of an ecological education is that one lives alone in a world of wounds" (*Round River* 165). They show what the Anthropocene really *is* far better than any facts and figures I could relate showing how humans have destabilized the Earth's natural climate cycles, pesticides and habitat destruction have led to species collapse, and so on. They indict and they console. They bring us face-to-face with the fact that while, sure, nature—the planet—will eventually bounce back ("probably with the bee"), in the meantime, on a very human time scale, within little more than two generations, we have set off the sixth mass extinction along with all its attendant untold suffering. Oh, and we've doomed ourselves into the bargain. Following Morton, I both do and don't feel the weight of my own culpability for that. Sure, in the grand scheme of things my role is small, but let's cut the bullshit, shall we? It could be a lot smaller.

In short, McCarthy's affect-saturated word-picture functions to some extent like W. J. T. Mitchell's imagetext—under whose compass also happens to fall the verbal-visual medium of graphic narrative.

AFFECT, VULNERABILITY, AND COMICS

Making specific reference to Richard McGuire's 2014 graphic novel *Here*, LeMenager writes, "The feeling-states that language can evoke through mimicked perception are externalized and simplified in visual narrative" ("Climate Change" 236). I would quibble with "and simplified"; rather, comics' poetics of sequentiality and text/image tensions introduce new orders of complexity (and an often irreducible irony) along its multimodal tracks, offering a space, as Hillary Chute has noted, "for ethical representation without problematic closure" ("'The Shadow of a Past Time'" 214). Furthermore, Kate Polak has capably demonstrated in *Ethics in the Gutter: Empathy and Historical Fiction in Comics* (2017) the importance of such formal matters as point of view and focalization to a comics reader's emotional/ethical engagement with the material.

Indeed, if affect has much to do with "that which escapes, resists, or exceeds language," pointing "to processes of potentiality and becoming, to vital forces and intensities, to physiological and biological matters that lie outside discursive structures" (Bean), then graphic narrative's text-image hybridity offers distinct advantages (twice as large a toolkit!) for unpacking such phenomenological realia. In short, as Veronica Vold maintains, "Comics studies opens the environmental humanities to a range of verbal-visual moves that can deepen interdisciplinary inquiry and offer new methods of analysis" (81).

And while it's fair to say that the Affective Turn has yet to touch comics studies the way it has other fields, since the 1990s, several scholars have tapped this approach to analyze comics works. A list of their contributions would include Daniel Worden's examination of the literary journal *McSweeney's Quarterly Concern* #13 (2004), devoted to graphic narrative works by numerous luminaries (R. Crumb, Daniel Clowes, etc.). Within its pages, Worden finds a consistent theme, from editor Chris Ware on down, drawing on "a common tradition in comics that centers on intimacy, shame, and masculine melancholia" likened to pornography ("The Shameful Art" 893).

The rich emotional repertoire of Japanese shoujo manga (girls' comics) all but cries out for an affect theory–based reading; Waiyee Loh answers the call with a wide-ranging formalist discussion of the genre's irregular and open frames, which enable the impassioned "lawless" movement of sentiments across the page. Its "free-floating text" unframed by balloons, Loh maintains, consists of "floating verbal signifiers that have no fixed referent and whose function is affective rather than discursive" (471–72).

Gesine Wegner investigates the deep affectual investment in graphic medicine (comics devoted to health care, illness, and to some extent disability) on the part of its practitioners and supporters, whose representational ambit extends "from mediating the emotional state after diagnostic mistakes, to considering the emotional well-being of patients, to expressing empathy as part of medical practice." But though she agrees that "the specificities of the medium allow graphic pathographies to narrate precisely that which cannot be expressed by words," Wegner cites a number of problems with such claims, first and foremost an unacknowledged ocularcentrism endemic to medicine itself ("Reflections" 62–63). For her part, Maheen Ahmed, editor of an essay collection devoted to child-animal relationships in comics, notes that such works are "layered with emotion and affect" (15).

Scholars have drawn on affect theory for readings of environmental racism in Jackie Ormes's *Torchy Hearts* (Vold); narrative empathy in J. P. Stassen's *Deogratias: A Tale of Rwanda* (Keen); cuteness and rage in the works of Julie Doucet (Richardson); repulsion and Ngai's "ugly feelings" in Jillian Tamaki and Mariko Tamaki's *Skim* (Luedecke); human rights issues in immigration narratives (Fernández L'Hoeste); and the shivers-inducing ecohorror of Junji Ito (see Tidwell).

But in particular it is a related, medium-specific line of inquiry, what I call comics studies' embodied turn, that has yielded the most valuable insights. Emerging from the feminist approaches advanced by Hillary Chute, Alisia Chase, Jared Gardner, Susan Kirtley, and others, this framework envisions the physical processes of comics production and comics reading as evocative of a shared human vulnerability.

As Chute writes in *Graphic Women: Life Narrative and Contemporary Comics* (2010), graphic narrative as a traditionally hand-drawn practice "registers the subjective bodily mark on the page" (183), rendering it "a gripping index of a material, subjective, situated body" (193).[26] In *Disaster Drawn: Visual Witness, Comics, and Documentary Form* (2016), she reminds that "the plasticity of [Keiji] Nakazawa's line ... is an index of its signature corporeality" (140), foregrounding "the embodiment of the creator in composing comics—an act of embodiment that translates to the page" (141). Chute further contends that negotiating traumatic and graphically violent material like Nakazawa's *I Saw It* (1972), "generate[s] readers' awareness of their own contingent, durational, embodied activity of *reading* and *looking* at the mark, the panel, the page" (141).

But Chute focuses too narrowly on comics dealing with war, massacres, and related atrocities, compelling as they are for her thesis. For one's "awareness of their own contingent, durational, embodied activity" may just as easily be activated by other sorts of material, from the three-hankie melodrama of many Romance comics to the spine-tingling horror of the aforementioned Ito and the porn stylings of, say, Gilbert Hernandez's *Birdland* (2000). These evoke the "body genres" discussed by cinema studies scholar Linda Williams, who investigates their particular capacities to elicit altered bodily states like sexual arousal, accelerated heartbeat, goosebumps, weeping, etc.[27]

Eszter Szép's *Comics and the Body: Drawing, Reading, and Vulnerability* (2020) in fact opens with a discussion of a harrowing scene in Miriam Katin's graphic memoir *Letting It Go* (2013) that has no direct tie to any battle (save perhaps for the struggle over incontinence). Yet this episode nonetheless produces an extreme affective response in the reader: "[I] was not prepared to see the naked body of the protagonist of this confessional narrative covered in her own excrement. *I winced*," Szép writes, adding, "Why is this such a challenge to bear? What is happening to my body while I am reading that book, that scene?" (1–2, my emphasis).

Apart from recalling to me my first encounter with the work of Mike Diana (which to this day twists my stomach, right down to each individual drawn stroke), Szép's nuanced analyses of works by Joe Sacco, Ken Dahl, Katie Green, and others underscore the interconnectedness of those who make and those who consume comics—since both parties do so with living, feeling bodies, bodies that can react with sympathy, revulsion, and no shortage of other responses. In this conceptualization, the artist's line becomes a kind of moist membrane, labile and porous, letting through manifold sensations whose emotional/physiological effects we can never wholly predict. Beyond that, Szép insists she is describing an interdependent sensual process shot through with ethical implications; we are far removed here from any dispassionate "detached reader" model. To complicate things further, Szép claims the material qualities of the comics' format (floppy, iPad, accordion book) also play an agentic role in reception; the medium is not just the message, it's an actor (almost a full partner) in a tripartite negotiation between selves. As she puts it: "The ethical encounter enabled by the performance of bodies of drawers and readers and by the body of the comic is an "affective transaction" between embodied minds and mindful bodies, and it can transform the participants taking part in the encounter by not only acknowledging but also experiencing the vulnerability of the self and of the Other in interactions with the comic" (8).

Building on Judith Butler's "shared precariousness," Ian Hague's phenomenology-informed comics scholarship and Katalin Orbán's "haptic vision" model of comics reading, Szép makes vulnerability—the fact that as bodies we are *ipso facto* subject to harm, pain, and eventual death—the fundament of her aesthetic/ethical schema. In this framework, graphic narrative (on the production and reception sides) reifies a universal human precarity.

Szép's empathetic framework turns comics into more than a communications medium, more than a bridge between separate subjects; here it's as if comics forms a shared artery, with creator/reader as conjoined twins. In her words, "Comics require the reader's openness to the touch of otherness. Actual physical contact and a metaphorical touch—that is, being affected and transformed—are both necessary for comics reading to become part of a dialogue centering on the experience of vulnerability, taking place between artist and reader, mediated by the comic" (16).

The embodied turn's "organic" model, premised on vulnerability, precarity, mortality, and a big-hearted blurring of borders between human and nonhuman actors, puts me in mind of Stacy Alaimo's transcorporealism. A key concept in new materialist environmental humanities alongside Mel Chen's animate matter, Jane Bennet's "vibrant matter," and Donna Haraway's "sympoeisis,"[28] transcorporealism too figures an ethical encounter between bodies—all bodies, and beyond. For Alaimo, selves are not integral or self-sustaining and nature is not passive, a mere blank canvas for human action. All—living and nonliving—is mutually constitutive; everything shares the artery. Therefore everything matters. *We are the asteroid*; we are also the rhizome—and with great rhizome comes great responsibility. As Alaimo conveys:

> Concern and wonder converge when the context for ethics becomes not merely social but material—the emergent, ultimately unmappable landscapes of interacting biological, climatic, economic, and political forces.
>
> Potent ethical and political possibilities emerge from the literal contact zone between human corporeality and more-than-human nature. Imagining human corporeality as trans-corporeality, in which the human is always intermeshed with the more-than-human world, underlines the extent to which the substance of the human is ultimately inseparable from "the environment." (2)

The reader can guess what comes next: If comics are embodied, that means that like all bodies, comics are also transcorporeal. The line (that trace of the drawer's body/vulnerability so closely scrutinized by Chute and Szép) is that porous membrane that extends beyond the page, beyond our skin, to the air we breathe and water we drink and the earth that feeds us. That food of the earth in turn is broken down by the microbiome in our gut without which we could no more survive than if the atmosphere vanished or the planet's climate soared beyond a certain temperature—as it's started to do now. In sum, we are the environment (not just the asteroid), and as we have been discussing, that environment is increasingly, catastrophically compromised in the Anthropocene. A distinctly transcorporeal art form like comics might just help to reorient us to those realities.

I think we see some of this happening in the page we were discussing earlier, from the "Indistinctions" chapter of *The Puma Blues*. The interrelation of the loon's call, Jake's memory of the unnamed Native logger in the Amazon, and Immer's motor (represented through a morphing sound effect that undulates in two streams across the hyperframe), binds the different human and nonhuman actors along a stylized "aural" track even as it transcends a fixed time, place, perspective, umwelt. In turn, the "visual" track offers a wealth of details as to Jake's moment-by-moment perceptions/thoughts: the landscape that shifts from Qabbin to Amazon; the view of his inner eye as he remembers the logger so vividly that he "actually thought I could hear *that* chainsaw devour *that* tree" (we even see the initials GE on the logger's hardhat); his expression hardening as he turns in the bottom tier to break the fourth wall, seeming to stare accusingly at the reader. The Jake-focalized panels' shapes, too, do their work: They have the thin verticality of tree trunks, mirroring the one the logger saws into without emotion, dronelike, in the top-right panel. Jake's panels even seem to "teeter" like a kapok about to tumble down. (The one Immer-focalized panel, at bottom-right, is square and does not "teeter.")

Aside from all this, we have a page here about the relationships and interdependencies not only of the main characters but of various anonymous and nonhuman actors who still play important roles: Jake, Gavia, the unseen Ruth (who's listening to Jake's narrative), the logger, the loon, the trees, the fog, the water, the motor, and so forth, all unified in their diversity by Zulli's page design with its delicately cross-hatched lines, which make clear (almost palpable) many synaesthetic overlaps of memory, sound, ontology; they seem to bleed into each other and intermix because they are all the product of the artist's pen, his ink, his precarious self. No less precarious than the reader. No less precarious than the world in which that reader resides, to whose destruction they are witness and accomplice. Because the page is about that too.

Murphy and Zulli's *The Puma Blues* offers some of the best evidence that comics boasts unique meaning-making capabilities for not only visualizing but *feeling* our "world of wounds" in ways that may well resonate with audiences inured to other media. (That's why I spend so much time on that series in this book.) Comics' transcorporeal embodied depiction of a damaged, polluted environment likewise finds its correlate in the writings of those who work at the queer-inflected intersection of disability studies and ecocriticism. Such authors, like Eli Clare, cast a skeptical eye at Romanticist evocations of "pristine" nature. In a startlingly radical passage describing a hike, he goes so far as to embrace—not bemoan—a ruined landscape: "I round the next bend and am suddenly in a new clearcut: stumps as far as I can see, the great heap of tree parts left behind, bulldozer tracks frozen into the dry mud. I don't want this to mean destruction but rather to be home" (*Exile and Pride* 27).

Advocating an ethic of "fractured wholeness" that "resists the pressures of normal and abnormal" and "defies the easy splitting of *natural* from *unnatural*," Clare makes explicit, nuanced connections between the environment in the Anthropocene and his life with cerebral palsy (*Brilliant Imperfection* xvii). Further, he likens ableist society's eugenicist fixation on "curing" disabled people with the desire to restore degraded landscapes to some fanciful Edenic state.[29] As he writes, "How would I, or the medical establishment, go about restoring my body? The vision of me without tremoring hands and slurred speech, with more balance and coordination, does not originate from my body's history. Rather it arises from an imagination of what my body should be like, some definition of normal and natural" ("Notes on Natural Worlds" 248).

Clare does not categorically oppose land restoration efforts for enhancing biodiversity, though his queer ecology perspective emphasizes that—as the

Inhumans discovered to their peril—much of nature is already inescapably imbued with the human (a point to which we will return) and that such policies need to be balanced with other "multi-issue disability politics." He concludes: "Simply put, the bodies of both disabled and chronically ill people and restored prairies resist the impulse toward and the reality of monocultures" ("Notes on Natural Worlds" 259).[30]

That complexity vis-à-vis nature also informs Mel Chen's transcorporeal work on chronic illness and chemical sensitivity. Writing that "toxicity straddles boundaries of 'life' and 'nonlife,' as well as the literal bounds of bodies" (218), Chen too explodes any naïve notions of a separation between living beings and the environment. Their relationship is rather as much of violence and harm as of restoration and healing, especially when we account for the countless man-made pollutants that have long suffused the "natural" world:

> There is a potency and intensity to two animate or inanimate bodies passing one another, bodies that have an exchange—a potentially queer exchange—that effectively risks the implantation of injury. The quality of the exchange may be at the molecular level, airborne molecules entering the breathing apparatus, molecules that may or may not have violent bodily effects, or the exchange may be visual, the meeting of eyes unleashing a series of pleasurable or unpleasurable bodily reactions, chill, pulse rush, adrenaline, heat, fear, tingling skin. (206)

If affect theory in general and transcorporealism in particular persistently underline the permeability of all flesh and material, how subjects are suffused with the environment in which they reside, an environment that pulses and lives and induces and hurts and kills, a suspension in which *Homo sapiens* forms but one floating pregnable particle, then I hold that the art of comics, whereby "the drawn line can be read as an initiation of a dialogue of vulnerability" has some crucial correlates to that framework (Szép 166). To say nothing of valuable tools to deploy in crafting narratives about how the vulnerability of our bodies is in contiguity with that of the natural world whose disappearance we are witnessing (and abetting).

If all this talk about precarity and disappearance sounds a little heavy, the naturalist John Burroughs put forth much the same idea as the transcorporealists over a hundred years ago and in more dulcet, reassuring tones: "The trembling gold of the pond-lily's heart and its petals like carved snow, are no more a transformation of a little black muck and ooze by the chemistry of the sunbeam than our bodies and minds, too, are a transformation of the soil underfoot. We are rooted to the air through our lungs and to the soil through our stomachs. We are walking trees and floating plants" (160).

In the next chapter we examine graphic narrative's "walking trees" and "floating plants" (some of them literally so). I urge my reader to remain open to the affective possibilities inherent in the comics medium to represent the vulnerability not only of bodies, but of nature itself.

Because they are the same.

2

NATURE, COMICS, AND THE MEGA-IMAGE

Norrin Radd/the Silver Surfer debuted in *Fantastic Four* #48 (Mar. 1966). He was created by Jack Kirby and Stan Lee (in that order)[1] as the space-faring herald of the dread godlike Galactus. In 1966, carbon particulates in the atmosphere as measured at the Mauna Loa Observatory stood at about 330 ppm.[2]

Moved by the humanity of the FF's blind friend Alicia Masters, the Surfer eventually turns on his master and helps save the Earth—but Galactus extracts a grievous price: Radd is condemned to remain eternally within the bounds of Earth's atmosphere. The stars would be denied him forever (*FF* #50, May 1966).

The stand-alone *Silver Surfer* series, launched in 1968, picks up the story from there. But as written by Lee, the Surfer was far from the soulless cosmic being that Kirby first envisioned. This Radd agonized over his fate and the many injustices of his adopted world in long faux-Shakespearean speeches as he floated along on his cosmic surfboard. Such scenes made the Surfer among the most tragic and the most absurd of figures in the superhero genre. Lee described his cocreation as a "space-born apostle" with "a certain nobility in his demeanor, an almost spiritual quality in his aspect and his bearing," which "graphically represent[ed] all the best, the most unselfish, qualities of intelligent life" (*Son of Origins* 206). Later commentators didn't quite agree. Charles Hatfield sees in the Surfer a "pathetic, blatantly Christlike hero" (*Hand of Fire* 136), while Sean Howe captures the figure's stark duality by calling him both "Sisyphus recast as a fallen angel" and a "hyperempathetic wanderer, encountering human foibles and spouting homilies with puppy-dog eyes" (90).[3]

Norrin Radd/the Silver Surfer unburdens his soul in Lee and Buscema's *Silver Surfer* vol. 1 #1 (Aug. 1968). © Marvel Comics.

The first issue of the new series features just such a maudlin soliloquy—intriguingly, one touching on the planet's environmental woes. Having buzzed several world capitals, sparking air defense alerts across the capitalist West and communist East, Radd retires to a barren mountain range. Skimming along on his board with his back to the reader, overlooking the massive crags (we are perhaps meant to think of Caspar David Friedrich's seminal Romantic painting *Wanderer Above a Sea of Fog*, ca. 1818?), the Surfer unburdens his soul. Over four rather histrionic panels, he declaims:

> In all the *galaxies*—in all the endless reaches of *space*—
> I have found *no planet* more blessed than *this*—
> No world more lavishly endowed with natural *beauty*—with gentle *climate*—with every ingredient to create a virtual living *paradise!*
> Possessed of *rainfall* in great abundance—*soil* fertile enough to feed a *galaxy!*
> And a *sun*—ever-warm—ever-constant—ever symbolizing new life, new *hope!*
> It is as though the *human race* has been divinely *favored* over all who live!
> And *yet*—in their uncontrollable *insanity*—in their unforgivable *blindness*—they seek to *destroy* this shining jewel—this softly-spinning *gem*—this tiny *blessed sphere*—which men call *Earth!* (Lee and Buscema, "The Origin" 6)

As depicted by artist John Buscema, Radd delivers this solemn diatribe with grand sweeping gestures and pained expressions; uttering the last few lines, he seems to gaze up directly at the reader, not unlike Jake in the *Puma Blues* scene previously examined. This emotional episode seems calculated to appeal to a post–*Silent Spring* sensibility—as indeed did much popular culture in the build-up to the first Earth Day in 1970. Still, the vision of a shiny space alien called the Silver Surfer, spouting eco-friendly platitudes about our "softly-spinning *gem*" whilst levitating on a surfboard above the Himalayas would doubtless inspire more ridicule than reverence for most readers over nine years old. (Perhaps not; the sensitive Surfer proved popular among college students and was embraced by some in the counterculture; see Howe 120.)

In any case, the *Silver Surfer* series represented one pole—call it the "direct affective appeal" pole—in the broad spectrum of superhero representation of the Anthropocene in the late twentieth century. The other end was occupied by topical "ripped from the headlines" stories about the threatened environment,

Aerosol sprays led to a dystopian future in Gerber and Buscema's *The Defenders* vol. 1 #26 (Aug. 1975). © Marvel Comics.

like floods, wildfires, and oil spills (as discussed at length in chapter 6 of this study). This too, of course, played on emotions like anxiety and eco-grief but used empirical data and (for superheroes) less hyperbolic language.

A notable example appeared in *The Defenders* #26 (Aug. 1975). "Savage Time!," written by Steve Gerber, centers on the testimony of the time-traveling thousand-year-old Vance Astro of the Guardians of the Galaxy, who has come from the thirtieth century CE. He narrates the history of Earth starting from his childhood, though for his 1970s audience Astro is of course talking about events in the present and near future. And they are grim. The decline of civilization, we learn, began with what many readers in this era would have recognized as man-made chlorofluorocarbons (CFCs) found in refrigerants and aerosol sprays and their effect on a specific portion of the atmosphere:[4]

> We made a very foolish *choice*, that's all . . .
>
> We decided we valued dry *armpits* and the 3-billion-dollar *aerosol* industry . . . over our flowers, our food, and ultimately our *health*. Oh, the scientists *warned* us . . . !
>
> They said the gas in those cans would break down the *ozone* layer—the world's protection from the sun's ultraviolet rays—but we didn't *believe* it. Not until the first *skin cancer* epidemic in 1982.

Not until a walk in the sun became so *deadly* that even to cross the street, we needed protective *clothing* over every square inch of our *bodies*. (Gerber and Buscema 15–16)

As artist Sal Buscema renders it, Astro's tale begins with him sitting on grass, leaning against a tree, and gesturing to the stars—but in the page that follows, we see no more trees or greenery, only a sweltering urban scene with citizens and a traffic cop in what look like scuba outfits, going about their day as the sun bears mercilessly down on them. Without really understanding it, the seven-year-old Joseito who read this in Edinburg, Texas, in 1975 was nonetheless deeply disturbed; I especially remember wondering why these people on the street were treating such a bizarre situation as if it were normal, banal. Even the cop looked bored. Why weren't they trying to fix this terrible problem, instead of just living and dying with it?[5] The middle-aged Joseote today wonders much the same thing about climate change.

So, two different visions of proliferating natural disaster from just before and after the first Earth Day in 1970: one more abstract and Romanticist in its leanings, the other hard-nosed and facts-based. One could say much about how these two Marvel products trace the evolution of superhero comics from their 1960s "Silver Age" incarnation (often overblown and bombastic) to their "Bronze Age" iteration (with its more existentialist, pessimistic outlook). But besides that, it seems to me they also signal a shift in the culture itself. As noted by the journalist Nathaniel Rich, US ecological awareness (which had been building since the industrial age, and which Rachel Carson did much to galvanize in the 1960s) launched a bona fide political movement by 1970. This led to real legislative achievements like the Clean Water Act (1972) and the establishment of the Environmental Protection Agency under Nixon. The catalyst seems to have been a new "broader understanding of the interconnectedness of ecological threats," so that disparate phenomena like land development, resource extraction, wildfires, roadside littering, species extinction, and eventually the ozone layer and climate change all came to fall under the category of "the environment" issue (8–9).

In this process, comic art played the roles of both chronicler and, to a considerable extent, shaper. Indeed, I agree with Sidney Dobrin that "it requires little effort to point out the deep-seated—though as of yet, rarely articulated—history of the comics form's engagement with representations of nature, wilderness, animal, human, environment and ecology . . ." ("EcoComix" 2). This section's ecumenical, highly selective survey presents evidence for that claim. I especially seek to highlight comics works that make plain an "environmental imagination," that is, an ethical orientation to the natural world (Vold 67),[6] as well as those that especially tap the medium's affective capacities.

THE MEGA-IMAGE

In their introduction to a *Journal of Cinema and Media Studies* special section on film and media studies in the Anthropocene, Jennifer Peterson and Graig Uhlin pose the Hitchcockian "vertigo zoom" as a cinematic correlate to life in the current era of anthropogenic natural cataclysm. This "dizzying confluence of human and nonhuman perspectives" can (depending on the person) feel both immediate and remote, as abstract as the particulates of carbon in the atmosphere and as concrete as one's home consumed by a wildfire, occurring simultaneously on geologic time scales and with appalling haste in the here and now. They write: "It is precisely the disorienting perspective of the Anthropocene, where previously slow-paced geological and climatological transformations appear accelerated to the scale of human action, that makes these connections apparent" (145). This strikes me as an intriguing example whereby art can invoke, mirror, compel *an Anthropocenic awareness*.

Graphic narrative can do no less; as a comics equivalent to the vertigo zoom, I propose the "mega-image" (splash, double-page spread, foldouts, strategically large frames/compositions, and the like), which punctuates narrative flow, often stopping it cold—the way Gerber and Buscema's outsized "banality of ozone depletion" panel in "Savage Time!" did for me as a child. It is such visual configurations of comics space, I submit, that through the medium's own potentialities perform a similar task to the vertigo zoom: They, so to speak, "bottle" the Anthropocene for our fixed regard.

Bigness often matters here. This imagery tends to be oversized, immersive, virtually transporting the reader into the storyworld[7]—while, weirdly, also repulsing her from the narrative through a forced recognition of the artificiality, the constructedness, of the presentation itself. As we know, comics excels at such paradoxes—and in thinking the Anthropocene, paradox is good.

The mega-image[8] nominally belongs to the realm of what Benoît Peeters calls the "rhetorical" mode of comics page layout, one artists "plac[e] at the service of a pre-existing narrative for which it serves to accentuate the effects." In this approach, "images of grand dimensions appear," including "at a particularly powerful moment which it is important to emphasize." But as noted, what I'm describing is stranger than that. For one thing, these moments subvert and transcend narrative as much as "accentuate" it. As we discussed, when the Inhumans in "Exodus!" disembark to explore their new lunar home, Byrne shows us that plot point as a full-page splash—the better for his readers to see and "feel" and dwell at length in the nigh-mythological enormity of the event.[9] At fourteen, I certainly took my own sweet time on that page.

Above all, the mega-image is contemplative, in the way discussed by Scott Bukatman in his analysis of Hellboy comics: "They invite a contemplation of the whole before (and/or after) one has absorbed the narrative content of the scene" (*Hellboy's World* 167).[10] The enthralling gargantuan visions of Jack Kirby, with figures practically leaping off the page (best enjoyed in the Treasury Editions format), are some of the most compelling examples. Bukatman notes that they capitalize on a "fundamental tension between the panel and the page to evoke awe or transcendence. Panels would enlarge, opening onto full-page panoramas that the eye would linger over or (even better) onto double-page spreads in which spectacle entirely overwhelmed narrative progress" (*Hellboy's World* 67).[11] As Bukatman phrases it further on: These are sequences that refuse their status as sequences, whereby "the forward flow of the comics reading experience is blocked" (*Hellboy's World* 170).[12]

To the extent that, as Thierry Groensteen argues, the more a page deviates from a given work's established patterns of layout, the more it will stand out, the "mega-image" can hold an especially powerful affective yield. For example, the first six pages of chapter 12 of Moore and Gibbons's *Watchmen*, Groensteen says, "have a remarkable impact" precisely because in the eleven chapters preceding, no such single-panel splashes had appeared. "The rhythm of the narration freezes," he writes, "and time is suspended over these images of devastation" (*Comics and Narration* 147).

That's another crucial ingredient: time. Weird time. For as Hatfield reminds us, comics' synchronistic undivided polyptych (i.e., single-panel splash page or spread) "tends to stress haste, intensity, near-simultaneity—or, oddly enough, the opposite: stillness and inertia" (*Alternative Comics* 53). He goes on to contend that an action-packed double-page spread from Kirby's *New Gods* makes use of composition and verbal/visual interplay to "captur[e] successive moments simultaneously; this is not a snapshot but a tableau" (55). Actually, I would say that it's *both* a snapshot and a tableau, instant and (implied) durée all at once, for "while comics appear to give us an atomistic conception of time as something that can be broken into discrete units, they actually present an interlacing of multiple temporalities" (Bukatman, *Hellboy's World* 171). This applies to divided (multi-panel) as well as undivided polyptych comics pages.

Such a seeming contradiction has its analogue in narratologist Gérard Genette's false binary between literary narration (figured as time, sequence, events, etc.) and description (space, stasis, "passive" setting). Just as subsequent scholars have rightly complicated that too-tidy formulation, pointing to examples of narrativized description and "descriptivized" narration along a continuum,[13] so too does the "mega-image's" double-voicedness call for a rethinking of such flimsy dichotomies as now and not-now, here and there, bodies and environments, stasis and movement, etc.

We see a similar discourse on the synchrony/diachrony of the single image in art history, in discussions of works that purport to capture a specific moment in time. For example, Caravaggio's life-size 1601 painting *Supper at Emmaus* seems to depict the precise instant when the resurrected Savior reveals himself to some stunned tablemates. But as Lorenzo Pericolo and others have shown through careful scrutiny, the master renders the different figures within their own distinct temporalities, such that "it could be said in an updated terminology that Caravaggio spliced together two different sequences of an episode to create what might be interpreted as the illusion of a diachronic development" (Pericolo 531).[14]

In like manner, the comics "mega-image" invites—nay, forces—contemplation of an overlapping "this and also this." Bukatman, once more, phrases it well; the "stasis" that he finds intrinsic to Mignola's *Hellboy* comics "creates something of a ruminative and intertextual space for the reader to occupy" (*Hellboy's World* 151). My claim is that this "ruminative and intertextual space" is greatly amplified in large-scale figurings that explode narrative progress even as they in a sense magnify/intensify it.[15] Let me repeat, though, that the "mega-image" does not have to present exclusively as a single-image page or spread; it can encompass a polyptych composition, provided that such provokes the noted contemplative pause (as attested to by some of my examples below).

What might all of this have to do with the Anthropocene? The opportunity for narrative suspension and rumination afforded by the "mega-image" in comics that addresses the natural environment and/or the ecological crisis, I want to strongly suggest, has affective potential for engaging with said crisis. At times shocking, always visually arresting, the large-scale picture that freezes a climactic action in midstride or alternatively seems to extend a quiet mood indefinitely (or both) makes the stakes crystal clear at the same time as it disorients and destabilizes the customary order. These scenes, I offer, are the culture speaking to itself about the Anthropocene; this is comics' version of "staying with the trouble."

Moreover, the "mega-image" answers Amitav Ghosh's dissatisfaction in *The Great Derangement* with Anthropocene art that fails to rupture conventional, predictable aesthetic norms, which in late capitalism are premised on individual subjectivity and a neoliberal "common sense." As noted by Hatfield and Bukatman, the not-so-static "mega-image" is by its nature multi-perspectival, polytemporal, open to a whole spectrum of applications. Nothing is foreclosed, certainly not a collective ethos of the sort Ghosh calls for.[16]

Perhaps more than anything else, the "mega-image" compels (demands) *attention*. In this sense it responds to LeMenager's prescription for the Anthropocene novel, which she describes as "at best a project of paying close attention to what it means to live through climate shift, moment by moment, in individual, fragile bodies . . . of reinventing the everyday as a means of paying attention and preparing, collectively, a project of staying home and, in a sense distant from settler-colonialist mentalities, *making* home in a broken world" ("Climate Change" 226).

The comics visions I now present of cataclysm, stasis, beauty, horror, the future, and the now are not all "mega-images," but I argue they contribute to LeMenager's project by centering an intense, zoomed-in awareness of home—in all its brokenness, woundedness, aliveness. Erin James notes one last contradiction of our current era: "The Anthropocene is both produced and mitigated by narratives and, at the same time, incapable of being narrated" (*Narrative* 5).

The following selections put considerable pressure on that claim.

FROM GASOLINE ALLEY TO GREAT PACIFIC

Frank King's newspaper strip *Gasoline Alley* (launched in 1918) is the first work of modern comic art that consistently refused to take nature as mere setting or background, instead embracing the environment's animate and agentic power over its protagonists, the small-town duo of father Walt and his adopted son Skeezix. King showcased this power most explicitly in his annual "autumn walk" episodes, which conveyed the season's nuanced hues on the largest canvas then possible for conventional comics: the Sunday page. Appearing most years in October or November, "this 'walk' marked not only the approaching close of the year, but also highlighted the changes to its principal characters over the past twelve months," according to Chris Ware. This is because, in another great innovation, King had introduced real-time continuity into the comic strip, such that a year for the reader equaled a year for Walt and Skeezix. The rhythms of their lives were thus closely tied to those of the seasons.[17] These "autumn walk" *Gasoline Alley* installments were also not particularly humorous; as Ware put it, "if there was any punchline to the strip, it was usually overshadowed by the natural beauty of the page as a compositional whole."[18] In other words, the large format and design unity of the page (twelve panels in "waffle iron" layout) were inextricable from the content.

The panels themselves tended to jump around locations a lot, eliding how Walt and Skeezix got to where they are. In one frame from October 21, 1923, Walt stands before a marsh, holding his son on his shoulder, and proclaims, "Isn't that a restful view, Skeezix?" In the next frame, they're in a forest with cascading yellow leaves, as Walt remarks: "Color even drops from the trees like rain after a shower. I could almost be a poet today!" (King).

An avid nature lover and hiker, King channeled his affection onto these Sunday pages, which unlike the more plot-driven dailies were an opportunity to "savor experiences and ruminate on life," explains Jeet Heer (iii). Nature is many things in these utopian works: wise guide, generous mentor, fantastic artist, sensitive friend. Many times, Walt compliments "Jack Frost" on his tireless work and lovely hues. "Nature is the best teacher of color," Walt says on November 4, 1928 (King).

Walt and Skeezix take their annual autumn walk in King's *Gasoline Alley* (November 4, 1928). © The estate of Frank King.

A minority of King's nature-themed Sunday pages that are not "autumn walks" introduce discordant notes. For example, in a funny/sad story from August 6, 1922, father and son chase a rainbow across the countryside, to see if they can retrieve the pot of gold at the end of it. After much travel, they reach their goal, only to find an ugly heap of garbage and discarded junk. "I always thought there was something phoney about that story!" Walt complains in the last panel. But a more optimistic Sunday composition from November 8, 1925,

Ka-Zar tries to stop an elephant stampede in a double-page spread in Thompson's *Marvel Mystery Comics* #11 (Sept. 1940). © Marvel Comics.

takes the "autumn walk" concept to remarkable new heights by having Walt and Skeezix in eight brisk panels traverse an entire year's worth of seasons, not just the fall. The mind-bending time-machine quality is enhanced by the *ostinato* of the panels, regulated as always by Walt's calm exposition: "Now the buds on the trees . . ." / "Now it's autumn, the time when . . ." / "And now winter comes along . . ." (King). In all these examples, the "mega-image" (here presenting as a polyptych) facilitates a lush, near-enveloping sensual experience with few parallels in the art.

My next example is, if not the first double-page spread in the comic book format, certainly among the very earliest.[19] "Adventures of Ka-Zar the Great," in *Marvel Mystery Comics* #11 (Sept. 1940), features a rollicking jungle adventure by writer/artist Ben Thompson, in which hero Ka-Zar/David Rand ("white man and the guardian of the wild Belgian Congo") must foil the destructive predations of India's Rajah Sarput, figured as little more than a nefarious racialized Other (B. Thompson).

At one point, the Rajah's slaves drive a raging herd of elephants through the jungle for him to kill, but Ka-Zar and his animal allies Zar the lion and Trajah the elephant arrive just in time to block their path; this is the moment captured in the double-spread. A towering (rather generic-looking) tree at the center, split by the booklet's crease, dominates the picture, which appears balanced between opposing forces about to collide. At left, we see over a half dozen panicked elephants rushing toward, on the right side, Ka-Zar and his friends. Vegetation, trees, and gradations of green and brown create various planes of depth; in the distance to the right, the Rajah sits atop his hunting elephant, which due to some odd perspective seems almost to be defying gravity. There is minimal narration and dialogue, the better to take in the joltingly large image, whose design contrasts sharply with that of the previous pages (made up of as many as eight panels). A tiny but brave Ka-Zar raises his hand to the "fear-crazed herd" with its "thundering hoofs," and yells, "Stop, my brothers! Turn into the West . . . Ka-Zar commands it!"

The "freeze-frame" quality of the spread arrests the forward motion of the story in ways we have already discussed, inviting the reader—at the mere turn of a page—to contemplate an unexpectedly expanded vista. The effect is akin to switching from a thirteen-inch television screen to theatrical CinemaScope in one breath. The suddenly panoramic scope allows the reader to newly appreciate that Ka-Zar (a blond Tarzan knock-off, down to his leopard-print loincloth) lives in a fabulously rich environment full of animate, diverse life.

Some of that life (stampeding elephants) is dangerous, its threat only enhanced by the larger format (the frightened herd fills up more than a quarter of the total real estate). The human hero and villain form only a part of that vast interconnected array; in this double-sized figuration they even appear decentered, dwarfed by the jungle, the animals, and the land. In one sweeping visualization, the narrative's relationships (heroic Ka-Zar, evil Rajah, natural world in peril) are crystallized, along with—potentially—the implications these carry for the reader's own ties to the real natural world off the page.

Creators have of course engaged with that natural world since the earliest days of modern comics, whether in the fantastic dreamscapes explored by Winsor McCay's Nemo, or the surreal Coconino desertscapes where George Herriman's Krazy, Ignatz, and Officer Pupp do their thing. More rare are works that foreground natural spaces and their denizens as a matter of course, the way King and Thompson do only occasionally. In this regard former park ranger Ed Dodd's popular nature-themed mid-century comic strip *Mark Trail* (debuted 1946) holds an important place in the history of the form. Even if more recent critics have labeled the strip "something of a byword for stultifying legacy comics" and sneeringly derided it as "weekday afternoon PBS meets your Boy Scout troop leader" (Rabiroff)—as if those were self-evidently bad things—Dodd's work brought exotic animals and plants into readers' living rooms years before television shows like *Mutual of Omaha's Wild Kingdom* did the same.[20]

Though it featured the adventures of a rugged nature photojournalist and his friends, the strip was characterized more by a deep fascination with the environment and an eagerness to share it. In doing so, Dodd went so far as to break with the conventions of mainstream storytelling. It was not an uncommon

A human-decentering midstrip cutaway in Dodd's *Mark Trail* (July 31, 1969). © The estate of Ed Dodd.

occurrence to cut away in the middle of a panel sequence from the protagonists to a close-up of some unrelated natural feature (usually an animal), thus decentering a human perspective. As Veronica Vold describes it, "This dynamic focalization serves to disorient the reader; it can sometimes be difficult to tell if the animals themselves are speaking or if an off-panel human character is talking" (71). See for example the *Mark Trail* for July 31, 1969, in which Dodd inserts a close-up portrait of a pair of seabirds in the middle frame of a three-panel sequence, making for an odd cutaway in an ongoing conversation among the principals (who neither comment on nor seem to notice the birds). These moments of casual rupture represent the diminutive daily strip's version of the "mega-image," prompting Vold to further comment: "In the formal tension between animal icons and humans as well as narrative content, *Mark Trail*'s panel sequence imagines a conservationist paradigm that insists on human reverence for and submission to the active interests of the more-than-human world. Its lyrical tribute interrupts any anthropocentric narrative flow" (71).[21]

Dodd's Sunday pages and comic book collections like *Mark Trail's Adventure Book of Nature* (1958) blow up that ethos to page-size proportions, further displacing the human hero. In fact, in many of these features Trail appears only in the upper-left minipanel as a sort of entry point for the reader into a nature documentary fully focused on its animal or plant subjects. In the Sunday page for January 26, 1969 (on Pennsylvania's state bird, the ruffed grouse), we see Trail only in that smallest first panel next to the title, hunting with a rifle in some snowy woods, while in the May 5, 1974, Sunday feature (on bees) he again pops up there in a close-up, with a worried expression as a bee buzzes close to his face. He is reduced to a cameo, a brief comedic bit, in his own series—the better to leave the other 90 percent of the page to the wonders of pollinator doings. In this regard, Dodd's much-mocked *Mark Trail* (deemed by later critics among the most square and pedestrian of series) is a radical work, bent on evoking a fully fledged posthumanist vision. (Take that, Charles Schulz!)[22]

Pogo (1948–1975) never went that far in defying anthropocentrism, but Walt Kelly's seminal strip has long held a reputation for doing more than any other twentieth-century comics work to facilitate an "environmental imagination" in the public.²³ That standing rests largely on Kelly's late work of the 1970s, when he explicitly promoted environmentalist causes, but in fact, his stories of Pogo Possum, Albert Alligator, and other "critturs" had long explored questions of interconnection in the fragile ecosystem of a lovingly etched Okefenokee swamp. Brian Cremins argues that "Kelly's emphasis on protecting the environment is the logical conclusion of his strip, the destination to which these tropes were leading him from the strip's earliest days" (39).²⁴

Kelly came to shape much of US environmentalist visual culture in its early phases with his 1970 poster *We Have Met the Enemy and He Is Us*, issued in commemoration of the first Earth Day. This shows Pogo gazing forlornly at the viewer, a sack and trash picker in his hands, while behind looms a polluted Okefenokee strewn with bottles, tires, a bathtub, and other garbage—not unlike what Walt and Skeezix discovered at the end of the rainbow. Only Pogo *lives here*. The mordant phrase "We have met the enemy and he is us"—a 1970 version of *we are the asteroid*—grew ubiquitous in the culture and was adopted as a slogan by the environmentalist movement.²⁵ The strip Kelly produced for the second Earth Day in April 1971 cemented the phrase into Pogo "canon." In two "widescreen" mega-image-y panels, Porky Porcupine and Pogo inch their way across an even more heavily polluted swamp ("It *is* hard walkin' on this stuff."). As the two sit gazing at the sad scene of devastation, Pogo delivers his famous line. They have no choice but to "*mak[e]* home in a broken world."²⁶

As touched on in my discussion of the Silver Surfer above, by the late 1960s concerns over the environment had reached a critical mass in the US. Fueled among other things by doomsayer books like Paul Ehrlich's *The Population Bomb* (1968), these anxieties to some extent even displaced Cold War worries over the bomb. In 1965, meteorologist Morris Neiburger had warned that civilization would collapse "not from a sudden cataclysm like a nuclear war, but from gradual suffocation in its own wastes" (quoted in Dunaway, "Gas Masks" 74).

Out of that affective tangle emerged the first Earth Day on April 22, 1970, organized by Wisconsin Senator Gaylord Nelson and a broad coalition of progressive groups. The event inspired over twenty million people across the country to take part and redirected the national conversation on the environment. A country riven over the Vietnam War, the civil rights movement, and counterculture could come together over the need for clean air, pure waterways, and safe natural spaces. For all its shortcomings,²⁷ Earth Day set an ambitious cultural and legislative agenda for the new decade—and delivered. Among that era's accomplishments, as noted, were Nixon's new Environmental Protection Agency (1970) and passage of the Clean Water Act (1972) and the Endangered Species Act (1973).²⁸

Among the initiatives held in conjunction with the first Earth Day was underground comix publisher Ron Turner's ecology-themed series *Slow Death Funnies*

(1970). (I devote a lengthy discussion to this series in chapter 4, while Leonard Rifas provides a wide-ranging examination of the 1970s underground's engagement with environmentalism.) Even Alfred E. Neuman appeared grinning in a haze of smog on the cover of *Mad* #146 (Oct. 1971), a "special polluted issue."

And while the mainstream had long touched on such themes through characters like Aquaman (created by Paul Norris and Mort Wiesinger in 1941), in the seventies the superhero genre really got in on the post–Earth Day zeitgeist; Silver Surfer and the Defenders were far from alone. In this regard, Denny O'Neil and Neal Adams's DC series *Green Lantern/Green Arrow* made for the most explicit and ham-handed example. As part of what Bradford W. Wright and others termed superheroes' "relevance" movement (which took in such mature themes as drug use, poverty, and pollution),[29] the blond archer Oliver Queen and ring-toting space cop Hal Jordan took on environmental injustice through a rather offensive "white savior" scheme that involved Queen dressing up as a Native American in "Ulysses Star Is Still Alive!" (#79, Sept. 1970); overpopulation in "Death Be My Destiny!" (#81, Dec. 1970); and industrial poisons in "Peril in Plastic" (#84, July 1971).

The high-water mark for the green movement passed, and a new conservative administration held sway in Washington starting in 1981. Environmentalism ceded ground to "meat and potatoes" issues like jobs and economic growth—as if one had to choose between them. In the comics as well, the ecological theme retreated to the margins of the scene, in independent series like *Ms. Mystic* (see Alaniz, "'Where Is My Soil?'") and *The Puma Blues*.[30]

One mainstream series from this era, though, bears mention for how it upheld a fully dedicated "environmentalist imagination" even within the limits of a culture that as a whole had moved on (to say nothing of superhero comics' own genre constraints). Some eight years after "Exodus!," John Byrne embarked on a new series for Marvel, *Namor the Sub-Mariner* (1990), starring a character created by Bill Everett in 1939. The ocean-based Atlantean Namor, historically as much villain as hero, had clashed with the human race before over its polluting ways, which had drastically affected his underwater kingdom. Namor even objected before the United Nations when surface-dwellers dumped chemical weapons in the ocean in "The World My Enemy!" by Roy Thomas and John Buscema, in *Sub-Mariner* #25 (May 1970, again around the first Earth Day).[31]

Byrne's series begins at a point when the world believes Namor dead. In secret, he resolves to plunder the priceless loot of the ocean's sunken ships and build a financial empire devoted to ecological restoration. As the book's recurring opening crawl puts it, "The wealth of eternal seas at his command, he has set up a new campaign of conquest . . . against the enemies of the environment itself!" In *Namor the Sub-Mariner*, Byrne's hero deals with rapacious petro-conglomerates, a massive oil spill engineered by eco-terrorists, and a towering mountain of sewage named Sluj. What stands out in the series—which suffered from clunky writing, weak characters, and subpar art from Byrne—is how it wears its environmentalist ethic very much on its sleeve. In the first issue, Namor explains his rationale:

> Humankind has treated the planet we share as if it were a single vast disposable resource.
>   It is not. The ecology which supports life as we know it is frail. Each day the surface dwellers damage it is a day that cannot ever be fully undone.
>   Yet, there is a chance that one man in the right place, at the right time, could work the miracle necessary to save this battered planet.
>   Provided, of course, he has sufficient power. I believe I have that power. Here, in the hidden wealth of the ocean floor.
>   The only power the surface dwellers truly comprehend.
>   Money! (Byrne, "Purpose!" 27)

Though it does not fulfill the potential of that premise, Byrne's *Namor the Sub-Mariner* sought to explicitly redefine the superhero within the context of the Anthropocene's complex systemic challenges, in the end showing up the genre's in-built disadvantages for such a task.

A more auspicious and successful attempt to do that very thing came in the guise of Roger Stern and Kerry Gammill's *Superman for Earth* (1991), an in-continuity DC one-shot in which the Man of Steel confronts the world's pollution, deforestation, and mass extinction with superpowers—only to come up woefully short. The liberal bromides and late-capitalist "fixes" he turns to next may ring hollow (for reasons already discussed above), but the graphic novella effectively parlays a reader's familiarity with the Superman mythos for an informative, fact-filled evocation of late twentieth-century environmentalist angst.

The story opens with a discomfited Lois Lane telling fiancé Clark Kent about her research to prepare for an upcoming international ecology symposium she will cover as a journalist: ". . . Acid rain, toxic waste, the greenhouse effect, species extinction [. . .] we've done some *terrible* things to this world . . ." (Stern and Gammill). Superman notices some of these effects while flying about; we learn that Metropolis's skies and Hob's river have become noticeably dirtier since Perry White's childhood and Superman's arrival—instances of solastalgia.

As he often does, Kal-El takes it on himself to lend a hand. But the hero's every attempt to address this crisis only reveals how multifaceted and fathomless it really is. In addition, Superman's efforts are all reactive:[32] The FBI and EPA ask him to help foil a toxic oil ring, so he does so; White complains about the polluted river, so Supes goes to sweep up garbage out of it; while doing that, he notices a leaking sewage pipe and seals it up; he spots illegal logging in the Amazon, so he stops it. "I don't think I've ever spent so much time on any one task before," he sighs.

The problem is too big even for the Man of Tomorrow, who discovers that modern ways of life in the US lie at the root of the country's environmental woes. For example, a scientific analysis shows that the partially cleaned river carries innumerable chemical pollutants (it's not just a matter of sunken old tires and shopping carts), while even a paper-recycling facility leaks deadly dioxin. "I can assure you," its director tells our hero, "our plant meets federal standards."

Appalled as he is by the ubiquitous presence of that dangerous substance, even in milk cartons and diapers, Superman flies again and again into a wall of neoliberal business-as-usual. Frustrated, he grouses: "Mills in Sweden are already using a safer oxygen-bleaching process in their paper production. But American mills have been slower to change. Instead, they've argued that the dioxin levels are too low to be a health hazard."

A scene in the Amazonian rainforest introduces still more complexity. It opens with a panoramic shot of dark-skinned loggers (perhaps workmates of the anonymous Native worker in *The Puma Blues*) chainsawing and burning the trees as terrified animals flee.[33] They are criminally clearing the land for a "great ranch"—presumably to pasture cattle for beef. Superman stops their operation cold; the federal authorities arrive to take the perpetrators into custody. Our hero lectures them (in Portuguese) with familiar platitudes about the rainforests as a "priceless resource" for the planet's climate and so on. But the logger foreman spits at his feet, saying, "Yankee pig! You level your own forests, and then preach to us to leave ours uncut! Do you expect us to *starve* to protect your world?"[34] As Lois responds when she hears of the incident: "The United States talks big about bettering the environment, but we set a wretched example, don't we? We're the most conspicuous consumers."

The story continues in this vein, with Superman repeatedly shown as not up to the task of solving this crisis, whether at a NIMBY protest objecting to the siting of a landfill; a new housing development in Smallville that is consuming farmland ("Where are all the people coming from?" Ma Kent worries); or Lois expressing doubts about having children once she and Clark marry, referencing debates about the ethics of childbirth in the Anthropocene (he answers that his alien genes may make that issue moot). "It's such a complicated problem," he concludes. "There are no easy answers. I'm afraid that what is needed is a major change in the way we live—maybe even the way we *think!*"

He's certainly right about that, but Superman's failures here of course owe as much to the market's approach to the genre as to any extratextual global state of affairs. In a deeply rooted convention, mainstream superheroes do not forcibly impose their will on society as a whole, even for its own good (as they perceive it)—if they do, they've become villains like *Watchmen*'s Adrian

Veidt/Ozymandias. So, the hero must uphold a sort of generic Prime Directive, lest *Superman for Earth* turn into a very different dystopian story, disrupting regular series continuity, damaging the hero's "good guy" brand, etc.[35] So in this novella, Superman is stuck, in ways that productively challenge and critique the genre along with the US way of life. Stern and Gammill's choice of the first, most iconic, "gold standard" superhero (as opposed to, say, Batman or Green Lantern) reflects their commitment to that task of deconstruction.

As such, the Man of Steel's most harrowing encounter with the reality principle takes place during an exchange with the chemist Professor Hamilton:

> **Professor Hamilton:** Our world's biosphere is so *fragile* in some respects . . . we may already be past the point of no return.
> **Superman:** Professor, you don't honestly think that life on Earth is becoming impossible?
> **PH:** Not at all! Barring some cosmic cataclysm, the Earth should continue to support life for many millions of years. But the life it supports need not include the species we presently know . . . not even the species *Homo sapiens!* There have been, after all, countless *extinctions* over the millennia . . . and they continue today!

The last lines of this clear-eyed assessment unfold in a text box accompanying a panel showing the cityscape of Metropolis, with its ultramodern skyscrapers, which match-cuts to a panel of equal size and shape depicting the Amazonian rainforest (initiating the aforementioned illegal logging scene). The visual-verbal interplay thus hints at a collapse of civilization and a return to primeval nature—as well as blurs the line between the two.

But the true horror of the dilemma comes home to the Kryptonian in an apocalyptic nightmare. Kal-El—himself a sort of climate refugee—witnesses the destruction of his home world, from which his parents spirited him away as an infant. Next, he gazes helplessly as his adopted planet transforms from verdant fields into a sprawling concrete jungle; the *Daily Planet* building rips through the earth as it grows to full size like some giant malevolent beanstalk. These urban canyons soon grow overwhelmed by garbage and fetid smog that kills people in their cars. "*Stop!*" Superman pleads directly at the reader. "Can't you see what you're doing?! You're poisoning everything—you're poisoning yourselves!" We see here the genre's repressed, latent horror (the reverse of the superhero's reflexive can-do optimism) brought uncannily to light. The epithet "man of tomorrow" takes on a bitterly ironic edge: Superman is left as the only living humanoid on a ruined planet, with only corpses, roaches, and rats for company.[36]

The Man of Steel witnesses humanity's fall due to pollution in Stern and Gammill's *Superman for Earth* (1991). © DC Comics.

Stern and Gammill make their climax Kal-El's address to the chaotic ecology conference, with all parties arguing and dragging their feet on action. Awed by his godlike presence, the delegates settle down and, along with a worldwide TV audience (citizens on the street, children in classrooms, the *Daily Planet* offices), listen closely as he declares:

> Anyone who has given the matter any thought must surely realize—that life on planet Earth is being threatened.... And that we, ourselves, are the source of that threat. [*We are the asteroid.*] On virtually every level, from the economic to the spiritual, humanity has been squandering its inheritance. Our rainforests, the very lungs of our world, are being destroyed. Plants and animals are becoming extinct faster than they can be studied. We cannot even begin to calculate what we are losing every year ... every day!
>
> [...] I cannot save the world by myself. A thousand supermen could not do all that is necessary to save the world. We are, all of us, part of the problem ... we must all be part of the solution.

That "solution" is the inadequate, individual-based, low-hanging neoliberal fruit that we covered earlier: New cross-border environmental initiatives are pursued after the conference (though we don't know if any of them will actually happen); Lois's apartment building sets up a recycling service; a woman carries her groceries in a reusable "world bag"; a new solar project is announced; Lois and Clark overhear a couple of strangers on the streets of Metropolis decide to walk rather than take a car because "it *is* a nice day ..." In the thirty-plus years since this story's publication, in the fifty-plus years since the first Earth Day, we've all seen how that sort of thing works out. All due respect.

I've spent this much space on the plot of *Superman for Earth* to detail how, for all its considerable shortcomings, it actually does do a serviceable job of covering point by point many of the critical concepts and issues the Anthropocene dredges up, in bite-size, reader-friendly, four-color format. That in the process it leaves the conventional superhero figure in somewhat of a shambles is just the icing on the cake.

That said, there were—there always are—strict constraints on how far such a publication could go in questioning the prevailing order. And so, right down to its notice that it is printed on recycled paper,[37] Stern and Gammill's earnest epic enacts and embodies the flawed, middle-of-the-road, hand-wringing liberal response to the Anthropocene in the late twentieth century.

It's left for me in what remains of this biased survey to briefly discuss those Anthropocenic comics "mega-images" that have stayed with me, in most cases for decades—though maybe "haunted me" works better as a description. I do not know why, exactly, these visions have seared themselves in my mind's eye, in some cases unmoored from their context due to the frailties of memory, except to say that they hold for me an affective power deeply intertwined with my personal growing awareness of the environment and all the trouble we've put it in. In a crucial sense, they helped wake me up. These are some of my own deeply felt emotion-pictures—my way as a lifelong comics reader of staying with said trouble.

I recollect, for example, that magnificent double-page spread from the climactic twelfth chapter of Don McGregor and Billy Graham's "Panther's Rage" in *Jungle Action* #17 (Sept. 1975). The Panther is caught in midleap, his beautiful, black-garbed body stretched across the width of both pages as Killmonger's forces attack the capital. T'Challa dispatches two villains (landing a punch on Macabre and strangling Karnaj) as explosions fill the sky about the towering necks of brontosauruses pressing their advance. It is an exhilarating Afrofuturist spectacle: dinosaurs versus lasers and jet airplanes, soldiers in traditional Wakandan dress, and a graceful superhero, muscles rippling, rushing to and fro amid the chaos. As McGregor puts it: "He seems to be *everywhere* . . . lashing out . . . *releasing* the rage that he has kept restrained for near a year" (248).

The spread especially partakes of what Andrei Molotiu terms "iconostatization" or "the move of a comic toward the stasis of an icon," an "all-in one-glance" impulse that exists in tension with the sequential dynamism that propels the eye from one panel to the next ("Abstract Form" 91). In this case the composition even resembles an actual iconostasis, comprising no fewer than seventeen panels in total. In a strip of nine small panels above the main image, we see fleeing citizens, crumbling infrastructure, the inept clowns Kazibe and Tayete cowering, T'Challa charging ahead. Balancing out the design, a strip of six small panels along the bottom show the injured M'Kabi struggling up from his hospital bed to gaze out the window with his wife Chandra.

These "framing" sequences serve both a storytelling function (to recount what is happening in the lead-up to the big image, as well as what may be taking place simultaneously with it) and an ideological one: to tie the superheroic sci-fi action directly and holistically to the many other characters and themes of "Panther's Rage." In this sense, the spread functions as an ecosystem with interdependent parts working together to create a fabulously complex unity.

I have long had a fascination with larger-than-human-scale life, of which fantasy comics have no short supply. I'm thinking of creatures like Lee and Kirby's malevolent Ego the Living Planet, debuted in *Thor* #132 (Sept. 1966), especially as rendered by John Byrne in *Fantastic Four* #234 (Sept. 1981). Or the strange organic fusion of pilot/starship from Archie Goodwin and Michael Golden's "Riders in the Void!" in *Star Wars* #38 (Aug. 1980). Don't forget the Acanti, a species of space-faring whales introduced by Chris Claremont and Dave

The sewage kaiju Sluj in Byrne's *Namor the Sub-Mariner* vol. 1 #7 (Oct. 1990). © Marvel Comics.

Krakoa the living island in Wein and Cockrum's *Giant Size X-Men* #1 (May 1975). © Marvel Comics.

Cockrum in *Uncanny X-Men* #156 (Apr. 1982). Who could forget Greg Irons's planet-devouring grotesque on the cover of *Slow Death Funnies* #1 (Apr. 1970)?

Maybe this predilection stems from an early love of kaiju movies, but as a kid, whenever these "super-sized" landscape-feature villains appeared on the covers of my favorite comics, I knew I was in for a treat. Many of these figures were an extension of the environment or *were* the environment, like Alpha Flight's first nemesis Tundra in Byrne's *Alpha Flight* #1 (May 1983) or *Namor the Sub-Mariner*'s aforementioned Sluj (debuted in *NSM* #6, Sept. 1990), which "when it rose from the waters there came a *stench* as *foul* as all the *sewers* of the world bursting as one!" (Byrne, "That I Be Shunned" 4). Byrne seemed to have a thing for these gargantuan monsters.

Among the most fully developed of these environs-scale characters is Krakoa the living island, which first appeared in the landmark *Giant Size X-Men* #1 (May 1975) by Len Wein and Cockrum. This has since been retconned, but at first Krakoa had an origin similar to Godzilla's: An "early *atomic test*" in the Pacific transforms affected flora and fauna into a mutant "*colony intelligence*" (Wein and Cockrum). Krakoa's trajectory from enemy to its role as habitat for a mutant nation (in twenty-first-century stories written by Jonathan Hickman) tracks a growing Anthropocenic public awareness—along with the yearning for a means to live in harmony with the natural world. In addition, the sheer size and umwelt of Krakoa-type figures poses challenges to conventional comics storytelling, prompting artists to experiment with or otherwise "queer" page layouts to accommodate them along with humanoids.[38]

Writer Alan Moore's 1980s revamp of DC's *Swamp Thing* (worthy of its own separate study) figures as perhaps the most fascinating and environmentally engaged superhero/horror/fantasy series of all time. Moore's reimagining of Alec Holland/Swamp Thing as an earth elemental and avatar of "the Green"[39] stands as the most brilliant of all retcons. The sentient Parliament of Trees, first seen in a double-spread in *Swamp Thing* vol. 2 #47 (Apr. 1986) drawn by Stan Woch, evokes what Rebecca Evans calls the "Botanosublime." A literary descendant of the world tree Yggdrasil and J. R. R. Tolkien's Ents, the series presents a radical vision of plant ontology that Sean Parson relates to the posthumanist aims of the Dark Mountain project: "The plant world seems to follow a slower, more intentional understanding of time, seen by the slow cadence of Swamp Thing's dialogue." It also resonates with recent studies in tree sentience and "plant cognitive ecology" by Suzanne Simard and Monica Gagliano (Pollan).[40] Moore and Stephen Bissette's "Rite of Spring" in *Swamp Thing* vol. 2 #34 (Mar. 1985) concludes a major story arc through an extraordinary sequence of "mega-images" that call for the reader to tilt the book ninety degrees in order to take in the double-page spreads representing Alec and Abbie's . . . well, I was going to say "love-making," and that's not wrong,

Swamp Thing's face transformed into a mega-image in Moore and Veitch's *Swamp Thing* vol. 2 #61 (June 1987). © DC Comics.

but the episode deals with content far more mind-blowing than that. Let's just say the earth moves.[41]

But no story from Moore's three-year run moved me as much as "All Flesh Is Grass" in *Swamp Thing* vol. 2 #61 (June 1987). A startling blend of drama, superheroics, and eco-horror, the tale finds Alec on JS86, a world of sentient plants. Since our green elemental manifests his body out of plant matter in his surroundings, the alien visitor sets off an apocalyptic disaster when he inadvertently absorbs millions of individual plant creatures. He becomes a towering horror that "did not know it was a horror" (110), a transcorporealist nightmare made up of mashed-together, terrified people. Only the intervention of Medphyl, the Green Lantern of this sector, saves the day.

Nonetheless, all the plant people traumatically incorporated by Swamp Thing are forever affected, from the disenchanted lovers Disma and Locliss to the alienated artist Shurlo to the priest Imrel, whose lagging faith is restored by the experience. Though these characters never formally meet each other, their wide-ranging connections and interdependencies are crystallized in a page by this issue's artist, Rick Veitch. It shows Swamp Thing's screaming face overlaid onto five panels over four tiers. This face also forms various landscape features populated by the other characters: His eyes are pools, his nose a mountain, his teeth tree stumps, etc. (115). Reminiscent of Arcimboldo, Moore and Veitch's virtuoso page design once more demonstrates the comics "mega-image's" capacity to weave together the Anthropocene's many multiscalar strands of disquiet, terror, tenderness, beauty, catastrophe, community, awe.

A similar poignancy suffuses the chilling episode in Frank Miller's *The Dark Knight Returns* (1986) when Superman fails to foil the Soviets' Coldbringer nuclear missile and suffers the effects of its nearby detonation. The explosion batters him about and blocks out the sun, plunging the world into darkness, robbing him of his powers' source. He quickly deteriorates into an emaciated, pallorous living zombie. Yet this appalling scene finds the gritty, hard-boiled Miller resorting to a rare lyrical key as Superman mourns not himself but the desecrated land: "You cannot *touch* my planet without destroying something *precious*. Even her *deserts* are abundant. There were *birds*, here, who she blessed with *chest feathers* absorbent enough to carry *water* for *miles* to their *children* . . ." (176).

The page that sticks with me, in its left half, freezes the instant when a floating Superman is pierced by lightning as he tries to reach the sun. The image participates in *The Dark Knight Returns'* storytelling strategy of using such "freeze-frame" visuals to judiciously "further the narrative or make clear symbolic points" (Wandtke 101). On the right side, in eight panels arranged in four equal tiers, Superman drops Icarus-like into a jungle. Skeletal, resembling his nemesis Bizarro or perhaps Frankenstein's Monster, he apostrophizes the

Superman reduced to a sunlight-deprived zombie in Frank Miller's *The Dark Knight Returns* (1986). © DC Comics.

earth itself, calls it "mother," begs it to release the sun's energy that "fuels us both" stored in the plants (178).

The imagery and text on this page have always struck me as indescribably weird, tragic, and beautiful. Lynn Varley's subtle painted color matched with Miller's cartoony mannerism is surely part of the spell. Like nothing before or since—there's certainly no scene like this in *Superman for Earth*—this astonishing episode cements the notion that the Man of Steel is bound to his adopted planet's environment through his very lifeblood. (He eventually manages to suck in the energy of the entire jungle, restoring him to health, saying, "You are ... so *generous*" [179]). What makes it all even stranger—productively so—is how the master choreographer Miller intercuts this scene with the ongoing violent chaos of Gotham City in the throes of a blackout. Yet again, comics design strategies allow the reader to propulsively, dizzyingly traverse multiple scales, even from panel to panel, in a vignette that works both as page-turner and as contemplative paean to lost nature.

Miller's penchant for "clear symbolic points" likewise informs a splash from a later work, the ecologically themed dystopia *Give Me Liberty* #2 (Sept. 1990) from Dark Horse. In the series' hellish satirical twenty-first century, a fractured, hyper-capitalist US despoils the planet until a sudden change in administration ushers into power a liberal environmentalist. He redeploys the country's "Pax troops" from their foreign wars to fight for nature. This issue finds protagonist Martha Washington, a Pax soldier, on a mission in Brazil to "defend what little remains of the forest from ruthless international fast food corporations" (Miller and Gibbons).

As this is a comic written by Miller, you never know what you might see when you flip the page, and as a young man I certainly found one page-turn in this issue both humorous and deeply unsettling. It opens to a splash depicting a giant war machine shaped like the Fat Boy burger franchise mascot, a sort of corpulent ventriloquist's dummy dressed in red with yellow polka dots, holding a soft drink and burger in its hands. Its mouth houses cannons that spray fire at tiny Pax troops; its thick legs tumble trees as it walks in the rainforest while Washington, in a one-person helicopter, fires back. The picture by artist Dave Gibbons is surreal, almost obscene somehow. And sickeningly funny, an effect enhanced by the cannon's sound effect "POOM POOM" mirroring the font of the company logo on Fat Boy's round torso (both are yellow). This page is like the Stay Puft Marshmallow Man sequence from *Ghostbusters* (d. Ivan Reitman, 1984), but hella darker. I know of few images that better capture the crushing banal perversity of the Anthropocene: rainforest into burgers. It more than answers Amitav Ghosh's call for art that screams about the reality of the now.[42]

Pax troops defend the rainforest from fast food corporations in Miller and Gibbons's *Give Me Liberty* #2 (Sept. 1990). © Frank Miller and Dave Gibbons.

Ron Lithgow/Concrete visits a clear-cut in Chadwick's *Think Like a Mountain* (1997). © Paul Chadwick.

From arch satire we turn to devastating realism (albeit in a sci-fi key) in Paul Chadwick's Concrete story *Think Like a Mountain* (1997). In this graphic novel, Concrete (i.e., Ron Lithgow's brain housed in an alien stone-like superbody)[43] consorts with an Earth First! eco-terrorist cell for a writing project. They bring him to Canada to view the remains of an old-growth forest after a clear-cut. In a two-page spread, the eye is assaulted by a land laid waste, innumerable stumps and debris stretching from horizon to horizon. At top left, Concrete and his companions meet Marge Wetherall, an itinerant artist whose "hobby" is marking freshly murdered tree remains with each specimen's birth and death year, based on its rings: 1775–1996, 1811–1996, 1530–1996, and so on. Marge describes herself as "an old woman capable only of empty, symbolic gestures" but hopes that someone someday will notice her memorial "and perhaps feel anger. Or shame."

Chadwick distorts the scale and perspective of this large image such that the shape of a wood pile behind Marge doubles as the curved horizon line; depending on how one views them, in that first portrait Concrete and the others look like giants compared to the ruined forest. But as we shift our gaze toward bottom right, we see a second depiction of the group in proper scale, wandering among the dead as Marge shows them around. At bottom left an eagle soars, its back to us (this could be the same raptor flying in the distance behind the first group). Apart from horror, the spread effects a strong sense of duality, of standing apart from or within nature itself, based on one's perspective. As argued by Adele

John Porcellino releases toxic fumes at a chemical plant in *Diary of a Mosquito Abatement Man* (2005). © John Porcellino.

Haverty Bealer, such scenes enact the series' transcorporeal ethos: "*Think Like a Mountain* is Chadwick's most sustained effort to show us Concrete's struggle to reinscribe his material body as the subject and the substance of an ecological body" (191). Produced during the 1990s Timber Wars of the Pacific Northwest (ably fictionalized by Richard Powers in his 2018 novel *The Overstory*), *Think Like a Mountain* lives up to its title's Leopoldian source.[44]

Moving now to twenty-first-century works: "Chemical Plant/Another World," an episode from John Porcellino's *Diary of a Mosquito Abatement Man* (2005) stands out for a scene of dystopian dread just as potent as Fat Boy in the rainforest—and all the more bizarre for its real-life basis. A collection drawn from the author's self-published autographic series *King-Cat*,[45] *Diary* chronicles his early job exterminating mosquitoes in Illinois and Colorado. In this chapter, the young Porcellino drives a truck at twelve miles per hour on his assigned route, a chemical plant, releasing pesticide gas into the air.

The sheer irreality of maneuvering his vehicle at 2:00 a.m. through "a flood-lit open-air city of pipes, wires, scaffolding towers and catwalks," a "maze-like compound" of "towering machines" with street names including Technology, Oxygen, and Progress, while he himself is spewing poison, profoundly unnerves our baseball-capped hero. In a page made up of two large rectangular panels, Porcellino depicts the eerie scene as his tiny truck plies the "jungle of machinery." Ever the consummate minimalist, he renders this industrial-scape

The waters rush in. Richard McGuire's *Here* (2014). © Richard McGuire.

as long tubes, vents, pipes, a sort of stripped-down Kirbyesque "technological sublime."[46] What's most haunting here are the people: in chem-suits and hard hats, going about their business, taking notes on clipboards, riding bicycles, "the slow, sad workers—drifting back and forth—or standing motionless as I passed. . . ." As in "Savage Time!," the Anthropocenic disquiet stems from seeing humans carry on as normal in a setting that is anything but.

We could read this "mega-image" as the natural follow-up to Chadwick's from *Think Like a Mountain*, representing the ultimate form of development that rises up on the bones of cleared forests. In the notes to his collection, Porcellino calls "Chemical Plant/Another World" "a document of one of the most surreal nights of my life"; it formed a step in his path to giving up that line of work forever.[47]

A graphic novel practically made up of "mega-images," Richard McGuire's *Here* (2014)[48] has drawn an unusual amount of attention from beyond the world of independent comics (or maybe it's just that in a post–*Jimmy Corrigan*, post–*Fun Home* world, comics releases get wider attention nowadays).[49] The book presents an alinear, kaleidoscopic narrative that juxtaposes multiple temporalities onto the same space—a corner of the house where McGuire grew up—for its entire two-hundred-plus pages (apart from landscape features, whether the house exists or not, and people's fashion, the author helpfully provides text boxes to ground the reader: 1992; 1899; 2314; 80,000,000 BCE, etc.) Several scholars have identified *Here* as a quintessentially Anthropocenic work for its felt sense of deep time and disorientingly posthuman storytelling. Referencing the novel, Erin James argues that it "nicely" illustrates the concept of solastalgia, "a useful reminder that terrestrial environments in the Anthropocene have taken on the instability of their aquatic peers. We can no longer step into the same *anywhere* twice in this era defined by radical, total, and complete change" ("Narrative" 196).[50]

I'm particularly taken by two double-page spreads in *Here*. In the first, a 1915 hyperframe contains panels of a resting bison in 10,000 BCE and a girl lounging on a rug in 1970. (McGuire fills his work with just such transcultural, trans-species parallels and repetitions.) The other shows, in the second-largest panel, floodwater streaming into the room through a broken window. The year reads: 2111. That's sobering enough in our era of rising oceans, but it's the other eighteen panels paired with this image (and seeming to respond to it) that are the most cutting. They are almost all insults: 1955 says, "Weirdo"; 1957: "Square"; 1963: "Dipshit." McGuire delivers perhaps the most fitting condemnation/put-down yet of we the asteroid.

Peter Kuper, also known for his vicious satirical demolitions,[51] channels his lyrical side in *Ruins* (2015). The graphic novel's troubled New York couple protagonists, George and Samantha, are fairly run-of-the-mill New Yorkers getting to know Oaxaca. The real star of the book is a monarch butterfly[52] on its migration from Canada to Mexico. In splash after splash interspersed within the human narrative, Kuper draws the butterfly as it flits over various Anthropocene "ruins": a strip-mining site in West Virginia; a Pennsylvania nuclear power facility evocative of the Three Mile Island disaster; farmworkers toiling in the Florida fields under a boss's tyranny; the aftereffects of Hurricane Katrina on New Orleans; a drive-by shooting in Monterey. One sequence also shows the monarch's perspective as it navigates using the Earth's magnetic field.

But *Ruins*' most stunning mega-image is its most unexpected: a gatefold spread late in the novel depicting George and Samantha on a visit to a Michoacán butterfly reserve where tens of thousands of these colorful creatures gather to breed. The spread is much better seen than described; more salient is Kuper's bold gambit to surprise the reader. I purchased the book without noticing the gatefold—until I got to that part of the story. It felt like bonus material, somehow; there was without exaggeration more comics here than I anticipated. The foldout section "literally moved beyond the dimensions of the book to evoke the euphoric," in Bukatman's words (*Hellboy's World* 69).[53] My experience found its analogue in George's grateful reaction to the swarm: "With so much destruction, I'd forgotten how much life persists. . . ." We both

The gatefold depicting George and Samantha's visit to a Michoacan butterfly reserve in Kuper's *Ruins* (2015) (detail). © Peter Kuper.

got more than we bargained for, our preconceptions dislodged—an intriguing instance of reader/character overlap.[54]

My final example, Joe Harris and Martín Morazzo's sci-fi satire *Great Pacific* (2012–2014) deals with the heir to an oil fortune, Chas Worthington,[55] who decides to stake a claim on a Texas-sized Pacific Ocean garbage patch and create a new country.[56] I found the series rather so-so, but there was no denying its engagement with the Anthropocene and furtherance of an environmental imagination. One large panel, from the first story arc, "Trashed!," landed particularly hard. It presents an enormous set of tentacles bursting from the surface of Worthington's island nation amid a spray of plastic bottles, caps, and other man-made debris. Our dumbfounded hero loses his footing before the monster, as the artificial "ground" gives way beneath him. In this image I'm getting notes of Jules Verne, with accents of sci-fi flicks like *Waterworld* (d. Kevin Reynolds, 1995), and a finish of parody. The borrowings and clichés unfold in the most real-world of settings, a synthetic continent choking life out of the ocean—but also serving as habitat for other life (see Roth). The self-referential panel alludes to the fact that *Great Pacific* is as much of an anthropogenic patchwork as the garbage island itself. To paraphrase Colin Powell: We broke the environment, and we own it.

I have centered nonhuman animals in my last few examples in part to segue to the next section, as well as to highlight the fact that when we speak of our modern transformation of nature, it's often to animals that we turn as synecdoche and victim (recall the pregnant orangutan in Indonesia). Comics are full of animals and animal-like creatures, so much so that even institutional exhibits about comics tend to feature them; see for example the Charles M. Schulz Museum's "Peanuts . . . Naturally" (2013);[57] the Billy Ireland Cartoon Library & Museum's "Power Lines: Comics and the Environment" (2021); and the New York Public Library's "INterSECTS: Where Arthropods and Homo Sapiens Meet" (2022), with art by Peter Kuper.

Drawing on critical animal studies, *Comics of the Anthropocene* emphasizes throughout its pages the degree to which animals in comics have figured as our closest and most explicit engagement with nature. It is to such representations that we now turn.

THE COMICS ANIMAL

The depiction of animals in graphic narrative[58] has long exhibited the paradoxical visual ubiquity and marginalization-as-metaphor John Berger regards as a hallmark of modernity. Of especial relevance: his discussion, in the 1980 essay "Why Look at Animals?," of the nineteenth-century French caricaturist J. J. Grandville's work, whereby animals *qua* animals all but disappear in a pictorial strategy to "people" dramatic tableaux and comment on social mores—a sort of "ani-drag." This near-total abnegation of the nonhuman image, Berger argues, served as a precursor to "the banality of Disney" (19). In Grandville, he contends:

> Animals are not being "borrowed" to explain people, nothing is unmasked; on the contrary. These animals have become prisoners of a human/social situation into which they have been pressganged. The vulture as landlord is more dreadfully rapacious than he is as a bird. The crocodiles at dinner are greedier at the table than they are in the river. . . . The dogs in Grandville's engraving of a dog-pound are in no way canine; they have dog faces, but what they are suffering is imprisonment *like men*. (19)

Ani-drag has predominated in the medium, across genres, since the modern form's emergence in the late nineteenth century; as noted by Michael Chaney, "Comics have theorized the animal by *performing* it since their incipience and contemporary productions show no signs of flagging" ("Animal Subjects" 44, my emphasis). Whether in such classic figures as Otto Messmer's Felix the Cat, Carl Barks's Donald Duck and family, or "edgier" and more recent antiheroes such as Robert Crumb's Fritz the Cat, animals in graphic narrative often partake of what Lisa Brown terms stereotypical "reverse anthropomorphism," its features codified by artists such as Will Eisner (inspired in part by the nineteenth-century physiognomic studies of Charles le Brun). She writes: "Images of animals are culturally coded and take on certain prescribed characteristics—especially in comics: the proud lion, the mischievous cat, the sly fox, the wise owl, the dumb bear, the untrustworthy snake" ("An Introduction" 4). Or as Chaney concludes: "The animal in such comics always functions as mere mask or costume, beneath which lies the human, whose universality is reaffirmed and reified in the process" ("Animal Subjects" 50).

Animals' hyper-(in)visibility in such a visual economy (reflecting their utter marginality) arises from their perceived radical otherness and concomitant speechlessness—as Jacques Derrida famously put it, their "bottomless . . . uninterpretable, unreadable, undecidable, abyssal and secret" gaze (12). Such a perception extends beyond the Western developed world, as evinced by Rupert Bazambanza's 2005 graphic novel *Smile Through the Tears*, based on the author's experiences in the 1994 Rwanda genocide. In his discussion of Bazambanza's work, Chaney registers that animals merely bear witness to the extreme limits of (human) experience; they appear as a "recurring image evocative of traumatic narration" ("The Animal Witness" 95).[59]

Even the more recent wave of animal-related or animal-centered comics works discussed by Chaney, David Herman, and others—including writer Grant Morrison's 1980s run on the DC series *Animal Man*; Murphy and Zulli's *The Puma Blues*; David B.'s *Epileptic* (2000); Morrison and Frank Quitely's *We³* (2005); James Vining's *First in Space* (2007), and McGuire's *Here*—while all clearly of a different order in terms of their environmental consciousness (often in a solemn, eco-catastrophic vein), must still grapple with Derrida's dilemma of on some level "speaking for" the "dead" animal or "animort" (62). As Jonathan Burt has written in regard to cinema: "The visual animal is caught in an argument over whether the animal should be considered on its own terms or understood through a network of human-animal relations" (188)[60]—an argument animals almost inevitably lose.

A voiceless, radically marginalized figure for whom anyone may speak recalls another such object of longstanding affective and ideological potency in Western culture: the corpse.[61] As anthropologist Katherine Verdery argues, "What gives a dead body symbolic effectiveness in politics is precisely its ambiguity, its capacity to evoke a variety of understandings" (29). Indeed, for most of the medium's history, animals have suffered repeated social deaths through the (mis-)representational ventriloquism of ani-drag (animals made to signify whatever the author chooses), reflecting their "dead" peripheral status in the larger world.

Shmoos slaughtered in *Li'l Abner* by Al Capp (1948). © The estate of Al Capp.

The foregoing underscores what Sarah Bezan identifies as a prevalent "framework of finitude" in critical animal studies, present too in animal-based comics for much of the medium's history (if only in latent form). Bezan sees in "finitude" a morbid if politically useful tool for advancing "a responsible and compassionate ethical paradigm that responds to the biopolitical (or thanatopolitical) state's violent and systematic slaughter of human, and especially nonhuman, animals" (192).[62]

In sum, the animal figure in graphic narrative is fully subsumed into what Chaney calls a "strategically parodic veiling of the human," a nonliving façade of otherness above which there often looms "the shadow of death" ("Animal Subjects" 45). In this regard, the animal *qua* animal disavowed by representation becomes available for mourning—at least for those willing to resist representational convention, to trouble the textures of said façade. The works I briefly examine now are just such a resistance, just such a troubling.

The shmoo, a white, diminutive, bowling pin–shaped animal, debuted in Al Capp's newspaper strip *Li'l Abner* on August 31, 1948. Inoffensive, docile, and eager to be killed for food and consumer products, the shmoos quickly upend life in the rural community of Dogpatch. In one 1948 strip, Mammie Yokum, Pappie Yokum, and Li'l Abner sit down to a dinner of shmoo steaks while several of the whiskered creatures stand around smiling. "Shmoos does *ev'rything!*" marvels Li'l Abner. "They gives milk, aigs, meat, an' th' eyes makes fine suspender buttons!!" The richly dressed store owner Soft-Hearted John, though, is furious: "But *ah'll be ruined ef ev'rybody has ev'rything they need!! Ah* cain't make any *money!!*" (Capp 17–18).[63]

The shmoos' abundance of benefits as a domestic animal becomes a threat to capitalism itself; in fact, they function as an allegory of socialism—a bold one, given the anti-communist era in which they first appeared. The strip's "solution" to this dilemma proved one of its more disturbing motifs: the frequent slaughter of shmoos, to the edge of extinction, in the name of preserving the Western free enterprise system. Capp's shmoos became a bona fide pop hit, spawning comics collections, many popular culture references, toys, music, and other merchandise, the animated TV series *The New Shmoo* (1979), and even a 1982 episode of *M*A*S*H*. The shmoo, through its evolving transmedial guises, became a parable on the exploitation and decimation of animal species in the Anthropocene.

Some of that affective charge—minus the satire—pervades children's comics on animal themes from the mid-twentieth century and after. Many of these also had transmedial lives: DC's *Rex the Wonder Dog* (1952–1959); the Gold Key series *Walt Disney's Big Red* (1962); and Dell's *National Velvet* (1962), *The Lone Ranger's Famous Horse Hi-Yo Silver* (1952–1960), and *Walt Disney's Water Birds and the Olympic Elk* (1956), the latter documentary comics in the *Mark Trail* vein. One of these I found especially moving for its tragedy-infused spirit of uplift: *The True Story of Smokey Bear* (from Western, 1969), in which Smokey is orphaned as a cub in a forest fire.[64]

These works all draw on an anthropomorphic framework in their depiction of animals, making those that manifestly resist the "ani-drag" approach of special consideration in the Anthropocene, an era in which nature is literally being remade in humans' image.[65] One example of this "animal as animal" mode, courtesy of one of the fathers of modern comics, is Will Eisner's "Izzy the Cockroach and the Meaning of Life" from his story cycle *A Life Force* (1988), which draws comparisons between a human being's struggles and those of a humble vermin.

Similarly, Finnish comics artist Hanneriina Moisseinen's graphic novel *The Isthmus* (Kannas, 2016) focuses on people and animals fleeing in the wake of the 1944 Second Soviet-Finnish War (a.k.a. Continuation War) through a realist, quasi-documentary mode that incorporates historical photographs. In the book's most heart-breaking scene, a calf is born in the middle of the agrarian Finnish Karelia region's evacuation as Soviet troops invade. Moisseinen shows its birth over several panels across four pages, in graphic detail made still more intimate by her delicate pencil technique. The farmers, seeing that the newborn is too weak to make the journey, take it away and shoot it. The cow mother, Rauha ("peace"), responds to her calf's disappearance with distress, though her frantic vocalizations do not appear on the page as sound effects ("moo" or the like). Instead, Moisseinen's cow "speaks" through speech balloons containing exclamation marks of increasing frequency. She

A frantic cow moos for her young in Moisseinen's *The Isthmus* (2016). © Hanneriina Moisseinen.

also exudes a watery discharge from her eyes, which a reader could interpret as tears of grief.[66] In any case, the association of animals with word balloons (traditionally reserved for human speech, even when—or especially when—delivered by an anthropomorphic mouse) powerfully conveys their subjectivity, emotions, and inner lives. As Aura Nikkilä and Anna Vuorrine indicate, "The animals in *The Isthmus* are not primarily represented as a source of livelihood, but as individual beings sharing the same lifeworld as the humans," opening a door to "interspecies empathy."[67]

Works such as Moisseinen's, in part focalized through the perspective of animals and thus providing imaginative access to their joys and sufferings, take on an added consequence in the age of the sixth mass extinction, when we are extirpating nonhuman species by the bushel. I delve at length on animal death and animal ontology in comics through the cases of Kamandi's insect companion Kliklak (chapter 5) and the many animal victims in the Black Panther storyline "Panther's Rage" (chapter 6), among others, but these themes run throughout much of this study. I consider such works as crucial opportunities for mourning the losses of the current era—but not only for that. As David Herman writes, "Animal comics have functioned, in effect, as a narrative technology for . . . (re)imagining the dynamics of self-other relationships that cross the species boundary" ("Introduction" 12).

3

COMICS AS ECOLOGICAL OBJECTS

Weaving our way toward the end of part I, I now want to consider the question: What makes comics ecological? Delimiting comics' status as "ecological objects" (whatever that might mean) may help us understand what the works we have examined so far—and what comic art in general—have to offer their readers in the way of greater engagement with a natural world (whatever *that* might mean) in an age of rapid human-induced change.

For starters, it's not simply a matter of finding comics that serve as vehicles for environmentalist messages, blithely calling them "eco-comics"/"eco-comix" and leaving it at that.[1] Sidney Dobrin, while introducing his collection *EcoComix*, brilliantly dispenses with that question. "It might appear straightforward," he writes, "to promote an axiomatic imperative through an ecocritical lens, to point to specific image/text artifacts and announce that they convey representations of the environment in some way or another." But he immediately contends, "To privilege ecocriticism as a methodology through which we might read comics is to promote a rhetoric that infantilizes image/texts as merely artifacts to be read rather than as dynamic representations of and constructors of cultural moments" ("EcoComix" 5). Elsewhere he adds, "Comics . . . don't merely depict images of the natural world, they often engage directly in ecocritical thought" ("EcoComix" 3).

What it might mean for comics to "engage directly in ecocritical thought"— simply in the course of being comics—is very much what I want to pursue here.

For this task I turn to the work of Timothy Morton, whom *The Guardian* calls "the philosopher prophet of the Anthropocene" (Blasdel). Through them, could we say more about how comics as comics can, if not represent Anthropocenic unrepresentables like deep time, mass extinction, climate change, global pollution ("hyperobjects," in Morton's parlance),[2] then at least help us to think them better? That might be the more valuable achievement, after all.

It would be folly to try and quickly summarize Morton's posthumanist, object-oriented ontology (OOO)–derived thought,[3] but drawing primarily from their *Ecology Without Nature* (2007) and the essay "You May Find Yourself Living in a Mass Extinction" (2016), I want to stress a few critical concepts.

First, Morton's philosophical program is in large measure a repudiation of the understanding of nature inherited from the Romantics, one premised on a subject-object relationship that sees the environment as separate, grand, pristine, sublime. In place of such thinking, they posit the "ecological," a radical "mesh"-like embrace of otherness coexisting, coequal, and overlapping with the self.[4] Like the bacteria in our microbiome, the nonhuman genetic material in our DNA, the microplastics ingested with our meals, or the pollution swirling in our air ("hyperobjects" again), we are already in a real sense coextensive with "nature," while "nature" is itself entirely suffused with the human (along with everything else). In this understanding, even man-made objects like Styrofoam and plutonium are "ecological." As Morton puts it, "The very idea of 'nature' which so many hold dear will have to wither away in an 'ecological' state of human society" (*Ecology Without Nature* 1).

Such a framework—equal parts utopian and terrifying—resonates with the arguments of environmentalist historians like William Cronon, who in his landmark 1995 essay "The Trouble with Wilderness, or Getting Back to the Wrong Nature," maintains: "Wilderness hides its unnaturalness behind a mask that is all the more beguiling because it seems so natural. As we gaze into the mirror it holds up for us, we too easily imagine that what we behold is Nature when in fact we see the reflection of our own unexamined longings and desires" (69–70).[5]

Moving on: Art plays a crucial role to inculcate in us moderns a sensitivity to the vagueness, "in-betweenness," and weirdness of the Anthropocene, its "subjunctive" quality. Because "not being able to be in the subjunctive is . . . a big problem for ecological thinking. Not being able to be in 'may' mode. It's all so black and white. And it edits out something vital to our experience of ecology, something we can't actually get rid of: the hesitation quality, feelings of unreality or of distorted or altered reality, feelings of the uncanny: feeling *weird*" (Morton, *All Art* 2).

We are to remain eternally in a state of disoriented suspension, like Jimmy Stewart hanging from the roof at the end of the first scene of Hitchock's *Vertigo* (1959; Morton loves to make pop culture references). After all, both ends of the ideological spectrum, from deep ecologists who worship (their idea of) nature to people who don't give a shit about nature, jettison the world's strangeness, its irreducible mystery (*All Art* 21). It seems that a bleak certainty (of whatever stripe) is the biggest impediment[6] to letting in a truly ecological thought.[7]

Morton pairs their assault on "nature" with a critique of ecomimesis in art, which they deem self-defeating. They advocate instead a self-referential, often conceptualist "ambient poetics" that bare not only the device but the very medium itself, the better to feel that vital "in-between" media often seek to paper over.[8] For example, building on the Russian formalists' concept of estrangement (*ostranenie*) and especially Roman Jakobson's "phatic statements," Morton champions "medial expresssions" such as writings that "highligh[t] the page on which the words were written, or the graphics out of which they were composed." These make contact conscious, they claim, since "when the medium of communication becomes impeded or thickened, we become aware of it, just as snow makes us painfully aware of walking" (*Ecology Without Nature* 37)[9] or annotations on a page jolt us into awareness of the ink impressed on paper or the pixels flickering on a screen. "How do you pronounce a crossed-out word?" they ask (*Ecology Without Nature* 45).

Calling attention to the medium blunts smooth communication. Indeed, Morton's question "Notice how the black marks on this page are separated from the edge by an empty margin of blank paper?" (*Ecology Without Nature* 37) recalls my discussion of the comics mega-image, with its contemplative pause and interruption of narrative flow.[10] (But we're getting ahead of ourselves.)

To sum up, a Mortonian "ambient poetics"–driven ecological art would privilege interconnectedness; a built-in awareness of its own construction so as to resist any straightforward ecomimesis; a "thickening" of its medial expression such that a consumer oscillates between varying modes of signification—or takes them all in simultaneously—even as they suspend disbelief; and a deep commitment to ambiguity, subjunctivity, multiplicity of meanings, and weirdness, the better to facilitate the philosopher's expanded notion of the ecological thought. An art that wears its artificiality on its sleeve. An art that is perhaps verbal, and visual, and somehow everything in between, all at once. In fact, an art that in a crucial sense is *all about* "in-betweenness." A profoundly "impure," ironic,[11] provisional, ambivalent, "contaminated" art, eternally flitting betwixt categories, a correlate to a nature that "keeps collapsing either into subjectivity or objectivity" such that "it is very hard, perhaps impossible, to keep nature just where it appears—somewhere in between" (*Ecology Without Nature* 41).

As my reader has long figured out, there is indeed such an art. You can practically picture it sitting there tranquilly, declaring, "Look no further, Mr. Kim. I'm your man." (Morton especially loves eighties pop references, as do I.)

So how does comics fit the bill?

It turns out that the harder task is proving that comics are *not* ecological in Morton's terms.

For starters, we have Ole Frahm's evocative work on the unreliability, uncanniness, and adulterated nature of comics. He writes:

> Comics remain between the categories of bourgeois aesthetics. They are neither literature nor art. They lack the depth of a novel, the richness of a painting, the density of a poem, the detailedness of a photograph, and the motion of film. That all this is missing is only natural; otherwise comics would not be comics. But they do not really lack these specifics of other media. Comics emerge from a mixture. As Art Spiegelman once put it: comics are a *com-mix*, a mixture of words and images.[12] As most people maintain, comics seen *as commix* contain rather too much than too little: too much is mixed up. ("Too Much")

He goes on:

> Comics as such are always self-referential. The words refer to the drawings, the drawings to the words. Which one is more true? The answer to this question cannot be found within the comics. "What do the images mean?"; "What kind of effect do the words have?"; "What is happening between them?" Comics have the capacity to raise questions about power. They expose the helplessness of all referentiality. And, comics expose the claim to show reality through signs, the totalitarian claim to end all struggles for "reality" by imposing *one* notion of reality . . .
> [Comics] mock the notion of *an* origin, of *an* original, that were to be signified by the heterogeneous signs. ("Too Much")

This is hardly an uncommon way to theorize the medium in comics studies. For instance, Benoît Peeters echoes Frahm when he discusses "the contradiction between narrative breakdown [découpage] and *mise en page* [page composition]."[13] In the "productive mode" of comics design, he argues, the tension between them is exacerbated, "the two aspects of the comic strip being put into operation simultaneously. One thus ends in a perpetually mobile result, which has for its primary effect the destabilization of reading." Hatfield is saying much the same when he calls comics a verbal-visual "art of tensions" (*Alternative Comics* chapter 2).[14]

More recently, in the introduction to a 2020 special section devoted to comics on the environment in the German comics studies journal *Closure*, Cord-Christian Casper notes:

> Comics are marked by specific "base distinctions," which, as Lukas Wilde has shown, observers can draw and re-draw constantly in their reading

process—for instance between more or less abstract, cartoonish signs. As a result of the need for distinctions of this kind, the aesthetics of comics appear as discontinuous, particularly when compared to media geared towards an impression of unambiguous reference. . . .

Comics offer conspicuously intransparent, repeating signs that foreground their fabrication and keep diegetic reality at arm's length. In bulk, these strategies make sure that represented ecologies are never fully subsumed under one mode of representation (10).[15]

We saw precisely this hydra-headed form of depiction in the lush, detailed ambient natural settings to which Walt and Skeezix devote their annual stroll, while our protagonists themselves King renders ever "cartoony." Comics, the art form of "too much," demands that the reader constantly distinguish between different levels of abstraction, style, virtuosity as a matter of course. Or as Scott McCloud relatedly put it, comics have "one set of lines to *see*, another set of lines to *be*" (*Understanding Comics* 43).

Without exaggeration, then, we can say that the more one looks for analogues in comics' formal properties to Morton's ecumenical "ecological thought," the more one finds them. Aaron Cloyd, examining wilderness, marginality, and the gutter in *Watchmen*, relates that "unlike a traditional novel that encourages a linear vision across the singular image of the text, comics require attending to multiple facets that are often disruptive of linear patterns" (236). In his Pierce-inflected reading of Jack Kirby's cartooning, Hatfield zeroes in on how it "activates a tension between iconic reading, based on assumptions of likeness, and symbolic reading, based on a knowledge of Kirby's distinctive conventions and codes" (*Hand of Fire* 46).

Much of what we mean by comics reading involves making just such quick distinctions between different registers of signification, different tracks, different modes, panel by panel and page by page. Except when it doesn't. Except when the work itself leans into the ambiguity, the "in-between" of these various regimes of visual-verbal signification, be it the "bloody" font of an EC Comics horror story or Chadwick's doubled-voiced spread in *Think Like a Mountain*, in which Concrete and his friends tower over the landscape and at the same time exist within it, are dwarfed by it.[16] Both apply, lending visual form to the "vagueness of kinda sorta finding yourself in the Anthropocene" (Morton, *All Art* 7). Terry Harpold plumbs similar depths in his analysis of the "middle voice" in Philippe Squarzoni's graphic novel *Climate Changed* (Saison Brune, 2012), whereby "image-text cum speech manages the ambiguous agency of the reader" (34), reflecting said reader's own participation in/anxiety over Anthropocenic processes.

Morton's medial expressions too find their correlate in Eszter Szép's "embodied vulnerability" model of comics production/consumption through the

Jess Thomas's cover for *Closure* #7 (2020).

former's attention to a music-derived "timbral voice," which "does not edit out its material embodiment" (*Ecology Without Nature* 40). Such a line of argument echoes (sorry) Szép's own lengthy analysis of the comics artist's corporeal trace in the artwork, as well as the physical presence of the comics work, which I discussed earlier.[17] Morton again: "The brilliance of ambient rhetoric is to make it appear as if, for a fleeting second, there *is* something in between" (*Ecology Without Nature* 50).

In sum, as Casper puts it, comics' "repertoire of devices, its image-texts relations, and its degrees of abstraction add up to a *formal* environment that takes up, transforms, and reflects the demarcations of the natural and the ecological that we live by" (1), such that they

> contest any image of nature in which a collective actor "humanity" is confronted with an external "environment" in the first place. Rather than a unitary storyworld, each panel can shift its allocation of human characteristics in the course of one movement across the gutter between panels. This attenuation of ecology as "types of origin" deploys the "weird signs"[18] of comics in the service of an equally "weird ecology." (3-4)

A "weird" art form amounting to a species of "weird ecology": quite the Mortonian evocation of ambient poetics.[19]

I point to three comics works as examples of the advantages and pitfalls of seeing comics as "ambient poetics"-type ecological objects, as a sort of ecosystem quite apart from though not unrelated to the reality that comics present as material objects.[20]

First I have in mind Jess Thomas's[21] cover to the aforementioned *Closure #7*. This lovely piece shows four panels formed by colorful foliage, in which deer, rabbits, birds, and other creatures placidly gambol. In other words, the comic's gutters present as vividly "alive," while the spaces framed by the verdure—dreary gray-tone images of spewing smokestacks, a dump, and other industrial settings—are "dead" or at the very least tainted, ruined, awaiting renewal. (*We are the asteroid.*) Some of the animal figures extend into the "dead zone" of the panels; a curious fox seems to trail a bridge of hued "nature" after it as it ventures deeper into the gray.

Casper celebrates the cover as one in which "gap and panel border, gutter and frame become one comics ecology as finely-tuned formal differences are subsumed by nonhuman life." Maybe. But I'm more attuned to something else he says: "Compared to this animated gutter, the framed images are a wasteland" (7). And there's the Romanticist rub. For such hard-and-fast dichotomies between "despoiled" urban spaces and "pristine" nature are precisely what Morton's anti-Romanticist philosophical project seeks to dismantle. This cover is Cronon's "Trouble with Wilderness" thesis visualized as a color/good versus black-and-white/bad composition—minus the critique. So, while Thomas's beautiful work may indeed enact a poetics of comics design that emphasizes connection and interdependency (both "pieces" of the image work together to make meaning), they only do so to convey the sort of message that upholds rigid human/nature hierarchies that are anthropocentric to their core. (It doesn't help that the animals, especially the cute bunnies and deer, recall a Disney movie.)

Further, though Casper reads it differently, for me the image reinforces rather than blurs the gulf between foreground (color gutters) and background (gray distant industrialscapes).[22] They don't appear on the same picture plane. That's another problem. To quote Morton again, "Whether we think of nature as an environment, or as other beings (animals, plants and so on), it keeps collapsing either into subjectivity or objectivity. It is very hard, perhaps impossible, to keep nature just where it appears—somewhere in between" (*Ecology Without Nature* 41). The *Closure* cover, sadly, erases the "in-between."

Thomas's piece reminds me of the Zone from the Strugatsky brothers' sci-fi novella *Roadside Picnic* (1972), famously brought to cinematic life by Andrei Tarkovsky in *Stalker* (1979).[23] In the story, mysterious aliens create bizarre Zones on Earth in which standard physics do not apply and inscrutable objects of unknown function (some very dangerous) pepper the landscape, which itself seems to flicker in and out of what humans understand as reality. But however strange and (that word again) weird as it appears, the Zone when regarded through a Mortonian lens represents something like the genuine totality of the Real, not some queer exception to it. (Or, if you will, it's all queer.) In contrast, Thomas's page design, despite its virtues, ultimately props up a Romanticist, deep ecology ghettoization of the places where most humans actually live, casting them as lost, forfeit, fallen from grace. Against such thinking, Morton declares, in an utterance recalling Eli Clare: "We choose this poisoned ground" (*Ecology Without Nature* 205).

Murphy and Zulli's *The Puma Blues*, a text I turn to more than once in this study, at times suffers from a similar impulse to dichotomize, which as discussed is not uncommon in works dealing with environmentalist melancholia, solastalgia, and eco-grief. But in other ways the cult 1980s series (in 2015 completed and collected by Dover Press) presents as an exemplary ecologically "ambient" comics work.

Resolutely experimental in form, *The Puma Blues* constantly troubles borders between comics and experimental cinema (the protagonist Gavia Immer spends several chapters watching a sort of experimental video documentary); comics and art (across the high/low spectrum); and especially comics and music—with liberal quotes from Bobby Capó's "Piel Canela" (1953), Jefferson Airplane's "White Rabbit" (1967), Peggy's Lee's "Is That All There Is?" (1969), and several songs from someone who looms very large in the story: queer icon David Bowie.

The two-page sequence—one could read it as a spread—that springs to my brain appears late in the narrative (Murphy and Zulli produced this material years after the series' cancellation, for the Dover compendium). At upper left, an aged Bowie croons "Where Are We Now?" from *The Next Day* (2013), while

Multiple eras/personae of David Bowie in Murphy and Zulli's *The Puma Blues* (1986–89/2015). © 2024 Stephen Murphy and the estate of Michael Zulli.

on the facing page we see the glam-rock era Bowie (in his dog-man persona) wailing "Future Legend" from *Diamond Dogs* (1974). Meanwhile, above the dog-man, astronaut Chris Hadfield sings his version of Bowie's breakthrough hit "Space Oddity" from *David Bowie* (1969)—which Hadfield performed on the International Space Station in 2013 ("Planet Earth is blue and there's nothing left to do"). Such ruptures of time/space, comics/music and fiction/reality typify *The Puma Blues*' "ecological" poetics of genre-mixing assemblage; here they accompany a mordant monologue by the middle-aged Gavia Immer on mass extinction, climate change, and myriad other environmentalist ills, updating his reader on how the Anthropocene has progressed since the 1980s: "As we brought about the end of nature/who knew nature was bringing about the end of us? [...] Nothing. Left. To do" (497–98).

Immer's grim soliloquy functions as the rumbling, persistent undertone to the playful, even funny, visuals (most of which are not delineated by panels) over the course of which Bowie morphs from his actual appearance as a sixty-eight-year-old at the time of the book's publication, to a singing Buddhist monk perched on melting ocean ice to various other guises. Murphy's text is the steady bass, Zulli's pencil drawings the wildly improvising sax. Ambient indeed.

Comics of course don't have to explicitly deal with the environment or the Anthropocene to count as Mortonian ecological objects. But it is also true that graphic narrative holds considerable "ambient poetics" advantages for representing some of the key concepts, frameworks, and phenomena linked to this era of global transformation. Certainly for me, no work in any medium has illustrated so powerfully and lucidly the mechanics of climate change, its place in planetary history, and the enormous stretches of time involved quite like German artist Jens Harder's *Alpha: Directions* (2009).[24]

An ecological opus in every sense of those words, it is nothing short of astonishing. Harder takes as his subject the first thirteen-odd billion years of existence itself, charting cosmic history from the Big Bang through the formation of the galaxies and planets, through the ebbs and flows of terrestrial climate and extinctions across the millennia, from the first single-celled organisms to the dinosaurs to—in its closing pages—the first Australopithecus.

In short, Harder produces a comics primer on deep time, a graphic narrative version of Charles H. Langmuir and Wally Broecker's *How to Build a Habitable Planet: The Story of the Earth from the Big Bang to Humankind* (1984/2012). In his discussion of such Earth system tracts and the difficulties of "thinking geological time," Dipesh Chakrabarty notes that they present "the history of life on Earth and the supportive Earth processes, all considered on geological if not astronomical scales," which foster a perspective on the planet "looked at from outside as if through a series of time-lapse photographs" ("Anthropocene Time" 24). He goes on to argue that "the protagonist of Earth system history is thus the Earth itself, not humans. Humans, in any case, come very late in that history.... In old Althusserian terms, the history of the Earth system is 'all process without a subject'" (25).

And what a process! On the one hand there is no story here; on the other, it is the only story, the greatest story, all stories, ever.

How does Harder do it? For one thing, by leaving out far more than he puts in. The fact is that even in a book of over 360 pages, he could only average about seven million years of history per drawing. "It's always too little, close to nothing," he sighed to an interviewer. "It will never be enough to show only a snippet of the whole" (Lorah). To stave off the threat of collapsing into incoherence posed by such a massive task, the artist resorts to an image dump derived from sifting through thousands of scientific and other sources, but one rationalized and aestheticized through "rhizomatic" page design (splashes, two-page spreads, endless subject-to-subject transitions, schematics) and minimally informative text boxes supplemented by more detailed appendices. Harder further familiarizes the unfamiliar through clever visual quotes that span everything from ancient mythology to contemporary popular culture, for example, Shiva in her Nataraja aspect (the dance of creation and destruction); Katsushika Hokusai's *The Great Wave of Kanagawa* (1831); medieval woodcuts; Francisco de Goya; works by German zoologist Ernst Haeckel, English paleoartist John Sibbick, and Czech

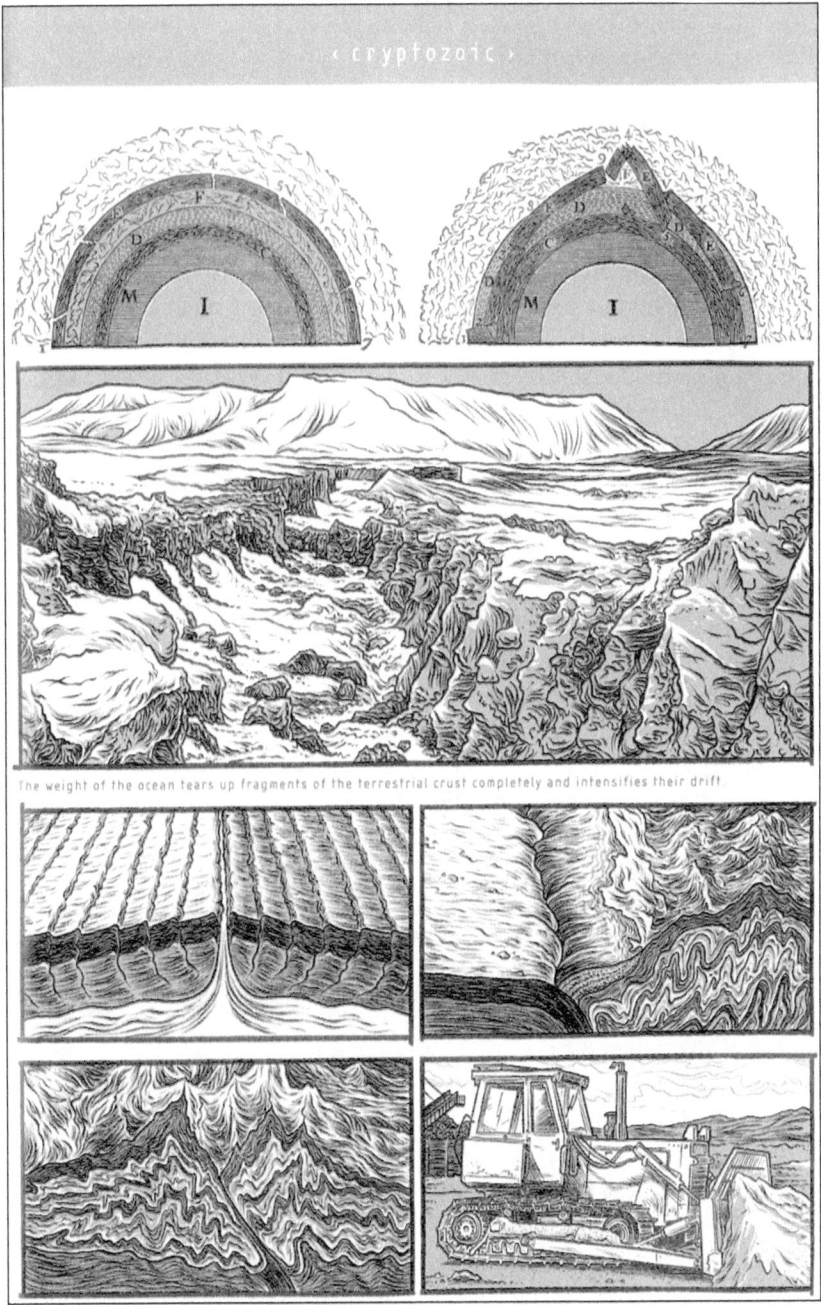

The deep past tied to the present in Harder's *Alpha: Directions* (2009). © 2024 Jens Harder.

illustrator Zdeněk Burian; McCay's Gertie the dinosaur; and Jim Woodring's Frank universe. And every few hundred million years, a mass extinction.

"Science comic" doesn't begin to describe it.

Alpha: Directions is the finest evocation of deep time ever set down in a work of graphic narrative, perhaps in any medium. Reading through its bravura set pieces brought back to me a similar feeling to when I first watched Stanley Kubrick's *2001: A Space Odyssey* (1968), in particular that spine-tingling moment when the proto-human hurls a bone into the air and as it falls back down to earth it transforms—via the most famous match-cut in all of cinema—into a spacecraft millions of years later. This extraordinary visual chronicle opens up kindred vistas of cosmic potential as it traverses mind-bending expanses of time for a lived sense of the universe's cold, beautiful, terrifying immensity. Harder takes you to church!

My first example comes from the book's section on the Archaen Eon, up to some 2.5 billion years before the present (give or take). Harder depicts this unimaginably remote period of Earth history (before the advent of life forms more sophisticated than microbes) in black ink with aquamarine tones. A page dealing with the tearing up of the planet's crust by the ocean's weight shows at the top tier two borderless half-circles representing the Earth: the first drawing is an intact globe, while the second's top layer has been ruptured. We may read the sequence as an action-to-action panel transition. The rest of the page lays down three more tiers made up of bordered panels in various sizes in which we see landscapes, what seem like close-up cross sections of terran crust as it is being ripped apart, and in the final frame a present-day earth-moving vehicle shoveling vast quantities of dirt in an off-page direction.

The inclusion of mundane construction machinery among other imagery of a time long before the emergence of *Homo sapiens* exemplifies Harder's approach in *Alpha* to relate the remote past to the here and now, to underscore how our presentist predilections shape our understanding of history. As he puts it, "I always had the wish to show not only the development of the world, but also the development of our view of the world" (Lorah). More subtly, the page design itself, made up of several subject-to-subject panels, advances that mission: the two eye-like "Earth" panels at top, paired with the rest of the layout, suggest a face (though not necessarily a human one; maybe something vaguely reptilian or alligatoresque). This Arcimboldo-ish composition, in fact, strongly recalls the previously referenced mega-image from "All Flesh Is Grass" in *Swamp Thing* vol. 2 #61 (June 1987), which maps a screaming Swamp Thing's face onto the page. As with all such compositions (and *Alpha* has no shortage of them), the artist leverages the visual/textual and linear/tabular functions of the comics page to produce ironicized "art of tensions" payoffs.

My last *Alpha* examples both take us back to the Cambrian Period of the Paleozoic Era, roughly 500 million years ago. In one "scene," Harder draws in black and terracotta several of the phyla that experienced a boost in their evolution in this age: mollusks, arthropods, amphibians, with their various tentacles, antennae, armored bodies, and corral shapes. Into this fray he throws in a panel of Woodring's cartoony Frank contemplating one of the pottery-like floaters of the Unifactor known as "jivas" (see Thielman). What startles and amuses more than anything about such a strange juxtaposition is how well these disparate worlds match on the page, an effect enhanced by Harder having several figures (mollusks and jiva) protrude slightly out from the panel borders. Unity in diversity, the past in the present, and vice versa.

Another page does similar work. This one shows innumerable prehistoric fish, a three-panel sequence displaying their evolution of jawed mouths and teeth, and in the final tier an image of Carl Barks's Donald Duck surrounded by hungry piscine predators (leering swordfish, sharks, lampreys). "Huh!" Donald exclaims. As seen here, among *Alpha*'s many virtues is its deft use of montage as a prompt to reflection, connection, laughter. To make a Mortonian 1980s reference, Harder's technique harkens back to the TV series *The Wonder Years* (1988–1993), which through intercutting likened the goings-on in the plot to classic films and television.

Finally, I should point out *Alpha*'s "untidy" panels, present throughout the work. Borderlines at panel corners constantly go well past the point where they meet their perpendicular fellows, giving off a less-than-neat impression. Comics artists will often erase such stray lines to maintain a cleaner, more "professional" look, but Harder leaves them as is. Yet this too adheres to the project's grander, holistic purposes. A reader (this reader) comes to feel as if he is taking in a comics work itself still in the process of construction, development, evolution—just like the world Harder sets forth (this world) is one of perpetual becoming. The journey is all. That kind of visual flair is how comics can subtly evoke . . . well, everything.

In the epilogue to the book, Harder writes, "With *Alpha* I tried to bring together for the first time all the visual representations from the assumed singularity point to the formation of the known universe. Similar to an illustrated Bible, as was previously published for the illiterate, only here now with a background in natural sciences in place of denominational constraints." It indeed helps that comics—an expansive, democratic, ecumenical art—need not suffer from "denominational constraints."

Part I has argued for comics as a medium uniquely suited to evoke, explore, and critique the daunting complexity of the Anthropocenic moment in global history, a moment when we are witnessing the destruction of nature as *Homo sapiens* has known it since the dawn of its time on Earth, a destruction *Homo sapiens* itself is bringing about day by day, year by year, particulate by particulate, degree by degree. (*We are the asteroid.*)

I've laid down a case for why comics, the hydra of the arts, is especially endowed for such a mission thanks to its multimodal, presence-absence, narrative/antinarrative, fake/real proclivities, its astounding comfort level with multitudinous meanings—with paradox, even. Among other things, this leads me to echo Armelle Blin-Rolland's call for an ecographics, that is, "an ecocritical approach . . . in which comics can engage with the porosity of human bodies as part of—rather than apart from—the environment and with the potential for ecological visions, contestations, awareness and imagination in this decentering" (110).

In a passage that could work as a description of graphic narrative itself, Morton averes, "All life-forms, along with the environments they compose and inhabit, defy boundaries between inside and outside at every level. When we examine the environment, it shimmers, and figures emerge in a 'strange distortion'" ("Queer Ecology" 274). The works examined in *Comics of the Anthropocene* "shimmer" in just such a Zone-like, boundary-flouting, ecological "strange distortion."

CONCLUSION: MUSINGS ON HOPE, OR REQUIEM FOR THE SAVAGE LAND

Timothy Clark reminds:

> As a possible global catastrophe arising from innumerable mostly trivial or innocent individual actions, including some which seem politically taboo, such as increased material prosperity, an expanding population or increased longevity, climate change does not present any one easily identifiable antagonist. Its causes are diffuse, partly unpredictable and separated from their effects by huge gaps in space and time. Climate change entangles itself with other environmental problems that seem to present no acceptable solution—the demands, for instance, of an expanding population for new and safely inhabitable space as against the claims to preservation of the habitats of increasingly scarce animals or plants.
>
> Can western eco-critics comfortably inhabit a stance from which to engage the environmental degradation latent in the hopes of millions of people in the Far East planning to buy a first car? ("Some Climate Change Ironies" 146)

I would have to answer no, first and foremost because by definition there exists no real way to "comfortably inhabit" the Anthropocene. (Your emissions-spewing mileage may vary.)

More directly, Clark brings us Western ecocritics back to an always-vital introspection. Does what we write and do matter in the face of such immensity—apocalypse itself? Could we be doing something else, something (as certain of my students put it) more "solutions-oriented"?

In a 2020 interview with Kim Stanley Robinson, *Jacobin*'s Derrick O'Keefe notes, "One of the *Ministry* characters wonders at some point, 'Were they fools to have tried so hard for words in a world careening toward catastrophe?'[25] Every writer working on the topic of climate, whether approaching it through fiction or nonfiction, probably has this thought from time to time."

Words, word, words, as Hamlet says.[26] Words like Johnny Cash's prescient "How high's the water, mama?" Words like *We are the asteroid*. Words like "futility," spoken by Stephen Falken in *WarGames* (he elaborates: "Nature knows when to give up, David"). In sum, as Jack says in the *The Puma Blues*: "My head was too full of words" (85). But words can also be used as Cronon uses them, to not let us forget that "far from inhabiting a realm that stands completely apart from humanity, the objects and creatures and landscapes we label as 'natural' are in fact deeply entangled with the words and images we use to describe them" ("Foreword" 20).

Words like "connection," "interdependence," or Morton's entangled "dark ecology."

Words like hope.

Not an optimist by temperament, I wince at that word. I tend to gravitate to Jenny Offill's cutting satirical vision in *Weather*; Lizzie's boss Sylvia tells her she'll call back soon, because right now "I'm about to send off this article, but I have to come up with the obligatory note of hope" (67). Discussing the novel, some of my students clung to that word as if it were a raft in a Category 4 hurricane, while others saw the joke. As one of them put it, "The use of 'obligatory' in some ways removes us from the debate of the justifiability of hope, as it implies that regardless of the sensibility of the notion, the people must be provided with their light in the darkness." To paraphrase another: If something is "obligatory" it's kinda meaningless.

All that said, Offill does name the website accompanying the novel obligatorynoteofhope.com. Parodically, sort of?

Instead of all that, I have perennially found myself in Senator Jefferson Smith's (Jimmy Stewart) camp, where lost causes are "the only ones worth fighting for."[27] My previous work in death and dying and experience with hospice has for me turned hope into something rather flimsy compared to other values for confronting the abyss;[28] hope is what transforms a story of Inhuman climate refugees driven to the moon just so they can keep breathing into a triumphalist exodus that ends with the birth of a baby girl who "should be so ... *human!*" Mainstream superhero serials, of course, have many such obligatory forms of hope (read: denial), like good defeats evil; people don't appreciably age; death isn't permanent; and all sorts of other nonsense. (But read on.)

So, hope, take a hike. The late Marxist critic Mike Davis, in the terminal stages of metastatic esophageal cancer, captured some of what I mean:

> To put it bluntly, I don't think hope is a scientific category. And I don't think that people fight or stay the course because of hope, I think people do it out of love and anger. Everybody always wants to know: Aren't you hopeful? Don't you believe in hope? To me, this is not a rational conversation. I try and write as honestly and realistically as I can. And you know, I see bad stuff. I see a city decaying from the bottom up. I see the landscapes that are so important to me as a Californian dying, irrevocably changed. I see fascism. I'm writing because I'm hoping the people who read it don't need dollops of hope or good endings but are reading so that they'll know what to fight, and fight even when the fight seems hopeless. (Dean)

Those are the words that move me. Hope, not so much.

And what about words and pictures? Might they go further, deeper?

I thought through some of this starting in 2016, as I embarked on the writing of this book, which took place over a peculiar stretch of time in my life. (See the conclusion to this volume.) Entering the final phases of composition, during the COVID-19 pandemic year of 2020 and beyond, things got even stranger. Mortonianly weird, one might say.

Words do have their uses, like for keeping track of our "progress" in the Anthropocene. The following twenty-first-century highlights reel, then, is meant as something between a Levinasian act of bearing witness and a *Harper's* Index: a litany of somberness, the occasional quirky story, and a lot of eco-grief in the recent past.

Awareness of what trouble we're in was growing (it always seems to be); the Oxford English Dictionary first included the term Anthropocene in 2014.

Sudan, the last male northern white rhino in the world, died in Kenya. The cover of the October 2019 issue of *National Geographic* featured an intimate portrait of Sudan with Joseph Wachira, one his keepers. Sudan and his descendants, the females Najin and Fatu (the last survivors of that subspecies), had for the last few years been under armed guard to protect them from poachers. The lineage of these animals stretches back some fifty million years, and they would soon be gone forever (some technological miracle of "de-extinction" notwithstanding—I warn you again, don't get me started).

"Eco-anxiety" made it into the Oxford English Dictionary in 2021.

A baby zebra called Hope died in a London zoo, apparently startled by fireworks (Woodyat).

In China, pandemic hysteria led to the mass killing of bats and destruction of their habitats out of the mistaken fear that they carried the virus (Dalton).

With Joe Biden in office, Lawrence Kudlow raged against the "radical green agenda" (Kudlow).

My natal state of Texas suffered a major power outage during a remarkably severe and long-lasting winter storm. People at South Padre Island worked feverishly to rescue thousands of sea turtles stunned by the deep freeze (Cavazos). The animals covered the floor of the convention center. A substantial and growing portion of the Texas power grid was taken up by Bitcoin mining, which along with NFTs and AI contributes mightily to greenhouse gas emissions, increasing the likelihood of such extreme weather events (see Calma).

For the first time, I taught a cinema and media studies course called Literature and Cinema of the Anthropocene at the University of Washington, Seattle. One of my students wrote, "The Anthropocene is the era when humans burn down forests with gender reveals."

Someone found an owl living in the Christmas tree at Rockefeller Center. They named the owl Rockefeller. The 2021 Marvel Studios TV series *Hawkeye* alluded to Rockefeller in its final episode, during which the eponymous hero (Jeremy Renner) discovers a feathered companion while he's dangling from the tree.

A Facebook user voiced their disgust at the Atlanta Botanical Garden's Holiday Nights: "My family thought I was the ultimate buzz-kill . . . all I kept talking about was the enormity of the light pollution and all the damage being done to nighttime ecosystem! The lights in the photo below are hanging from trees and were choreographed to loud music! Botanical gardens have an immense opportunity to educate the public by setting an example, yet they turned an urban old growth forest in the middle of the city into a botanical Disneyworld."[29] Similarly, during an event for Texas Governor Greg Abbott's 2022 reelection campaign at the Quinta Mazatlan World Birding Center in McAllen, Texas, they set off fireworks. Quinta Mazatlan not infrequently holds events for large groups, like weddings, at a site nominally intended as a sanctuary for birds where they could, you know, take a break from humans.

Climate activist Wynn Bruce of Colorado died by self-immolation in front of the US Supreme Court. Someone tweeted: "This act is not suicide. This is a deeply fearless act of compassion to bring attention to climate crisis." I thought of Jan Palach.

Three months later, the Supreme Court gutted the Environmental Protection Agency's powers to regulate emissions under the 1970 Clean Air Act. In 2024, the court overturned its own long-standing *Chevron v. Natural Resources Defense Council* decision, further eroding the federal government's ability to regulate polluters and address climate change.

Celebrities including Taylor Swift and Kylie Jenner were branded "climate criminals" for their profligate use of private jets. Some of their trips lasted barely seventeen minutes. (Oh, sorry, my bad. I meant "three minutes.") Jenner posted to Instagram a picture of herself and her boyfriend in front of two private jets on an airport tarmac, with the caption, "You wanna take yours or mine?" "What's the point of keeping track of carbon footprints when a single celebrity's footprint rivals that of Godzilla?" somebody groused. What seems often lost in such discourses is that transnational fossil fuel/agribusiness conglomerates like Exxon and Monsanto spew orders of magnitude more emissions than any celebrity.

In a development anticipated by the aforementioned *Superman for Earth*, Tosi Mpanu Mpanu, the Democratic Republic of Congo's lead representative on climate issues, announced his country would auction off vast tracts of old-growth rainforest to oil and gas interests. The funds raised would help Congo's struggling economy and address its poverty crisis. "That's our priority," Mpanu said. "Our priority is not to save the planet" (Maclean and Searcey).

Democrats passed on a party-line vote and President Biden signed the weaselly named Inflation Reduction Act, the largest-ever national investment in green energy and renewables, which sought to transition to a post–fossil fuels economy—though without resorting to what economists deem the most effective tool for such purposes: taxes and carbon caps.

Lewis Lapham wrote with his usual eloquence in *Lapham's Quarterly*: "Eighty-five percent of the carbon now present in the atmosphere is the value added during the course of my lifetime, 2.5 trillion tons, roughly equivalent to one thousand times the total weight of all the fish in the sea. I was 50 years old before I knew it was there, much less understood it to be a problem" (14). Lapham was born in 1935.

Category 4 Hurricane Ian carved huge chunks out of Cuba and Florida.

The Southwest sweltered under the worst "megadrought" in 1,200 years. Reservoirs all but emptied. The fire this time. A winter of severe storms and atmospheric rivers left California with a near-record snowpack, mostly ending the drought but leaving it vulnerable to serious flooding.

That same issue of *Lapham's Quarterly* ("Climate," 2019) reminded me that George Perkins Marsh had seen this coming as far back as 1864:

> The ravages committed by man subvert the relations and destroy the balance which nature had established between her organized and her

inorganic creations; and she avenges herself upon the intruder by letting loose upon her defaced provinces destructive energies hitherto kept in check by organic forces destined to be his best auxiliaries, but which he has unwisely dispersed and driven from the field of action. (42)

I say again: It is the biggest, the only story in the world. Which only makes it more disheartening when other stories shoo it from the headlines: COVID-19, Russia's invasion of Ukraine, the overturning of *Roe v. Wade*, inflation, President Biden's cognitive abilities, the 2024 election, Trump's lies. Those stories are all important and compelling, but me, I'm with Tony Soprano, weeping over the ducks. As Andreas Malm fumes: "It should be the movement of movements, at the top of the food chain, on a mission to protect the very existence of the terrain on which all others operate, but the question is—as so many have pointed out—whether it can attain that status and amass a social power larger than the enemy's[30] *in the little time that is left*" (394).

In the little time that is left.

Musing on such matters as I sped along in my Honda Fit with its fairly good fuel economy, listening to Jennifer Atkinson's podcast *Facing It*, about how we're already living in "climate overtime," there it was again: the "obligatory note of hope."

As it does throughout the culture, and as satirized by Offill, hope in the Anthropocene makes for a salient theme in many contemporary comics. There it is in Richard Monastersky and Nick Sousanis's "The Fragile Framework" (2015) on the Paris Climate Talks: "The job of finishing the task will fall to future generations." And in Patrick Kindlon and Marco Ferrari's series *Frontiersman* (2021), about a retired eco-superhero who returns to the fight to save a forest: "Maybe the kids have the right idea." Even the conceptualist Ilan Manouach's Shapereader story *Arctic Circle* (2016) deals with scientists in the Arctic investigating climate change.

Other works bracingly reject hope. I have particularly in mind a number of pieces in Last Gasp's *Slow Death Zero: The Comix Anthology of Ecological Horror* (2020), published on the fiftieth anniversary of both Earth Day and the launch of Ron Turner's venerable underground comix series. Turner himself, in the form of his avatar "Baba Ron Turner," welcomes the reader on the inside front cover, proclaiming the anthology's theme: "(what else?) real-life man-made horrors we idiot humans are perpetrating on our fragile planet. . . ." Coeditor Jon B. Cooke adds in the introduction: "Is this the end of the world? Sure feels that way with this shit-show each of us is trying to muddle through, whether politics, pandemic, or—especially—the environment. It's, like, what's a person to do facing all this insanity?" ("Welcome").

Well, how about escape into *virtual* reality as the world crumbles? That's the premise of Rick Veitch's story "Tiny Dancer," in which a decrepit humanoid wanders a blasted urban hellscape in search of food while his brain is fed constant visual stimuli by corporations. In this product-placement-heavy inner space, our hero can fall in love, marry his sweetheart, and fight for Mark Zuckerberg against rival conglomerates to defend a utopian world that exists only in his colonized mind. Veitch revs up the homage to EC horror comics with a story host, the "gutbucket guru" Mr. Mind Candy (modeled on Turner), here to "squeez[e] out another shit-frappe tale of *eco-suicide!*" (73). In such Anthropocene narratives, the destruction of the world for callous gain is a foregone conclusion; we have gone way beyond "climate overtime" here. Nor do the certainties of genre offer any respite. Imagine Tarzan's jungle razed for a palm oil plantation or a cow-grazing pasture.

In point of fact, something very like that happened, back where we started this book, in 1980s Marvel.

For me, of the hundreds of comics titles I've consumed, the thousands of stories traversed, Bruce Jones and Brent Anderson's run on *Ka-Zar the Savage* (1981–1984) bubbles up to somewhere very near the top. Which seems strange, since besides this I've never counted "jungle action" stories among my favorites.

Longtime Marvelites need no reminding that Ka-Zar/Kevin Plunder—a new iteration of the Golden Age hero discussed earlier[31]—dwells in the Savage Land, a hidden prehistoric jungle in the heart of Antarctica inhabited by dinosaurs and many other species extinct elsewhere on the planet, as well as by various tribes of *Homo sapiens*. The blond knife-wielding Ka-Zar and his fierce sabertoothed tiger companion Zabu serve as protectors of this paradise hidden from the outside world by a veil of clouds.

As I said, this was not the kind of material that usually appealed to me. But most likely drawn in by the arresting image on the cover of our hero, his cat, and Shanna the She-Devil grimly charging forward against a red sky, my thirteen-year-old self picked up a copy of *Ka-Zar the Savage* #1 from the stands anyway, sometime in 1981.

The first thing I discovered inside was the beautiful art by Anderson and inker Carlos Garzon, which strongly evoked Al Williamson's work (Garzon, I knew, had inked Williamson on the recent Marvel comics adaptation of *The Empire Strikes Back*). Second, it quickly became clear that the title's name was a misnomer; Ka-Zar had never seemed *less* savage in his entire four-decade span. He was no longer speaking in gruff monosyllables as he did in the 1940 spread we discussed earlier, nor as in the black-and-white Marvel magazine *Savage Tales* of the early 1970s (where I'd also seen him). This Ka-Zar was basically a snarky, quip-happy hippy, a long-haired Archie Andrews in 10,000,000 BC, searching for a higher purpose in life while caught—especially in the early issues—in a love triangle with a blonde and a brunette. I was intrigued.

The opening of Jones and Anderson's *Ka-Zar the Savage* #1 (Apr. 1981). © Marvel Comics.

It turned out that the personality change was just an entry point to grander explorations. The series opens with Kevin's somber contemplation of a woolly rhino being mauled by a wolf pack. A text box muses, "The rules never changed, only the combatants. No judgements were made, no sides taken. The grass fed the rhino which fed the wolves which fed the big dinosaurs which left their droppings which fed the grass. The chain was as endless as it was timeless. The rhino would not be missed. The law would not be questioned" (Jones and Anderson, "A New Dawn" 1). But regarding this violent scene from afar, Ka-Zar does question the order of things. He soon plunges into a full-blown existential quandary, which his partner Shanna dismisses as a "mid-life crisis" (10).

The Savage Land, with its echoes of Verne's Pellucidar, Burroughs's Africa, and Raymond's Mongo (racialized colonialist baggage in tow), forms a vibrant backdrop for what develops into a young misfit's journey of self-discovery. Kevin and Shanna come off as counterculture nonconformist types who live off-grid—*way* off-grid. They have fled modern urban life, what Shanna calls a "cage" (3), to a prelapsarian world of astonishing diversity, beauty, and danger. In these early issues, our hero, in search of the missing Zabu, discovers a path to the neighboring and far larger wilderness of Pangea, filled with unknown cultures like the Lemurans and species such as the winged bird-people of Aerie Shalahn. First glimpsing Pangea as he overlooks a verdant, sun-swept landscape, Kevin experiences a moment of "sheer magnitude and awe-inspiring grandeur" (12).

Though as seen in the series opening, Jones and Anderson don't gloss over the ugly realities of such locales, either, in ways that resonate with Morton's dark ecology. One must still kill or be killed. At one point, Ka-Zar and Zabu hunt down a gnu-like creature for their dinner. When Kevin discovers his prey's calf lying nearby, he destroys it to spare it needless suffering—though this horrifies Princess Leanne, a Lemuran city-dweller who then refuses to eat (28). In addition, all is not well with Pangea, which suffers unaccountable phenomena like frequent earthquakes and islands forming and disappearing with astounding speed. Shalahn leader Lord Typ describes it as "severe climatic and ecological changes. Weird animals and plant mutations are appearing. Our geography is altering and we don't know why" (Jones and Anderson, "To Air" 6).

Smart, self-aware, and infused with an ecological bent, Jones and Anderson's *Ka-Zar the Savage* brought together elements of jungle adventure, 1930s sci-fi, screwball comedy, and an environmentalist angst that anticipated later discussions of the Anthropocene in the wider culture. In ways analogous to what I argue in this study's chapter on the Wakanda of *Black Panther*, the Savage Land *spoke* in this series; it had a richness and living presence that made reading Ka-Zar's monthly adventures a rare sort of joy.

Which only makes the ultimate fate of that milieu all the harder to take.

The absolute eradication of both the Savage Land and Pangea by fire and ice—down to the last dinosaur, the last tribe, the last leaf—unfolded over three issues starting in *Avengers* #256 (June 1985) by Roger Stern and John Buscema. The cause: a supervillain, of course. Supervillainy is one of the genre's hyperobjects, massively distributed in time and space. Supervillains do what they do because they do it, and always will.

To be more specific, the culprit is Terminus, a 150-foot armored humanoid with a staff of nigh-atomic destructive power who cracks open and tosses aside huge seafaring vessels like child's toys. This intergalactic "loathesome scavenger of worlds" (Stern and Buscema, "This Power" 18) comes to the Savage Land in search of Celestial booty and other long-buried tech. Why does he do this? Who knows? The same old will to domination, resource extraction, whatever. "*Such is the power . . . such is the right of Terminus!!*" he says (22). Right.

Ka-Zar is lucky to survive a blast from the giant's staff. The rest of his party—a scientific expedition—is incinerated. The mechanical monster destroys Shanna and Kevin's thatched-roof home without even noticing, by stepping on it while on his way through the jungle to somewhere else (Stern and Buscema, "Holocaust" 3, 7). (The kaiju-like imagery gives a foretaste of the "Fat Boy" war machine attacking the rainforest in *Give Me Liberty*, discussed earlier.)

The middle chapter in *Avengers* #257 (July 1985), tellingly titled "Holocaust in a Hidden Land!," opens with Ka-Zar helplessly splayed out on the turf, stirring back to consciousness as the Avengers (including Captain America, Wasp, and Black Knight) tower over him in a double-spread. An amused Hercules holds a struggling Zabu by the scruff (2–3).

Ka-Zar and his family are thus utterly decentered from their own storylines, in their own domicile; "Some jungle lord, huh?" he gripes at his failure to stop Terminus (5). It all makes sense, of course. This is the Avengers' title and the threat in question will require superpowers to deal with, like those of the demigod Hercules and the Titan Starfox. The team has tracked Terminus to the Savage Land and intends to defeat him. Nonetheless, the battleground is Kevin and Shanna's home and that of countless other life forms reduced to the status of near-anonymous victims (such circumstances were often the concomitant of superpowered beings visiting the Savage Land, e.g., the X-Men). Like the woolly rhino dispatched by wolves in *Ka-Zar the Savage* #1, they "would not be missed." In fact, Terminus is described as "almost an elemental force" (Stern and Buscema, "This Power" 20); appalling as this extinction-level event is to witness, the story presents it as "natural"—kill or be killed on a grander scale.

It is certainly superhero business-as-usual, just with a much higher body count. Such seemed par for the course in the 1980s, with genocide and apocalyptic events happening with some regularity at both Marvel and DC: Dark Phoenix wiped out the entire D'Bari race (five billion souls) in *X-Men* #135 (July

Terminus destroys the Shalan aerie in Stern and Buscema's *Avengers* vol. 1 #257 (July 1985). © Marvel Comics.

1980); Galactus annihilated and consumed the Skrull homeworld—with lots of Skrulls still on it—in *Fantastic Four* #257 (Aug. 1983); to say nothing of the cosmic-scale bloodbath of the *Crisis on Infinite Earths* megaseries (1985–1986), in which universes dropped like flies.[32]

So, when Terminus's staff cleaves the rocky plateau separating the Savage Land from Pangea, it's only a matter of time before this "world-pillaging creature" (Stern and Buscema, "Holocaust" 6) rips the nature refuge apart, disrupting its ancient Atlantean climate-control technology as he digs for treasure.

What profoundly dismayed this seventeen-year-old first-time reader, though, was the almost-cavalier dispatch with which the story killed off beloved civilizations/species/ecosystems. It takes a mere six panels on one page, in a modified grid pattern, to off the Aerie. (Lemura's apocalypse on the previous page took only five panels.) The bird-people's extinction doesn't even merit a mega-image (Stern and Buscema have other plot points to hit, after all): Terminus is spotted, the winged denizens try to fly away, by tier three it's all over as the "raging atomic storm" that precedes the titan reduces everything and everyone to blackened husks.[33] A text box announces: "And even as the last of them plummets from the heavens, their centuries-old city melts away, like a candle thrust into a blast furnace!" (16).

What unspeakable waste, I thought. That final panel especially haunts me: charred bewinged corpses falling from the skies, burning Icaruses daubed out by inker Tom Palmer with pokes of a brush and ink splatters, like some nightmare version of Kirby Krackle. They drop onto a molten red inferno, a whole host of birds frightened to death by fireworks.

Evidently the Lemurans and Aerie Shalan[34] are not the Inhumans; no FF-vouchsafed exodus to the moon for them.

The Avengers arrive in their quinjet just as Terminus is completing his ecocide by afterthought. The narrator elaborates: "Like some merciless, wrathful god of old, he stands triumphant in the very center of Pangea, a land once green and vital . . . a land now in its death-throes!" (17).

The heroes' victory is swift in coming. Black Knight/Dane Whitman's enchanted blade slices through the giant's arm, depriving him of his staff; Hercules strips away the villain's armor. Inside we find a corpulent, puny, Jabba-like being; like the Martians in H. G. Wells's *The War of the Worlds* (1895), Terminus was but a superior mind with a weak body enhanced by hi-tech machinery. The link to Wells seems more than coincidental, as the "ravager of a thousand worlds" (22) shares a fate similar to that of the Martians laid low by mere Earth microbes. As Hercules puts it, "For all his power, once he was downed, he was helpless before the forces of nature! Those very forces which he unleashed sealed his *doom!*" (Stern and Buscema, "Pyrrhic Victory!" 4). In the Anthropocene, such a description does not just augur our future; it captures our day-to-day reality.

Terminus's wrecking of the region's environment-regulating system leads to a continent-wide blizzard and final catastrophe. A mourning Ka-Zar informs Captain America/Steve Rogers that the damage is total. Earthquakes set off during the attack "snuffed the volcanos that warmed my Savage Land. The Antarctic has reclaimed everything. It was all gone in a matter of minutes.... My wife and I managed to save only a few tribesmen" (3). The men stand in frozen wastes; the no longer bare-chested Kevin wears a parka along with the other mere mortals. "Yeah, it's hard to believe that yesterday this was a tropical rain forest" says an unnamed pilot (1).

One detail stood out to me: Kevin says *my* Savage Land. Not *the*. Decades of lovingly tended continuity, a deep investment of history and care, an intimate connection with the earth, a bottomless solastalgia, all reside in that possessive. In that *my* lie untold broken hearts. It embarrasses me not at all to admit mine was one.

Of course, Ka-Zar cannot really grieve; it's not his title (which had been canceled the year before). This is the Avengers' turf. So, he resorts to quite the understatement. Boarding a helicopter to leave, he only says, "[I]'ve spent most of my life in these hidden jungles. It's going to take me a while to get used to the fact that they're gone" (4). Those platitudes seem woefully inadequate in response to such devastation—but then again, what words could ever not be?

Let's face it: Stern and Buscema's opus does not achieve what Hillary Chute calls "a phenomenology of memory and trauma" capturing both the "interior and exterior trauma" of life-shattering events as seen in Keiji Nakazawa's *I Saw It* (1972), an autobiographical manga about the US's atomic bombing of Hiroshima (*Disaster Drawn* 125). It doesn't have time to, and the stakes are of course much lower in a fictional superhero narrative.

Still, this is a superhero narrative that speaks directly to the sort of real and precipitous transformations and unimaginable losses now underway in the Anthropocene. I argue too that, *mutatis mutandis*, the Terminus storyline to a degree mirrors Nakazawa's poetics, themselves premised on what Chute considers the conventional "exaggerated" renderings of manga to convey an all-too-real event of unprecedented violence and death; such a representational strategy "throws into even greater proportion the catastrophe of 'the real' in this narrative" (126). As Chute explains: "In Nakazawa's re-creation of his own Hiroshima experience as a graphic narrative created in Japan's most widely popular style, he structures his text around the productive tension between form (here the overstated idiom of manga) and content (the indubitably traumatic and gravely serious subject of the devastation of the US bombing of Hiroshima)" (128).

I would quibble with "overstated," as that term means different things in different cultures, but certainly something similar is happening in "Holocaust in a Hidden Land," with its unparalleled and harrowing earthly destruction contrasted and to an extent contradicted by (1) the presence of primary color–garbed superheroes and (2) the expedited, unceremonious annihilation of whole species/ecological regions. It both does and doesn't seem to matter. We return to Morton's "subjunctive mood": *You may find yourself living in a mass extinction.*

Two other facets of the Terminus storyline bear mention; these also relate in particular to how the superhero genre, with its own "overstated idiom," addresses the end of nature. To begin with, let us return to Ka-Zar and his supporting cast being outclassed by superpowered interlopers. *Avengers* #256–58 is a colonialist narrative in the direct sense: The meta-humans arrive, push aside the natives, do their business, destroy the landscape. (Superheroes are different from us. Yes, they have more powers.) The actual denizens of Pangea and the Savage Land (i.e., the field of battle) have no say in the matters of superior beings.

The Avengers put the local "jungle adventurers" in their place almost immediately, as noted. The latter say and do very little, besides get rescued by the long underwear brigade. That striking hierarchy is cemented when Kevin and the pregnant Shanna bicker over whether she should join in the fight against Terminus. Avengers' chairperson Wasp/Janet Van Dyne shuts them down: "We don't have time for arguments! Neither of you is going and that's final!" (Stern and Buscema, "Holocaust" 14). So that's settled.

For Peter Coogan's taxonomic purposes, Ka-Zar exemplifies the figure of "liminal genre status" who interacts with superheroes but is himself not of like ability, operating "at the borderline of both the jungle and superhero genres" (52–53). But at the end of the day, this is the Avengers' world, in which Greek gods like Apollo drop by the mansion on a chariot drawn by flying horses to deliver Hercules a change of clothes (Stern and Buscema, "This Power" 2). Cool as it is to fight dinosaurs with a knife, it's hard to compete with veterans of the Kree/Skrull War, who also saved the multiverse from Korvac and Thanos. So "regular" humans like the Savage Land's protectors are effectively marginalized, silenced. Before I reread the storyline for this analysis, in fact, I had forgotten that Ka-Zar and Shanna say anything at all in the final chapter; I just had a mental image of them as parka-wearing refugees on a helicopter speeding them away from the continent (Shanna in fact does not appear in this issue at all).

All of which is to say that this is ultimately a story of resource extraction on Indigenous land. Terminus is a tin-plated Ulysses Klaw invading another Wakanda to seize its stores not of vibranium but of alien gadgets. The Avengers seek to right this particular wrong, but it's not like they're against resource extraction in principle (they need to fuel the quinjet with *something*, don't they?). They fight, in other words, in the name of restoring the "natural" order of capitalism—which, ecologically speaking, is like the red Kryptonian sun: source of "our" strength and nourishment, cause of our eventual destruction.

In the middle of all this, Shanna, Ka-Zar, Zabu, the Lemurans, Aerie Shalan are all victims of environmental injustice. Stern and Buscema demote the Savage Land to what Steve Lerner calls a "sacrifice zone," whose severely degraded environment forces its population to "make disproportionate health and economic sacrifices that more affluent people can avoid" (5). In a variation of Rob Nixon's "slow violence," the Savage Landers join the ranks of such locales as Louisiana's "Cancer Alley," a stretch along the Mississippi River so dubbed for its intense state-sponsored development by the petrochemical industry (which many blame for abnormally high cancer rates there).[35]

To its credit, the Terminus storyline acknowledges at least some of this, by focusing on the fallout of the calamity, in part through the theme of belatedness. The final chapter, in *Avengers* #258 (Aug. 1985), titled "Pyrrhic Victory!," adds a layer of complexity to the standard triumphalist superhero narrative by showing Captain America haunted by everything that went wrong in the mission, everyone not saved. The star-spangled national symbol apologizes to Ka-Zar, saying, "I wish we could have stopped Terminus sooner, but—!" (4). On the flight back home, Hercules wonders why Cap is feeling so glum. They should be celebrating; after all, they just saved the world from a cosmic supervillain. "That's not much comfort to his victims!" Rogers replies. "We should have been there sooner!" (5). The hand-wringing over tardiness continues back in Avengers' Mansion in New York, when Rogers berates a federal official for suspending the team's security clearance, depriving them of needed information as they were investigating the Terminus case. Timely intelligence would likely have saved lives, a livid Cap complains (9).

The extended discussion of tardiness functions as a frontal assault on superhero identity. If there's one thing that superheroes do, it's get there just in time, usually "faster than a speeding bullet." As Scott Bukatman puts it, "The best of them move with more than swift efficiency, their poise and elegance also speaking a kind of poetic appropriation of space" (*Matters of Gravity* 190). In the classic Sheldon Moldoff cover to *Flash* #1 (Jan. 1940), Jay Garrick stops a bullet at the last possible instant before it perforates a woman. He doesn't dress like Mercury for nothin'.[36]

But in the Anthropocene it's always too late; it's already happening. *Climate overtime*. Heroes, governments, they're always too slow. We are always fighting the clock and always losing. Losing life, losing species, ecosystems trickling, bleeding away.

In the little time that is left.

The *Avengers'* Terminus storyline presents some sobering lessons. On the one hand, it implies that superheroes—not regular people—are the only ones who can deal with existential threats to the environment. But on the other, when it comes to existential threats to the environment, superheroes always arrive too late, always fall short, the apocalypse hits anyway. Innocents die. The Savage Land is toast.[37]

Because we are the asteroid.

The comics case studies discussed in depth in part II—again, whether or not they directly reference the Anthropocene and whether or not they fall into the orbit of Morton's hypertrophied uncertainty principle—"are determined by a web of interactions, a formal ecology that requires environmental imagination before any consistent storyworld can be reconstructed" (Casper 4). The chapters cast a wide net in terms of genre, approach, and mood as they seek to delve more deeply into how graphic narrative has explored and reflected the ecological crisis since the first Earth Day. (In the book's conclusion, I turn the lens inward, to examine Anthropocene comics of my own home region of the Pacific Northwest.)

And so, I end part I with a plea to my reader, that they give due consideration to the words of a person whom some have likened to a real-life superhero, and who has to some degree embraced that role.[38] At the January 2019 Davos World Economic Forum, teen activist and face of the global climate justice movement Greta Thunberg put matters thusly:

> Adults keep saying: "We owe it to the young people to give them hope." But I don't want your hope. I don't want you to be hopeful. I want you to panic. I want you to feel the fear I feel every day. And then I want you to act.
>
> I want you to act as you would in a crisis. I want you to act as if our house is on fire. Because it is.

Just "words, words, words"? I "hope" not.
And in their spirit:
Act like your Savage Land is burning.
Because it is.
Don't be the asteroid.
Be the world.

PART II

4

HOW MANY TREES HAD TO BE *CUT DOWN* FOR THIS CHAPTER?

R. CRUMB AS IRONIC ECO-ELEGIST

Robert Crumb's "A Short History of America," first published in 1979 in the environmentalist journal *CoEvolution Quarterly*,[1] unfurls over twelve stately page-wide panels, building up to a devastating portrait of ecological doom. The first frame shows what some might consider a "pristine" unpeopled woods and meadow: deer calmly amble, flocks of birds fill much of the sky. In the next images, train tracks cut through the terrain, tearing a diagonal wound that steadily widens as grass and trees disappear, telephone wires spring up, roads are paved and repaved, fences sprout, and streetlights, signs, buildings, cars, gas stations, and every sort of urban detritus take over from horizon to horizon, all nonhuman animal and plant life long gone. The concluding text box—"What next?!!"—betokens even worse to come.

Crumb's relentlessly pessimistic before-and-after (panel nine, in which the last tree vanishes, has always hit this reader especially hard) functions, among other things, as a literalistic parody of Ralph Waldo Emerson's contention that

> Nature is thoroughly mediate. It is made to serve. It receives the dominion of man as meekly as the ass on which the Saviour rode. It offers all its kingdoms to man as the raw material which he may mould into what is useful. Man is never weary of working it up. He forges the subtile and delicate air into wise and melodious words, and gives them wing as angels of persuasion and command. More and more, with every

The opening of "A Short History of America" (1979). © R. Crumb.

thought, does his kingdom stretch over things, until the world becomes, at last, only a realized will,—the double of the man. (20)[2]

More directly, it incarnates in comics form the much-bemoaned postwar mania for development Russell Baker, in a 1963 op-ed for *The New York Times*, dubbed "The Great Paver":

> His dream, which we would dismiss as implausible if concocted by one of Ian Fleming's villains, is to pave the entire United States with concrete and asphalt. He envisions a nation buried under six-lane, limited-access turnpikes. When the last blade of American grass is buried, he plans to go on to pave Europe. Then Asia. And on and on until the whole planet is coated in cement. Today America—tomorrow the world. (378)[3]

Furthermore, "A Short History of America" stands out from Crumb's oeuvre—and certainly belies his reputation as a "raunchy" provocateur—for its avoidance of overt references to sex and/or drugs, and for its seemingly "serious," even tragic, mood. The only "rape" here is of the landscape.[4] Such a sobering, easily understandable and unimpeachable message perhaps helps to explain why this work stands alongside "Keep on Truckin'" (1968) and Crumb's cover for Big Brother and the Holding Company's album *Cheap Thrills* (1968) as his most reproduced and anthologized;[5] "Short History" has appeared as a poster;[6] in several Crumb-themed collections, including a color version near the beginning of the *R. Crumb Handbook*, setting the tone; more recently in innumerable internet iterations;[7] even in *American Earth: Environmental Writing Since Thoreau* (2008), edited by 350.org founder and environmental activist Bill McKibben, who in his introduction notes that "in the years around the first Earth Day [in 1970], every radical expressed themselves on the ecological crisis, and Crumb . . . was no exception" (590).[8]

A key question in Crumbology, however, comes down to precisely what any given "radical expression" by the artist means. It turns out not so easy to pin down Crumb's "message," even in so relatively "straightforward" a piece of environmentalist agit-prop as "Short History." For one thing, people in it all seem equally to blame—i.e., equally blameless—for nature's extirpation.[9] We see no one picketing or protesting the tearing up of the land and banishment of the birds; no government steps in to regulate and conserve at least some of the "original" setting (as actually happened). Instead, a nameless force ("the Great Paver") drives the ineluctable process of uglification to an apocalyptic end. "Short History" thus amounts not to history, exactly, but more to a dramatically satisfying work of misanthropy; we may boil down its message to "humans suck, they ruin everything; a plague o' both your houses."[10]

Such a stance of the absolute outsider virtually defines Crumb, seriously compromising the efficacy of any progressive politics his comics might advance. As Brandon Nelson argues in a 2018 essay, "Rather than appealing to a revolutionary artistic and political mode by condemning the social and political establishment, or scoring points at the other end of the spectrum by propping up traditional power structures, Crumb criticizes and destabilizes the utopian ideals inherent in both reactionary and radical aesthetics of his and previous eras" (140).

Gary Groth has likewise identified "an unresolved conflict between Crumb's serious attitude toward his art and his attitude toward seriousness" ("Introduction" xi), which Crumb himself confirms: "There's a tension between wanting to get as close to the truth in some form of expression as you can, and being too serious" (Groth, "Introduction" xi).

And yet, few things seem more "serious" than the ecological devastation, disappearing species, unsustainable population growth, and human-induced climate change of the Anthropocene. To address them, even satirically, is to confront one of the greatest ongoing disasters of planetary history—deemed by most scientists, in fact, a sixth mass extinction.

This chapter suggests a resolution to the perceived "conflict" and "tension" between Crumb's "serious" concerns and his politically inert disavowal of action as it pertains to the environmental crisis: a resolution we might call Crumb's role of ironic eco-elegist. As discussed by Jessica Marion Barr, Patricia

Rae, and other scholars, the contemporary eco-elegy descends from the modern, post-WWI elegiac form, with its resistant politics couched as grief over unjust losses and dread of more to come (Barr 197). Similarly, the eco-elegist proleptically expresses anticipatory grief when she "mourn[s] past losses such as habitat destruction and species extinction, and ... also warn[s] against the kind of absences we will be mourning in the future should present losses be allowed to continue" (Barr 197). Crumb does comparable work, addressing these losses in characteristic style: with snark, scatological humor and ironic detachment premised on contempt for *Homo sapiens* as a species.[11]

Crumb's expressions of irreverent "ecological angst," an underexplored strain both in his work and underground comix in general, appear in both explicit and figurative forms throughout his oeuvre, though most scholars have seen them as a subset to larger themes like the Cold War nuclear threat and his attack on modernity. While drawing on such insights, I maintain focus on Crumb's environment-themed comics from an ecocritical perspective, with an emphasis on one of his longest stories, "Whiteman Meets Bigfoot" (1971). Examining material from roughly four decades of Crumb's cartooning, noting such influences on his thinking as deep ecology and postmodernist discourses, I aim to trace the development of the artist's bleak (albeit tongue-in-cheek) expressions of postwar environmental dread—Robert Crumb as ironic elegist for the death of nature—and suggest that such a stance need not diminish the eco-elegy's power to "spur an ethical impulse to act" (Barr 195).

THE ECOLOGICAL CRISIS, UNDERGROUND COMIX, AND CRUMB

In the late 1960s, during a period that saw the launch of the *Whole Earth Catalog* (1968); the founding of Friends of the Earth (1969); and the first Earth Day (1970), Ron Turner, "ex-Ceylon Peace Corps member/ex-Bakersfield engineer/ecology freak" (Green 93) and at that time a graduate student at San Francisco State University, discovered underground comix. Patrick Rosenkranz, in his *Rebel Visions: The Underground Comix Revolution, 1963–1975*, recounts how Rod Frieland, a printer at the Berkeley Ecology Center, suggested Turner start a "comic book on ecology" as a benefit venture for the center (128). Turner launched his company, Last Gasp Eco-Funnies, and published the first issue of its anthology *Slow Death Funnies*[12] shortly before the first Earth Day, which took place on April 22, 1970. The title, which lasted eleven issues published through 1992, would become the underground's most prominent and striking example of environmental consciousness-raising, tackling issues such as pollution, cancer, the AIDS crisis, nuclear energy, and climate change.[13]

Greg Irons's cover for *Slow Death Funnies* #1 (1970). © R. Crumb.

The cover of *Slow Death Funnies* #1 shows how Turner was willing to go far beyond Walt Kelly's *Pogo* (a newspaper strip then notable for its ecological focus): A ravenous monstrosity, with a cityscape for a back, straddling the globe, gouges out great chunks of earth and pops them into its maw, while greedily reaching for the moon. Inside the comic, the reader discovers this image reproduces the final panel of Greg Irons's three-pager "It Grows," a blend of essay and EC horror featuring an unstoppable contagion. The fourth panel on page 1 declares, "Like a terrible tidal wave, it spread over the earth, leaving behind it bleak, ravaged desolation. It found it could eat anything. It spawned and ate and grew, and the delicately balanced wheel of life began to grind to a shuddering halt." Irons continues, "In seeking the 'good life' we have created a toxic, alien environment which threatens our very existence," and concludes, "Even as our choked planet shudders and gasps for it's [sic] life breath, it reaches out into space, expanding, seeking more raw material to appease it's [sic] insatiable appitite [sic]. . . . Will the festering cancer of Western civilization[14] consume all life?"

A Crumb story in the inaugural *Slow Death Funnies*, "Smogville Blues," replaces Irons's humorless approach with tragicomic farce. Introduced with the phrase, "And now for a little pep-talk . . . ," the opening panel shows straight man Flakey Foont traversing a crowded, smog-choked city, griping, "Everything has become such a fucked-up mess. . . . I can't stand it anymore. . . . I really can't." A despairing Foont decides to help reduce the population by committing suicide—but jumps off a bridge with no water under it (we see trash and a dead fish on the ground) and sinks into mud. As a cavalier Mr. Natural explains, "Hey, Flakey! Don't you know they've drained the bay to quench th' parched throats of th' citizens of Los Angeles?" (a reference to California water diversion schemes).

Enraged, Foont demands concrete solutions for the environmental crisis, but Mr. Natural responds only with a plethora of platitudes ("Mother Nature will prevail"; "behind every cloud there's a silver lining"; "life will go on somehow") in text-heavy speech balloons extending over three panels. The white-bearded guru concludes: "Now get out of my sight and don't come back until you've cleaned up this goddamned hell-hole!!" giving Foont a kick in the posterior for good measure.

The story, however, concludes with a cynical twist. A thought balloon reveals Mr. Natural's true feelings: "Poor Flakey! Bless his heart! Thank god somebody's worrying about it!!" The "pep-talk," then, serves not to solve anything (nature is still doomed), but only to sardonically appeal to the reader's sentiment over Foont's "good heart." "Smogville Blues"—subtitled "How many trees had to be *cut down* for this comic book? A moot point!"—depicts environmental disaster as no less apocalyptic than Irons's grotesque Earth-straddling "cancer," but where "It Grows!" ends with a question, challenging the reader to engage with the problem, Crumb's piece forecloses hope. Mr. Natural patronizes squares

The conclusion to "Smogville Blues" (1970). © R. Crumb.

like Foont ("Poor Flakey!") who think we can actually make any difference at all. We might as well just have a laugh as the planet burns.

Nuclear planetary annihilation[15] likewise serves as grist for a send-up of real-world anxieties in another Crumb one-pager, "Mr. Sketchum" (1970). The eponymous bespectacled hero, while mailing his cartoons to Bertrand Russell,[16] falls victim to an H-bomb attack on his city. Plans ruined—along with, presumably, much of humanity—a vaporized Sketchum complains, "Now I'll never know if Bertrand Russell liked my cartoons." The *Dr. Strangelove*-like buffoonery in the face of atomic doom both mocks and confirms fears of the ultimate Cold War catastrophe; Crumb vents and defuses them at one stroke.

As Hillary Chute points out, "Underground cartoonists, including founders of the movement such as Crumb, made comix the arena in which they could visualize disaster" (*Disaster Drawn* 149) through what she calls "an atomic haunting" (151). However, she downplays the role humor and irony played in such expressions, seeing "the atomic *reality*" (151) not in the undergrounds but rather in such "serious" autobiographical works as Keiji Nakazawa's *I Saw It* (1972, about his experiences as a child during the Hiroshima bombing). Despite accounting for the frequency of nuclear-anxiety imagery in Crumb's works (147), Chute here overly discounts the potent ways parody and absurdity—as opposed to more "realistic" approaches—capture the particular madness of the atomic age (with Stanley Kubrick's aforementioned classic a prime example).[17]

Similarly, Crumb's double-edged treatment of the environmental theme in "Smogville Blues" and "Mr. Sketchum" (his lampooning of a dead serious subject) may seem facile compared to more "weighty" approaches, but to argue so is to overlook the central, multivalent, politically charged, in short revolutionary role irony played in underground comix. As Les Daniels wrote in the early 1970s: "If some underground comix are pure propaganda, the best of them are distinguished by an irony denoting skepticism at the notion of any simplistic solution. Such comics are equally likely to overstate their case for the purpose of shock, a type of exaggeration that the undergrounders use as a major comedy device, gleefully secure in the belief that it will pass over the heads of the uninitiated" (166).[18]

Charles Hatfield has written the most incisively on this facet of the undergrounds; though he does not define precisely what sort of irony he means, he is describing a fundamental tension between form (comic book) and content (adult material) when he writes: "Many of the comix books were awash in irony, based on the appropriation of popular (or once-popular) characters, styles, genres, and tropes for radically personal and sometimes politically subversive ends" (*Alternative Comics* 18).[19] Furthermore, he identifies Crumb's comix in particular as "inherently ironic, in a manner not unlike that of the Pop artists before him. Indeed, this is his signal contribution to American comics: the ironizing of the comic book medium itself" (12).

Thus Crumb, along with other underground artists—including Gilbert Shelton, Trina Robbins, Larry Welz, Denis Kitchen, and Ron Cobb[20]—took on the ecological crisis with varying degrees of irony, despair, satire, and sobriety, though always with an anti-authority bent reflecting their disdain for government. Such a radical stance proved rather misplaced, given that, as noted, in this very era (the Nixon and Ford administrations) "the federal government was moving most quickly, strongly and effectively to address environmental problems" (Rifas 140), with the passage of the Clean Air Act (1970), the formation of the Environmental Protection Agency (1970), passage of the Clean Water Act (1972), the Endangered Species Act (1973), and other measures.[21]

Let's turn now to examine the particularities of Crumb's environmentalism in more detail.

CRUMB AND "DEEP ECOLOGY"

Crumb articulates his well-known contempt for postwar modern life—and its toll on the natural world—as early as 1959, in the letters he wrote as a fifteen-year-old. Corresponding with a friend on July 9, he describes a journey from New York to visit an acquaintance, Stan Lynde:

> It took about half an hour to get to Massapequa Park, which is a typical "suburbia," USA! Miles and miles of modern ranch style homes with neat little lawns between neat little streets, with convenient little shopping centers neatly distributed throughout. Frightfully boring set-up, although most people like it that way, men out with their power-mowers whistling as they walk them along. . . . The wives lazily reading magazines and sipping drinks while relaxing on contour chairs, etc. . . . (I. Thompson 40)[22]

In this and throughout his oeuvre, Crumb associates "real" nature with blessed isolation, an escape from the loud chaos of cities and the flipside to his hatred of "progress."[23] A March 8, 1961, letter in the form of a first-person comics story depicts the young Crumb's ruminations on his beloved jazz records and art as he ambles through a calm wooded area, encounters speeding traffic ("voom") and eventually gets run over by a train (splat)—all encroachments into an otherwise peaceable natural setting (I. Thompson 141–44).

The middle-aged author, now living in rural France, would later elaborate on these lifelong feelings in a 1999 interview:

> In America, it's very difficult to find, unless you own thousands of acres of land yourself, it's hard to get away from people. You have

to go to national parks. You drive, you pay, you go in. All the trails are marked; there are other people. Campsites are full of people. You really have to work hard to get away from people in the United States. As big a country and as wide open as it is, it is hard to get out to the wilderness. You have to go in your car and drive a long distance, and be really committed. When we lived in California, it was sort of out in the country, yet all the land around us was private property.[24] Here, I just walk up there. . . . Unique! What a country! (Laughs)[25] I tried very hard to find a place like that in California, where I could go out to nature, but it was too difficult! I used to go down along this creek, and these farmers would come and chase you out: "Whaddaya doin' down here?" "Oh, just walking around, is that OK?" "Eh, naw, not rilly." "Why not?" "Well, ya know, we have to pay a lot of insurance, if you get hurt or something like that, we gotta pay, blablabla." (Laughs) (Mercier 222, ellipsis in original)

Such lamentations resonate with a strain of late twentieth-century environmentalist thought broadly labeled ecocentrism or deep ecology,[26] which couches a radical critique of modern life within its defense of "wilderness" (a highly subjective term). Note, for example, how Crumb's grousing over the difficulties of getting away from people find their correlate in Bill McKibben's writing:

There's no such thing as nature anymore—that other world that isn't business and art and breakfast is now not another world, and there is nothing there except us alone.

At the same time I felt lonely, though, I also felt crowded, without privacy. We go to the woods in part to escape. But now there is nothing except us and so there is no escaping other people. (*The End of Nature* 76–77)

Discourse like this has deep roots, from Emerson, Henry David Thoreau and his writing on wilderness, to George Perkins Marsh and John Muir in the nineteenth century to Aldo Leopold and Dave Bower in the twentieth, as well as to the modern environmentalist movement launched in the 1960s by the publication of Rachel Carson's *Silent Spring* (1962).[27] As refracted through countercultural expressions like underground comix, such thinking amounted to the blunt "demonization" of modern machines (R. White 178) and economic expansion, which its detractors felt had severed an ancient and benign relationship with nature. At its worst, deep ecology thinking could descend into outright nihilism, misanthropy, and ecofascism.[28]

Eco-angst in "The Desperate Character Writhes Again" (1971). © R. Crumb.

Apart from the danger of such self-defeating rhetoric and acts, Jeffrey Stark argues, movements like deep ecology suffer from a fatally anti-science, postmodernist stance, which offers "quaint spiritualistic assertions about nature" instead of ethical reasoning (270). He explains:

> For postmodern environmentalism, the essential connection to existence is manifest in the authentic individual who resists participation in all repressive and externally imposed contexts, including social interaction operating under taken-for-granted norms of daily life. This includes a rejection of all conventional restrictions or obligations, whether or not the individual agrees with them. In this framework, community *is* repression, community *is* inauthentic. At best, what postmodernism implies is communities without unity in which all persons are united in their alienation and isolation and can do little more than pursue private virtues. (272)

While he has never come out as a deep ecologist, it is striking how well this description applies to the über-nonconformist, modernity-despising, alienated artist Crumb. Related themes and imagery appear with considerable regularity throughout his career, even in incidental or unpublished works. "Leave the City" (a color drawing in a 1967 sketchbook) shows a besuited urban "schlub" figure walking astride tram tracks on a smoggy metropolitan street, about to fall victim to a train, while his thought balloon depicts presumably longed-for trees, sun, and a meadow (Crumb and Poplaski, *The R. Crumb Handbook* 126). Urban detritus and the polluting, filth-spewing smokestacks of factories often form a backdrop, as in "King of Motor City?" (one of them boasts the banner, "Great United Shitworks, Inc.") in *Motor City Comics* (1969) and the Mr. Natural strips Crumb produced for the *Village Voice* in 1976.

They appear too in the one-pager adorning the back cover of *Home-Grown Funnies*, "The Desperate Character Writhes Again" (1971), with its naked neurotic "who sheds bitter tears for the human race!!" Against a dark industrial landscape, with bulging eyes and scraggly hair, he harangues:

> The dum shits! The stupid fucking sons of bitches!! Those fucking assholes!! sob
>
> They're ruining it for all of us! They're destroying our planet! Those blind, arrogant bungling fools! Those viscious [*sic*] power-hungry insane maniacs!
>
> They should all be killed! Even now they continue to create even more and greater methods of destruction!! Why? Why? How can we stop them? Or is it . . . is it . . .
>
> *Is it too late?*

Underscoring the sardonic, half-serious tone, the homunculus-like "Desperate Character" walks off in the last panel, concluding his tirade with "I don't know . . . I just don't know. . . . Fuck it!"[29]

A Crumb cover for the alternative ecological newspaper *Winds of Change* (1980). © R. Crumb.

Two Crumb projects from the 1980s in particular exhibit his environmentalist proclivities. Early in the decade he joined the staff of the Yolo County, California, alternative ecological newspaper *Winds of Change*, working as art and layout editor (Holm xix). There he produced a number of striking, ecologically themed illustrations, including a skeletal farmworker guiding a crop-dusting bat in a field (cover of *Winds of Change* vol. 2 #4, 1980).[30] In general, however, as Crumb told Fantagraphics publisher Gary Groth in a 1988 interview, he felt artistically stifled:

> I couldn't go along with doing creative work that's decided by some dour bunch of politicos at this point in my life, even if I believed they were right. When every decision is made by a committee or consensus it becomes hard to do anything interesting or exciting, because when it comes down to it, this one objects to something, that one objects to something, and when you come to an agreement all that's left is the most bland piece of mashed potatoes. It was like that when I worked for *Winds of Change*. They always wanted to present what they thought were positive alternatives to the ways things are. It always had this dreary, goody-goody aura of we're-gonna-eat-tofu-and-sit-around-singing-folk-songs-together. Politically I agreed with those people, but working with them was so tedious and annoying, and they were utterly humorless. . . . I tried to do these really strong political cartoons, like Thomas Nast, putting down agribiz and stuff, and everybody said I was too negative. General agreement that I was too negative. [*Laughter*] (Groth, "A Marathon Interview" 46)

Another venture, more in keeping with Crumb's anarchist politics and poetics, involved his illustrations for the tenth anniversary edition of Edward Abbey's *The Monkey Wrench Gang* (Dream Garden Press, 1985).[31] This eco-terrorist novel, a cult favorite among radical environmentalists that may have even inspired the early development of Earth First! (Woodhouse 185), gave Crumb a much freer hand in his renderings of industrial sabotage. In one illustration, of the nighttime partial dismantling of a soil compacting machine, the artist even took license to show the gang's one female wrecker, Bonnie Abzug, bent over her work, derrière prominently displayed (Abbey 83).

Taking into account, along with the foregoing, Crumb's much-celebrated 2009 *The Book of Genesis*, especially the early chapters with their detailed renderings of an eco-topian Garden of Eden, the reader may agree with Marc DiPaolo that "environmentalist themes permeate [Crumb's] body of work" (273). In the next section we discuss Crumb's longest and most sustained comics exploration of this recurring preoccupation.

"WHITEMAN MEETS BIGFOOT"

Imagery of satyrs (goat-human hybrids) and "wild men" (civilization's other) goes nearly as far back into the European past as we can see. The Wild Man, according to Timothy Husband and Gloria Gilmore-House, reflected wide-ranging beliefs in "aberrational human forms" and "monstrous races" described by, among others, the fifth-century BCE historian Herodotus, as well as the rise of new, highly ordered Christian social structures in early modernity, which a savage "shadow figure" helped to define (5–6).

Similarly, US "wild man" lore took shape on the late nineteenth-century frontier, as an emblem of "freedom" and counterpoint to advancing "civilization" from the continental East. Increasing industrialization exacerbated the process. Since the 1950s, alleged sightings and media depictions of Yetis, Abominable Snowmen, and related "Sasquatchiana" represented a "modern update of the traditional wildman," writes folklorist Joshua Blu Buhs (196).

Such a cultural idée fixe betokened postwar anxieties—in particular over changing definitions of manhood—serving as a frame for "grappling with this new world, of resisting the cultural arrangement, and of accommodating oneself to it. The magazines, books, and movies in which the wildman appeared flattered the mostly male, mostly working-class audience's sense of self-worth, denigrating the womanly art of shopping and championing traditional notions of character" (Buhs 200).

We should not underestimate the enduring centrality of such myths to the US national character, pervading even children's literature. An especially stark example: Maurice Sendak's "psychoanalytical" picture book *Where the Wild Things Are* (1963), a fantasy of escape from domesticity to a community of monsters in a far-away land, in which the young protagonist Max dresses like a wolf.

But no "wild man" gripped the country more immediately than that US pop culture obsession of the 1960s and 1970s: Bigfoot. Purportedly sighted by loggers in Northern California as early as 1958 (Buhs 198), the shy, hirsute giant saw an explosion of media coverage after the release of Roger Patterson and Bob Gimlin's faked Bigfoot footage, shot in 1967 near the California-Oregon border (200). We could indeed call the 1970s the Bigfoot decade, when the figure came to dominate popular discourse.

Tapping into the national mood, "Whiteman Meets Bigfoot" (1971) portrays as only Crumb can modern man's deteriorating link to nature, a process intersecting with questions of race, sex, the human/nonhuman borderline,[32] and male inadequacy. Taking up the majority of *Home Grown Funnies* #1, extending even onto the inside back cover, the twenty-two-page epic represents Crumb's most detailed, tragicomic statement on the ecological crisis—uncharacteristically, a statement not without hope.

Rooted in the author's childhood memories of watching Irish McCalla in the *Sheena, Queen of the Jungle* television series in summer 1956,[33] the story imbricates femininity, nonwhite identity, and animality in a sort of raunchy ecofeminism *avant la lettre*.[34] As Maria Mies and Vandana Shiva write: "An ecofeminist perspective propounds the need for a new cosmology and a new anthropology which recognizes that life in nature (which includes human beings) is maintained by means of co-operation, and mutual care and love. Only in this way can we be enabled to respect and preserve the diversity of all life forms, including their cultural expressions, as true sources of our well being and happiness" (6).

By personifying a dying environment in the form of a gigantic, furry, sexually voracious "abominable snowgirl," Crumb brings together most of his major themes (with the exception of drugs, which he implies people in cities consume precisely because of their alienation from nature). As he told an interviewer: "Angelfood McSpade was a goddess, a vision of perfect, primitive sexuality.... The 'Yeti' in 'Whiteman Meets Bigfoot' is a further development of this theme. ... The lusty Amazon sex goddess who lives naked in the jungle.... You figure it out ..." (Duncan 121, ellipses in original).[35]

Crumb contrasts this prelapsarian vision with Whiteman, a modern, strait-laced, barrel-chested male citizen (seemingly modeled on his ex-Marine father) plagued by violent erotic urges. When first introduced in "Whiteman" (*Zap Comix* #1, 1967), the figure can barely keep these drives in check: "My real self deep down inside.... The raging, lustful beast that craves only *one* thing! *Sex!*" But in "Whiteman Meets Bigfoot," we see a more benign version: younger, thinner, more "puny." The "lovable honky" is taking "his yearly two weeks from the salt-mines" with his wife and family, driving his "spankin'-new '71 Winnebago Renegade." Yet even here, at the beginning, Whiteman vaguely longs for something more than the twentieth-century city can provide: "Ah, the life of an explorer! I tell you what, Louise, if we didn't have so many bills, I'd just quit my job and hit th' road 'n' just be a nomad, wanderin' from place to—" "*Fergit it*, Marco Polo," his wife interrupts. "We owe enuff on this goddamn jeep to keep us in debt 'til doomsday!"

That evening, the family hooks up "at a campsite in one of America's great national forests," and although the kids, Dick and Jane, prefer to watch *Mission Impossible* on TV, their father insists they go on a hike. While on this trek in the woods, Whiteman gets separated from the children and kidnapped, tossed into a sack by a hulking, hirsute anthropoid. Text boxes over the next two panels, echoing the stereotypical speech of "primitives" (sans articles), inform us that "Bigfoot run like the wind for hours!" and "Bigfoot take Whiteman to his home deep in the mountains." The next morning, this creature presents Whiteman to its "tribe." They immediately react with their form of laughter ("Horch horch!";

"Guhunk hilk hilk!"), rolling and farting on the ground. A female then rubs her overflowing genitalia all over the human's face, almost gagging him ("No! Please! I'm a happily married man! I—blub blb!").

Soon, as a text box says, "Bigfoot gives his daughter to Whiteman as a mate. The family says goodbye and the newly wedded couple goes off to make their own nest." With escape impossible, Whiteman settles in for the night, straddling his furry "bride" for warmth. One thing leads to another, and when our hero discovers he has an erection ("C-could I actually be sexually aroused by this mountainous hairy ape-like beast?"), nature takes its course. In the act, Whiteman has his epiphany: "Wow! Louise was never like this!! Yetti, you're incredible!! Ya make me feel like a real man!" As Brandon Nelson notes, Crumb here promotes the act of sex "as an aesthetic tool, so base and animalistic that it can exist outside the realm of social hierarchies, consumerist impulses, and political posturing" (144).[36] Whiteman literally fucks his way back to nature—or so the story claims.

Six weeks later, a long-haired, bearded, bedraggled Whiteman (resembling the hippies he routinely despises) lounges with "Yetti" in the woods. He wears rags and has lost his glasses, another marker of civilization. To his grinning, oblivious mate he soliloquizes:

> I've learned so much! More than I ever learned in ten years working for General Dynamics! When I think of the *shit* I used to take from those jerks! How useless and futile it all was! [. . .] Living here in the woods hasn't been easy for me . . . I've never had to fend for myself in the wilds like this . . . But it's surprisingly simple, once you learn how . . . So much simpler than life back there . . . I feel so much more alive than I've felt in years!

Notably, in Whiteman's journey, smell plays a determining role from the very first panel. In the title, the word "Whiteman" appears in a sleek, bespoke typeface connoting modernity and perhaps superheroics, with our hero's face as an accent (looking hyper-polished, as if made of metal). In sharp contrast, the word "Bigfoot" below presents as furry, pockmarked flesh that reeks with curvy "smell lines" and hovering flies. These "stink flies" also accompany the Bigfoot that abducts the human, while Whiteman himself often makes remarks such as "Ugh! What a stink! Gag!" (as Yetti introduces herself by presenting her genitalia) and "Phew! She sure *smells!!!* Kind of like it almost . . . musky animal odor . . ." (as Whiteman starts to get aroused on his wedding night).

Like sex, then, the olfactory forms an atavistic link to our animal nature, as it did for early sexologists like Havelock Ellis, Richard Von Krafft-Ebbing, and Sigmund Freud, who, as David Huebert notes, surmised that "the human species' ascension up onto hind legs and the subsequent turn away from olfactory eroticism might in fact have caused the proliferation of human neurological disorders [Freud] encountered in the modern populace." In fact, Huebert concludes, "a more mentally healthy creature might be one that engaged more deeply with smell" (132). Here the father of psychoanalysis and the obstreperous undergrounder see eye to eye (or, if you will, nostril to nostril).

The rest of "Whiteman Meets Bigfoot" recounts our hero and his paramour's return to civilization, which immediately misjudges their relationship: "rescuing" him so he may resume his previous life, incarcerating her in the Abominable Snowman Research Center for scientific study. After only two weeks back in modern America, though, Whiteman (now dressed in slacks and a long-sleeved shirt) is reduced to sitting passively before a television, when a fortuitous call from Dr. Greyface at the ASRC reunites him with the forlorn Yetti, imprisoned in a dungeon-like cell. "Oh, God," he laments when he sees her, ". . . sob choke. . . . It's all my fault! What a fool I was to bring you back here! sob whimper. . . . In six short weeks I'd forgotten what a fucked-up mess civilization is!! Sob . . ." Yetti is soon fellating Whiteman (still wearing a coat and tie).

Although Dr. Greyface sees a rich research opportunity in Whiteman—"We've got to have him put under psychiatric care immediately!! [. . .] I'm afraid his whole experience with the snow-woman has had a traumatic effect! He should prove a most interesting case study, I should say!!"—the interspecies couple escapes, with Yetti bounding over traffic, her lover in tow. Not long after, we see a key image for Crumb's intersectional representation of his "wild woman": In a large panel taking up more than half the page, the "hot chick" Yetti clop-clops down a city street in tight jeans, a wig, sweater, and boots, to stares and catcalls. Whiteman, spewing sweat drops and gazing round nervously, mutters, "This is embarrassing! I can't stand to be conspicuous!" In disguising his animal-wife to more easily traverse the city, Whiteman visualizes Crumb's sexist, racist fantasy: an amalgam of urban and pastoral in the striking figure of a nonwhite, steatopygic woman of limited intelligence that stirs the envy of other men ("Man, that dude sure has his hands full! Haw Haw!!").[37]

The image invites comparison with "Whiteman Meets Bigfoot's" only other panel of comparable size:[38] the splash page that begins the story. Here our man finds himself at the wheel of his Winnebago, relaxed, unashamed, with his bored-looking wife. (He travels in the opposite direction—left to right—of what Crumb draws in the later picture of the bewigged Yetti.) Here, too, a male passerby (also in the southeast quadrant of the panel) expresses his admiration—but not for Whiteman's woman; instead, he digs the wheels: "Jeezo! What a rig! Lucky guy!" The two scenarios set up a telling contrast between different modes of manhood and libidinal engagement: one public, conventional, industrial, and observing the proprieties (vehicle), another private, deviant, amalgam, blurring nature and culture and thus prompting shame—yet all the

Whiteman and Yetti draw stares in "Whiteman Meets Bigfoot" (1971). © R. Crumb.

more alluring for it (Yetti). Significantly, one of the leering dudes in the Yetti panel resembles the *Zap* version of Whiteman himself: He wears a fedora-like hat (yet another marker of the civilized self), while our hero by this point has long abandoned his, getting around bare-headed.

The opening splash page to "Whiteman Meets Bigfoot" (1971). © R. Crumb.

Back to the direction of travel in each panel alluded to just now, which bears additional comment. Just as Thomas Cole's *The Oxbow* (1836) and other protest landscapes of the westward expansion era represented the encroachment of white populations from right to left (read: East to West) to denote the conquest of the North American continent and (as artists like Cole saw it) the despoilment of nature,[39] so do Yetti and Whiteman's traveling right to left in the aforementioned image, as well as in the work's penultimate panel as they make their final break for freedom, signal a return to the—swiftly receding—wild.[40] Conversely, the opening splash with its left-to-right direction of movement marks the opposite: constraint, narrowness of horizons, confinement—an effect enhanced by showing Whiteman and Louise's tiny bodies looking out from inside the metal "prison" of the Winnebago (we see even less of the man admiring the RV; he looks positively cramped in his smaller car). Modernity means life in boxes (cars, buildings), watching boxes (television). Thoreau redux.

The "snow woman's" physical struggle with the Winnebago over six panels, as Whiteman tries to help her board ("Push, Yetti!") underscores the antagonistic relationship of animal/machine. Her large frame gets stuck in the door, her weight almost tips over the vehicle, finally she leaves it ruined, its wheels bent. The clamor attracts a livid Louise, who poses to her husband the story's climactic moral dilemma. As Whiteman agonizes in a thought balloon, "I can't just get up and walk out on my family.[41] . . . Oh, Lord, what'll I do? What'll I do?"

In the end, Yetti makes the choice herself, absconding with him by foot—again, right to left, breaking the panel borders—and making good their escape ("Whew! That was easy!"). A final panel shows the couple in an idyllic forest, Yetti lolling lazily on her back. She cools her head in a stream, a newly "hippified" Whiteman astride her, scratching her neck: "*And so, Bigfoot took Whiteman back to the woods where they lived happily ever after!!*" Apart from repeating the sexually accessible prostrate female pose noted earlier, the scene recalls nothing so much as Pieter Brueghel the Elder's *The Land of Cockaigne* (1567) and related "paradise of plenty" imagery, with Crumb substituting love and sex for food.

Nelson, through a feminist lens, sees "Whiteman Meets Bigfoot's" conclusion as rehearsing a familiar Crumbian fantasy in which "the straight men are granted a sexual trophy at the end, seemingly as compensation or consolation for the humiliations they have been made to endure, provided usually in the final panel by an inert, purely accommodating female who receives his sexual attention with unawareness or slobbering gratitude" (144). With its long-haired, half-dressed Whiteman (face unseen) and the ever-naked Yetti (beaming a smile), the final panel also represents a utopian, Garden of Eden–like fusion of human and animal. Whiteman's torn remnants of

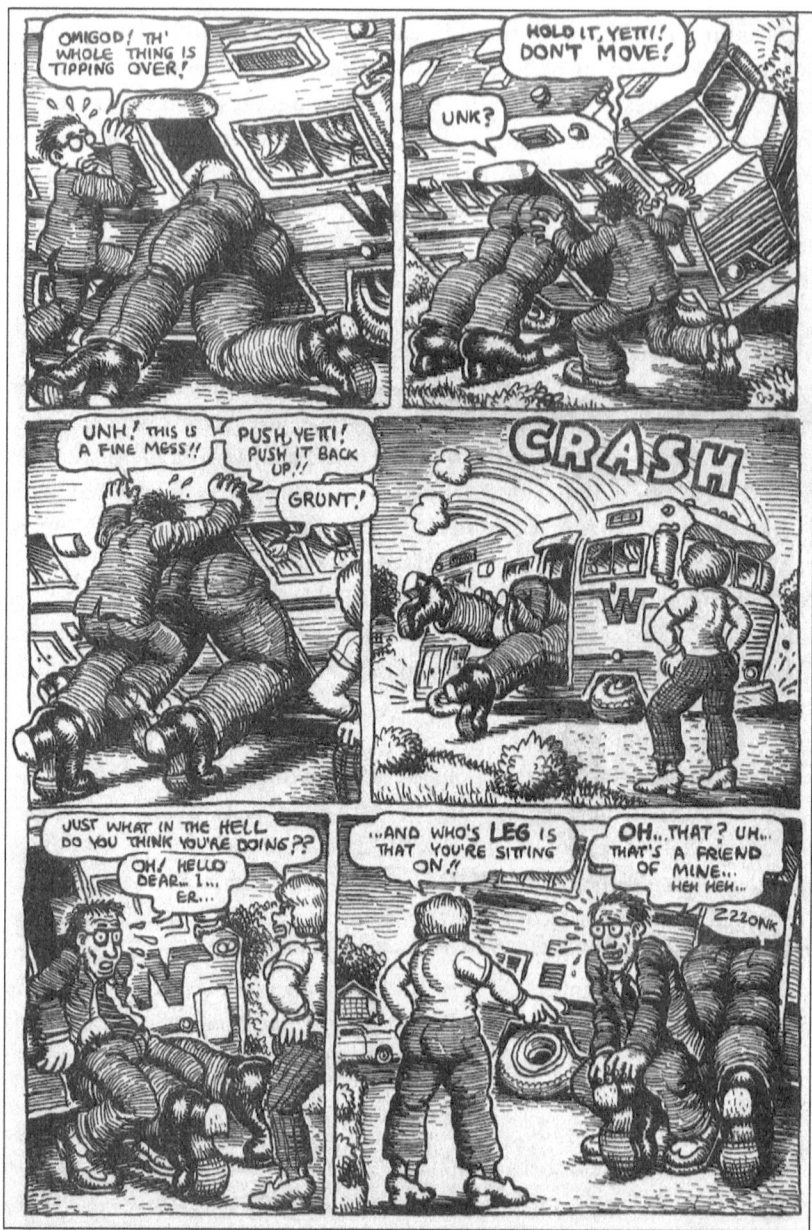

Yetti's struggle with the Winnebago. "Whiteman Meets Bigfoot" (1971). © R. Crumb.

shirt and pants signify the vital transformation proceeds apace, away from domestication and back toward the "wild."

Yet such a self-aware, exaggerated "happy ending" is no less of a Crumbian fantasy.

The conclusion to "Whiteman Meets Bigfoot" (1971). © R. Crumb.

CONCLUSION: MUST WE BURN CRUMB?

This chapter has tried to show that, despite (or in addition to) a reputation for unsentimental, sardonic, sexist satire, over the course of his career Robert Crumb has in his comics work consistently voiced distress over the state of the natural world, and especially the role of modern consumerism in its destruction. As he told an interviewer in 2015: "All that stuff, the whole ecological crisis and all that. That worries me" (Limnios). This preoccupation led Crumb, in 1988,[42] to return to his most straightforward statement on the issue, "A Short History of America," and add three new panels depicting a trio of possible futures: "Worst-case scenario: ecological disaster"; "The FUN Future: Techno Fix on the March"; and "The Eco-Topian Solution."

Like the original twelve-panel version, this extended "Short History" functions among other things as parody and update of Thomas Cole's *Course of Empire* (1833–1836), a five-painting cycle tracing the evolution of an imperial power from its "savage" origins to its arcadian/pastoral state to "consummation" and collapse. A key difference: Crumb's added panels (at least one of them, anyway) dare to envision the possibility of a livable future.[43]

Partly racist, sexist, misanthropic, and pessimistic works on the environment such as "Short History of America," "The Desperate Character Writhes Again," and "Whiteman Meets Bigfoot" viciously mock and ironicize postwar anxieties about modernity's zero-sum approach to the ecological crisis, but I submit they hardly evince the notion, voiced here by Nelson but shared by other critics, that Crumb presents "a borderline nihilistic assertion that all ideology and social persuasion is ruinous and devoid of ethical value" (140) or that "There is an intellectually inert quality to Crumb's representation, an outrage expressed in grotesquery and surrealistic exaggeration, but with no implied interpretation, and, perhaps thankfully, no proffered solution" (143). We need, it seems to me, to differentiate between irascibility, contrarianism, curmudgeonliness, and nihilism. Problematic and noncommittal as they are, the noted works come from a place of outrage, even melancholy, not a "moral vacuum" (140). As Christine McKenna better captures it: "Crumb's concern about the bigotry, pollution, illiteracy and corruption that he feels are poisoning this country is mirrored in his Expressionist depiction of America as a country in the process of decay, a corroded, withered and gnarled place" (162). Grosz, Goya redux.

Such concerns, as this chapter sought to demonstrate, have a long history in US culture. Most immediately we may tie them to deep ecology/ecocentric discourses that emerged into public awareness at the height of the counterculture era, though their origins date to much earlier. As such, Crumb's stance is vulnerable to the critique of deep ecology: that among other flaws it traffics in a false urban/rural dichotomy and an essentialized vision of nature/"wilderness" that ignores nonwhite populations that have often occupied "pristine" lands for untold millennia. (As I noted near the outset, "Short History of America" is more about hating people than loving nature.) Rebecca Solnit in her essay "The Thoreau Problem" puts it this way:

> Those who deny that nature and culture, landscape and politics, the city and the country are inextricably interfused have undermined the connections for all of us.... This makes politics dreary and landscape trivial, a vacation site. It banishes certain thoughts, including the thought that much of what the environmental movement dubbed wilderness was or is indigenous homeland—a very social and political space indeed, then and now....
>
> Conventional environmental writing has often maintained a strict silence on or even an animosity toward the city, despite its importance as a lower-impact place for the majority to live, its intricate relations to the rural, and the direct routes between the two. Imagining the woods or any untrammeled landscape as an unsocial place, an outside, also depends on erasing those who dwelt and sometimes still dwell there, the original Americans. (972–73)

The foregoing leads me to value Crumb's nature-themed work not for its upholding of such untenable ideological fictions as "wilderness," but for what he does so well throughout his oeuvre, what he seems almost congenitally predisposed to do: not take things too seriously. Nicole Seymour has hailed the rise of an "irreverent ecocriticism" that forsakes the maudlin phrasings and counterproductive hand-wringing of much environmentalist discourse. Such works, she writes, "largely reject the affects and sensibilities typically associated with environmentalism" like "gloom and doom ... guilt, shame, didacticism, prescriptiveness, sentimentality, reverence, seriousness, sincerity, earnestness, sanctimony, self-righteousness, and wonder—as well as the heteronormativity and whiteness of the movement" (*Bad Environmentalism* 4–5). As she has also argued, "A comedic stance entails flexibility and humility, those qualities required for humans to coexist with non-humans, or maybe even for us to contemplate our possible demise. And it might be the best stance at a point when humans suffer from doomsday fatigue, or an overload of 'tragedy.' A comedic, irreverent stance would thus entail adaptation on the part of ecocritics and 'regular' humans alike" ("Toward an Irreverent Ecocriticism" 63).[44]

It strikes me that, as ironic elegist for the death of nature, Crumb brings that gonzo, antisocial, sacred cow-tipping, and yes, often offensive irreverence Seymour welcomes as a tonic for discussions of how we are killing our fragile environment day in, day out. In fact, as seen in his farcical interactions with the "tofu-eating" *Winds of Change* staff, Crumb can't seem to help ironicizing (or "queering") the standard ecological narrative of utopian striving on the one hand, apocalyptic damnation on the other. All of which seems to me a more productive approach to the cartoonist than zero-degree critical dead ends like this:

> By couching obscene depictions of violence and sexuality in the style of American comics produced earlier in the twentieth century, and by reproducing offensive racial and sexual caricatures absent of any obvious attempt to condemn or interrogate them, the works of R. Crumb represent an aesthetic of perpetual and apolitical obscenity that favours the collision of discordant styles and themes as its method for ultimately achieving ideological nullification and correspondingly unfettered indulgence and gratification. (Nelson 140)

That said, Nelson's reading does bring to mind a colleague who told me about how they were once discussing the work of Robert Crumb in office hours with a Black female student. Holding back tears, she explained how much the work hurt her, how painfully it ripped open racial wounds and demanded to know why she should be required to read it in a college literature course. One might answer: "its oppositional stance and critique of white heteronormative hegemony"—though as Rebecca Wanzo has persuasively argued, Crumb "not only comments on the white racist gaze, but very explicitly interpellates a reader who is 'in on the joke' being told" (*The Content of Our Caricature* 173). However, what if that reader belongs to one of the historically othered groups Crumb represents in dehumanized fashion? To attack what Whiteman stands for is one thing; to do it while wallowing in Yetti's racialized, misogynistic, "noble savage" depiction quite another. As Wanzo concludes, "[Crumb] is taking the underground sensibility of recasting Americana, but he does not actually revise the representations" (177).

So, with all that, why read Crumb, whose work Nelson decries as perhaps nothing more than "personalized pornography writ large" (140), at all?

Why not burn Crumb?

The reference, of course, is to Simone de Beauvoir's 1953 essay "Must We Burn Sade?" Apart from many cutting insights on one of Western civilization's great monsters—such as this: "On the eve of his adult life he brutally discovered that a reconciliation was impossible between his social existence and his private pleasures" (47–48)—de Beauvoir answers her own question in the negative, by concluding, in part, "What constitutes the supreme value of [Sade's] testimony is that it disturbs us" (95).

While important to vigorously critique Crumb, to acknowledge the violent reactions his work provokes (practically by design) as well as the harm it can and does do, I have chosen to champion him here precisely for his capacity to disturb, for his potent—and, crucially, *irreverent*—challenge to intellectual complacency on the death of nature for which each of us bears our share of blame. A satirist like Crumb, hurtful as he is, helps us feel *the obscenity at the heart of the Anthropocene*, its desecration of both human and nonhuman life—without sinking into mournful keening, itself a piece of that complacency.

But you know what, screw all that. Given the artist's legendary recalcitrance, it feels most apt for me to close by giving Crumb the final word. So, on nature, from his "Litany of Hate":

> Nature is horrible. It's not cute and lovable. It's killed or be killed. It's very dangerous out there. The natural world is filled with scary, murderous creatures and forces. I hate the whole way that nature functions. Sex is especially hateful and horrifying, the male penetrating the female, his dick goes into her hole, she's impregnated, another being grows inside her, and then she must go through a painful ordeal as the new being pushes out of her, only to repeat the whole process in its time. Reproduction—what could be more existentially repulsive? (Crumb and Poplaski, *The R. Crumb Handbook* 386)

5

"WINNER TAKE ALL!"
CHILDREN, ANIMALS, AND MOURNING IN KIRBY'S *KAMANDI*

For Leona, Amelia Earhart, and Conchita, our second generation.

Jack Kirby's "The Gift!" (*Kamandi* vol. 1 #16, Apr. 1974) opens with a harrowing scene. The young blond hero, Kamandi, prowls the catacombs beneath a postapocalyptic Washington, DC. Grim-faced, shirtless, clutching a rifle, he wonders, "*What* kind of place is this?" At his approach, in the splash page's foreground, we see gnarled, grasping human hands (in the distinctive blocky, angular style of Kirby's 1970s work),[1] looking as if about to seize the "Last Boy on Earth" (1).

Turning the page, the suspense breaks, revealing a sorry spectacle. In a double-sized spread, Kamandi stands before a set of cages holding a mass of half-naked *Homo sapiens*, limbs and heads spilling out of the bars,[2] grabbing at food and ladling water out of buckets, their expressions frantic, dulled, tormented, grotesque. These pathetic creatures' only utterances: cries of "Grraaar!" and "Yowr!" Kamandi has stumbled on a research lab, in a world where, except for him, all humans have lost their reason and their dominant place in the natural order. A sign cruelly reinforces the point: "Experimental Animals/Bio Chemical Research Section/Unauthorized Persons Not Admitted" (2–3). When the desperate beast-people snatch at Kamandi, he yells at them in contempt, "*Stop* pawing at me, you mindless idiots! It's *not* my fault you're here!" (4).

Reacting in characteristic fashion—angrily, violently—Kamandi reveals himself as the child he is. Yet despite frequent tantrums before the humans

An "animal research lab" in *Kamandi* vol. 1 #16 (Apr. 1974). © DC Comics.

and human-animal hybrids he often encounters, the youth notably develops a tender fondness toward Kliklak, a gigantic grasshopper (of regular intelligence), which in the series' second year briefly serves as his companion and mount. In a storyline that culminates with Kliklak's mortal wounding and mercy killing at Kamandi's hand, Kirby draws a stark contrast between his hero's response to most therioanthromorphs in his insane world (many of which, admittedly, want to kill him) and this "normal" inarticulate beast. In so doing, the artist constructs a vision of childhood, maturity, and the place of animals centered on the experience of trauma.

Said trauma, in turn, metonymizes the fraught relationship between humans and the environment they were still despoiling a scant four years past the first Earth Day.

THE "FERAL TALE" AND THE LIMITS OF HYBRIDITY

Conceived as DC comics' response to the original *Planet of the Apes* film series,[3] Kirby's *Kamandi: The Last Boy on Earth* (vol. 1, 1972–1978)[4] posited a postapocalyptic scenario of inversion, in which anthropomorphized animals of various sorts become the intelligent top species, with humanity cast as their cattle, pets, and as seen above, research subjects.[5] "Men are just *animals* now,"

Kamandi says, in one of many such laments. "—Herded—hunted and sold—by the very beasts they *once* mastered" (*Kamandi* #12, Dec. 1973, 2).

The title became among Kirby's most sentimentally and morally invested; along with fantastic and satirical elements such as hyperintelligent dolphins, the genius dog-man Dr. Canus, nuclear-powered androids, giant bees, and Watergate-worshipping apes, the series made mankind's mistreatment of other life forms and the natural world a consistent theme. In story after story, the adolescent Kamandi explores an American continent drastically altered after some unexplained catastrophe, with little purpose besides seeking out other reasoning humans like him, while traversing various rival animal-man nation-states whose conflicts meld the futuristic (ray guns, genetic science) with the medieval (gladiatorial games, cargo cults). As Charles Hatfield notes, such an adversarial vision of nature entwines "imaginary geography and Kirby's envisionment of wild boyhood," which is essentially Romantic, "combin[ing] androgynous beauty with a ferine scrappiness" ("Kirby's Post-Apocalyptic Child"). The sullen orphan (his grandfather murdered by wolf-men) fights to survive in a world where environment and child mirror each other in their disordered, out-of-control condition, with natural splendor countered by constant eruptions of savagery and death; as Hatfield aptly puts it, "*the boy entails the setting*" ("Kirby's Post-Apocalyptic Child").[6]

And while others make mention of Kamandi's constant "shock and awe" existence in an "Earth A.D." (i.e., "After Disaster"),[7] the insights put forth by Hatfield and Craig Fischer (who sees the hero's plight as that of "a disposable animal") push the furthest on the productive question of Kamandi's dual identity as child/beast.

Indeed, as argued by Hatfield, *Kamandi* represents a late twentieth-century manifestation of the feral tale, described by Kenneth Kidd as "a literary but still folkloric narrative of animal-human or cross-cultural encounter, in which animals figure prominently" (*Making American Boys* 3). A discursive frame to both "dramatiz[e] but also manag[e] the 'wildness' of boys" (1), the feral tale troubles the line between human and nonhuman in its figuration of "the white middle class male's perilous passage from nature to culture . . . from boyhood to manhood" (7) in tales ranging from Rudyard Kipling's *The Jungle Book* (1894); to the pulp series *Bomba the Jungle Boy* (1926–1938) by Edward Stratemeyer (writing as Roy Rockwood);[8] to Maurice Sendak's *Where the Wild Things Are* (1963), which signals a "recuperation of the feral boy as a normative subject" in children's literature (6).

Significantly, Kidd traces the modern manifestation of the feral tale, which tends to represent animals as both threatening and nurturing (8–9), to psychoanalysis's interest in feral children. Bruno Bettelheim, for example, strongly linked prepubescents and animals (S. Baker 123) and saw in the feral tale a bridge between extreme trauma as exhibited by Holocaust survivors and the behavior of emotionally disturbed and autistic children (Kidd, *Making American Boys* 131). Zoe Jaques further argues that, given "the ontological instability of separating human and animal" (11) in a post-Darwin era, the terms "child" and "animal" come off as similarly reductive (26). These approaches partake of what Jacqueline Rose calls childhood's teleologically inflected construction as a mere formative stage leading to a rational and coherent adult mind, rather than an identity in its own right (13). Michael Chaney concludes, "The device of animal representation becomes in itself a signifier of children—those cultural primitives among us for whom Western theology's insistence on the subject-object disparity between man (Adam) and animal does not apply" ("Animal Subjects" 48).

In sum, the feral tale authorizes a blurring between animals and children often effected in comics through visual-verbal interspecies blendings, or as Mark Heimermann calls them, "hybrid bodies in a hybrid form (word-image)" (238). While most commonly seen in what Paul Wells dubs the "bestial ambivalence" of theriomorphic and therianthropic figures (72), e.g., "funny animals," we see a striking and more subtle instance in a later chapter of Kirby's "The Gift." Our boy hero, now incarcerated in the same research lab as the brutes encountered previously, becomes an object of fascination for Professor Hanuman,[9] a gorilla-man seeking to enhance the intelligence of "dumb animals" (i.e., humans) through a serum known as Cortexin.

During an artillery bombardment by the gorillas' archenemies the tigers, Kamandi manages to escape the collapsing prison along with several inmates (or "micro minds," as he derisively calls them). They imbibe spilled Cortexin in the water they wade through as they flee and immediately show signs of elevated intelligence. Kirby counterpoints these vignettes of dawning higher-order awareness with excerpts from the diary of Dr. Michael Grant, a pre-disaster human scientist from which Professor Hanuman draws inspiration for his animal experiments. In the story's climax, the professor marvels at the animals' feats, to the accompaniment of Dr. Grant's narration from beyond the grave:

> I saw an animal curb its fear and successfully elude capture by guards.
> An animal halted his headlong flight to help another who was injured....
> There seemed no end to it. A female escaped because a fellow animal sacrificed his safety for her!
> Animals of wonder! Animals of nobility! And the most magnificent was Whiz Kid! He'd picked up a fallen weapon and used it to defend himself! ("The Gift" 19)

Blurring the animal/human boundary. *Kamandi* vol. 1 #16 (Apr. 1974). © DC Comics.

These scenes of past-present melding make for quite the heady mixture: Grant's diary passages (presented in text boxes as visual "shots" of his cursive handwriting) refer to the chimps of his prelapsarian experiments, which we are given to understand led to the super-intelligent fauna that now populate the series' North American continent. But the concurrent images show Kamandi and his fellow *Homo sapiens* escaping, negotiating the battlefield, fending off gorilla soldiers, already exhibiting signs of impressive intellect. Multiple strata of story map the then onto the now, literalizing the adage "history doesn't repeat itself, but it often rhymes,"[10] with the "most magnificent" Kamandi now taking on the role of "Whiz Kid," the smartest chimp who leads his fellow prisoners to freedom. Comics' hybrid imagetext strategies thus enact not only an uncanny mirroring of current and historical events but a blurring of animal/human/child identities as well—Heimermann's "hybrid bodies in a hybrid form." In "The Gift," Kirby's "feral tale" approach ultimately suggests that the various species may not differ much from each other at all.[11]

That said, as Chaney argues about animal representation in comics:

There is a limit to all of this hybridity . . . which seizes the animal, not surprisingly, at the vanishing point of the human, but not the other way around. The primacy of human speech and mobility makes the primacy of animal appearance secondary, perhaps even inconsequential. If you look just like a horse, but walk around, wear a cowboy hat, a badge, and carry a side arm, you are more of a sheriff than a hybrid of any kind. ("Animal Subjects" 47)

From *Krazy Kat* to *Fritz the Kat* to *Kamandi*, cartoonists superficially reinscribe species distinction only "to finally celebrate and naturalize the superiority of the human (as defined by the Enlightenment) as well as the insuperable difference separating the human from the non-human" (47). Chaney here isolates the use and emptying out of the animal image for aesthetic/political ends, a process described by, among others, John Berger (as I discuss in chapter 2). Hence, Kirby's multifarious animal-people (intelligent dolphins and killer whales, dog-men, tiger-men, gorilla-men, etc.) in essence fulfill the anthropomorphic function I have elsewhere called "ani-drag";[12] they wear their animality like an elaborate mask. As Wells characterizes the strategy, "Animal metamorphosis . . . privileges cross-species engagement, cross-dressing, gender-shifting and the performance of identity as a method by which unreal settings and impossible situations may be used as a vehicle to play with contemporary issues" (66)—though as he drily understates: "The animal might be evacuated" (83–84).

But while certainly true of figures such as the father-substitute Dr. Canus, not all animals in *Kamandi* participate in Berger's "pressganging." Beasts of burden, including horses, oxen, and mutated fauna such as giant bees do not gain supra-normal intelligence from swallowing Cortexin or through any other AD means. They remain "dumb," speechless animals—arbitrarily so. It seems that enough fans expressed puzzlement at the distinction[13] that Kirby felt compelled to take up the subject himself in a 1974 letters column.[14] He wrote:

> Why, in the world of Kamandi, do I discriminate among the animals, giving some the intelligence of Man and others less sentient awareness? Why must the stately horse serve as transportation for a smelly, old gorilla? Why must the bird remain a beautiful dum-dum? . . .
>
> To my mind, the hooved animals and our feathered friends would have to undergo changes too extreme in nature to reach a civilized statehood. It would pain me to know that a wonderful animal like the horse had endured a millennium of back-aches in order to sit in a chair and drink his coffee at the television set. I would crack up and roll on the floor if a sincere and intelligent turkey were to run for congress. (*Kamandi* vol. 1 #17, May 1974)

Aside from Kirby's odd sentiments on what constitutes "changes too extreme" to allow for certain animals to be portrayed with humanlike intellects—given that he makes the hooded business titan/slaveowner Mr. Sacker a snake—the explanation falls rather short as plausible "science." This despite the fact that Kirby bases his premise on "a variety of authoritative articles written by qualified men who have speculated on the form life must take in order to acquire intelligence as we know it." (Apparently none of those men was Jonathan Swift—see this chapter's endnote 5.) Rather, it seems obvious that—as in *The Planet of the Apes*—animals of conventional intelligence in *Kamandi* are there to serve such vital narrative functions as conveyance, threat, labor, and food. Not anthropomorphically "pressganged" or "evacuated," their animality not rendered "inconsequential," these beasts in a sense remain free to be what they are.

One of these creatures in particular would come to play a central role in one of the series' most heart-wrenching episodes.

"WINNER TAKE ALL!"

In "Winner Take All!" (*Kamandi* #14, Feb. 1974), Kirby addresses the subject of animal-human ethics in particularly stark terms: The adolescent blond protagonist finds himself competing in a perversely gladiatorial "Sacker's Sweepstakes" race, with raucous crowds of ani-people placing wagers on the outcome and cheering on their champions. In a sickening reversal typical of the series,

Kamandi confronts impossible odds, reduced to the bare life of a beast (not unlike those "micro-minds" in Professor Hanuman's laboratory), total slave to a higher species, compelled to perform against his fellow humans. His role differs little from that of a dog forced to fight another dog.

Kamandi's opponent: Bull Bantam, another loutish semi-articulate astride a fearsome buffalo, who barks such scintillating dialogue as "Me stomp you *deep* into ground!" (11). The "beater of women," equal parts odious and pugnacious, sparks Kamandi's ire for his ill-treatment of Spirit (sister of our hero's lost love, Flower). When the bully's comeuppance finally arrives, it does so on the racetrack, as the enraged boy beats the larger man to a pulp with his bare hands, sputtering, "I've just been *aching* to pay you off! Stupid—arrogant—pampered—brutal little *tyrant!*" (12). Their final melee unfolds over two pages (one of them a nine-panel grid) as Kamandi, his face a rictus of fury, pummels the villain senseless to a cascade of "Pow"/"Bam!" sound effects (up to three per panel) and explosive power lines. The scene's savage dynamism (blurred fists flying, blond hair aswirl) underscores Kirby's "violent, conflictual understanding of story" (Hatfield, *Hand of Fire* 8), as well as what Glen Gold sees as the "underlying rage" that fueled so much of Kirby's art (67).[15]

Speaking of which, one aspect of that art in particular drives the scene's propulsive energy: the veteran Kirby's oft-remarked "blocky" 1970s expressionism, described by Hatfield as "angular modernist severity bordering on the grotesque" (*Hand of Fire* 73), which redraws the balance between "pictorial realism and cartoon stylization" (72). Disdained by some,[16] this style—precisely through its mannerist excess—is largely what makes *Kamandi* work so well as children's fantasy. What Alexi Worth calls a Blakean "forcefully wrong presentation of human anatomy" (70), enhanced in no small measure by breathless dialogue and triple exclamation points, abets an ingenuous mood that readily marries the surreal to the prosaic, the "innocent" to the harrowing, talking dolphins to tragedy and death. Its oddness somehow evokes a child's horror at the appalling violence and instability of the world, along with her awe at its fundamental beauty; a naif sublime. Kirby's art here, with bodies abstracted to graphic essences and pure kineticism, expressions distorted to absolutes, makes *Kamandi*'s otherwise over-the-top subject matter ("The Human Gophers of Ohio!") uniquely engaging. Among other things, the series demonstrates the inextricability of graphic narrative's content and form.

Kirby's art further augments an effect isolated by comics writer Gerard Jones pertaining to how young readers process representations of trauma and loss. Discussing violence with a teen fan at a 1994 comics convention, Jones has a revelation about the true appeal of his work to this audience:

I'd seen fight scenes as a necessary evil to induce kids to read the more valuable contents of my stories—but now I'd made the most meaningful contact with a reader of my career *through* the fights. The characters, plots and themes mattered, but the truly affecting, truly transformative element of the story was the violence itself. The violence had helped a timid adolescent tap into her own bottled-up emotionality and discover a feeling of personal power. (5)

For Jones, comic-book violence functions as recuperative, therapeutic—even, troublingly, adaptive. It certainly does so for Kamandi himself (and his readers?) after repeated traumatizations, bodily injury, and psychic strain. And what unnatural shocks his flesh has been heir to: By this point in the series, Kamandi has lost his dear grandfather and entire family; his love interest Flower; numerous friends and allies in the unforgiving hellscape of Earth AD, with new comrades Dr. Canus, Ben Boxer, and Prince Tuftan to replace them—a mirror to Kirby's life "defined by conflict and, paradoxically, by camaraderie" (Hatfield, *Hand of Fire* 6). We therefore need not begrudge Kamandi (and vicariously, his fans) the emotional outlet of throttling his enemies. The boy's momentary—and bloody—victory over Bantam balances the scales just enough to restore his self-worth. Trembling, sinews taut, towering over his defeated foe, the boy even feels sympathy for the bully: "But it *isn't* all your fault! The Sacker's company *made* you what you are!" (12).

However, violence in this series always takes place within a larger social context—which Kirby makes brutally manifest almost immediately after his hero's triumph. The final panel on this same page (the largest, full-width) shows a diminished Kamandi in long shot, Bantam prostrate before him, and the racetrack stadium crowd wildly cheering, "*The 'long shot' wins!*" "*Yahooo!*" (12). In "zooming out" from the previous panels' tighter shots, Kirby effects a devastating deflation by exposing the battle royale for what it always was: mass entertainment and a gambling opportunity. Incensed, Kamandi hurls abuse at the throng—but by the next panel has given up. "What's the use," he muses, walking away, "to *them—I* am the animal—" (13). In short, victory means nothing to a slave.

But something the sullen Kamandi does care about lies broken nearby: his beloved mount Kliklak. In the next few pages, "Winner Take All!" shows the full consequences of violence in Kirby's world, as Kamandi faces a problem he cannot beat with his fists.

Introduced in "The Devil" (*Kamandi* #11, Nov. 1973), the gigantic green grasshopper Kliklak terrifies the leopard-men pirates who captured him in the wild, but it befriends our blond hero, who at this point has also become the property of Mr. Sacker. With only four legs and behaving more like a skittish horse,[17] the giant insect allows itself to be saddled by Kamandi, who schemes to ride it away to freedom. "I thought you were going to gobble me up at first. But, you turned out to be real *friendly!*" he says, patting the goliath. "I'll call you *Kliklak*—okay?" (Kirby, "The Devil" 5). The creature's only utterance thereby becomes its name.

In David Herman's scale of animal representation in comics, Kliklak (along with horses, bees, and cattle in the series) lands somewhere on the "Umwelt exploration" side of the spectrum, with its emphasis on "the lived, phenomenal worlds of non-human animals themselves" and how these "reshape humans' own modes of encounter" ("Storyworld/Umwelt" 167). Though not an intelligent anthromorph like Tuftan or Professor Hanuman, Kliklak does have a personality: nervous, rambunctious, frolicsome. In his first interaction with Kamandi, he nearly destroys the boy's hideout by leaping and crashing through it—only to playfully bump the boy's backside to continue the "game" ("The Devil" 6). He ranks among Kirby's most odd, endearing creations.[18]

But by "Winner Take All," which opens in *medias res*, Kliklak has already suffered grievous injuries in the "Sacker's Sweepstakes" race through bombardment and heavy gunfire. Further battered by Bantam's charging buffalo, he lies dying on the battlefield as the humans settle their score. Turning angrily from the rowdy crowd, a bruised Kamandi at last takes note of his wounded friend. The sad truth quickly crystallizes, despite the boy's denials: Kliklak cannot be saved.

When Sacker's leopard-men deem the animal's injuries too severe for veterinary aid, they move to shoot him. "*No! No! Wait—!*" Kamandi cries, pleading to spare his friend (13). "Kliklak's *trying* to get up! *There!* You *see?*" But soon, even he must admit there is no hope: "He's in *terrible* pain—he's *suffering*—a-and I *can't* help him—" Remarkably, a leopard-man answers: "Yes you *can*.—I'll give you my *rifle*—" (14). This astonishing act of trust (Kamandi could use the weapon against them), along with the leopards calling Kliklak "he" (rather than "it" or "devil," as before) and even referring to the insect as "your friend," cements the notion of the animal's status as a near-equal, deserving of a merciful end. Kirby here presents a rare moment of community between humans and enemy animal-men in the series, authorized by the solemnity of death. The leopard even instructs Kamandi to aim for a soft spot between the eyes for a quick kill.

"I-It'll take *all* the guts I have to do this—but it's the *only* thing left to do—" the boy mutters, taking the rifle. "*Goodbye*, Kliklak—I'll *try* to make this as quick and painless as I can—!" He aims, fires—and it is over (14).

Throughout this maudlin scene, Kirby reinforces both its tragic mood and radical portrait of trans-species empathy through composition and layout. Let us focus on the climactic six-panel grid on page 14. Panels one and two: Kamandi's initial panic is signaled through his posture and fearful eyes—rarely would he ever

Killing Kliklak. *Kamandi* #14 (Feb. 1974). © DC Comics.

appear more like a scared, helpless child. He strokes the giant's head, as it struggles weakly on the ground. Here he tells the leopards Kliklak is trying to get up.

But as we shift to the next tier,[19] we see the start of a transformation over the next four panels. Now the depth of Kliklak's suffering finally dawns on Kamandi; panel three shows his face in extreme close-up, half of it cut off, the closest shot of the page. With deep scratches on his cheek, jaw set, he now looks man-like, steadfast, determined. The frightened kid has vanished. In the fourth panel, where he takes the rifle, he looks grim, eyes narrowed, gaze fixed on Kliklak, whose head juts out in the foreground. In the penultimate frame, as he hoists the weapon to shoot, Kamandi resembles an automaton, his eyes jet-black and empty, doll-like. Kirby accentuates the "robot" effect by making Kamandi's arms unusually rigid; the barrel swings into position with a semicircular motion line, like some mechanical device. All the same, the stiff posture somehow only makes Kamandi appear more haunted, driven. In sum, the page masterfully represents the phases of grief, from denial to acceptance—and on to euthanasia.

Beyond that, Kirby reinforces the pathos of the scene throughout the last four panels by depicting Kamandi and the leopard-men frontally and looking slightly down. The boy aims the rifle in our general direction, with the shot itself, in close-up, going off down and to the side. Such bending of the fourth wall secures an intimacy with the reader, a connection based on the universal human encounter with death. The scene, like few others in the Kirby corpus, devastates and wounds.

Which makes what follows all the more risible.

"Winner Take All's" final part, "The Last Mile!," opens with a splash page and the series' customary chapter introduction: "The echo of Kamandi's shot *fades* in the tragic air, and with its passing, a strange but noble heart *stops* in midbeat. Kliklak suffers no more. Here, in this distant land, he's found peace only in death" (15).

As Kamandi grieves over Kliklak's dead body in the foreground, we see the sweepstakes' award ceremony go into full swing, complete with parade float ("Sacker's Salutes its Prize-Winning Animals!"), brass band, balloons, and motorcycles (15).[20] Scantily clad women bear the victor the "Sacker's crown of champion," fresh clothes, and the ultimate jackpot, a "delicious yum yum layer cake." The ludicrous spectacle[21] only heightens the hero's gloom, expressed in the bottom tier through a dead-eyed stare once more directed at the reader (16).

Despite the leopard-men's advice that he cheer up and enjoy "Happy Time," the "sulking animal" refuses all blandishments. Kamandi recalls historical microfilms of victorious thoroughbred horses similarly rewarded with floral wreathes, concluding, "This is the same!—The *same!*" (16).[22] When Spirit appears to present herself as another of his trophies, he goes berserk, screaming,

"Happy Time" begins. *Kamandi* #14 (Feb. 1974). © DC Comics.

"*We're people!!* Get that? You *can't* give us away as prizes!" (17); the outburst earns him a rifle butt to the head, and unconsciousness.

In short, the demise of Kliklak leads to a full-blown existential crisis. The giant insect, far from a mere servant or interchangeable mount, registers in Kamandi's conscience as an equal partner in his struggle to survive; his loss plunges the boy into deep despair. Kliklak goes down bravely in battle as a comrade, similarly to how Homer describes the death of Pedasus, a battle horse slain in much the same manner as fallen human warriors during the siege of Troy. As Berger notes of the poet's treatment of Pedasus and his master in death: "Both are equally transparent in Homer's eyes, there is no more refraction in one case than the other" (9).

Certainly, the portrait of Kliklak, a minor supporting character who goes in and out of the hero's life in four issues of an ongoing series, will not equal Kamandi's in psychological depth and sophistication, all the more so because the creature cannot speak. Yet Kirby's decision to render the animal as animal while still allowing for readers to sympathize with its suffering and death opens a space for what Herman calls "narrativity constituted on different grounds," that of nonhuman life's imagined engagement with the world ("Storyworld/Umwelt" 178). Unlike with the killing of countless nameless ani-men in *Kamandi*, Kliklak's death moves in part because we are allowed to experience it with him (to the extent, as noted, of having the merciful rifle pointed in our direction).

But of course, as also noted, Kliklak dying matters because it matters to Kamandi, through whom all events in the series are focalized. Kirby demonstrates this most subtly, through composition, just before the actual death scene. Let us return to the large panel that punctuates the ending of Kamandi and Bantam's battle on page 12. Kirby signals the stakes for his boy hero by positioning him in the exact center of the frame, back to us, confronting the cheering crowd. Various story elements radiate out from him: His foe lies face down on the track to the left; the buffalo strides away to the right. We see a portion of Kliklak's green head in the foreground. It appears as the largest object, reflecting the ethical dilemma at hand (should we spare our loved ones needless pain, even it means killing them?); Kamandi's back turned foreshadows that he will indeed have to consign his friend to death and somehow move on. Here as in so many other episodes, the series yokes science fiction and melodrama to Levinasian contemplations of the Other.

The death/killing of a beloved animal represents for some a troubling trope in children's literature, in its most reductive form a sort of way station on the road to growing up. Kamandi's killing of Kliklak to spare him further suffering finds precedent in Fred Gipson's *Old Yeller*, a 1956 novel for children in which the adolescent hero Travis famously shoots the eponymous family dog, who has contracted rabies. The film adaptation of *Old Yeller* (d. Robert Stevenson,

USA, 1957) further popularized the sad death scene, injecting treacly pathos onto the spare description of its source:

> It came clear to me then that Mama was right. We couldn't take the risk. And from everything I had heard, I knew that there was very little chance of Old Yeller's escaping the sickness. It was going to kill something inside me to do it, but I knew then that I had to shoot my big yeller dog.
> Once I knew for sure I had it to do, I don't think I really felt anything. I was just numb all over, like a dead man walking....
> I reloaded my gun and called Old Yeller back from the house. I stuck the muzzle of the gun against his head and pulled the trigger. (152–53)

Apart from the striking parallels with the slaying of Kliklak,[23] this laconic passage, from near the end of the novel, exemplifies a familiar (albeit problematic) boy's rite of passage in US culture. So maintain more than a few children's literature scholars: Drawing on John Bowlby, Sigmund Freud, and Judith Butler, Eric Tribunella sees Old Yeller's death as key to Travis's gender formation, whereby the boy must "purchase" heterosexuality at the expense of "actually murder[ing] his beloved dog, which itself repeatedly suffers tremendous wounds while saving the boy he loves" (31). The logic of the story dictates that "in killing the object of proto-erotic attachment Travis finally becomes a man" (37–38).

Related to the dead/wounded child trope (Kidd, "A Is for Auschwitz" 126), what Tribunella calls the "enabling injury" (xiv) of trauma produced by the child's encounter with the (often Darwinian)[24] violence of life acts as a sacrifice of sorts to the god of growing up; we see its Freudian premises in the emphasis on renunciation and suppression as the price of personal growth. As Tribunella starkly puts it: "The striking recurrence of this pattern suggests that children's literature, and indeed American culture, relies on the contrived traumatization of children—both protagonists and readers—as a way of representing and promoting the process of becoming a mature adult. It is as if loss generates the escape velocity of youth" (xi).

In short, he concludes of such messages as *Old Yeller*'s: "To be mature is to be wounded" (xiv). The ethical pitfalls—if not outright sadism—of such a stance have prompted its critique as needlessly traumatizing and triggering. They moved Katharine Capshaw Smith, in a much-cited 2005 forum on the subject in *Children's Literature*, to read the "wounded child" trope, including the "kill what you love" scenario, as a perverse fantasy of adults that makes of the innocent child trauma's ultimate victim *and* ultimate survivor, both fragile and strong (116).[25]

Kamandi's traumatizing loss of Kliklak thus stems from a long tradition of authorial barbarity aimed at child readers, to harden them against "extratextual realities" (Tribunella, xii), i.e., artistic terrorism as "tough love." That Kirby's boy hero, trapped in an ongoing bimonthly series, suffers emotional and physical trauma of every sort on a regular basis only makes us sense all the more strongly the fundamental perversity involved—as well as appreciate how it paves the way for some terrific melodrama and fantasy. It goes without saying, too, that an issue later Kamandi seems to have effectively forgotten Kliklak, so preoccupied is he with current shocks and dangers. (Here the sacrifice, perhaps, is to the god of serial production.)

I do want to suggest, however, that the death of Kliklak and Kamandi's concomitant grief bear other layers of meaning beyond that of the aforementioned children's literature trope, ones that speak directly to late twentieth-/early twenty-first-century environmental angst.

CONCLUSION: KLIKLAK'S GAZE

If, for Kidd, the twentieth-century feral tale—"by turns heroic and melancholic"—is "fundamentally a story about maturation" (*Making American Boys* 11), then in the third decade of the twenty-first century, we can say that graphic narrative has itself arrived at some sort of culminating "maturation" as well. Thanks to the burgeoning field of comics studies and an explosion of industry productions impossible to generalize about, we can no longer wholly subscribe to Charles Hatfield's 2007 view that "certain underlying beliefs—such as the idea that comics are specially 'children's' reading, or are automatically accessible to most child readers, or necessarily partake of the welcoming 'simplicity' of childhood—have yet to be seriously questioned or historicized" ("Introduction" 8). We are questioning. We are historicizing. Viva comics!

More specifically, as I have tried to show, an examination of Kirby's *Kamandi: The Last Boy on Earth* only reminds that there was never anything *de rigeur* childish or simplistic about comics to begin with, even in their most commercialized "genre" incarnations. In this conclusion, then, I want to reflect on how a sophisticated visual-verbal text such as "Winner Take All!," while fulfilling some of the (fraught) expectations for young readers' literature in its era, also comments productively on such matters as trauma, mourning, and mass extinctions that have purchase in our own era of climate change.

To begin, and hopefully without overly psychologizing Kirby, I want to speculate on Kliklak's personal significance for his creator. Glen David Gold, in an essay drawing on Kirby's experiences as an infantryman in World War II, calls him "a genius of trauma" (67). While growing up in New York's prewar Lower East Side came with plenty of hard knocks, Gold emphasizes how the artist's experiences in the European theater helped shape his mature vision. Private Jack

Kirby landed at Omaha Beach in summer 1944, some ten days after the Allied invasion, with the Eleventh Infantry, Company F. Here he both witnessed and committed mass killings that would forever influence his view of the world. Gold suggests part of the power in Kirby's wartime accounts to his family "came from him not being able to actually tell these stories," how he often talked around or changed key details, "meaning his eye continued to glance away" (74).

Kirby did tell interviewers one coherent narrative about what he called his "worst" wartime experience—notably, one involving an animal victim. On a scouting mission to a bombed-out, abandoned French town, Private Kirby enters a damaged hotel with a charred front door. Inside, he discovers a badly injured dog that emerges from the rubble and confronts him, without growling or whimpering, with what seems a reproachful stare. As he recounted:

It was like he was saying, "You did this to me."
Oh, I felt so guilty.
I felt just terrible and so hurt, because to me it was like an accusation by a dumb creature that didn't care why I was there. . . . All he knew was that I was there and he was hurting. . . . I lowered my rifle and it limped past me out of the wreckage and onto the road. He kept giving me these dirty looks, terrible dirty looks (quoted in Gold 75).

I do not mean to reduce "Winner Take All!" to a mere expiation of its author's guilt, decades on, for a wartime dereliction of decency (why didn't Kirby put the animal out of its misery with his rifle, as does Kamandi?). But surely Kirby's "worst" war memory, of a grievously wounded animal's gaze, made its way in some fashion into the Kliklak storyline. Only here the hero can do the right thing—even if "it'll take *all* the guts I have to do this."[26]

But what precisely is it about the suffering of a "dumb creature" that could produce such a lasting, reverberative effect on an artist's work long after the encounter? Here I think we see most clearly that the depiction of Kliklak's death and Kamandi's grief overlaps with a central malaise of both the 1970s and our own age, an age of great die-offs on land, sea, and air.

In a series so focused on environmental degradation ("a great disaster has *changed* the world"),[27] launched a scant decade after the publication of Rachel Carson's *Silent Spring* (1962) and just two years after the first Earth Day had pricked the nation's conscience regarding the ecological crisis, the putting down of a beloved animal readily takes on an added patina of melancholy for a dying planet. All the more so when the animal in question is a mutant, produced through unnatural processes (radiation) set in motion by man.

Though the term "Anthropocene" (denoting the age of human-caused mass extinctions, global pollution, and climate change) would not come into prominent use until the early 2000s,[28] Kamandi's mourning for his friend resonates with our own time's anxieties over a very real unfolding "great disaster." (Once more, "the boy entails the setting.") We may read *Kamandi*, in fact, as a comics precursor to modern-day cli-fi;[29] the famous cover and opening spread of the series' first issue (October 1972) show the hero on a raft, plying the waves of a New York City reclaimed by the Atlantic, Statue of Liberty bobbing in the background: "This is *not* the New York I saw in the micro-film library!" the boy marvels. "*The city is gone!*—Covered by the sea—!" ("Kirby, "The Last Boy on Earth" 2–3). Kirby's postapocalyptic vision[30] incarnated an ecological dread just stirring in the early 1970s, which has blossomed since into an all-too-recognizable alarm over a nature grown exceedingly precarious. Reading it in the age of the sixth mass extinction (this one largely human-caused), Kliklak's death thus stands out from previous animal-killing narratives in children's literature as a late twentieth-century metonym for a dying Earth.

That it can function so, I submit, has much to do with the rise of conceptual modes that emphasize the autonomy, individuality, and self-worth of nonhuman beings vis-à-vis our own species. Writing on one of those modes, posthumanism, Bidisha Banerjee notes it "offers a questioning and reframing of human subjectivity based on the principles of community bonding which allows us to look at strangerhood and otherness in new and challenging ways" (400). In short, Kliklak—whom, crucially, we read as a kind of nonhuman person and partner, not merely as a generic "beast"—represents an instance of what Jacques Derrida terms *l'animot*, a neologism signaling an "irreducible living multiplicity of mortals" (41). In his landmark 1997 lecture-turned-essay "The Animal That Therefore I Am (More to Follow)," the great deconstructionist critiques an anthropocentric Western culture that counterposes the "general singular" of the animal to the presumptive heterogeneity of *Homo sapiens* (40–42). To upend such thinking, Derrida posits *l'animot* (a play on both *animaux* ["animals"] and *mot* ["word"]). He sees in the move an ethical imperative to restore a sense of respect, if not reverence, to creatures much abused due first and foremost to their lack of human language. He writes: "It would not be a matter of 'giving speech back' to animals but perhaps of acceding to a thinking, however fabulous and chimerical it might be, that thinks the absence of the name and of the word otherwise, as something other than privation" (48).

Certainly, Private Kirby's nameless injured dog, with its accusing stare, communicated volumes to him without the need for words. Similarly, Kamandi's despair over Kliklak's death arises largely from his compassion for the animal's speechless suffering. Its capacity to express pain and the boy's sensitivity to it represent an instance of trans-species connection with repercussions for how readers (especially young readers) relate to the state of the natural world as they develop their social bonds. Tribunella, indeed, sees many episodes of animal/child encounter in children's literature as "exemplar[s] of a secure, successful, and a pleasurable attachment in contrast to the typically more embattled attachments" with fellow humans, especially adults (46). No wonder they experience the loss of the ideal "bestial relationship" so profoundly.

From Virginia Woolf's posthumous 1942 essay "The Death of the Moth," in which she recognizes her own death fears in an insect's mortal throes—"One could only watch the extraordinary efforts made by those tiny legs against an oncoming doom" (374)—to Michael McCarthy's 2015 book *The Moth Snowstorm*, an elegy for Woolf's selfsame English lepidoptera driven perilously toward extinction,[31] the dying animal points beyond itself. In turn, the mourning of nonhuman lives, even fantastic and fictional ones, further demonstrates their "affective power vis-à-vis the human observer in [their] material, observable form,"[32] as argued by George Ioannides in his discussion of the dead animal in cinema (108), and by Julia Schlosser on "the visual language of loss" and the dead animal in photography.[33] Even in vicarious settings such as that of "Winner Take All!," we "grieve with them not necessarily because they are humanized, but because they do transcend boundaries of kin and kind by becoming integral to our lives as social partners rather than as resources" (Weil 115).

Further, phrases such as "affective power" and "transcend boundaries" as they relate to representation signal yet another way in which animals point beyond themselves, to an extradiegetic quality Steve Baker links to Derrida's concept of the supplement:

> The visual language of the animal, however minimal or superficial the degree of its "animality," invariably works as a Derridean supplement to the narrative. It is apparently exterior to that narrative, but it disturbs the logic and consistency of the whole. It has the effect of bringing to light the disruptive potential of the story's animal content. It limits the extent to which the narrative can patrol and control its own boundaries. (139)

To sum up, the animal body—already a form of narratival excess—takes on additional signifying layers when depicted as suffering, dying, and dead, directing the reader both "outwardly" (connecting it with modern disquiet over global species collapse) and "inwardly" (to those great intimate zones of liminality: childhood, with which it shares its feral origins,[34] and the agony of mourning). Speechless, it nonetheless speaks "for" the dying world from which it emerged and "to" the traumatized child who fitfully struggles to grasp the cataclysm of its passing. In saying goodbye to Kliklak, Kamandi parts not only with his "innocence," but with a portion of the wildness that constituted them both.

Whether such "shock" episodes in children's literature perform culturally beneficent work, contributing to the child reader's personal development as "a kind of inoculation" against the "toxicity of loss" (Tribunella xii), seems a different sort of judgment call. But more expansively, I would say "dying animal" stories function as ground-level commentaries on crashing fauna populations with which child readers—as the future of our species—will have to contend someday.

"The boy entails the setting": In a world out of balance, unstable, gone ecologically insane, many feel they can only grieve—a helplessness not unlike Kamandi's on the Sacker's Sweepstakes racetrack, during "Happy Time."

"Winner Take All!" tells us that in a dying biosphere, with animals' lives at best mere commodities, the Kliklaks of the world are doomed.

From that truth we can shield our kids for only so long.

6

WAKANDA SPEAKS

ANIMALS AND ANIMACY IN "PANTHER'S RAGE"

> Posthumanism possesses a deeply utopian bent. Its practitioners sometimes proceed as if the breeching of ontological categories were in itself affirmative or transcendent. Yet violence is omnipresent, part of the world's fabric, the provenance of plants, animals and materiality itself. Storied matter possesses many genres, including horror.
> —JEFFREY JEROME COHEN (36)

In "There Are Serpents Lurking in Paradise," chapter 9 of the "Panther's Rage" storyline (*Jungle Action* #14, Mar. 1975), King T'Challa/Black Panther and the forest-dweller Mokadi stumble upon a sorry sight: an oil slick choking a river deep in Wakanda's remote Serpent Valley. As the two gaze from overhanging tree branches, a text box proclaims, "The scent of *oil* is overpowering, spreading black, leprous fingers. The river *struggles* to continue its *ageless flow*— / The struggle has been *lost!*" (Sedlmeier 186).

They soon discover the black ooze's source: The villain N'Jadaka/Killmonger and his crew created the slick to immobilize and capture dinosaurs, which they will weaponize in a bid to seize the Wakandan throne. A splash page shows the primeval giants struggling against the crude-contaminated waters as men in boats cast nets over them. The leader of the operation looks on, grinning: "*Killmonger* is in good spirits. The day has gone *well*" (Sedlmeier 187).

Writer Don McGregor and artist Billy Graham here pause in their sprawling, multiyear epic to comment on an extractive, domineering mindset toward nature, one heedless of consequences. The narrative, however, does heed—and to a remarkable degree: Over the course of six panels, in the midst of other human-centered business, we zoom in on a tiny bird (resembling a grebe)

T'Challa and Mokadi encounter an oil slick. *Jungle Action* #14 (Mar. 1975). © Marvel Comics.

stuck in the sludge. One of Killmonger's henchmen, himself pushed into the muck by his master, tries to save the trapped creature ("frail figures *merged* in . . . *tragedies*"), only to be censured by the villain: "Tayete, if we lost time saving each *helpless stray* on our road to *greatness*— / we would never *reach* our destination" (Sedlmeier 188).

As strongman and lackeys stride off into the distance, we maintain focus on the foreground and its feathered, sinking, doomed victim: "The graceful wings flutter. Weak bird-trilling seems to ask what has happened to the gift of *flight*. / . . . [I]ts plaintive death-cries are *lost* in the *vastness of events*. / As usual!" (Sedlmeier 188). A few pages later, at the climax of a battle between the Panther and a Tyrannosaurus rex, we once again, over three thick-bordered panels, zero in on the oil-encrusted bird in its last moments, as its eye closes forever. "A few *crucial* elements of the scene are missed," the captions say. "For some, night does *not* arrive. As usual" (197). The page makes for a startling contrast in scale: The towering T-rex collapses from a *coup de grâce*-by-boulder in the two largest panels, while in the smallest, the bird suffocates silently, unnoticed, unmourned.

The episode recalls the human-decentering "cut-aways" in Ed Dodd's mid-century comic strip *Mark Trail* (discussed in part I). As Veronica Vold maintains, such odd panel sequences evoke "a conservationist paradigm that insists on human reverence for and submission to the active interests of the more-than-human world. [Their] lyrical tribute interrupts any anthropocentric narrative flow" (71).

In any case, animals of all sizes suffer violent deaths throughout "Panther's Rage." But as punctuated by that echoing "*as usual!*," McGregor and Graham insist that there are no "insignificant" casualties in the unending war between man and nature. To underscore that point, they seize on an image which by 1975 would have struck many US readers as depressingly familiar.

Multiscalar animal death in *Jungle Action* #14 (Mar. 1975). © Marvel Comics.

SANTA BARBARA

On January 28, 1969, a Union Oil well six miles off the coast of Santa Barbara, California, catastrophically malfunctioned. Despite attempts to cap it, the well blew, spilling between 22,000 and 220,000 gallons of oil into the ocean each day for the next eleven days (Spezio xvi–xvii), creating a slick thirty-five miles long along the coast and killing thousands of birds, fish, and sea mammals. At the time, it was the third-largest oil spill in the country's history (Nash et al. 22).

Citing a study by the Santa Barbara–based General Research Corporation, A. E. Keir Nash and his coauthors noted in 1972:

> By February 3, six days after the blowout, oil had spread over 251 square miles of the [Santa Barbara] Channel. Eighty-six square miles were covered with heavy, dark oil, the remainder by a lighter film. By February 5, Santa Barbara County beaches were blanketed with a layer of crude oil which was several inches thick in most places. Its odor was noticeable several miles inland; 660 square miles of the Channel were covered—160 square miles by the heavy, dark oil. (22)

By the end of April 1969, more than three million gallons (about seventy thousand barrels) had spilled, a black stain stretching from Santa Barbara to the nearby Channel Islands, as far away as Pismo Beach (ninety miles north) and Malibu Beach (sixty-five miles south) (Nash et al. 22). "The thing I remember most about it was the noise of the waves breaking on the beach ended," author Robert Sollen told *The Los Angeles Times*. "The water was heavy and lubricated with oil. There was a total silence" (Grad).

In the end, according to geographers K. C. Clarke and Jeffrey J. Hemphill:

> Eight hundred square miles of ocean were impacted, and 35 miles of coastline were coated with oil up to six inches thick. The oil muted the sound of the waves on the beach and the odor of petroleum was inescapable. The ecological impact was catastrophic. Rescuers counted 3,600 dead ocean feeding seabirds and a large number of poisoned seals and dolphins were removed from the shoreline. The spilled oil killed innumerable fish and intertidal invertebrates, devastated kelp forests and displaced many populations of endangered birds. (159)

Dead and suffering animals dominated media coverage of the Santa Barbara spill, spurring public demands for government action to safeguard the environment from similar disasters. Much of the imagery featured oil-smothered birds. On February 6, 1969, *The Los Angeles Times* led with "Drifting Oil Smears

Beaches for 12 Miles" in screaming bold, with a photograph of a blackened cormorant and caption reporting that the animal was "beyond saving" (Spezio 137).[1] As historian Kathryn Morse notes:

> *The Los Angeles Times*, the *Washington Post*, the *Boston Globe*, and *Time* ran photographs of the rig, the slick, the makeshift oil booms, the beaches, and volunteers and workers bathing oily grebes (diving birds that spend almost all of their time in water). *Newsweek* included a dying cormorant (a coastal seabird), along with workers raking up oil-absorbent straw. *Life* published images of two grebes, one dead, one being bathed. Reports and images emphasized a sense of tragic, heartbreaking helplessness. Volunteers watched, the *Los Angeles Times* reported, as cormorants "tried vainly to clean one another off with their beaks," and then died from ingested oil. Fleeing well-intentioned rescuers, birds headed into the surf. "Falling into the black liquid," the report read, "they lay in the ooze, crying weakly." In June *Life* covered the spill's effects with photographs from San Miguel Island off the coast. Pictures included an oil-drenched seal pup stranded in slippery rocks. The island, the reporter wrote, provided "the black vision of the dead world which may come." (129–30)

In a McLuhanesque twist, technical advances in home entertainment may also have played a role in viewer emotional engagement with the tragedy; historian Teresa Sabol Spezio argues, "With the spread of color television technology, many Americans experienced an environmental catastrophe in color for the first time. The contrast between the blue water, white sand beaches, and multicolored plumage of birds and the oil that now covered them shocked the viewing public" (131).

Workers spreading straw along the slick to soak it up, bulldozers scraping the top layers of beaches, contaminated sand being trucked away, and heroic volunteers desperately scrubbing oil off animals became familiar fare on TV screens and newspapers for the duration of the disaster[2] (setting the mold for reportage of such events in the future). The immediacy of the coverage and something more ineffable, maintains historian J. Brooks Flippen, broke through a late-1960s public consciousness in ways previous natural catastrophes had not: "The disaster was, in fact, no greater than several oil tanker spills the world had suffered[3] but, with the scenic beauty of the Californian coast as a backdrop, it still made for great television. Birds covered with sticky oil struggled for life; dead seals floated ashore; enraged Santa Barbara housewives cried for the cameras" (25).[4]

Whatever it was, Santa Barbara had a galvanizing effect on a US environmentalist movement[5] that had remained relatively quiet since the eruption following Rachel Carson's 1962 publication of *Silent Spring*. "It shocked Americans, placing environmental protection on the front burner in a way it never had been before, turning a concerned public into an activist one" (Flippen 25). Investigations into the disaster first and foremost demonstrated that (1) the cozy relationship between the federal government and the oil industry had led to and exacerbated the disaster[6] and (2) there existed no federal policy on preventing and containing such spills.[7] President Richard Nixon, inaugurated just eight days before the well blew, faced heightened pressure to lead proactively on the environment—which, to put it mildly, had not formed one of the central pillars of the Republican's successful campaign.[8]

To further encourage the administration, Senator Henry "Scoop" Jackson (D-WA) introduced the framework for the National Environmental Policy Act (NEPA) on February 18, 1969, less than a month after the spill (Spezio 144). It passed the Senate with a unanimous voice vote in July; then it passed the House with a vote of 372 to 15 in September. The president signed it into law on January 1, 1970, at his residence in San Clemente, California, along the Pacific coast about 160 miles from Santa Barbara itself (Spezio 152–53). Among other things, the act mandated public input and environmental review for all federally funded projects and led to the creation of the Environmental Protection Agency (EPA) later that year.

Activists built on this groundswell, further pressuring the young administration to take seriously the safeguarding of the environment. More than twenty million people in the US (or one in ten of the population) took part in the first Earth Day on April 22, 1970 (Rinde); the conservative but pragmatic Nixon made the environment a centerpiece of his first State of the Union address and in his first term signed several other landmark pieces of environmentalist legislation, including the Endangered Species Conservation Act (1969); the Clean Air Act (1970); the Water Quality Improvement Act (1970), which made oil companies fully liable for cleanup of spills; and what became known as the Clean Water Act (1972). In his second term he signed the Endangered Species Act (1973).

In the words of Russel Train, a former Republican judge who had helped create the World Wildlife Fund and who as head of the Task Force on Natural Resources and Environment had urged Nixon to lead on the issue: "Serious students of the environmental movement agree that the Santa Barbara oil spill was the single incident that crystallized the amorphous concern for the environment into an international movement" (Spezio 143). LeMenager goes further, making of the event a sort of green litmus test: "Santa Barbara offers us an ideal lab for questioning the relative conservatism—or radicalism—of the multifaceted movement that came to be known as American environmentalism" (*Living Oil* 33).

Thus, by invoking in their dinosaur-hunting scene the birds smothered to death at Santa Barbara—those who perish "*as usual*" to maintain our modern lifestyle—McGregor and Graham were tying superheroic "jungle action" to real-world headlines of the ecologically conscious early 1970s. Such politically charged imagery taunts the reader with the challenge: "Why do you put up with this?"

But it does more. In fact, as I will argue, "Panther's Rage" fulfills an ecological vision of animals, land, and resources only implied in its protagonist's origin story.

"MAN-MADE JUNGLE"

"Wakanda! It is a nation of *paradoxes*," writes McGregor. "Technology existing with primitive traditions . . . and *not always* coexisting peacefully" (Sedlmeier 97). A hidden African nation harboring the only known stores of a fantastic metal, vibranium, which fuels its astoundingly advanced society, not only nodded to the decolonization movements then ongoing in real-world Africa; it also reflected Marvel's (specifically artist/co-creator Jack Kirby's) "growing interest in the collision of ancient civilizations and futuristic technologies" (Howe 86). Such innovations also broke with sordid and longstanding representational practices directed at nonwhite races in comics. In the words of Cathy Thomas, "Wakanda's techno-organic jungle disrupts past depictions of African primitivism and Black natives who, for instance, supported Tarzan. The jungle is reclaimed as a site of Black self-reliance, self-sufficiency, and self-determination" (79).

Thomas here refers specifically to Wakanda's most outré environmental feature, the "man-made jungle," which debuted along with T'Challa/Black Panther, the first black superhero, in *Fantastic Four* vol. 1 #52 (July 1966). Writer Stan Lee and Kirby heighten the drama of the "jungle's" first appearance through suspense: As the eponymous quartet (plus Wyatt Wingfoot) speed over lushly overgrown terrain at the king's invitation, Reed Richards/Mister Fantastic proclaims, "The jungle looks so *primitive*—so undeveloped! Are you *sure* we have reached *Wakanda* territory?" The king's emissary responds, in part, "You would do well to remember . . . in this land, things are not always as they *seem!*" (Sedlmeier 12). The foliage parts, and the ship suddenly enters a bizarre techno-space that defies understanding, an instance of what Charles Hatfield calls Kirby's "technological sublime."[9] Utterly enthralled, the guests can only strive at words to describe the spectacle:

> Richards: It's truly a *jungle*—but like nothing ever spawned by nature! It's a *man-made* jungle!
> Emissary: Indeed you are *correct!* The entire topography and flora are electronically-controlled *mechanical apparatus!* The very *branches* about us are composed of delicately constructed *wires*—while the

The first appearance of the "mechanical jungle" in *Fantastic Four* vol. 1 #52 (July 1966). © Marvel Comics.

flowers which abound here are highly complex buttons and dials! Even the *boulders* can be heard to hum with the steady pulse of *computer dynamos!* (Sedlmeier 13)

Our first glimpse of the mechanical "jungle" highlights—extraordinarily so—what Adilifu Nama calls "a high-tech African Shangri-La where African tradition and advanced scientific technology are fused together to create a wonderland of futuristic weapons and flying machines" (43). But this panel also presents a readerly conundrum: None of the emissary's descriptions match what we see. No "branches," "flowers," or "boulders" appear; rather, crystalline shapes, contained explosions, and psychedelic machine-tubes, of a sort that would not feel out of place in the alien Galactus's mother ship, confront our senses.

How to account for such an oddly drastic disjunct between the dialogue and image, as if Lee and Kirby were depicting two different spaces independently of each other? Perhaps owing to the so-called Marvel Method, whereby

The evolution of the "mechanical jungle." *Fantastic Four* #311 (Feb. 1988). © Marvel Comics.

scripter and artist worked mostly separately,[10] art here conflicts mightily with text; Kirby's imagery is much weirder, even opaque, reflecting the "psychic unstitching, the mind-bending excess" of the 1960s, as Hatfield puts it (*Hand of Fire* 154). (This rendering in fact anticipates Kirby's late baroque style of *The Eternals* and *2001: A Space Odyssey* from ten years later.)

The most obvious explanation, it seems to me, stems from the fundamental paradox implied by the oxymoron "man-made jungle."[11] Its unnerving hybridity—nature as human construction—evokes a melding of objects the modern mind defines as opposites; to imagine it requires an imaginative feat akin to Romantic Negative Capability.[12] In short, Thomas's chimeric, overdetermined "techno-organic" has no predetermined visual correlate, hence Lee and Kirby's disparate results.[13] Wakanda's "man-made jungle" is a Mortonian ecological hyperobject *par excellence*.

Future Marvel creators and artists, too, often seemed uncertain of how to approach the concept. They would portray T'Challa's creation in very different and inconsistent ways, underscoring its instability, unrepresentability, and sublimity. John Buscema essentially takes a pass; his depiction of Wakanda's "man-made jungle" in *Avengers* #62 (March 1969) simply duplicates Kirby's original from *Fantastic Four* #52 (Thomas and Buscema, "The Monarch" 2). In another version, from *Fantastic Four* #311 (Feb. 1988), the concept is broadened; it presents as a typical jungle setting, from whose foliage spring up communication and surveillance devices, as well as weapons—a different sort of nature/tech blend (Englehart and Pollard 19, 22).[14] More recently, Ta-Nehisi Coates and Brian Stelfreeze, in their 2016 story arc, "A Nation Under Our Feet," portray the "man-made jungle" as T'Challa's scientific lab/botanical garden.[15]

Over decades of Black Panther continuity, Wakanda would shift identities and aspects many times. In their celebrated mid-1970s storyline, McGregor and Graham turned their vision to the land itself and away from the "man-made jungle," which served as mere metonym for a vast African nation of multiple and contradictory ideas—as multiple and contradictory as our feelings over nature itself.

"PANTHER'S RAGE": WAKANDA AS ECOSYSTEM OF MEANINGS

In the groundbreaking thirteen-issue "Panther's Rage" (*Jungle Action* #6–18, 1973–1975),[16] McGregor along with artists Rich Buckler, Graham, and others, brought a new maturity and sophistication to King T'Challa/Black Panther. In the storyline, hailed by fans and critics as a proto–graphic novel unfolding bimonthly over two years, T'Challa battles revolutionary upstart Killmonger and his cadre of mutated henchmen, at the same time dealing with doubts and divisions within his own court. Taking place entirely within the borders of the fictional kingdom, remarkable for its almost exclusively Black cast, McGregor et al.'s epic imparts on Wakanda and its people a degree of detail and topographic variety unbroached by creators Lee and Kirby, whose vision had bordered on that of the colonialist "jungle hero."[17] As comics scholar Rebecca Wanzo puts it, "Panther's Rage" proved "the first major step in decolonizing the character. The story arc introduced long-form epic storytelling to Marvel comics and is considered by many to be the story that allowed T'Challa to develop as a character and Wakanda as a place" (Wanzo, "And All Our Past Decades").

Indeed, "Panther's Rage" for the first time explored the country's quite varied geography, which manifests as Afrofuturist paradise, open savannahs, prehistoric wilderness, fetid swamp, snowy waste, futureshock battlefield, and commanding waterfall, among other settings. The storyline even includes detailed maps in its back pages, the better to keep track of such locales as "Killmonger's village (N'Zhadaha)," "Panther Island," and the "Woods of Solitude."[18]

As noted, the role of the "man-made jungle" in "Panther's Rage" is largely reduced to an "underground computerized complex" and weapons manufacturing center infiltrated by Killmonger's "death regiments." Graham's depiction skews to the minimalist and bare, with a few flourishes and shapes all that remains of Kirby's techno-sprawl (Sedlmeier 127).

Instead, "Panther's Rage" shifts much of the action to the outdoors, far from Wakanda's urban capital, to rural settings where McGregor and Graham trouble the line between African "authenticity" (through a Western gaze) and sci-fi adventure. We see a good example when T'Challa and his comrades attack Killmonger's village, whose thatched huts and crude paling fences resemble the "Tarzan"-era works Thomas decries.[19] But in combat, "*hydraulic systems* strip away the *façade* of primitivism," as the villain Lord Karnaj puts it; the thatched huts reveal a metallic structure beneath, out of which scramble troops with laser rifles (Sedlmeier 134).

The storyline makes animals and the country's natural splendors (and perils) much more the focus, particularly when T'Challa tracks Killmonger's movements through various environments for several chapters. Here Wakanda itself becomes a central, animate, agential character that the increasingly beset, exhausted, and injured T'Challa must traverse and appease. His is also an inner journey, a vision quest. As the critics Tucker Stone and David Brothers write: "The Panther moves deeper into Wakanda's hinterlands, discovering truths about his country that he either didn't believe in, or was completely unaware of in the first place." In sum, "Panther's Rage" puts Wakandan geography at center stage—doubly so; during his grueling journey back to civilization, its changing landscapes mirror the protagonist's growing desperation and will to triumph. To a degree not seen before in superhero comics, the natural setting entails the character.[20]

Of the many examples one could cite, these especially resonate with me as both supplying genre thrills *and* doing the figurative labor of landscape-as-mirror: a long footbridge extending into the fog-filled distance over a dizzying chasm, toward the Land of the Chilling Mist, as T'Challa embarks on his journey (Sedlmeier 148); a two-page spread of T'Challa warding off a pack of wolves in the snowy wastes (158–59); a pain-induced reminiscence of T'Chaka, the hero's father, on a "golden afternoo[n]" by the water (206); an idyllic interlude with his US lover Monica Lynne, in twinned silhouettes against a sunset suffused with pink, orange, and lavender before the big final battle (222); and the storyline's most iconic image, T'Challa tossed down the waterfall where he first knows defeat at the hands of Killmonger (59, 63–65) and where he must confront him again at saga's end (252–57).

Our discussion of the Wakandan landscape brings us to the Romantics, whose legacy, as historian William Cronon contends, "means that wilderness is more a state of mind than a fact of nature" and, further, that "the state of mind that today most defines wilderness is *wonder*" ("The Trouble with Wilderness" 88). Such wonder, according to W. K. Wimsatt, stems from a metaphysics "of an animate, plastic Nature, not transcending but immanent in and breathing through all things," adding, "to discount for the moment such differences as may relate to Wordsworth's naturalism, Coleridge's theology, Shelley's Platonism, or Blake's visions: we may observe that the common feat of the romantic nature poets was *to read meanings into the landscape*" (83, my emphasis). Nature in this understanding is both a subjective "state of mind" that reads meanings into things as well as an independent force that moves the beholder-poet; as Geoffrey H. Hartman describes it: "Not an 'object' but a presence and a power; a motion and spirit; not something to be worshiped and consumed, but always a guide leading beyond itself" (290).

Let us not forget, though, that contemporary understandings of landscape (both our personal witnessing of it and as genre painting) owe much not only to the Romantic poets but to the history of Western imperialism. W. J. T. Mitchell, in fact, calls landscape "something like the dreamwork of imperialism," disclosing both "utopian fantasies of the perfected imperial prospect and fractured images of unresolved ambivalence and unsuppressed resistance" ("Imperial Landscape" 10).[21] He also acknowledges that "landscape is a medium not only for expressing value but also for expressing meaning . . . most radically for communication between the Human and the non-Human" (15)—in the sense that it constantly mediates between the cultural and the natural.[22]

For Laguna Pueblo author Leslie Marmon Silko, the act of designating a landscape itself betrays modernity's imagined severance from nature:[23]

> The term landscape, as it has entered the English language, is misleading. "A portion of territory the eye can comprehend in a single view" does not correctly describe the relationship between the human being and his or her surroundings. This assumes the viewer is somehow outside or separate from the territory he or she surveys. Viewers are as much a part of the landscape as the boulders they stand on. There is no high mesa edge or mountain peak where one can stand and not immediately be a part of all that surrounds. (32)

In chapters 12 through 15 of "Panther's Rage," when T'Challa pursues his nemesis across numerous distinct and remote regions of Wakanda, McGregor and Graham depict their hero less as Mitchell's imperialist master of all he surveys and more in Silko's terms—as part of the natural environment with which he nonetheless must contend on equal footing. Gracefully stalking in jungles, trundling through barren snowscapes, scaling mountains, the Panther (whose

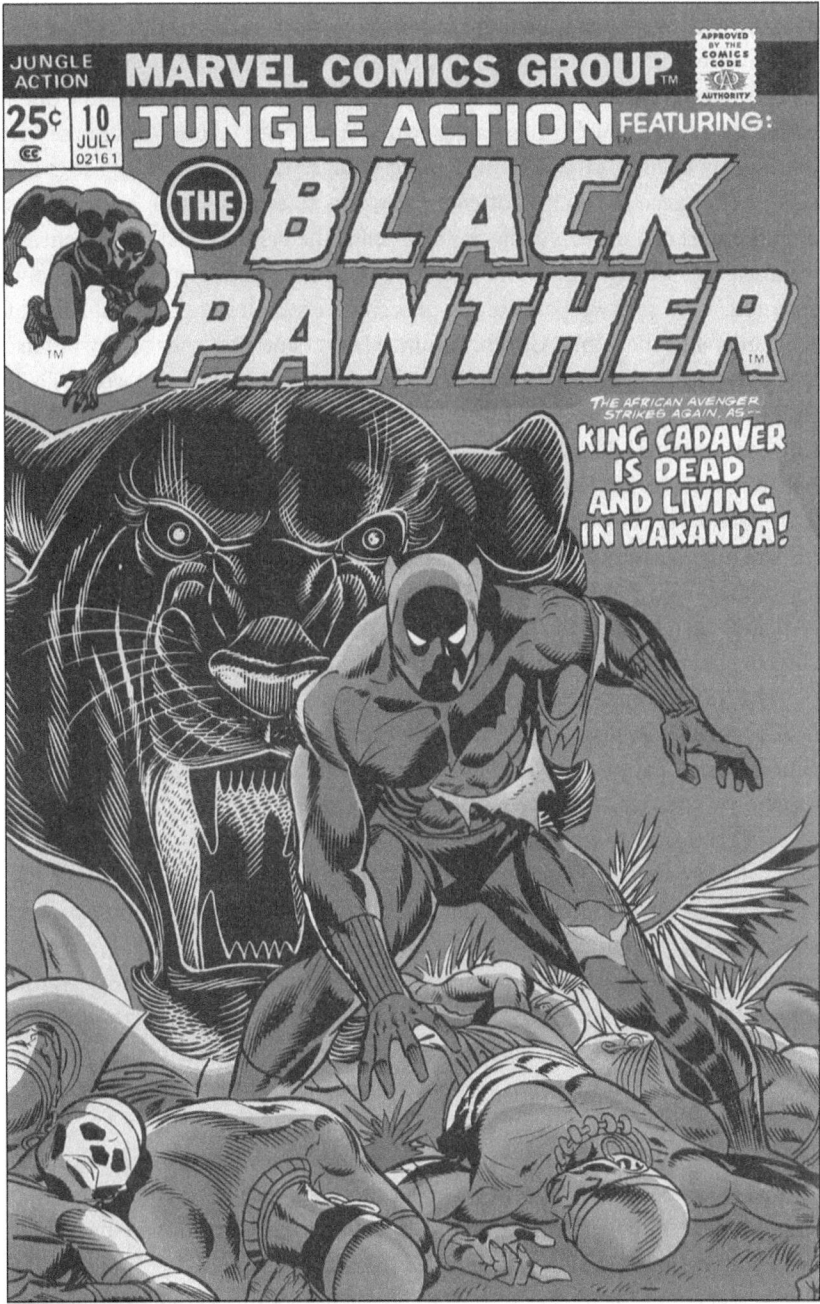

Throughout "Panther's Rage," T'Challa's costume is ripped to shreds. *Jungle Action* #10 (July 1974). © Marvel Comics.

superhero identity already blurs the human/animal boundary) "fits in" with these rustic settings in ways a more "futuristic" hero such as Iron Man would not.

The authors enhance this "naturalistic" effect in two ways: through the often extreme violence of T'Challa's battles with animals (see below), and the severe traces this violence leaves. For in "Panther's Rage," the hero's costume does not stay in one piece for long; it often deteriorates to tatters within a few panels after the start of a melee. As the costume tears, the Panther's dark skin beneath routinely suffers deep gashes and blunt force trauma, muscles rippling and blood smeared.[24] We see two particularly gruesome examples at the conclusion of the battle with the White Gorilla (Sedlmeier 177) and the "collage of wounds" that overwhelm the hero during his encounter with the thorn-covered villain Salamander K'ruel (204).[25] Stone and Brothers call such episodes "education through suffering." T'Challa in fact appears with costume ripped on more than half the covers of the "Panther's Rage" storyline, namely *Jungle Action* #6, #9, #10, #12–14, and #15. Through such visual-verbal devices, T'Challa "blends in" with his irregular surroundings rather than standing apart from them, as when he tracks the villain Sombre through the dense jungle of Serpent Valley (Sedlmeier 180) and when he surfs the back of a flying pterodactyl, his remaining scraps of costume flapping in the wind, mirroring the dinosaur's wings (215).

As Eliot Borenstein puts it, "No doubt we need to pay attention to McGregor's style, but we should not let his logorrhea distract us from the actual scenes that provoke him to such prolixity, and from what those scenes are about. Yes, McGregor loves words, but those words are often in the service of a preoccupation with bodies. In particular, with bodies in pain" (169).

Nothing conveys the savagery of McGregor and Graham's vision of life and death in the wild like Black Panther's gory, flesh-ripping, blood-spewing struggles against animals—an incomplete list of which includes dinosaurs, wolves, a crocodile, Venomm's snakes, and Killmonger's jaguar Preyy. While long a staple of the "jungle action" genre, Stone and Brothers argue these forays into graphic ultraviolence allowed the authors to dodge the Comics Code's strictures against "lyrical journeys into flayed skin," which would otherwise have applied were the combatants exclusively human.[26]

Whatever their motivation, these episodes—especially those resulting in animal death—function as tests for T'Challa's resilience in his mission, as well as reminders of the victims felled by Killmonger's revolution (whether a bird drowned in oil or a gorilla-god impaled in battle). Yet these descriptions only begin to account for the many variegated meanings and associations nonhuman animals bear or invoke in this narrative. Let us examine three instances of animal encounter—two of them violent—in "Panther's Rage."

On the opening page of chapter four, "But Now the Spears Are Broken" (*Jungle Action* #9, May 1974), the young boy Kantu is charged by a raging black rhinoceros

Visual/verbal tension in "Panther's Rage." *Jungle Action* #9 (May 1974). © Marvel Comics.

(Sedlmeier 97). The Panther immediately leaps into action, straddling the three-thousand-pound beast, whose unexplained aggression[27] leads T'Challa to drastic measures. Over five panels, the lithe hero swings from a branch, once more grabs hold of the rushing animal (which had shaken him off before), and exerts his superhuman strength on its neck. Artist Gil Kane draws the Panther and rhino exceeding the bounds of the panel borders in the largest, central frame, as they seem to erupt out of the page toward the reader. Color plays an important role as well: Mostly yellow backgrounds heighten the excitement, the in-the-moment stakes, while the Panther's black/blue costume offsets the veritable wall of gray of the rhino's body. The hero's efforts succeed, killing the pachyderm, and in the final panel a drained T'Challa leans languidly on the animal's corpse.

So, we see, at any rate—but a reading of McGregor's characteristically overdetermined text boxes shifts our perception of the event. They proclaim, in part:

> Fingers taut, he takes *hold*. This grip must not weaken else he will fall *beneath* these pounding hooves— / —left *maimed* and *bloody* under their tread. And how, he wonders, would that affect his *kingdom*, held in turmoil as it is by the chaos of Killmonger's *brutal insurrection*. / Erik Killmonger. Mustn't forget the Erik! / Yet, Killmonger does fade from mind, replaced by the task at hand . . . an *insane* task . . .
>
> —inspired by *American* "B" Western *mythos* of Hopalong Cassidy vintage and others, seen on idle Saturday afternoons at *Avengers' Mansion*. / The Panther bulldogs this 1 ½-ton monstrosity— / carving it into the mire . . . and *snapping* its vertebrae! (Sedlmeier 99)[28]

McGregor's free indirect speech, no less than his stream of consciousness, alters the significance of the titanic tussle between hero and beast. T'Challa's anxieties over the ongoing insurgency in his kingdom; his reluctance to demonize his enemy; even memories of his time in the United States, where he watched Western hero Hopalong Cassidy,[29] all figure into this critical do-or-die moment. The scene demonstrates the crucial role played by text-image interaction in comics, how the medium's multimodal "double track" can enliven and deepen even the most formulaic fare. But it also shows how the rhino acts as more than mere unthinking antagonist; rather, the animal body—despite or even because of its eminent threat—sparks thoughts and associations in T'Challa that would not have occurred otherwise. The charging rhino in its final moments thus facilitates both superficial genre thrills and a real-time trace of T'Challa's mind in motion.[30]

An even grander scope of animal signification asserts itself in chapter 8, "The God Killer" (*Jungle Action* #13, Jan. 1975), as T'Challa navigates the snowbound Land of the Chilling Mist on the trail of the villain Sombre. In these wastes, the scientifically minded king confronts nothing less than the source of one of Wakanda's religions.[31] McGregor and Graham construct the setting so as to highlight its metaphysical dimensions: The Panther stalks his prey across the white wastes beneath a multicolored, aurora borealis–like effect in the sky. The text box reads, "It is a night when a man can *reach* and believe he can *touch* the stars— / —that he is *part* of the cosmological scheme of things! / A night when a man could believe he is an *integral part* of the universe. / Not omnipotent. Not *superior*. / Just *unique* and unto himself" (Sedlmeier 170).

The description, recalling Silko's lack of division between subject and landscape, blurs the human/nonhuman realms and prepares the ground for the "*staggering*" (Sedlmeier 170) sight that comes next. T'Challa climbs a precipice, to an overlook. From there, the astounded Panther glimpses a plain strewn with bones, in which a troop of mammoth, agitated White Gorillas howl at Sombre's promise of a ritualistic sacrifice (171). Snaggle-toothed, red-eyed, long-clawed, standing at least twelve feet tall, they only somewhat resemble their ordinary namesakes and inspire fearful worship: "They are overpowering. *Ancient specimens* to some forgotten era when early Wakandan legends were at their *birth*" (172).

The White Gorillas are *sublime*; they dissolve borders between self and other no less than does the "magical" northern landscape. As one engages T'Challa in battle, with its towering bulk of furred muscle and fearsome fangs, the terrifying monster seems to exact worship. McGregor's very descriptors are biblical: "He is *staggered* by its *immensity!* This is no god of love or charity. This is a *vengeful god*, rising full and malevolent—*demanding its tribute!*" (Sedlmeier 172).

Which only makes the outcome of their clash seem all the more tragic—albeit, by the logic of the superhero "jungle action" narrative, inevitable. Yet something more than the fulfillment of generic expectations is going on in the White Gorilla's downfall; T'Challa here kills more than an animal, and something other than a god. The scene literalizes a process akin to that which cultural historian Steve Baker sees as vital to "free" the animal from human preconceptions of it as "pure" emblem of the real:

> The visual stereotyping of the animal necessarily focuses on its body, and my concerns over notions of "how animals should be seen" are that they seek to fix the image of that body in an image of nature, taking both to be an unproblematic reflection of reality. It is therefore the image of the animal body, I suggest, which needs *to be taken out of nature and rendered unstable as a sign*.
>
> Only when the animal body is taken "out" of this myth of nature does it become clearer what culture has invested in the animal. Once the body

is regarded as abstract, conceptual, arbitrary, unstable, and not as the site of a fixed "real," it is more easily recognized as a prime symbolic site: the very site of identity. (*Picturing* 223, my emphasis)

We may liken what Baker describes as the animal's imprisonment in the "natural" (that which for many "transcends" signification) to the White Gorilla's casting in the role of god. Once T'Challa—after much physical struggle and bodily injury—manages to grievously wound the giant, he declares, "My *legends* have been given the vulnerability of flesh, Sombre—and have *lost* their grandiose mythology!" (Sedlmeier 176). Ultimately, the Panther coaxes his foe over the precipice, where it plummets to a grisly death, gored through the chest by a sharp animal bone. (The beast-god's body is literally decentered; upside-down, skewered through the heart, its feet protrude from the middle frame into the top tier, as if "fallen" from there.) In the final panel, T'Challa lies battered and spent on the icy ground. McGregor's pronouncement on this resolution captures the immensity of the act: "The death of this god is stark and barren—and as *ugly* as most violent, senseless death. The Panther is consumed by a sense of his own *mortality*. / He has killed a *myth* . . . and his life is *lessened* by the act. He has *lost* part of his past without anything to replace it in the future" (177).

The Wakandan scientist-king's face-off with the mythic white deity ends as most such "jungle action" set pieces do, with the beast's violent demise. But the episode—vouchsafed, again, with T'Challa's blood—also allegorizes the modern disenchantment of the animal, its diminution since the Enlightenment to mere sentiment or meat.[32] It is a dethronement, a desublimation comparable to deicide. Or more precisely, semiocide.[33]

The final animal encounter in "Panther's Rage" I will examine would seem to reinstate nonhuman life to the realm, if not of divinity, then certainly to that of "unknowable" Otherness—an emblem of the Real (and thus a different aspect of the sublime). In the tenth chapter, "Thorns in the Flesh, Thorns in the Mind" (*Jungle Action* #15, May 1975), a profusely bleeding T'Challa finds himself strapped to a pair of trees in the swampy Serpent Valley, prisoner of K'ruel. His gruesome injuries, which include thorn punctures all over his body, induce a degree of pain that "makes *articulate* speech impossible" (Sedlmeier 203). In this tormented daze, he sinks into a warm memory of whiling away a golden afternoon with his father (which I alluded to earlier).[34]

But T'Challa's reverie is soon "obliterate[d]"—a newt is scrambling down his body, lapping at his blood. A page of five red-bordered, descending horizontal panels against a hyper-frame of the Panther's gloved hand (riddled with thorns) show the green and yellow scaled creature clinging to a finger, then progressing down his forearm, bicep, shoulder, and face. "Blood and saliva, both life essences, drip from its ridged mouth," the caption notes (in an echo of the

The death of the godlike White Gorilla. *Jungle Action* #13 (Jan. 1975). © Marvel Comics.

Tyrannosaurus rex the hero defeated earlier), while its large yellow eye stares off-panel against the hyper-frame's solid black background (Sedlmeier 207).

This seems, to say the least, an odd development in the middle of "Panther's Rage," a fast-paced epic of grand emotions and life-or-death thrills and chills. The stakes—as well as T'Challa's fearful reaction—seem all out of proportion;

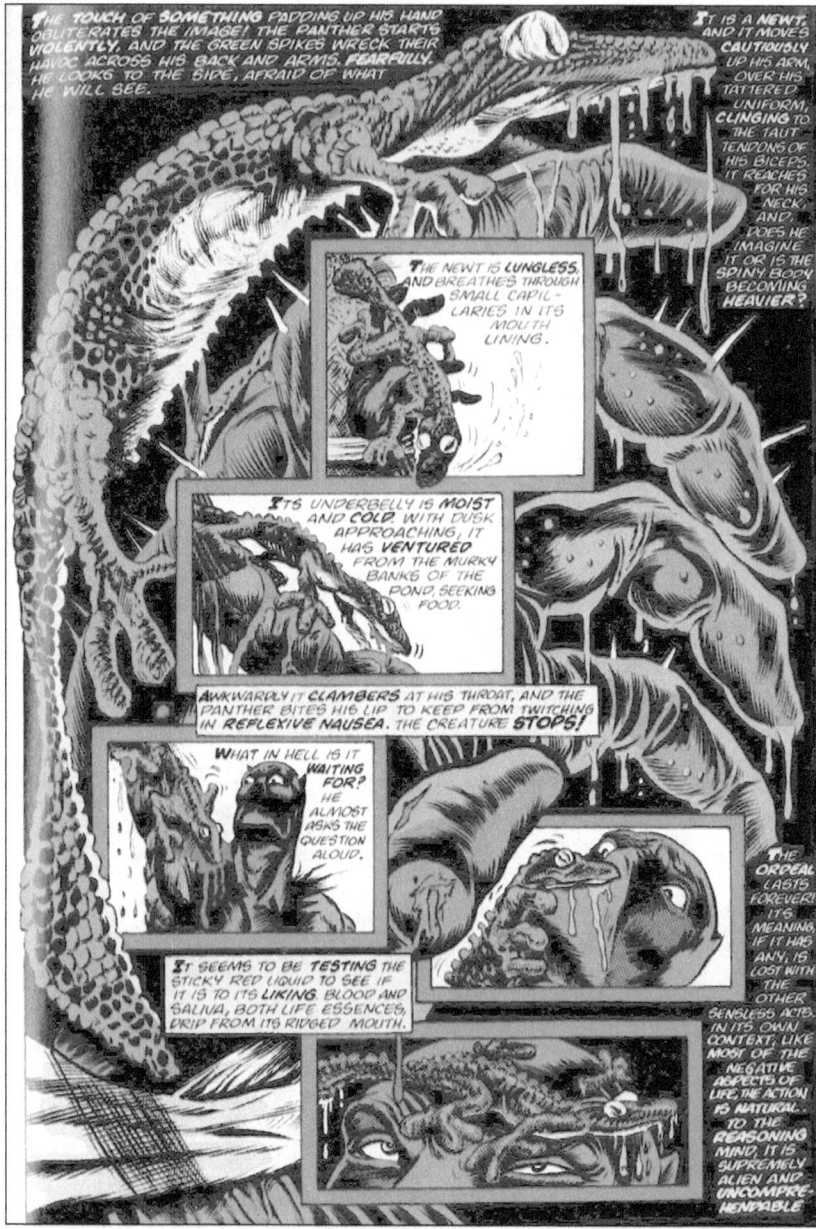

The "newt." *Jungle Action* #15 (May 1975). © Marvel Comics.

is Wakanda's throne now threatened by a tiny pond dweller? McGregor's text, meanwhile, comes off as both evasive and weirdly nature-documentary pedantic: "The newt is *lungless*, and breathes through small capillaries in its lung lining"; "It seems to be *testing* the sticky red liquid to see if it is to its *liking*"

(Sedlmeier 207). The scene fashions a mood of suspended "otherworldliness," an effect heightened by the strangeness of the situation; the hero's repulsion and befuddlement ("What in hell is it *waiting for?* He almost asks the question aloud"); and the episode's interstitial position between much grander events of the narrative.[35] As the drooling petty demon stares directly into the cross-eyed T'Challa's face, then crawls on his forehead, the final caption reads: "The *ordeal lasts forever! Its meaning, if it has any, is lost with the other senseless acts. In its own context, like most of the negative aspects of life, the action is natural. To the reasoning mind, it is supremely alien and uncomprehendable*" (Sedlmeier 207).

This text appears as yellow set off against black, accentuating the ordeal's "alienness," which McGregor relates both to the natural and to the "negative aspects of life." Negative in that nature stands in binary opposition to the "reasoning" human mind—dubious as that sounds. In short, we are presented here with nature as absolute Other. As with the "unaccountable" rhino charge before, the animal acts as an animal, motivated by its own inscrutable impulses, free of man's interference. The newt thus appears in its "wholeness"—simply as newt. Such an image brings up an important consideration put forth by naturalist and author Aldo Leopold: "We can be ethical only in relation to something we can see, feel, understand, love or otherwise have faith in" (*A Sand County Almanac* 214). The newt, due to T'Challa's extreme and helpless circumstances, has made it onto his radar for a true contemplation, as an equal. (And an amphibian, with its particular sensitivity to environmental changes, would seem a good representative for or extension of nature itself.)

But another problem rears up: The newt as Other renders it conceptually inert. As ecocritic Mimei Ito warns: "Essentialization of 'otherness' in images leads to a mode of animal representation in which otherness in the animal identity tends to be essentialized, just as the word *animal* essentializes the idea of animals in general" (127). To avoid such visual essentialism of the animal other, "which is the very presupposition that ecology wants to problematize" (132), Ito argues we should "abandon the very idea of otherness itself in order not to essentialize the visual and the natural" (133).

I argue that the multimodal representational strategies of comics offer significant advantages for accomplishing precisely that (resistance to essentialism), with the newt in "Panther's Rage" a particularly good example. For one thing, in Graham's rendering, the critter weirdly resembles something more like a baby alligator; the visual-verbal discrepancy subverts the straightforward meaning of the signifier "newt." Secondly, the text presupposes, infers but does not access the newt's inner world—"*it is supremely alien and uncomprehendable.*" We see only its actions, not its subjective life. (Thought balloons would have made for a very different story!) At the same time, a reader takes McGregor's quasi-scientific assertions and philosophical musings into account in consuming the art, making once more for a doubly valent, unfinalizable aesthetic experience. As discussed at length in part I, comics art often operates this way, destabilizing clear-cut meanings (even of "otherness") through text-image tension.

Thus, more often than not, from gorilla gods to rhinos to newts, animals in "Panther's Rage" occur, in the words of political theorist Jane Bennett, not as objects but as "vivid entities not entirely reducible to the contexts in which (human) subjects set them, never entirely exhausted by their semiotics" (5).

CONCLUSION: WAKANDA SPEAKS

In their influential and innovative storyline, McGregor et al. portray Wakanda's wilderness as both threatening and threatened. Dead animals appear over and over: a strangled rhino, an impaled gorilla, a decapitated Tyrannosaurus rex, a humble bird trapped in an oil slick. Such imagery, as I have argued, tapped into a dawning collective angst over the death of nature in the decade before the term Anthropocene first started emerging in US public discourses as a means to frame the enormity of the problem. Such comics works of the 1970s Marvel/DC Bronze Age typified an era in which the superhero genre sought a new political relevance, often exploring progressive themes such as the ecological crisis.[36] Events like the 1969 Santa Barbara oil spill *spoke*—they showed that in the postindustrial age a reckoning with environmental apocalypse was coming due. Time was short to stop what Ta-Nehisi Coates calls the "Dream" of whiteness from "plunder[ing] not just the bodies of humans but the body of the Earth itself" (*Between the World and Me* 150), from putting a "noose around the neck of the earth" (151).

There is a moment in "Panther's Rage" when Wakanda itself speaks, in human language. Just before the oil pollution scene whose discussion began this chapter, T'Challa meets, interacts with, and misapprehends the mysterious jungle inhabitant Mokadi. Bald, short of stature, with a perpetual grin on his face, Mokadi risks associations with minstrelsy figures such as Stepin Fetchit (a.k.a. Lincoln Theodore Monroe Andrew Perry). But his dialogue reveals a cutting intelligence and wisdom of a different order:

> **Black Panther:** Are you even aware there is a land *beyond* the mist that *hovers* over this valley?
> **Mokadi:** And if I *was*, what would I see?
> **BP:** A *beautiful* land. / *Sunsets* and *dawns*. Exquisite gardens and superbly crafted palaces and homes and *shrines*.
> **M:** And what do they *stand* for? *More* than these trees? *More* than this river ... which once ran free and clear and now chokes on the *miseries* you and this Killmonger have brought *with* you. (Sedlmeier 186)

This scene, as much of an odd narratival digression as the newt episode, provides a crucial perspective to T'Challa's journey. What exactly is he fighting for? What ultimate values does he uphold? Is human scale too shallow a container for the things that truly matter? Mokadi supplies answers to none of these questions; as unexpectedly as he appears out of the Serpent Valley's jungle mist, he soon vanishes again. The Panther is left to wonder (on the same page that shows the oil-slicked bird's demise): "Was he ever really there?" The text then reads: "He has heard the word mokadi before. To the *Bomitaba tribe* in the *Likuala region* of Africa the term means . . . / spirit. / . . ."[37] Who were you, Mokadi? A thought mirror or sage pygmi?" (Sedlmeier 197, some ellipses mine).

In short, Mokadi is the "spirit" of Serpent Valley, a personification of the wild; like the newt (only much more human-looking), he acts as an emanation of the natural world itself. And like the newt, he is there to show T'Challa his place.[38]

The role of Mokadi in of all places a bloody superhero adventure serial resonates with recent interdisciplinary research into so-called animacy and/or vibrant matter theory, from scholars working in posthuman anthropology (Eduardo Kohn, Helen Kopnina), political theory (Jane Bennett), queer theory, critical animal studies (Mel Chen), and ecocriticism. This approach to life/nonlife relations sees all matter as "storied," or as Serpil Oppermann and Serenella Iovino put it, "a material mesh of meanings, properties, and processes, in which human and nonhuman players are interlocked in networks that produce undeniable signifying forces" (quoted in Cohen 25). Jeffrey Jerome Cohen elaborates: "Forming a biosemiotic web through which forests become sites of shared cognition, plants and animals possess an animacy that can alter human perspectives and disrupt the equation of being with being human" (28).

In her book *Vibrant Matter: A Political Ecology of Things*, Bennett emphasizes the "negative power or recalcitrance of things" (1), both living (trees, animals) and not (stones, bottle caps).[39] To orient attention to the nontheistic "agentic capacity" (9) of things, she claims, means "*to experience* the relationship between persons and other materialities more horizontally," so as to—echoing Timothy Morton—"take a step toward a more ecological sensibility" (10).[40]

As seen from such samplings, much of this work centers on an ethics of care for human and nonhuman life, itself stemming from a postindustrial vision of profound interdependence:

> The world is also "enchanted." Thanks to this living semiotic dynamic, *mean*-ing (i.e., means-ends relations, significance, "aboutness," telos) is a constitutive feature of the world and not just something we humans impose on it. Appreciating life and thought in this manner changes our understanding of what selves are and how they emerge, dissolve, and also merge into new kinds of *we* as they interact with the other beings

that make the tropical forest their home in that complex web of relations that I call an "ecology of selves." (Kohn 16)

To sum up, animacy conceptualizes the ways matter *affects* across the life/nonlife divide, troubling it. In her study of the discourses surrounding the April 2010 Deepwater Horizon oil spill in the Gulf of Mexico (at 210,000,000 gallons [4.9 million barrels], a slick several orders of magnitude larger than its 1969 predecessor), Mel Chen notes:

At bottom, the overbearing use of *dead* and *killed* functioned as an admission that a toxic spill was a *lifely* thing: lifely, perhaps, beyond its proper bounds. The well itself was alive, and not only because something had flowed out of it with such vivid animation. It was a threat to life in the Gulf, as well as to a *way* of life. This occlusion of life over marginal life speaks, as I see it, to the inadequacy of lifely notions as a framework for governance, medicine, and vernacular affect and makes room for a concept like animacy, which encodes forces without being beholden to the failing categories of life and nonlife. (227)

This is what I mean when I say the Santa Barbara disaster *spoke*, and popular fictions like "Panther's Rage" picked up its call. The violence, devastation, and death toll of the Anthropocene quite literally *speaks volumes*, prompts a response. For as Bennett cautions, "in a knotted world of vibrant matter, to harm one section of the web may very well be to harm oneself" (13). All the same, as Cohen mentions in this chapter's epigraph, mass death holds sway in our era, on a planetary scale, to an almost banal degree. It can serve as only partial consolation, the fact that the natural world is, after all, red in tooth and claw—a fact McGregor and Graham have plenty of generic license to wallow in—which dry-eyed environmentalists such as Paul Shepard have long insisted we remember:

The traditional insistence upon the overwhelmingly tragic and unequivocal nature of death ignores the adaptive role of early death in most animal populations. It presumes that the landscape is a collection of *things*. In this view the dissolution of body and personality are always tragic and disruptive, and do not contribute to the perfection of an intelligible world. But death, as transformation in a larger system, is an essential aspect of elegant patterns which are orderly as well as beautiful: without death growth could not occur, energy could not flow beyond plants, nutrient substances would be trapped forever. Without death the pond, the forest, the prairie, the city could not exist. The extremely complicated structure of living communities has yet to be fully explored, but constitutes a field pattern. Plants and animals participate in them without question in an attitude of acceptance which in human terms would be called faith. (207)[41]

Cold comfort when gazing on a grebe drowned in oil, and in any case an age of mass extinctions goes beyond a "field pattern" in any normal sense.

In what remains of this chapter, I want to discuss how animacy functions—what ethics of interdependency it fosters—in Black Panther continuity. Let us begin with the derivation of the word "Wakanda." According to an 1894 Bureau of American Ethnology report, among the US Plains Indian peoples it was a word for Great Spirit: "The ancestors of the Omaha and Ponka believed that there was a Supreme Being, whom they called Wakanda. They did not know where He was, nor did they undertake to say how He existed . . . Wakanda means 'the mysterious'" (quoted in Manseau).

Whether conceived as such or not,[42] then, the very name Wakanda betokens a far-reaching, agential actor, with or without an anthropomorphic "spokesperson" such as Mokadi. Wakanda hides from the world; Wakanda cultivates the Panther and White Gorilla cults; Wakanda, uniquely on Earth, grows the heart-shaped herb that gives its kings and queens their supernatural powers.[43] Wakanda speaks.

No more forcefully than through vibranium—the ultimate "vibrant matter." Vibranium: which moves nations, drives economies, masses armies and hi-tech holograms in its defense, lures neo-colonialists like Ulysses Klaw to kill T'Chaka, setting in motion the entire arc of the series protagonist himself. For critic Teju Cole, the substance overflows the banks of its own diegesis: "What is 'vibranium'? Too simple to think of it as a metal, and tie it to resource curses. Could it be something less palpable, could it be a stand-in for blackness itself, blackness as an embodied riposte to anti-blackness, a quintessence of mystery, resilience, self-containedness, and irreducibility?" Picking up that thread, Reynaldo Anderson reminds how sooner or later the ethical mission of Afrofuturism redounds to the human: "Black speculative work is serious, necessary work. It provides a compass so we—black people—can forecast and do what is needed to take care of ourselves, our communities, and our environments" (Barber 140).

In chapter 3 of Coates and Stelfreeze's "A Nation Under Our Feet," the Griot informs Shuri in the Djalia (the plane of ancient memory) that "Wakanda was great before it had things, and its secrets are older than any vaunted metal." Its greatness, as in Silko's vision of the Hopi landscape, owes to its conversation in all senses: of story, of place, of life: "Nothing is overlooked or taken for granted. Each ant, each lizard, each lark is imbued with great value simply because the creature is there, simply because the creature is alive in a place where any life at all is precious" (42).

Precious indeed, that which could survive—come to terms with—the Land of Chilling Mist, the dank depths of Serpent Valley, the vertiginous heights of Warrior Falls.

In "Panther's Rage," Wakanda the land, no less than the nation, found its voice.

7

"DEATH DRIVE" TO LOS ALAMOS
PUMA BLUES AS ECO-MALE-ANCHOLIA[1]

It is the privilege of man to revolt against nature and make himself sick (N. O. Brown 84).

Gavia Immer sits in his government-issued cabin in year-2000 Massachusetts, as military planes drop tons of lime in the Quabbin Reservoir "to compensate for the effects of acid rain" (Murphy and Zulli[2] 27). He starts to watch a trove of experimental videotapes produced by his late father, setting in motion the primary narrative trajectory in writer Stephen Murphy and artist Michael Zulli's *The Puma Blues* (1986–1989/2015), an independent comics series presenting a starkly pessimistic sci-fi vision of ecological catastrophe in a near-future USA, where mutated manta rays sweep through the skies, the Four Horsemen of the Apocalypse roam the Southwest desert sands, and nuclear catastrophe looms.[3]

Part environmentalist fable, part dystopian nightmare, the series like no other resonated with the zeitgeist of the era that gave us the Chernobyl accident, the Bhopal disaster, and the Exxon Valdez oil spill.[4] "It was a child of its age," writes Stephen Bissette, "a tapestry composed of ecological activist ire, various New Age belief systems, wholly invented species (key among these the flying manta rays, which became emblematic of the series) and visitations from mythic beings and archetypes" (529), while Alex Dueben calls *Puma Blues* a "missing link—a pop culture precursor to DC's Vertigo Line, *The X-Files, Twin Peaks* and a thousand other creative works" ("The Michael Zulli Interview").[5] Largely ignored in its time, Murphy and Zulli's cult series anticipated the anxieties over climate change and the eradication of the natural world in ways akin to what Aaron Cloyd, writing about a much-better-known 1980s comics classic, describes when he notes, "While definitions of wilderness in the late 20th century advocated for a separation between humanity and these places, *Watchmen* complicates this structure, questioning if humanity can continue on without accessing that which has been relegated to the margins" (241).

Focused, especially in its first third, on Immer's fraught relationship with his dead father, the five-hundred-page opus (in 2015 expanded, completed, and reissued through Dover Press) lends itself particularly well to an Oedipal reading. I will, however, go further, to argue that *The Puma Blues* functions no less as an overdetermined visual-verbal expression of post-Freudian environmental melancholia and white male angst at the turn-of-the-twenty-first-century Anthropocene. In this chapter I examine, among other portions of the series, the "dream" chapter "Amidst Wings" and the (original, interrupted) concluding story arc "Under a Deep Blue Sun," in which Immer visits Southwestern US nuclear test sites, for a consideration of the ways graphic narrative uniquely represents the psycho-drama of life at the end of nature.

"THE HIROSHIMA OF MY ILLS"

Gavia Immer is a mess, watching videos and listening to Iggy Pop (*TPB* 150–51)[6] while the world burns. Like his absurdly overdetermined name (Latin for "common loon"),[7] he comes off as more than a bit pathetic, moping about at the story's beginning in a trench coat through a winter urban setting. Handsome, gaunt, unshaven, with a limp mop of hair, as rendered by Zulli he resembles a gritty New Waver. A text box in his voice notifies the reader: "February 23, 1997 marked the first year anniversary of my father's death and I didn't know how the fuck to deal with it, nor even if I could. I barely knew my dad. I wanted very much to know my dad" (2).

This morose, Gen X Hamlet seems harmless enough until a sudden eruption of violence: He assaults an elderly homeless man on the streets, ripping off a chunk of his ear with pliers (3–4).[8] As it happens, the self-aware Immer has his own ready-made explanation for the brutal acting-out: A therapist ("actually my mom's therapist") "informed me that my world (that is, the reality I chose to accept) was an 'unpainted canvas,' that it was 'flat, featureless, devoid of highs or lows, emotions or meanings,' that my projected image was a 'slick, dull, façade,' like I was a frictionless dude"—because the young man, whom the therapist labels an "emotive thug," "wasn't allowing [himself] the opportunity to react to anything" (2). He goes on, "the old guy became the focal point of my repressed emotions, my anxious channeled release—the Hiroshima of my ills" (3).

The quasi-psychoanalytic language culminates a few pages later, when Immer describes "the events of February 23, 1997," as an instance of "displacement," which he partly defines as "the shifting of an emotional affect from an appropriate to an inappropriate object" (9). This rather loosely translates Freud's term *Verschiebung* ("displacement"), the detachment of cathectic energy "from one idea to another"; as LaPlanche and Pontalis describe it, displacement is "particularly noticeable in the analysis of dreams," and "also to be observed in the formation of psychoneurotic symptoms and, in a general way, in every unconscious formation" (121).[9]

In any case, the story then literally "displaces" the action by fast-forwarding—through the "match-cut" recitation of the song[10] Immer forces the old man to sing—to the year 2000, after our angry young hero has wandered and flailed for some time, "[ridden] shotgun for MX missiles for two years" (*TPB* 21), and landed as a government agent at the Quabbin, tasked with directing his rifle-like "Mitsubishi-Ruger displacer" at "animute or biomute" (the mutant flying mantas) so as to teleport them to an unknown location (8). Or, as he himself muses, he may simply be vaporizing them.

Then, at the urging of his mother, and with time to burn due to the aerial lime dispersal, Immer starts watching his father Ganz's tapes, as "an initial attempt at confronting the loss I'd been running from for several years" (*TPB* 27). What explodes on his screen is a fractured cascade of images and jump cuts, news excerpts and found footage (alien abduction, religious iconography, nature documentary, Chernobyl), mass culture détournement, and home-made performance complete with demon and Hitler masks. Ganz introduces the work himself, staring directly at the camera, imploring the viewer to enact a culture-wide *Vergangenheitsbewältigung*,[11] or "coming to terms with the past" (28) to avoid the fast-approaching destruction of the world.

The world of *Puma Blues*, it should be noted, has good reason to feel on edge: In 1996, white nationalist terrorists assassinated then-president Jack Kemp[12] and set off a nuclear bomb that destroyed Brooklyn (*TPB* 39–41). Hence the rage- and anxiety-fueled imagery of atomic explosions in Ganz's tapes (239 and passim). In Freudian terms, the videos are a condensation of 1980s eco-apocalypticism, which exaggerates and distorts but does not lie. What needed coming to terms with was the present.

In fact, in the last decades of the Cold War, atomic anxiety formed the background rumble to the national psyche; even thanatologists noted the phenomenon. Robert Kastenbaum and Ruth Aisenberg, in their 1976 textbook *The Psychology of Death*, titled a subsection "Why Is There Now a Surge of Interest in Death?" The authors lead off their answer with "Because *we face the prospect of mass death*" (193). As Kenneth Keniston put it:

> The Bomb and what it symbolizes has set the tone for this generation, even for the majority who made a semideliberate point of trying not

to think about it. There are relatively few young Americans who, upon hearing a distant explosion, seeing a bright flash of light, or hearing a faraway sound of jets overhead at night, have not wondered for a brief instant whether this might not be "It." (quoted in Shneidman 180)

Edwin Shneidman, in a chapter titled "Megadeath: Children of the Nuclear Family," went so far as to wonder whether "many of the current generation might not fall under the category of psychological *Hibakusha* ('explosion-affected persons')" (183), a term applied to survivors of the Hiroshima and Nagasaki atomic bombings.[13] One scene serves as emblematic of the era: Immer, wearing a Cerebus[14] T-shirt, rewinding the tape ("click") over and over to the moment when the Brooklyn bomb goes off, watching the mushroom cloud on an endless loop, a "repetition compulsion" accentuated by his father's commentary, "the Final Hour . . . / the Final Hour . . . / the Final Hour . . ." Text boxes in Immer's voice read, over seven panels and two pages, "Somewhat vacuously . . . / I sit pondering the implications of desensitization . . . / my mind collapsing upon itself . . . / again . . . / and again . . . / and again . . . / until I feel composed entirely of cloud" (*TPB* 62–63).

The imbrication of posthumous paternal "bonding" with nuclear-age dread lends fresh meaning to Immer's declaration that "the old guy became the focal point of my repressed emotions, my anxious channeled release—the Hiroshima of my ills"; he is in fact "displacing" his father onto the homeless man.[15]

Gavia Immer, the common loon, sits in his makeshift bunker, drinking beer, watching cryptic experimental videos left behind by his dead father, trying to mourn him, and slowly losing his mind. The situation sets the tone for *The Puma Blues* as a whole (Immer is a man beset by depression and ecological angst, searching throughout the series for something he either can't identify or can never find) and recalls Freud's assertion in "Mourning and Melancholia" that for the melancholic, object loss entails ego loss; the withdrawn object is cathected and narcissistically identified with rather than abandoned. In Freud's much-quoted formulation, "the shadow of the object fell upon the ego" (249).[16] Judith Butler further develops the notion that grief undoes the self when she writes, "On one level, I think I have lost 'you' only to discover that 'I' have gone missing as well" (*Precarious Life* 22).

Grief is never easy, of course, but Immer's task is made all the more arduous by the anarchic video antics of his father, who, like the ghost of Hamlet Sr., presents his son with puzzles and codes to decipher, and a challenge to fulfill—parental passive aggression from beyond the grave. As Ellie Ragland notes, in contrast to the Lacanian symbolic father of law, "the real father is the dead father who returns to haunts us, to poison desire, to mock us with our inadequacies or theirs" (95). At one point, Immer angrily talks back to the screen: "I don't need this. / I don't need this, Dad. / Leave my fucking world-view *alone*" (*TPB* 225).[17]

The Puma Blues' portrait of bereavement grows all the more poignant when one takes into account that writer Stephen Murphy based it on his own struggles in the wake of his emotionally remote father's death in February 1980, when the author was twenty.[18] As Bissette put it, the series was "in part an expression of Gavia Immer's (and Steve Murphy's) grief over the loss of a parent" (527). Murphy explores these at times painfully conflicting feelings in his comics blog *Contains Traces of*,[19] in which he refers to *The Puma Blues* as the "Tomb o' Clues"—"because that's what it's become for me: Evidence from the dead. From my subconscious . . . and the dead within."[20]

His father's death sent Murphy searching for a puma in Quabbin Reservoir, despite his understanding the irrational, quixotic nature of such a quest: "I think it was that sense of impossibility that led to my . . . longing, I guess. Longing . . . or sadness. Was it part of an overall state of depression? Maybe."[21] (In the original series, Immer is stalked by a puma, which he never sees.)

Murphy's grief, triggered by a difficult father's passing and echoed in Immer, opens the floodgates to something beyond Cold War fear of the bomb, to full-blown ecomelancholia: "I couldn't stop thinking about the state of the world: rainforest loss, species extinction, global warming, AIDS . . . All the things that permeated *The Puma Blues*."[22] He felt like he "wasn't doing enough to help save the world."[23]

The series' representation of Immer's deranged, despairing wake for both his father and nature, in particular its deeply gendered aspects, occupies the next section.

ECO-MALE-ANCHOLIA

Gavia Immer is depressed, stricken by the same Blakean "invisible worm" as his late lamented father, the same as many of us living in the age of mass extinctions, of climate change—in short, of the death of the natural world (with all the baggage such a term bears; see my part I) as it more or less existed before the industrial age. Private and global fuse. As Bissette writes, "The conflation of ecological crisis and personalized mortality stalked Murphy like a predator. The death of the self; the death of planet Earth—is there a difference, really?" (530). The Murphy avatar in his blog tells the unseen therapist, "I've come to think that the postapocalyptic landscape most likely represents my world . . . after Joe's death. / . . . blown to bits."[24]

Yes: blown to bits. The condition thus described goes by different terms: eco-grief, solastalgia, ecomelancholia, etc.; it involves contradictory, often self-lacerating emotions, as discussed by Ashlee Cunsolo and Karen Landman in the introduction to their *Mourning Nature*.

Harold F. Searles, in one of the earliest (1972) psychoanalytic explorations of the ecological quandary, saw humankind as a depressed patient (364) and even as a schizophrenic (367–68). Moderns use technology, he claimed, as a salve for the ache of separation from the natural world (367), in the perverse, self-defeating aim to prop up a Romantic mirage of a sadly vanished past:

> We equate the idealized world of our irretrievably lost childhood with a nonpolluted environment. We tend erroneously to assume that nothing can be done about the pollution of the present-day environment because of our deeper-lying despair at knowing that we cannot recapture the world of our childhood and at sensing, moreover, that we are retrospectively idealizing the deprived and otherwise painful aspects of it. The pollution serves to maintain an illusion in us that an unspoiled, ideal childhood is still there, still obtainable, could we but bestir ourselves and clear away what spoils and obscures its purity. In this sense, pollutants unconsciously represent remnants of the past to which we are clinging, transference-distortions which permeate our present environment, shielding us from feeling the poignancy of past losses, but by the same token barring us from living in full current reality. We can feel not that we have lost the world of our childhood, but that, omnipotently, we have spoiled it and are choosing to go on increasingly to spoil it through our polluting of it. (365)

The notion of culpability for our ongoing Anthropocenic sins makes resolution a thorny problem, not only for the planet, but for our mental health; in the words of Nancy Menning: "We must mourn not only what we have lost, but also what we have killed or otherwise destroyed. . . . When one feels complicit (directly or indirectly) in the loss being mourned, guilt entwines with sorrow, complicating the grieving process" (40). Proceeding from Freud's concept of anticipatory mourning, Joseph Dodds agrees that these fraught psychic processes often lead to our further injuring the very thing we grieve: "We might expect individuals and societies to adopt positions of consciously not caring about the environment or even our species survival, or becoming actively destructive and self-destructive, as a defense against the mourning yet to come. Alternatively we may engage in a premature anticipatory mourning, falling into a despair preventing the very action which might avoid the feared loss, while there is still time" (124).

Such symptoms—punishment, outward aggression, self-sabotage, depression—point to a fundamental disconnect that reverberates, free radical–like, throughout the psyche. As the writer Jay Griffiths, echoing the tenets of deep ecology, evocatively puts it: "When wild lands are lost, so is metaphor, allusion and the poetry that arises in the interplay of mind and nature. To lose your land is to lose your language, and to lose your language is to lose your mind" (quoted in J. Baker 58).[25]

What particularly interests me about how these fraught modern stresses manifest in *The Puma Blues* is their decidedly masculine framing. Immer is not just depressed; he is a depressed middle-class US white male, a recognizable literary archetype of the 1980s, cousin to the disaffected youth of Jay McInerney and Brett Easton Ellis, or of the even more unhinged teens in Tim Hunter's *River's Edge* (1987). Immer howls his laments to the heavens, then retreats into cold silence ("I don't need this, Dad"). He "cries for love" along with Iggy Pop like a college-age slacker in a rented basement, drowning his sorrows, communicating with the outside world only through a Zoom-like video monitor, the rest of the time consuming through the media the dreary factual evidence of a collapsing environment (much of this data are reproduced in *The Puma Blues* series' paratextual pages).[26] He craves affection but lashes out (especially against his dead father) whenever someone ventures too painfully close to his wounded ego. He spends most of his time alone, in the wilderness, winding up (in the 2015 ending) as a disabled hermit in Alaska as the world finally comes to an end.

His recitations of nature loss, right up to his death, come off as both genuine *cris de cœur* and as little more than juvenile grousing—mostly because, as an antihero, Immer is inert, ineffective, and inconsequential. He complains and objects but does nothing concrete about any of it. He joins no Monkey Wrench Gangs, organizes no demonstrations.

His critiques of postindustrial, post-nature life are cutting and exact, his accusations just, but his sense of his own complicity and sadness paralyzes him, retards any action—except once, when a middle-aged Immer finds himself in New York in 2011, in the middle of the Occupy Wall Street protests.[27] Wearing an FU T-shirt, he harangues a group of young men in New York, trying to rouse them: "Hey, man, why are we hanging around doing nothing?! / Let's fuck shit up like they do in Europe! / Show these rich wall street bastards we mean business!" The men ignore him, turning back to their smartphones. Still, a text box in Immer's voice notes, "If only for one hopeful, focused moment, I was elated" (*TPB* 492).

Immer then, on his own, vandalizes Walter Modica's 1989 statue *Wall Street Bull* (a.k.a. *Charging Bull*) in the Financial District. He spray-paints the anarchist symbol on it. The results: prompt brutalization and arrest by the police, and getting "on the state's radar" (*TPB* 494). This, pitifully, constitutes the whole of Immer's political and/or environmental activism.[28] A failed Raskolnikov, he mostly stews in his own impotence.

And not only him. *Puma Blues'* other major male character, the literature professor Jack, is also ineffectual—though, notably, he does not suffer from paralysis. Fortinbras to Immer's Hamlet, he belongs to a radical eco-terrorist cell ("a militant Audubon" [*TPB* 74]) investigating the government's machinations with the manta rays—which at one point brings him into conflict with his new friend Immer (67). No less beset than Immer by Cold War anxieties, Jack too has nightmares of nuclear Armageddon—though when he shares one with his class, a female student subjects the dream to crude Freudian reductionism (57).

But perhaps the biggest contrast with Immer is Jack's "manliness," marked by his thick beard, broad shoulders, and cowboy affectations. He dresses the part, riding a horse onto the off-limits Quabbin, "surrounding [himself] in an essence of maleness" and machismo, as his partner Ruth mockingly puts it; she even compares him to Clint Eastwood (*TPB* 79–80). During their interactions, the older Jack calls Immer "kid" (123); when his horse rears at Immer, Jack tells him "she don't like boys" (121). Soon after, he physically overpowers Immer, chloroforms him into unconsciousness (337), and fires a handgun at the flying rays, drawing blood (343). In the chapter "Deconstruction," he even takes part in an eco-terrorist action, demolishing a sign announcing a proposed site for luxury condominiums in a rural setting (206). In sum, Jack presents as a man of action, willing to risk his life and career for his environmentalist principles—a foil to the "all talk" Immer.[29]

None of that matters, however. The he-mannish Jack, no less than the "boyish" Immer, both come up sadly short of effecting real change. The world still burns.

Murphy and Zulli underscore the two's shared powerlessness in a chapter with a bifurcated narrative structure titled "Double Burn": At one point, the pages split into upper and lower tiers separated by a wide black gap, with each tier representing Immer's and Jack's points of view, respectively. They go about their day, in their own homes, with televisions playing. The soundtracks and "double screens" eventually converge: Both men are watching the same program—which happens to be a news broadcast about ecological collapse. As correspondent Tatjana Rebsamen reports, part of the Antarctic ozone hole has shifted to the lower part of South America, "another dramatic consequence of the *accelerating greenhouse effect*," possibly leading to "a new surge of *environmental refugees*" (*TPB* 371). She goes on with this litany, her face preternaturally composed, concluding the chapter:

> Meanwhile, marine biologists *again report* a substantial *decrease* in the amount of plankton found in the waters of the Drake passage between South America and the Antarctic peninsula.

From the chapter "Double Burn." *The Puma Blues* (1986–89/2015). © 2024 Stephen Murphy and the estate of Michael Zulli.

Plankton, which form the basis of the ocean's food chain, have proven acutely susceptible to increases in ultraviolet radiation brought on by the ozone loss.

From plankton, the food chain leads to *krill*, the tiny shrimp that in turn is the principal food source of squid, fish, penguins, seals, and many whales.

The numbers of krill, too, continue to drop precipitously . . .

As the collapse of this ecosystem sweeps upward in waves . . .

By all estimates the local populations of fur seals and fin whales have been reduced

by half . . .

while there have been no sightings

of humpback whales

at all

Elsewhere today, the. (372)

The sequence, a McLuhanesque mini-dystopia, highlights the dissociation and disconnection from nature emblematic of the television age, while the perfunctory "elsewhere today, the" points to the distraction and limited attention accorded the environmental crisis even as the damning facts themselves raise the greatest alarm (one would think). More than anything else, though, given the foregoing, the "two screens into one" episode depicts how Immer and Jack—"manly" or not—run headlong against the wall of the reality principle. *The Puma Blues*, in fact, spirals even further downward into dystopic "depression" from this point, its narrative fractured, storylines imploded or dropped, tone grown even more morbid, oneiric, and despairing.

The next chapter, "Thin Skin," starts with a stylized view of Earth from space, presents a disjointed parade of fragments, dream imagery (dolphins and fish, Immer's parents as "owl people," erotica, trees, nuclear waste in the oceans, etc.), ever-expanding gutters, and overlapping sentence fragments to plumb the depths of the hero's defeatism. "My world has become the theory of montage" states one unattributed text box (presumably Immer's disordered musings) (*TPB* 382), while on the next page the same female correspondent as before announces, "—iatric association has released findings suggesting that persons with thoughts about *death* or fears of *death* tend to have more nightmares than others." Such "defenseless" people, she goes on, suffer from "thin or permeable boundaries" (383), comparable to "people vulnerable to schizophrenia," who "may have troubles telling reality from fantasy and dreams" (384).[30] As Joe McCulloch interprets this chapter's experimental techniques and page designs: "Text swarms like flies, italicized captions representing media narration while other captions capture the allusive, stream-of-consciousness thoughts of the reclining, booze-addled narrator/protagonist, lamenting the state of a dying world accessible only in montage."

In other words, "Thin Skin," through highly unconventional graphic narrative, depicts the near-suicidal breakdown of a mind besieged, overwhelmed—crushed—by the sheer undeniable facticity of the Anthropocene, a mind that by the end can only quote David Bowie—"I wish we could swim / Like the dolphins / Like dolphins can swim"[31] as it sinks into stupor (*TPB* 389–91). On the final page, negative space predominates, panels and text effaced, showing only birds (nature) and manta rays (post-nature) plying the absolute white, like bits of disembodied memory (392). Had *The Puma Blues* ended here—with the very form of the comic "fallen apart"—readers may well have interpreted this finale as Immer succumbing to self-slaughter, perhaps through overdose.

Such does not happen. Following another dream issue, "Amidst Wings," the series "jump cut[s] forward two years, West twenty five hundred miles" to find Immer in the southwest (*TPB* 420). A partly "unassembled" page—panels of differing shapes, some canted, with uneven, inconsistently wide gutters—resolve into a fragmented view of the neon-lit words "Golden Nugget" (the sign atop a casino, seen from a window). Over these panels, text boxes declare: "*Howling winds*— / I have seen the best minds of my generation sucked dry through the lamprey hole of Life Fear and Big Control" (416) and so on, an echo of the

From the chapter "Thin Skin." *The Puma Blues* (1986–89/2015). © 2024 Stephen Murphy and the estate of Michael Zulli.

familiar opening lines to Allen Ginsberg's "Howl" (1955–1956): "I saw the best minds of my generation destroyed by madness, starving hysterical naked, / dragging themselves through the negro streets at dawn looking for an angry fix."

The partial views and Ginsbergian text continue—"Bought sold TV herd lull the pastures safe hereafter, who gives a fuck today?" (417)—until a "master shot" splash page shows the once-more long-haired Immer, smoking naked in the dark with a lover sleeping in bed beside him. We learn Immer has survived cancer: "Six months ago a tumor the size of an eyeball was cut from my left arm. / I didn't think I'd live / I never thought I'd die / to see this day / fucking like there's no tomorrow" (*TPB* 421).

The representation of Kate, an eighteen-year-old video rental store clerk who becomes the focus of Immer's lust, suffers from the same "male gaze" objectification and framing as the other women in the series, none of whom are full-fledged characters;[32] for Immer, the woman is little more than a sensual experience.[33] In a nod to Reagan-era "Just Say No" mores, he even reduces their encounter to "three weeks of sex so unsafe a few more of these fascist years it'll be made illegal" (421).

That sort of masculinist braggadocio sits awkwardly with what readers recognize as the same old despair, now recast as simmering anomie and fatalism. No matter how far he runs, flails, wanders, Immer cannot escape the Anthropocene. This chapter's mostly black backgrounds, bleeding to the edge of the page, convey as much, making for quite the departure from the brighter scheme of the two previous dream episodes. If anything even more morose and embittered, Immer wanly smiles as he *looks* out his window at the shiny glitz and flash of late capitalism, in the form of the casino and city lights, but *sees* something very different. As text boxes unfold:

> Living on the ledge of vulnerability.
> Looking outside what I see becomes all I know—*nightfall*.
> The cutting down of rainforests, planetary heat-up, the spread of atom-death, AIDS . . .
> I *hate* humanity
> But I know it's *inhuman* to do so.
> A voyeur of despair, I feel idiot compassion for a world I can't take care of . . . (*TPB* 422–23)

Apart from incarnating Kristeva's adage that "the depressed person is a radical, sullen atheist" (5), the sequence stands out for the *immediacy* of Immer's experience. The window has replaced the TV screen of previous chapters; a filter (the broadcast media) has been removed. Immer seems to have stepped closer to a direct confrontation with the dying world, seen it as if firsthand, lost all hope—but also found moments of peace. His tryst with Kate recalls both the "men and women copulating in the cemeteries of Milan," which Albert Camus cites as one of the "old pictures" of panicked disaster in *The Plague*, but it also alludes to the "tranquility so casual and thoughtless" that also attends Apocalypse, which Camus describes as well (38).

Against the urban lights refracted on the wall of his dark room, Immer contemplates the burning cigarette in his fingers, like a candle steadily exhausting itself, or perhaps a distant rainforest aflame (the smoke wafts out of the panel). His interior monologue continues:

> Gone.
> Up in . . .
> Oh, we may save a few of the larger and more spectacular species in zoos but substantial numbers of smaller species are doomed
> for lack of interest.
> Every day I witness *the state of the world*:
> Deforestation is accelerating, deserts expanding
> temperatures rising, immunities falling
> For the first time in history we are altering the atmosphere itself . . .
> We're fucking ourselves and everything else on this gone blue planet.
> We're too far strung on scar impressions
> to feel much of anything . . . (*TPB* 450)

The final three lines appear over a close-up of Kate's midriff; the same hand that held the cigarette now touches the scar just below her breast (a scar strongly resembling the craters Immer sees at the bomb test sites later in the chapter). The implied violence (cigarette, scar) I address further on, but now let us concentrate on what these passages emphasize above all: a new, unmediated responsibility signaled by the first-person plural: "We may save," "We're fucking ourselves," "We're too far strung." Immer has gone from passively consuming third-person reports on nature's ruin to more acutely feeling his share of the blame for it. (Aside from the occasional burst of anger and self-flagellation, he still does not act.)

In a similar vein, Margaret Ronda finds in a guilty conscience the abiding psychic condition of the human subject in contemporary US "post-nature" poetry. Analyzing Juliana Spahr's "Gentle Now, Don't Add to Heartache" (2005), she writes:

> For Freud, melancholia's pathology lies in the fact that these self-reproaches are out of proportion to the original loss. The melancholic punishes himself out of narcissistic and sadistic impulses that

become improperly outsized in relation to the original loss. "Gentle Now" presents a different form of melancholia, where the speaker's self-accusations are both entirely appropriate and never adequate. It is the loss itself that is outsized. "Gentle Now" lingers in self-punishing grief because there is no way to cope with or atone for the sense of human culpability that emerges here, no way even to grasp its material or psychological consequences. Spahr suggests the only viable work is to return, again and again, to an imagined realm of origins, in order to fathom this very imperceptibility, this withdrawn loss. This recursive structure of wishdenial, recognition of guilt, and ceaseless heartache offers a powerful account of how the determined, aggrandized human agency of the Anthropocene might be experienced—the feeling, that is, of thinking "nothing but us."[34]

Ronda's description of brokenness and blood guilt for loss pervades *The Puma Blues*, a work first published at a time when the term Anthropocene was not circulating beyond a small group of atmospheric scientists and climatologists,[35] but when the felt sense of urgency, of disaster-near-beyond-repair, was spiking in the middle of the Reagan era. Everything one did was feeding the problem; doing nothing perhaps fed it most of all. Stacy Alaimo's discussion of the body's interdependence with the environment (natural and otherwise) gets at the dilemma:

> As the material self cannot be disentangled from networks that are simultaneously economic, political, cultural, scientific, and substantial, what was once the ostensibly bounded human subject finds herself in a swirling landscape of uncertainty where practices and actions that were once not even remotely ethical or political matters suddenly become the very stuff of the crises at hand. (20)

Murphy and Zulli's series, like no graphic narrative before or since, intimately catalogs the mental toll taken by the great dying, when all connections fail, species collapse, the oceans rise, and the planet goes up in smoke. "Who greenhoused all as we slept apart," Immer soliloquizes, "the weave now fraying, circle broken; she watches as small fleeting shadows curl, her greatest gift undone [. . .] / As we become apart from her / She takes away a part of us, / Person, planet" (*TPB* 418–19). Immer's funk over a lost "maternal" connection with Earth presents as so bottomless, his helplessness so total, his retreat from life so absolute (even as his body goes through the motions, e.g., obeying libido), it seems as ineluctable as an instinct. Indeed, Immer's downward spiral points us to one of Freud's most controversial and poorly received concepts.

DEATH DRIVE TO LOS MAMA-MOS

Gavia Immer mourns a father he never really knew and has trouble relating to other human beings, particularly women; most of the time, he agonizes over the environmental crisis. Late in the original series, in an arc titled "Under a Deep Blue Sun," Murphy and Zulli put him on a motorcycle road trip to escape it all, only to wind up at the twentieth century's heart of darkness itself. I argue that we may read Immer's journey to this point (*The Puma Blues*' original ending, or at least when the serial ceased publication in 1989) as the inexorable process of the death drive, which takes him on a spiritual and emotional downward spiral to the very edge of the end of the planet: the nuclear bomb test sites in New Mexico and Nevada.

The theory of the death drive, "one of the first great landmarks in Freud's ways of 'changing his mind'" (Zilboorg xxviii),[36] appears in *Beyond the Pleasure Principle* (1920). It emerged from reflections on the "traumatic neuroses" experienced by soldiers in World War I. These compulsions to revisit or repeat the trauma, Freud hypothesized, largely resulted from a broken wish fulfillment dream mechanism (*Beyond the Pleasure Principle* 37). This eventually led him to a startling, more speculative conclusion that an instinct exists "*inherent in organic life to restore to an earlier state of things*" (43)—i.e., to a primordial stage of pre-animate matter. "It must be an *old* state of things," Freud writes, "an initial state from which the living entity has one time or other departed and to which it is striving to return by the circuitous paths along which its development leads" (45).

In other words, notes Liran Razinsky, death functions as an inherent drive, like sex (140); this does not mean that an organism explicitly "wants" to die, rather that it wants on an unconscious, instinctual level to experience "its own death" and resists any force preventing it from "a return to the preorganic that is not immanent to itself" (141).[37] Such philosophical formulations opened Freud to charges of unscientific mysticism; Razinsky sees in the theory an "almost mythical" psychological determinism (144), while Todd Dufresne deems it "an untestable piece of mythology" that has "entered popular psychology as assuredly as the 'Freudian slip'" (17). And those are the kinder, gentler critiques.[38]

Defenses of the concept, fewer in number, rarely rise to the fervor exhibited by Norman O. Brown in his book *Life Against Death* (1959), written in the throes of the Cold War: "Freud was right in positing a death instinct, and the development of weapons of destruction makes our present dilemma plain: we either come to terms with our unconscious instincts and drives—with life and with death—or else we surely die" (xviii).[39]

Such seems Immer's own thinking, eye goggles on, freak flag flying, like Peter Fonda's Captain America astride his "iron horse" on a "Blue highway drift" (*TPB*

The Four Horsemen and the bomb. *The Puma Blues* (1986–1989/2015). © 2024 Stephen Murphy and the estate of Michael Zulli.

425) through a desert landscape. We are given to understand that, inspired by Ginsberg and Walt Whitman, he abandoned his Quabbin cabin, explaining, "And so, on the verge of another nervous breakdown / I entered America's twisted winds" (424). But this is a journey inward as much as westward; in the

Kate, Immer, and the Horsemen. *The Puma Blues* (1986–1989/2015). © 2024 Stephen Murphy and the estate of Michael Zulli.

New Mexican and Nevadan sands, Immer enacts both a dark vision quest and a return to primordial origins in ways that strongly suggest the death drive.[40]

Zulli visualizes the morbid mood through numerous *mementi mori*: a hanging cardboard skeleton left behind at the cabin (424); roadkill (426); a rhinoceros poached for its horn, dolphins strangled in fishing nets, a clear-cut forest, stumps still smoldering (449); and the Four Horsemen themselves, led by the skeletal Death (427). The imagetext connotes an instinctual process, something inevitable and fated: Across seven page-wide panels, text boxes read, "Driven / always driven / always pushing it a bit *too far* / Vital signs unraveling / across the howling landscape," while the art shows a "bird's-eye" view of the road gradually straightening out or "flattening" (like vital signs) as Immer's tiny bike propulses steadily closer to the right-hand borders, disappearing in the last panel (455–57).

A double spread of eight page-wide panels, arranged along four tiers, goes so far as to illustrate Freud's hope, at the close of *Civilization and Its Discontents*, that "eternal Eros . . . will put forth his strength so as to maintain himself alongside of his equally immortal adversary" (144), i.e., the drive to aggression and self-destruction. Six of the panels, with conventional borders, show the Four Horsemen racing through the desert left to right, with Immer on his bike overtaking them. The second tier consists of two panels with jagged borders, which while separated by the page fold together make up one ultrawide image: Kate and Immer in bed, enjoying a postcoital reverie. This darker panel,

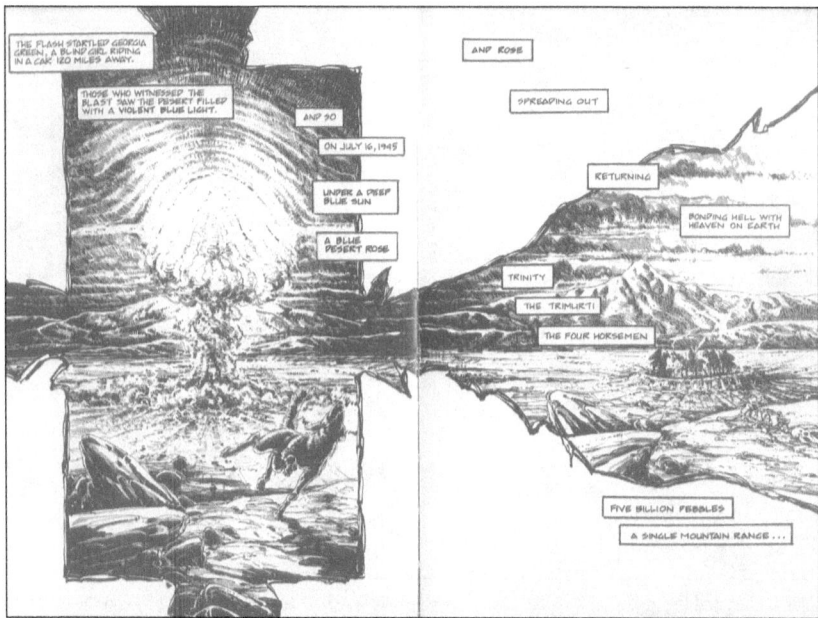

The Trinity explosion. *The Puma Blues* (1986–1989/2015). © 2024 Stephen Murphy and the estate of Michael Zulli.

contrasting with the bright light of the desert sun in the other frames, also stretches beyond the modular layout of the pages' grid, nearly to the edge of the book, as if crudely pasted onto the page (it even partly obscures the panels above and below) (*TPB* 442–43). In their eternal conflict and complementarity, Eros and Thanatos reflect different ontologies, this spread contends: Death seems more "teleological" and driven, while life breaks the expected pattern, slips through the cracks, "timeless."[41]

The Eros "meta"-panel has a bleaker association: It resembles another such book fold–spanning image from a few pages before, depicting the Trinity explosion. The world's first nuclear bomb was set off on Monday, July 16, 1945, at 5:29:45 a.m. in the New Mexican desert. As recounted by historian Ferenc Szasz:

> The heat at the center of the blast approximated that at the center of the sun, and the light created equaled almost twenty suns. At ten miles away people felt a blast of heat equivalent to standing about three feet from a fireplace. Where the fireball touched the ground, it created a crater half a mile across, fusing the sand into a greenish gray glass that was later termed atomsite or trinitite. Every living thing within the radius of a mile was annihilated—plants, snakes, ground squirrels, lizards, even the ants. The stench of death lingered about the area for three weeks. (83)

Murphy and Zulli depict this moment through a vertical rectangular panel covering most of the left-hand page, showing the mushroom cloud rising and an unfortunate coyote in the foreground, caught in the explosion. Text boxes read, in part: "Those who witnessed the blast saw the desert filled with a violent blue light. / And so / On July 16, 1945 / Under a deep blue sun / A blue desert rose / And rose / Spreading out / Returning / Bonding hell with heaven on Earth."[42] Some of these captions float apart from the panel, which "spills" in four places (from top, bottom, right, and left); the rightmost "effluent" spreads across the fold to the right page, creating another panel (despite the absence of any formal gutter) in which we see the long-dead bones of the coyote and a crater with the Four Horsemen in it. The "spilled" panels appear against a white background (*TPB* 430–31). The Trinity blast thus violently "rips" the fabric of time and space, seemingly gouging the very materiality of the page; this baroque panel, like the aforementioned double-spread portrait of Kate and Immer, also looks crudely "pasted on." Eros and Thanatos coexist, birthing each other.

Through such strategies, I submit, "Under a Deep Blue Sun" represents the culmination and climax of *The Puma Blues*' "eco-male-ancholia" theme; much of it reads as the masculine psyche's grappling with its ego ideal as well as the disavowal of its others, figured in everything from the dying and dead animals to Kate's objectified body to nuclear fire (called "man's fire" [429]), until—calamitously—the male psyche can disavow no more.

For one thing, all this time at the Trinity site, Murphy relates in Immer's interior monologue a facts-laden mini history lesson on the bomb and its testing. This Apollonian, "rational" recitation, complete with unflattering anecdotes about the fathers of the atomic age (physicists J. Robert Oppenheimer, Enrico Fermi, Edward Teller, etc.), drips with Oedipal venom, but it also recapitulates the "official" (read: male) story of the nuclear dawn.[43] The takeaway message for Murphy and Zulli comes down to a series of panels in which Immer reaches his goal, dismounts, undoes his jeans, and urinates down into the Trinity crater itself. The captions declare: "Bladder through cock is all I can answer / In the name of the poison, poison and more poison end end end" (*TPB* 433).

This acidic incantatory display, dripping with disdain, belies the fact that Immer's deepest vitriol and sorrow is aimed not at "fathers" at all, and not even at his own father's memory. Rather, as hinted by the close resemblance of the pissed-on crater to Kate's nipple (shown previously in close-up), we see now that Immer's long death drive to hell is in fact a return to (m)other. To begin with, according to Joseph Dodds, "we might understand the phrase of 'Mother Earth' as indicating that our experience with the planet relates in some way to our experience with our (m)other, not only involving feelings of love and being held. A Kleinian perspective might suggest a phantasy of an infinitely giving earth-breast we feel entitled to suck on with ever increasing intensity without limit" (123).

And while Jan Baker identifies "the desire for a retrogressive merger to an idealized state, a return to the safety of the womb" (56),[44] Julia Kristeva points out in *Black Sun* that "Freudian theory detects everywhere the same *impossible mourning for the maternal object*" (9). In the final analysis, this impossible mourning, the ambivalence, vexation, and desire toward the lost object we have been charting in *The Puma Blues* maps less well onto the father than it does onto both mother (Immer's biological mother, Theodora Fein) and *the* mother (dying nature)—and this in often startling ways.

For Immer, as noted, resents what he cannot save as much as he mourns it. The resultant guilt produces still more resentment as well as a narcissistic persecution complex (of the "Leave me alone! I can't do anything about it!" variety). Baker describes it thus: "We believe our environment-mother to be bountiful and limitless, but we also experience her as vengeful, dangerous and frustrating, capable of destructive, natural catastrophes," all of which complicates "the terrible grief because of the damage we have caused our loved ones and to our environment-mother, in this case, damage that, horrifyingly, can no longer be rectified" (J. Baker 58–59).[45]

This paradigm in mind, let us examine the final episode of "Under a Deep Blue Sun," when Immer visits Mercury, a "secret town" of government workers at the edge of the Nevada nuclear test site. Based on Murphy's "bone-chilling" real-life experience (Bissette 530), the visit takes our hero on a bus tour of the test range: "We descend onto the most heavily bombed spot on the planet" (*TPB* 471). Immer takes the tour "because the bomb is one of those unfathomables that shapes our existence, a duality of medicine and poison that has lent a sort of desperate fragility to our lives and to all life" (465), but the reception he gets is anything but reverent of such pieties. "Today's gonna be fun," says Ernie, the middle-aged tour guide, giving him (and the reader) the thumbs-up as Immer boards the bus (466). As the vehicle traverses a devastated moonscape, Ernie cheerily explains the history of the site and its hundreds of nuclear bomb tests, blithely points out the many craters left behind ("There's a nice one. / There's another nice one" [479]). Symptomatic of profound nuclear anxieties, yes, but also bathetic, oneiric, absurd. "I half expect to see a melted clock somewhere," Immer muses, spotting a warped train bridge—part of a "nuclear town" built to measure the effects of the blasts on infrastructure (472). Perhaps no image seems more surreal than that of life, in the form of a sparrow, flitting among the craters (479).

Invited to inspect a ground-level blast site up close, breezily told they would expose themselves to "less radiation than a chest x-ray" (480), the visitors disembark.

Immer visits an atomic bomb crater. *The Puma Blues* (1986–1989/2015). © 2024 Stephen Murphy and the estate of Michael Zulli.

Three wide panels, decreasing in size from nearly half a page (at top) to about one-fifth of a page (at bottom) depict Immer's encounter with the crater and his response (481). The largest panel, in long shot, shows the mammoth cave-in, resembling the Grand Canyon, partly in darkness; Zulli draws the clouds in the distance with a distinctive mushroom shape. The long-haired Immer stands at the lip with his back to us, like a parody of Caspar David Friedrich's *Wanderer Above a Sea of Fog* (ca. 1818)—the modern subject before the abyss. His black jacket and light jeans mirror the crater's light and shadow, while the close-ups of Immer's face with eyes closed in panels two and three show how the crater's ridges mirror his hair blowing in the wind, a similarity enhanced by Zulli's use of Duoshade to highlight both. In fact, Immer, the crater, and the cloud form an organic whole; in the dominant panel, their positioning suggests an upside-down triangle—or demonic Trinity. Text boxes convey Immer's account:

> ... And then I looked out across the crater, a petrified mirage ... My thoughts recoiling, this couldn't possibly be real ... I couldn't possibly be standing here ... [...]
>
> When the warm breeze blew from across the crater it felt good, a welcome caress cooling the perspiration that had formed upon my arms, my neck my (481)

Before we discuss what interrupts Immer's train of thought, and what ensues, note the comforting sensations linked to the crater ("warm breeze"; "it felt good") couched in quasi-maternal, quasi-erotic language ("a welcome caress ... upon my arms, my neck"). The suggestion conjures up feminine associations, particularly the women in Immer's life.

As mentioned, the scar from a cigarette burn on Kate's body not only resembles the Trinity crater into which our hero relieves himself, it also carries abusive overtones: "She's got this scar just below her left ribcage where a past lover once pressed a lit cigarette / allowing it to tear and sear downward for half an inch before he bore down on it hard enough to put it out" (*TPB* 421). Thus Kate as Earth, Earth as victim of male violence, or perhaps of sadomasochistic play (Kate tells Immer only that she "liked" it when he touched her scar [453]). Murphy and Zulli further connect Kate to the Nevada Test Site through—again—her body: in a dream she rides a giant caracara, which she describes[46] as "bigger than I am, but not by much," implying they are one and the same.[47] Kate as bird, bird (sparrow) as seen by Immer bounding in the craters, (feminine) life amid (masculine) death.

Through another woman who arouses Immer's desire, the Chinese government liaison Suki Mideng, the series racializes the otherness of women. And though they don't engage in heteronormative sex, Suki and Immer do have a highly eroticized (and rather ludicrous) symbolic coupling when they both partly disrobe so that he may hand over a baby manta ray, from his arm to hers. "Mmmm . . ." she responds. Immer helps put her jacket back on, with a sheepish look at his commander, the nonplussed Lieutenant Europa Buckley (*TPB* 302–4). Perverse sexuality, then, represents the "sense of unity, sense of desire" that overcomes the "separateness [that] arouses anxiety" related in Immer's journal (301). (The young man had drawn a yin-yang symbol on the very page where he wrote those lines; the fact that Suki wears a yin-yang enamel pin seals the "fatedness" and "love at first sight" quality of their meeting; they even complete each other's sentences [300–301]. Immer, though, never sees her again except in dreams.)

As Freud, too, reminds us, the repetition compulsion owes to an unconscious desire to return to an "original" state, seeking unity with that from which one separated—or at least its substitutes. (Andy Summers puts it more crudely: "Every girl I go out with becomes my mother in the end.")[48]

Ms. Theodora[49] Fein,[50] Immer's mother, appears sporadically throughout the original series' twenty-three issues.[51] Significantly, she and her son never meet in the flesh; their communication takes place over video monitor,[52] hinting at her emotional remoteness (and his). Indeed, at times she seems to fall just short of Winniciott's "good enough mother" role, so short as to exhibit signs of misanthropy. She makes light of Brooklyn's nuclear destruction (21); challenges (one might uncharitably say henpecks) her husband in his video ("*Oh, cut the shit, Ganz!*" [29]); and, lighting a cigarette, coldly bullies her only child in the middle of his personal crisis: "I do not believe you. You *know* you're lying" (214). Their relationship perhaps sees its ideal crystallization in the image of Fein yawning onscreen as Immer says, "Hi, Mom. / Am I waking you?" (200) during a late-night call. Fein herself admits that she may not have been the most "hands-on" of mothers when she flippantly refers to "Immer 'n Fein's distanced approach to child-rearing—trickle-down Dr. Spock—hands off, fingers crossed . . . valium handy" (210).

The character's introduction, early in the series, is also telling. This time it is she who wakes her son up with a call. Before Fein appears on the monitor, a robot operator—with oddly saucy programming—informs Immer of the caller's identity: "Tu madre. / Tu mere. / Deine mutter. / Tvoh mat.' / Yo' mama."[53] A weak joke, but the curious defamiliarization of "mother" as a translinguistic concept underscores the ambivalent nature of motherhood in this series, in ways that resonate with the larger psychosexual themes I have been pursuing.[54]

For our purposes here, the other side of the equation from motherhood is not fatherhood (in any case already discussed), but *babyhood*. Strikingly, babies and offspring of various kinds also undergo estrangement in *The Puma Blues*:

Note the woman testifying in Ganz's video that aliens abducted her baby (232); and the manta nestling Immer hands over (303); the Nevada Test Site's tour bus driver, who has a deformed hand, is called "an atomic baby?"(480); the redoubtable Fein, smoking, looks out her city cab window, sees members of a youth group who wear gas masks as part of their street gear, and thinks, "Those children[55] . . . / their hair tangled and strewn about by their gas masks . . . / remind me of those frenzied *monsters* from that children's book by Maurice Sendak" (59); finally, Immer is seemingly "reincarnated" as an alien fetus after his death (522), "original" paradise regained.

Before then, Immer only sees that ideal state in dreams. In the chapter "Amidst Wings," his dream-self emerges, Venus-like, from the surf, reborn as a naked man (*TPB* 403). He describes the experience as a Romanticist parable of the Fall: "I saw what I knew to be real—caught a glimpse of another truth—but had difficulty in maintaining the view" (402–4). The alluringly naked dream Suki soon appears, though her reception proves anything but kind: "This kid starts crying at the slightest provocation," she says, in Mandarin (409).

In sum, then, Nature presents as the cold, rebuffing mother and Immer as the helpless child, yearning to return to the "preorganic state" of her womb, uttering language equal parts sexual and retrograde: "I want back to the immersion tank / Thumb back in my mouth / [. . .] I want the feel of being inside you again" (385).

To reunite, reenter, step off into her embrace . . .

All filters removed, then, in communing with the Nevada bomb crater, Immer has a direct, unmediated confrontation with the horror, the Real, (m)other.

And then he recoils.

A design of three page-wide panels, a fairly close analogue to the crater page, shows him jolting from his reverie and backing away, as if he had almost jumped from the precipice. "My God," the text boxes say, "What / the fuck / am I doing / out here?" (*TPB* 482).

As psychoanalysts have long argued, the death drive does not entail literal suicide;[56] however, in the case of Immer, to take that last step and reunite with the preorganic state (read: mother) would indeed have meant his more-than-symbolic death from the plunge. In such a scenario, then, it is the incest taboo that ignites his last spark of self-preservation.

In its wake, the original series' climactic moment brings yet another "displacement": Death, in the guise of a skeleton in a suit, smoking a cigarette, walks out of the desert and greets Immer with "Hola, chico" ("Hi, kid"). The other horsemen, too, have caught up with our hero at last. Their leader then declares, "La tierra esta la notre" [*sic*] (482). When Immer fails to understand, Famine translates, gazing at the reader, "The Earth is ours, *meatpie*" (484). They all ride off, leaving Immer to stare after them in shock and desolation.

What has happened here coincides with the line of interpretation we have been following. The fact that Death smokes strongly recalls Fein, who rarely seems to go without a cigarette; his condescending manner to Immer strengthens the link. Furthermore, the words Immer cannot grasp[57] return us to Fein's multilingual introduction by the saucy robot; all the more so since, as in that early scene, Murphy botches the foreign language: "La tierra esta la notre" is ungrammatical gibberish; "La tierra es nuestra" would be standard Spanish for "The Earth is ours."[58] Neither can we discount the figure who clarifies the meaning, however contemptuously: Famine, who though described as male seems quite gender-indeterminate; with a cowl, eyeliner, and mole or beauty mark, he resembles an overweight woman—an evil matron.

In sum, I read all these details as symptoms of Immer's newly erected repression in reaction to the trauma of his encounter with the (m)other, which, siren-like, nearly leads him to the ultimate de-individuation. The Four Horsemen, that clichéd cultureme for Apocalypse, function as screen objects for Immer's fixated anxieties and fears about the true inexpressible terror, which caused him to flinch at the crater's edge. The horsemen are refractions, shards, projections, condensation of Immer's guilt, anger, desire, and a million other emotions provoked by nature's passing. Similarly, all along, Immer's real mourning has not been for his dead father, but for the dying (m)other constitutive of his identity—indeed, of all our identities. The foregoing bespeaks some of the endlessly fraught territory the ego must navigate in confronting the Anthropocene and what it means.

As Norman O. Brown characterized a similar struggle: "Man is the animal which has separated into conflicting opposites the biological unity of life and death, and has then subjected the conflicting opposites to repression. The destruction of the biological unity of life and death transforms the Nirvana-principle into the pleasure-principle, transforms the repetition-compulsion into a fixation to the infantile past, and transforms the death instinct into an aggressive principle of negativity" (104).

Rachel Carson put it less technically, though no less insightfully, at the dawn of North America's modern environmentalist movement: "Everywhere was a shadow of death" (2).

CONCLUSION: "POOR LITTLE WHITEY"

Gavia Immer inherits a video to ponder and a legacy of Dada activism from the late father he hardly knew. Guiltily, he rejects both.[59]

He deteriorates into despondency, but as we have seen, sorrow for the patriarch he betrays[60] is but the tip of a (rapidly melting) iceberg. *The Puma Blues*, which "proffered a jazz-like comic book meditation on our culture's headlong rush toward ecological disaster" (Bissette 530), has much to say above all about panic and futility and enervation and remorse in the face of everything the Anthropocene is and does, to the planet and to us.

The tools of psychoanalysis help to decipher some of that morass. Immer, a character whose narrative trajectory in large measure proceeds from the death drive,[61] I've argued, synonymizes said anguish for his lost father with the mourning for a lost Earth—which on a deeper level engages his far more complicated relationship with both his actual mother and the environment (m)other, who is "bountiful and limitless" but also "vengeful, dangerous and frustrating" (J. Baker 58).

By way of conclusion, however, I feel it worthwhile—perhaps even incumbent—for us to circle back and consider more closely: Whose panic? Whose futility? Whose enervation? Whose remorse?

The Puma Blues, after all, makes distressingly explicit the elaborate psychological scaffolding of misdirection, bad faith, and disavowal on which Immer's (and our own) encounter with nature is structured. This largely explains our seeming inability to save it; we don't (can't) see what's there—a cataclysmic, tragic failure of imagination in the face of the nonhuman.

But the matter I want to close with touches on what seems an equally crucial failure. This reading seems more amenable to Jungian than Freudian premises, given that it involves a collective-unconscious, national, and ideological mechanism of disavowal.

Because it turns out "our" imagination *fails before the human too.*

Just like (m)other, in Murphy and Zulli's graphic narrative, whiteness represses—until the repressed returns, overtly or symptomatically.

I proceed from the trend within ecocriticism and the environmental humanities to "decolonize the Anthropocene," whereby whiteness and capitalism present as chief bugbears, whether in the racist outlook that fueled John Muir and other early environmentalists' dehistorized sublime vision for the US national park system (Outka 167); the role of white patriarchy and settler colonialism in the forced relocation of Native peoples (Whyte 133); and in apportioning responsibility moving forward (Haraway).[62]

The depths of racial presumption, the penetration of a white framing of the world, how various virulent and pervasive forms of a white nationalism determine what's seen and not seen—even in "progressive" cultural productions such as *The Puma Blues*—are in large part what these studies seek to interrogate, expose, and dethrone.[63] An urgent project, particularly given the way the series we have been examining depicted a puma literally wrapped in the US flag on more than one occasion.[64] How indeed do the authors of this work, as well as the characters inhabiting it, conceive of the land they so elegize and grieve? For as Richard Dyer noted in his landmark book, *White*:

From the first, the properness of the White occupation of the North American continent (and indeed of other territories to be colonized) was argued in terms of the fact that the indigenous people did not cultivate the land, did not order it and therefore did not realize the true human (but we will now say white) purpose towards creation. White cultivation brings partition, geometry, boundedness to the land, it displays on the land the fact of human intervention, of enterprise. The frontier, and all the drama and excitement its establishment and maintenance entail, is about the act of bringing order in the form of borders to a land and people without them. (33)

The Puma Blues does something similar: It brings lyrical order to a land, animals, and people it construes as having none. And the bringers of this order are white. We've already discussed how the series struggles to represent women as rounded characters; we should also note that all the major characters are white,[65] and the few-and-far-between minor figures of color, like Suki and Ruth, are shrouded in a nigh-excruciating air of mystery and mystique. Others include Ben Weinstein, a Jewish childhood friend seen only in flashback, "who, like Dad, was somewhat possessed by racial haunting, adrift on ancestral tides" (*TPB* 83). Uh-huh. Meanwhile, Ernest, an android chauffeur with metallic skin, presents as a familiar type: the socially awkward white male introvert. In a disconcerting echo of Gavia and Fein, the haughty heiress Mrs. Malcomson coldly dismisses him so he may "follow [*his*] compulsion" (52), which appears to be to befriend animals in the forest (60–61) and eavesdrop on Jack and Immer (128–31). And then there is Immer himself, as noted earlier the white male ecomelancholic *sans pareil*.

But what of Dyer's people "without (b)order(s)," the Indigenous Americans? Intriguingly, they too appear through a kind of "racial haunting," at the margins and interstices, through incidental phrases and metaphors, in short as symptoms of a fundamental repression. Very early on, the saucy robot operator informs Immer that "it was the Nipmuck Indians who named this valley 'Qaben,' meaning 'a meeting of the waters' / —just thought you might like to know" (*TPB* 18). Much later, Immer finds a flint arrowhead on the reservoir grounds. Through a series of match-cuts, we see a Native American, presumably the one to whom the arrowhead once belonged, calling his trained falcon (310–11). A double portrait in juxtaposed panels, which closes the sequence, seals the suggestion of a white escapist fantasy: Immer and the Nipmuck are one (313).[66] In the experimental chapter "Thin Skin," the name of the most famous Apache appears as a marker for worldwide species extinction: "Death howls of a million Geronimos" (377). And a late sequence featuring Southwestern coyotes makes brief mention of "the Indians who once lived here" (438). *Just thought you might like to know.*

Of course, it is "Under a Deep Blue Sun," with its Southwestern setting, that most readily brings the uncanny racial repressed back into the light. The bomb testing range in Nevada that Immer visits was forcibly carved out of Western Shoshone territory, where "between 1951 and 1992, the United States and Great Britain exploded 1,054 nuclear devices both above and below ground there," according to Winona LaDuke, who adds, "Western Shoshone is the most bombed nation on earth" (26). (Recall that Immer echoes that language.)[67]

Patrick Sharp, in his study of the Laguna Pueblo author Leslie Marmon Silko's dystopian novel *Ceremony*, maintains that its Southwestern milieu alone, along with a Native point of view, functions as a rebuke to the lies of the hegemon: "By situating Tayo's story in a recognizable historical setting instead of the future, Silko provides a powerful critique of the usual SF assumption that a nuclear catastrophe has not happened in the United States. With the radioactive contamination, blasted landscape, and cultural devastation at Laguna Pueblo, Silko did not need a future setting to imagine a nuclear wasteland" (124).

Nor, I would argue, does *The Puma Blues*. Yet the perspective remains resolutely white. No person conclusively identified as Native American appears in "Under a Deep Blue Sun." The most tantalizing possibility: a person of indeterminate gender whom Immer chats up on the road immediately after relieving himself in the Trinity crater. The aged figure, in hat and poncho, walks up, singing the pop standard *Piel Canela*[68] in broken Spanish ("M'importa tú y tú y tú / y nada mas que tuuuuuu" [*TPB* 434]). With a devious leer, piercing the reader with their gaze just like Famine, the elder tells Immer, "Outside is in" (435). Not only does this phrase restate the opening of "Thin Skin"—"When the outside / gets inside" (373), a description of Immer's emotional breakdown—but the "cascading" design of this sequence, with almost every panel overlapping the one beneath, imparts a surreal atmosphere prefiguring the *rencontre* at the crater (434–35). Confirming this is no coincidence, the person walks away, saying, "Remember what you have seen," with the final panel positioning them and Immer in the same places relative to each other (435) as in the panel where Immer stares at the receding horsemen later on (485).

Whiteness, too, must always guard against "the outside" getting in, with all the connotations of racial mixing involved. But the impossibility of keeping "the outside" outside, as we have seen in various senses throughout the series, casts Immer into a racial melancholia (along with all the others he suffers).

Decolonizing the Anthropocene means that when Immer says, "I *hate* humanity" (*TPB* 423) for killing nature, we should ask which humanity he means—i.e., which humanity he *should* mean. When Murphy and Zulli show what appears to be a pubescent Asian poacher armed with a rifle (449), we should wonder who is the instrument, who is the end-user, and who really deserves blame for the taking of the (likely endangered) animal. When Jack, hearing a common loon in the Quabbin, is triggered into remembering "an Indian felling a tree with a chainsaw" in the Amazon, and the sounds of that chainsaw morphs through the magic of comics into the roar of Immer's boat engine ("RRRRRR" [93]), we should connect the dots.

The specific psychopathologies of whiteness and maleness don't account for the whole of the Anthropocene, or Capitalocene, or Chthulucene (or whatever). But as *The Puma Blues* shows, they're no small part of the problem, either.

Conclusion

THE PACIFIC NORTHWEST IN WORDS AND PICTURES

Having ranged far and wide in this book, from Yetti's bosom to the blasted heath of a future earth, from Wakanda to the bombed-out Shoshone desert homeland, in my conclusion I want to stay closer to home: the US Pacific Northwest.

In 2003, straight out of grad school, I moved to Seattle to work at the University of Washington. Before my job interview the previous winter, I'd never ventured to the PNW; it's pretty far (distance-wise, demographically, culturally, and by virtually every other measure) from the Rio Grande Valley of South Texas, where I grew up, and Berkeley, where I did my graduate work.

An astonishing city. From the air, you get an impressive sense of Seattle's stupendous greenery, an interpenetrating urban/forest blend[1] at the foothills of the Cascade Range, all dominated by a dormant volcano named Mt. Rainier (the Native peoples call it Tahoma). On the ground, you find yourself looking up and up at the towering trees, everywhere. Like Special Agent Dale Cooper marveling at the Douglas firs.

Within weeks of our arrival, I got quite the education in the power of the ecosystemic forces in this region. Long before I learned the term "atmospheric river," we experienced an incredible rainfall, the sort I'd never known. I'd been in hurricanes, but this was different, more impressive in its cumulative power, building up over days and days, nonstop. Streaming rivulets, the sluice of the sky torn open. The rain refused to end. The water rushed in torrents down ditches, gullies, drains, every available path. It turned out that in that period, my first full month in the city, Seattle saw its wettest October day of all time.

Just over five inches of rain had fallen in that twenty-four-hour period (the twentieth of the month), according to the National Weather Service.[2]

Most of the time, though, as we learned, the rain here is more like a constant mist. Often you don't even notice it. Seattlites walk around without umbrellas, mindless of the moisture in the air. It's just the atmosphere. Many times I've been walking down the street and noticed a glint of sun catching droplets in the air and realized, "Oh, it's raining." And walked on.

A complete outsider, over two decades I grew to love the Pacific Northwest. I love how you can be driving at the highest point on Interstate 5, just north of downtown, and catch a glimpse of the Cascades to the East and the magnificent Olympics to the West, with Lake Union sprawled beneath you. I love that we have hundreds of islands scattered throughout Puget Sound. I love that we enjoy the most extensive ferry system in the country, made up of watercraft with Native names like *Tillikum* and *Kittitas*. I love that we are next door to the Olympic Peninsula, a massive old-growth rainforest. I love our unique alien starship–shaped public library designed by Rem Koolhaas. I love that a couple of hours away we have two other stupendous cities: Portland, Oregon, to the south and Vancouver, British Columbia, to the north. I love to take visitors to Gas Works Park, a restored, decaying industrial works overgrown with blackberry, with a killer view of the city. I love spending time with the Fremont Troll under the highway (a very hippie public art installation) and the real-life Lenin statue from Slovakia nearby. I love that Seattle has a vibrant and flourishing drag culture. The greatest Fourth of July of my life I spent at the gay dance mecca R Place: A drag queen sang patriotic songs to a techno beat as we boogied our asses off. Honestly, I have never loved my country as much I loved it that day, in this city.

What I don't love so much: With all the money sloshing around this town (Boeing! Microsoft! Starbucks! Amazon!), we still have appalling levels of inequality, which were only exacerbated by the 2020 COVID-19 pandemic. I don't love the lip service paid to diversity as working-class people of color are disproportionately priced out of the city due to the high cost of living. I don't love Seattle's shameful history of redlining and the whole PNW's white supremacist settler colonialist roots. I don't love the thoughtless gentrification that has wiped out whole neighborhoods of shops and cultural institutions, like Xanadu Comics and the Harvard Exit Cinema and the Bauhaus Café, with its imposing portrait of Walter Gropius at the entrance. All gone.

In any case, over time, we learned how to properly pronounce "Spokane," "Des Moines," and "salmon" (my then-wife and I pronounced the *L* as in the Italian and Spanish cognates, so sue us) and picked up phrases like "Seattle (N)ice." In dribs and drabs, I also absorbed some of the history of the place.[3]

I learned, for example, that in the mid-nineteenth century the first white settlers were welcomed and aided by the local Salish peoples, who had populated the region for at least ten thousand years. They called this area Whulge (or Whulch), a Lushootseed word meaning "saltwater." Chief Seeathl (a.k.a. Si'ahl), of the Duwamish and Suquamish tribes, facilitated the newcomers' settlement; they named their city in his honor. The Treaty of Point Elliott (1855) set the terms of the new order. The Donation Land Law, passed by Congress in 1850, attracted countless more settlers with guarantees of up to 320 acres of free land (for white men). Within ten years the Natives would be driven out of the city (Seattle Board of Trustees Ordinance No. 5, 1865), save for purposes of work as servants and laborers. The Duwamish, which today number about seven hundred, have never gained federal tribal recognition.

In 1853, right on what is now Seattle's Pioneer Square, Henry Yesler fired up the first steam-powered sawmill in Puget Sound, launching a new era of utter transformation for the region. For human and nonhuman life that depended on the forests now being indiscriminately felled, it was an era of disaster that has never ended.

Washington became the forty-second state in 1889. Seattle made its mark on the modern world with the Alaska-Yukon-Pacific Exposition in the summer of 1909, which helped develop the grounds of the University of Washington, and 1962, with the Century 21 Exposition (a.k.a. Seattle World's Fair), which brought us the Space Needle and monorail. Almost thirteen thousand Japanese Americans in Washington State were rounded up and imprisoned during World War II. To this day, the Panama Hotel in Seattle's International District holds the belongings of many Issei and Nisei families who never returned from imprisonment.

Today, Seattle, as I said, is a prosperous city that caters to millionaires, billionaires, and world-famous corporations and disgracefully tolerates high levels of inequality, especially for BIPOC. Washington State has the most regressive tax system in the nation, punishing the poor and making the wealthy wealthier. Go Seahawks.

It bears repeating that, however one may sugarcoat it, the arrival of white people in the Pacific Northwest meant the decimation of old-growth forests, dispossession of Natives, pollution from horizon to horizon, and wide-scale death for nonhuman life. Among other things, this area was intensely—furiously—logged in the nineteenth century, to clear living/farming space. You can see the consequences compellingly illustrated in Portland filmmaker Kelly Reichardt's *First Cow* (2019). It opens in a sparse modern-day PNW landscape, denuded of mature trees, before flashing back to its 1820 setting in a lush old-growth forest.

"Only Heaven alone can describe those years—timber!—the challenge of it, the appalling labor, the deeds and misdeeds in its name," wrote historian Edwin Van Syckle in *They Tried to Cut It All*:

In the 64 years from the first going sawmill Grays Harbor cut something like 31 billion feet of marketable lumber . . .

In 64 years the first huffing-puffing sawmill grew into an array of timber-hungry, timber-devouring giants, pouring smoke, and distressing days and nights with the screech of machinery, the roar of saws, and the inevitable whistles which pierced or rumbled at dawn and dusk, and at noon sent the crews to their lunch pails. The mills were insatiable. (256)

Robert Michael Pyle, the great elegist of this region, has catalogued much of the destruction. In his 1986 book *Wintergreen: Rambles in a Ravaged Land*, he paints a portrait of the Willapa Hills in southwest Washington, an ecosystem repeatedly logged, depleted, and mismanaged over generations:

The woods of Willapa have been ravaged, along with its soils, rivers, and communities. It's a simple tale in many ways—great trees gone, boomtowns busted, fragments of forests struggling toward a kind of recovery, only to be logged again, too much, too fast. But the telling of it cannot be done simply. It carries too much satisfaction and pain, injury and age; it holds too many promises and lies; it weighs with too much labor and hope, profit and loss, heroism and hypocrisy.

In the end, it's just people and trees, money and time. And it's living with what we have wrought, coping with how the axe has fallen. . . .

This is a land of logging. The fact lives with us, supports many of us. We live with logging; many live for logging. (146)

It's still being logged. As are forests all over Washington. Those enormous trees I saw from the air when I first arrived? The vast majority of them are third- or fourth-generation growth, at most a few decades old. The Olympic Peninsula's Duncan red cedar, with a diameter of about twenty feet, is over a thousand years old.

Even the state agency designated with managing the publicly owned forestlands is legally obligated to maximize their return, meaning it too is in the business of logging (Pyle, *Wintergreen* 149). So, whether for private profit or the public "good," the trees—which house entire ecosystems—keep falling and falling. I moved away from Seattle in 2019 and today live in rural Washington near state-managed lands that are routinely logged. Every once in a while, you see a clear-cut. I've seen a number of them not a mile from where I'm typing this.

The nation as a whole last paid close attention to the deforestation in the Pacific Northwest during the so-called Timber Wars of the 1980s/'90s, when activists faced off against lumber companies over some of the last remaining stands of old growth. The northern spotted owl, native to this region, depends on old-growth for survival; some vilified it because its protection "kills jobs." (Untrue: logging jobs were growing scarce for many reasons that had nothing to do with the owl, like automation and overharvesting.)[4]

Richard Powers deals with some of this in his 2018 novel *The Overstory*. During a protest action, a Klamath elder declares, "Everything happening here was already known. Our people said long ago that this day would come. They told of how the forest was about to die, when humans suddenly remembered the rest of their family" (336).

The Great Decline of the rest of our family is also registered by the crashing of salmon populations in the Pacific Northwest. This has been happening since at least the 1890s. Overfishing, the damming of several rivers, pollution, and climate change that raises the water temperature are just some of the culprits. Only recently has some of this damage started to be reversed, with the removal of some dams and barriers like culverts. These grudging concessions were hard-won, over decades, by activists and Native tribes from state and federal governments. Today, over a million people a year visit Seattle's Ballard Locks to see migrating Chinook, sockeye, and king salmon swimming from the Pacific Ocean upriver to spawn. The locks' fish ladder system has an underwater window for easy viewing.

When these salmon make their way through a man-made canal to Lake Washington, adjacent to the city, they encounter a polluted waterway—though one much cleaner than in 1950. Around that time, as recounted by Matthew Klingle in his environmental history *Emerald City* (2007), Seattlites had grown fed up with the raw sewage and other contaminants spewing into their lake, a major site for recreation. Still, some saw the pollution crisis as "a stalking horse for an intrusive super-government" (228) and resisted the necessary reforms. In the 1960s, a solution was implemented: Redirect the human and industrial waste flows to the Duwamish River in the city's south. This area, mostly populated by Native people, immigrants, and nonwhites, did not have the political muscle to resist the despoiling of the river, which became one of the country's dirtiest. In 2001 the Environmental Protection Agency declared it a Superfund site. Cleanup will take several decades more. As Klingle puts it, "The rise of modern environmentalism often [goes] hand in hand with environmental inequality. . . . Lake Washington rebounded, the Duwamish River deteriorated, and, in the end, the poor and minorities suffered" (228).[5]

One more piece of environmental history: the American Smelter and Refining Company (ASARCO) plant site in Tacoma, an industrial town just south of Seattle. This dates to the 1880s. For almost a century, the site—Pierce County's biggest employer—smelted and refined copper, its smokestack (at over 570 feet, the world's tallest) spewing a toxic plume for miles around. It dumped over eleven acres of smelting byproduct into Puget Sound. In 1985, when the plant shut down, the EPA declared the sixty-seven-acre site among the most polluted in the entire country. The smokestack was demolished in 1993. While parts of the site remain contaminated with arsenic and lead, the EPA and Tacoma residents transformed eleven acres of slag into Dune Peninsula, named after Frank Herbert's terraforming-themed novel.[6]

Recent years have brought an increasing awareness and urgency of the ecological crisis in the PNW and the world; in particular, the 2021 summer heat dome (discussed below) concentrated attention. During his brief campaign for the 2020 Democratic presidential nomination, Governor Jay Inslee billed himself the climate change candidate. Seattle thinks of itself as pretty green; its nickname is "the Emerald City" and its hockey team is called the Kraken. It plays at Climate Pledge Arena. Yes, they really called it that, because supposedly it's a carbon-neutral facility. A lot of locals roll their eyes, but apparently it's true.

Artists have responded to the crisis, too, like Seattle's Maria Phillips, whose *Hidden in Plain Sight* (2019–2020) I visited at the Bellevue Arts Museum, across Lake Washington. The show comprised works made from plastic consumer items, like food containers and grocery bags. A similar piece, Danish artist Thomas Dambo's *Nordic Swan* (2015) adorns the entrance to Seattle's National Nordic Museum. Dambo fashioned the larger-than-life swan from three hundred mayonnaise containers and other materials. In 2023, Seattle's government settled a case over the recognition of the rights of nonhuman life, agreeing that it had to clear waterways to allow salmon to pass (Andreoni).

Among the saddest environmental stories of the twenty-first century in this region is that of Talequah, a member of the Southern Resident killer whales pod, which lives in Puget Sound. Numbering about seventy, the orcas are local celebrities. In summer 2018, Talequah (a.k.a. J35) was spotted pushing her stillborn calf with her snout along the water. She kept doing so for over seventeen days, prompting much media coverage over the "mourning" mother. Orca numbers in the Salish Sea have been falling for years, and newborns especially have the odds stacked against them: Too few salmon means little sustenance to begin with, while pollution in the Sound means mothers pass on poisonous toxins to their babies with their milk. Talequah gave birth to another calf in 2020; it seemed to be doing well.[7]

Talequah's story puts me in mind of the late Oregon-based writer Barry Lopez's essay "Apologia" (1989), about the many dead and dying animals he encounters on a road trip—some killed by him:

> In Idaho I hit a young sage sparrow—*thwack* against the right fender in the very split second I see it. Its companion rises a foot higher from the same spot, slow as smoke, and sails off clean into the desert. I rest the walloped bird in my left hand, my right thumb pressed to its chest. I

feel for the wail of the heart. Its eyes glisten like rain on crystal. Nothing but warmth. I shut tiny eyelids and lay it beside a clump of bunchgrass. Beyond a barbed-wire fence the overgrazed range is littered with cow flops. The road curves away to the south. I nod before I go, a ridiculous gesture, out of simple grief. (*About This Life* 114)

As I explored in chapters 5 and 6, the death of nonhuman life—intended or not—lies at the heart of what it means to be modern. Some kill more than others, it's true. But all do. The ancestors of the trees around me had their old lives taken from them through violence to make this city, this region, into a center of human domination and despoilment. And we, the inheritors of that legacy, are left to make ridiculous gestures out of simple grief. Like this book, maybe.

That, at any rate, is how I read the lyrics in "Maybe Sparrow" (2006) by Tacoma's own Neko Case:

> Oh my sparrow it's too late
> Your body limp beneath my feet
> Your dusty eyes as cold as clay
> You didn't hear my warning

WEATHER, WEIRDNESS, GOOP: PNW COMICS

Perhaps as an extension of this region's interpenetration of city and forest, the nearness and bigness of its trees, the endurance of its Native cultures, its overcast climes, and long dark winters, the Pacific Northwest has also developed a reputation for "weirdness"—and danger. We are known for our Bigfoot devotees, as well as for having more than our share of serial killers per capita. Not only can we boast UFO enthusiasts, we even launched the mid-century UFO craze itself in 1947, when pilot Kenneth A. Arnold allegedly spotted a formation of "flying saucers" near Mount Rainier (R. Lee).[8] The secessionist Cascadia movement—which would forge a new country out of Oregon, Washington, and parts of Canada—bears more than a whiff of our white supremacist settler colonialist roots. Until protesters toppled it after the 2020 murder of George Floyd, Seattle's Lake View Cemetery had a Confederate veterans memorial.

The rep for eccentricity goes way back, to turn-of-the-nineteenth-century figures like Portland's Ernest Darling, an acquaintance of Jack London, who styled himself a "Nature Man" subsisting exclusively on fruits and nuts. There was also Joseph Knowles, who pushed back against a purported "crisis in white manhood"

Seattle cartoonist John Ross "Dok" Hager's Umbrella Man. *The Seattle Times* (ca. 1910). © The estate of John Ross Hager.

by living unaided for an entire month in southern Oregon's Siskiyou Mountains in 1914 (K. Berger). Such stunts prefigured reality TV shows like *Alone*.

Phenomena like this seem to suggest that living in such a remote place, with so many trees, mountains, and water, makes people a little nuts. Pyle opens his book *Where Bigfoot Walks* with the words "Something is definitely afoot in the forests of the Pacific Northwest" (1). David Lynch has perhaps captured the local mood best of all, in his landmark *Twin Peaks* (1990–1992/2018), with its haunting phrase "The owls are not what they seem." The dual-edged nature of our *genius loci* is embodied in Lynch's series by the quirky Margaret Lanterman, a.k.a. the Log Lady (Catherine E. Coulson)—but also by Bob (Frank Silva), the demonic homicidal spirit that takes root in a family riven by sexual violence.

Rain-addled weirdos dot the landscape of PNW comics too, starting with a character created by cartoonist John Ross "Dok" Hager: Umbrella Man a.k.a. Old Sport. A white-bearded ancestor of R. Crumb's Mr. Natural, he appeared from 1909 to 1925 in his distinctive bumbershoot headgear with his sidekick Kid the duck on the front page of *The Seattle Times*, often paired with the weather report. Hager based the figure on Robert W. Patten (1832–1913), a beloved local eccentric, jack-of-all-trades, raconteur, and Civil War veteran who lived on a houseboat on Lake Union (see Blecha, "Robert W. Patten"; and Tumey, *The Umbrella Man*). Robert Hale (1918–1983) continued the trend as the first TV weather reporter in the Pacific Northwest; he jazzed up his coverage with live cartooning on-air starting in 1955 (Blecha, "Hale"). Throughout the history of PNW comics, we see an entanglement between humans and atmospheric phenomena, with the rain in particular. Ron Austin and Louise Amandes's *Bezango, WA* (2015), a documentary on cartoonists in this region, even has a poster by Pat Moriarity that features Umbrella Man and Kid in a downpour beneath dark clouds.[9]

This peculiar mix of weather and weirdness: You see it in everything from Jim Woodring's the Unifactor, the setting for his Frank stories, a "dreamlike world filled with deserts, forests, minareted castles, hot-air balloons, a devil, and the occasional cylindrical chicken" (Thielman)[10] to Charles Burns's homeless mutated youth living in Seattle's Ravenna Park in *Black Hole* (2005), from Gary Larson's *The Far Side* to Simon Hanselmann's drug-fueled Meg, Mogg, and Owl stories. You see it every year at Seattle's Short Run Comix and Arts Festival, in works by local authors published by Fantagraphics, Starhead Comix (1985–1999), and *Dune*, or in defunct publications like Seattle's first underground newspaper, *The Helix* (1967–1970), the *Seattle Weekly* and the comics quarterly *Intruder*, as well as their living counterparts *The Stranger* and *Scarfff*.

If there's a style associated with this region, it's what Paul Tumey, in a 2014 overview titled "The Seattle Underground Comics Scene Is Alive and Oozing," calls the "goop art school." This embraces "the strange, the fleshy, and the repulsively moist," as exemplified by the "twisted, organic forms" of James the Stanton (*Gnartoons*); Lynda Barry (who attended Olympia's Evergreen State College); Roberta Gregory (*Naughty Bits*); and Peter Bagge (*Hate*), as well as the works of Max Clotfelter, Tom Van Deusen, and Ben Horak. Tumey traces the style (which "feels like the love child of Big Daddy Roth and Hieronymus Bosch") to the work of the legendary Basil Wolverton himself, who lived in Vancouver, Washington.

More on the "weird" side of the spectrum, historian cartoonist Seth Goodkind's *Predators and Prophets: A Comic History of Pacific Northwest Cults*

(2015/2020) provides an incisive primer on such individuals and groups as the Indian Shaker Church, the Rancho Rajneesh and Brother XII, and Oregon's Temple of Oculus Anubis. In contrast, the late master comics satirist Michael Dougan's "Piggly Wiggly" (1988)[11] centers on the banality of the ecological crisis. In it, a middle-aged man at a grocery store balks at using plastic bags for his produce, saying, "This kind of waste is turning our protective ozone layer into . . . Swiss cheese!" In the next panel he mutters: "That reminds me . . . we have to get some swiss cheese" (5). The end. David Lasky's *Stay Safe in the Heat* (2019) sets yet another tone. A publication of the Collaborative on Extreme Event Resilience at the UW School of Public Health in collaboration with Public Health—Seattle and King County, the eighteen-page comic used public focus groups and interviews to identify populations most at risk during extreme heat events and target them with important information, provided in multiple languages. Meanwhile, Eroyn Franklin's quasi-autobiographical "The Cabin" (2018), a.k.a. "Get Away," addresses a different sort of menace figured by the Pacific Northwest's remote woodland spaces. It deals with a woman alone in an A-frame cabin in the forest, contemplating among other things her own sexual objectification by men.

In the next few sections I share some insights gleaned from talking to several PNW artists of my acquaintance. They had a lot to share about this place and how it's changing in the Anthropocene.

MEGAN KELSO'S UNREQUITED LOVE

What I've been describing, that sense of rooted strangeness coupled with vulnerability, the trees holding some vague threat of gendered violence that suffuses this region, was first brought home to me by born-and-raised Seattlite Megan Kelso. During a talk to promote her 2006 release *The Squirrel Mother: Stories* at Third Place Books in the Ravenna neighborhood, she discussed and showed images from her "Green River," partly based on the experience of working at a local hamburger joint, Dick's. It opens with a tired-looking young woman serving food at an outdoor counter to a balding, bespectacled man: "When I was a teenager in Seattle in the Eighties, the Green River Killer raped and murdered at least forty-eight girls" (145).

Over the next two pages, we see the woman serving other customers (all presenting as men), finishing her shift, and waiting at a bus stop as the narrator further describes the notorious Green River Killer, Gary Ridgway, who terrorized the region for over two decades and in 2003 pleaded guilty to killing forty-eight women. Kelso lines the tops and bottoms of the pages with panels of Seattle area landmarks: Black Diamond Road, Sea-Tac Airport, the Meeker Street Bridge, Star Lake Road, and so on, all under those familiar low gray clouds . . .[12]

Recognizable Seattle-area landmarks in Megan Kelso's "Green River" (2006). © Megan Kelso.

"Green River's" word-image tension (the utter routine of a food service job versus remote rural spaces versus facts about a real-life serial killer) makes for a profoundly disturbing portrait of a place—a portrait in which every man (especially the balding fellow, whom we follow into his car) is presented as a potential rapist and killer, where every young girl could wind up violated and dead in the woods somewhere. "Now I'm thirty-six and living in New York City," Kelso concludes.[13] "I surprised myself by wanting to see [Ridgway] hang" (147). Years later, a friend who works in Eugene, Oregon, told me that when he moved there a local told him, "Oh, you'll love it here. It's a nice place to live." The local then added something to the effect of "It's just that every once in a while a woman goes missing" or "Every now and then we lose a woman." That anecdote brought me right back, with a shudder, to Kelso's hauntingly powerful story.[14]

In 2013, in my capacity as chair of the executive committee of the International Comic Arts Forum (ICAF), I helped invite Kelso to our conference that year in Portland. She took part in a roundtable titled "Comics and the Pacific Northwest." During that event, Kelso said something that has always stayed with me: She described her relationship to this land as one of *unrequited love*.

Over the years we've talked about what she meant by that, and in summer 2022 I finally got to interview her about it. She started by referencing the afterword to her 2010 graphic novel *Artichoke Tales*, in which she writes, "'Place' is not a character in this book. I dislike that conceit. But place did indeed turn out to be the essential idea of *Artichoke Tales*." She elaborated:

> I've always been sort of irritated when you hear writers especially say, yeah, like, Los Angeles became a character in the novel. And for years, I would hear authors say that, like on *Fresh Air* and stuff, and it always kind of stuck in my craw. . . .
>
> [It] was very clear in my mind that I didn't think of place as a character because a character is someone that has relationships with the other characters in a work. And a place is not . . . there's an impersonality. It's impersonal. It doesn't have feelings for the creatures that live in the place. And yet the creatures that live in the place have feelings for the place. And to me, that's the essence of unrequited love. The feelings are not returned. And while I can imagine someone arguing with me, that perhaps that's a very Western, non-Indigenous way to think about it,[15] the fact remains that if there's an earthquake or a flood, *nobody should take that personally*. That's the earth doing what the earth does. It doesn't care about us (personal interview; my emphasis).[16]

Kelso clarified that she feels a deep love for the Pacific Northwest,[17] where she was born and has spent the vast majority of her life, and where her hiking-obsessed rock-climber parents familiarized her with many beautiful, wide-open spaces. Still, in this era of climate change, she resists romanticizing those experiences. At a later roundtable,[18] Kelso explained:

Megan Kelso's *Crow Commute* (2021), overlooking Climate Pledge Arena at Seattle Center. Photo by José Alaniz. © Megan Kelso.

I sometimes wonder when I see people who become obsessed, who go into the mountains all the time, that maybe it's a form of denialism. Because when you're out in "nature unspoiled," it can maybe be easier to think, "Oh, maybe it'll turn out okay, maybe we'll be okay." But I think the real battle is where most of us actually live: in cities. And trying to preserve the places that we densely inhabit and everybody finds necessary for life. So, I'm torn about the whole "experiencing the sacred in the mountains" thing.[19]

Kelso took that hyper-local ethic of a here-and-now groundedness for her most complex project, *Crow Commute* (2021), a public art installation overlooking the aforementioned Climate Pledge Arena at Seattle Center. Eighty-five feet long and made up of twenty-one etched stainless-steel panels, each ten inches tall and four feet long, the piece functions as a panoramic map and timeline of the city and its history. Cawing crows fly throughout, while individual scenes depict a crowd streaming out of a 1969 concert (at that very site) by Seattle's own Jimi Hendrix and Kurt Cobain singing in his house in 1993. Other luminaries shown include local Black Panther party member Carolyn Downs; Larry Reid, curator and events coordinator at Fantagraphics Bookstore & Gallery; and Vi Hilbert, a member of the Upper Skagit tribe and tireless conservationist of the Lushootseed language. Indeed, several transliterated Lushootseed words appear in the piece.

This was no casual choice by the artist. *Crow Commute* may be read in any order, but its central panel (the eleventh) is distinguished from all the others by both its location and its unique yellow color. Kelso here references the land on which Seattle Center itself rests, which before white colonization was a prairie cleared with fire by generations of Coast Salish people. "They would burn it from time to time to keep the trees back," she explained to me. Working on this project greatly affected Kelso's sense of her home region—a place she realized she had viewed most of her life from an exclusively white perspective: "I realized how I was so completely ignorant of the Indigenous history here, of all those prairie areas that only existed because for thousands and thousands of years they were managed that way. They didn't just naturally occur" (personal interview).

I've visited *Crow Commute* many times, in different weather and seasons. I bring out-of-towners to see it, the way I show them Gas Works Park and the Fremont Troll. It's already become a Seattle landmark, a testament to Kelso's unrequited love for this place.

T EDWARD BAK: ALL IS SACRED

Originally from Colorado, Portland's T Edward Bak bills himself on his website as "a cartoonist and illustrator exploring the psychogeographic and biogeographic crossroads of culture and ecology." Indeed, unusually for US comics artists, Bak tends to work at the intersection of biology, (natural) history, comics, and art.[20] Since the early 2010s he has labored on a multivolume, highly stylized comics biography of Georg Wilhelm Steller (1709–1746), a German naturalist who took part in the 1733 Second Kamchatka Expedition under Vitus Bering, which crossed Siberia, made it through the Kamchatka Peninsula in the Russian Far East, and reached modern-day Alaska. Bak's research and presentations related to the project have taken him to the Boomfest International Comics Festival and the State Ethnographic Museum in St. Petersburg, Russia; the Georg Steller Institute in Germany; and the California Academy of Science's Institute for Biodiversity Science and Sustainability, among other institutions. He also spent four years in an environmental studies program, focusing on habitat biology and geographical information systems (GIS), at Portland Community College.

Having gotten to know Bak personally, it's easy for me to see an affinity between him and the historical Steller, an intellectual devoted to exploring and cataloguing the wonders of nature who found himself caught in the middle of vast imperial, extractive, even violent processes. As noted by historian Ryan Tucker Jones, "For Steller, the act of doing natural history—describing nature— was holy work, transcribing the work of God into written form" (48). But that wasn't the ultimate aim of the expedition, one of Tsarist Russia's most expensive ventures, which (among other things) extended policies on the forced labor of

Kamchatka's indigenous Kamchadals, then bloodily suppressed their uprisings. The colonizers' hunger for animal pelts—which they sent back to the crown in a lucrative trade—decimated the Kamchadals' way of life. Myriad other environmental harms followed.

Yet despite what Jones calls Steller's "metaphysical protests" (53) against the cultural and environmental consequences of the Russians' expansionist conquest of Kamchatka, during the years of the expedition he made important studies of flora and fauna. For all his Protestant piety, which sharply contrasted with his fellow explorers' Russian Orthodoxy, Steller first and foremost was a scientist and man of reason. As Bak's Steller tells a friend in *Island of Memory* (2013): "The human being is merely another expression of nature—a leaf on the branch of an infinite oak! It is human vanity—rather than empyrean design—that situates man at the apex of creation, Johann!"

Steller's story resonates with the sentiment expressed in the introduction to Bak's 2020 nonfiction collection *Not a Place to Visit*:

> While traveling through western North America my mind is often simultaneously overcome with the beauty of landscapes and with the horrifying truthfulness in the flippant phrase, "Nothing is sacred." Consider for a moment the resignation with which the modern world accepts this bizarre notion. *Nothing is sacred.* Our children grow up embracing and embraced by this conceit while becoming as accustomed to mass extinction as [to] active shooter drills.

The pieces in *Not a Place to Visit*[21] bear out that Steller-like protest to a benumbed materialist outlook on the fragile ecosystems that sustain life on Earth. "Voices of Celillo Falls," made in collaboration with writer Sarah Mirk, eulogizes a major salmon fishing site on Oregon's Columbia River, which Native peoples had relied on for millennia. It was erased by the Dalles Dam, built in 1957 despite protests. "Not a Place to Visit" starts with Bak's musings on his occasional job as a porter on a replica sternwheeler plying the Columbia on a pleasure cruise along a course originally mapped by Lewis and Clark, which led to larger contemplations of modernity's flawed relationship with the natural world: "The vessel itself is a *microcosm* of global capitalism, little more than a *symbol* of *contrived nostalgia* designed to eclipse the *nature* of the *river*. The ship is driven (by 'hidden' engines operating beneath the surface) thru a *devastated environment* towards no real destination)."

As Bak explained in 2022, his work is less focused on cataclysmic events like climate change and more on "initiating curiosity about nature in the reader" ("Nature and Climate Change"). One of the ways he does this is through delicate ink and watercolor animal portraits, like a page from *Sea*

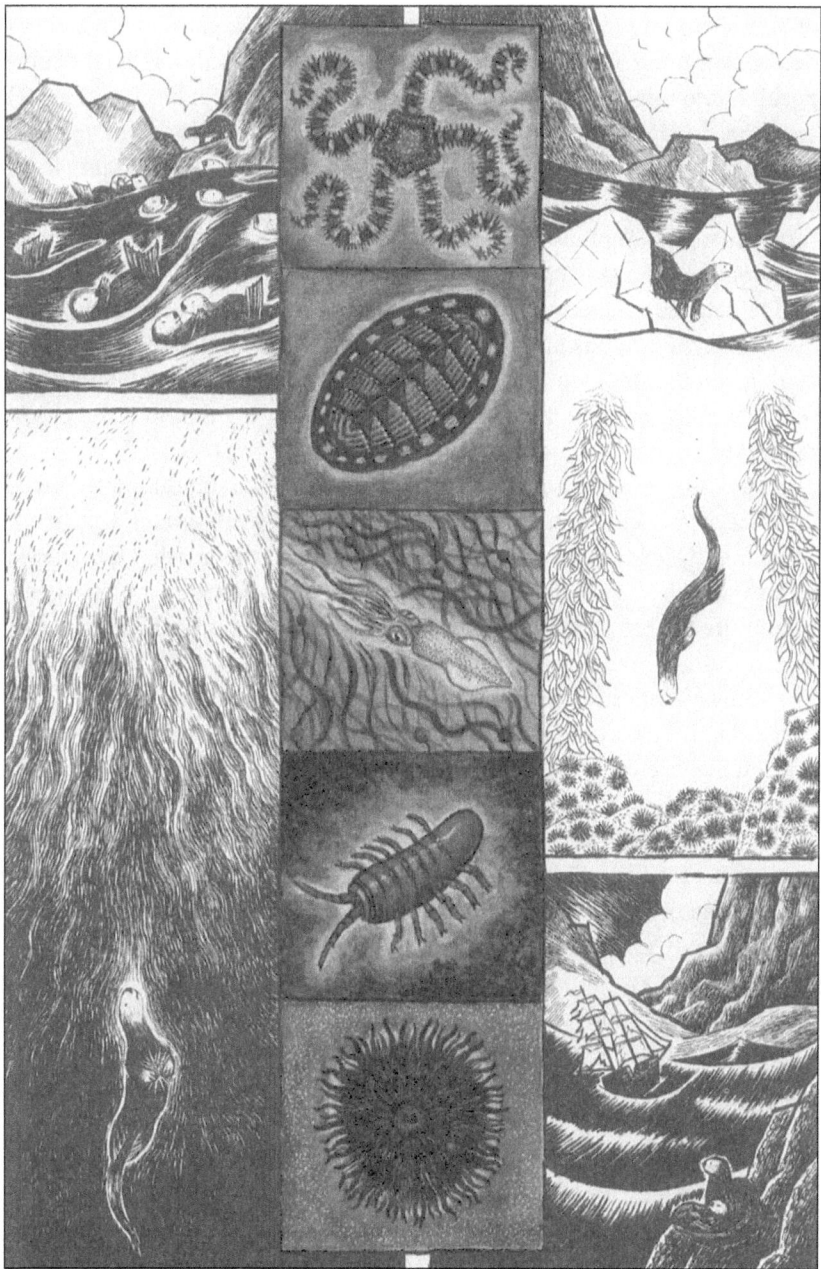

The sea otters in T Edward Bak's *Island of Memory* (2013). © T Edward Bak.

of Time Chapter 1 (2022) depicting sea lions and seals, paired with Steller's notebook jottings. Or the silent page in *Island of Memory* that splits the composition into three vertical columns, two of which show (in black and white) sea otters floating on the water and diving for sea urchins. The third, in color, presents close-ups of their prey: daisy brittle star (*Ophiopholis aculeata*); lined chiton (*Tonicella lineata*); opalescent squid (*Doryteuthis opalescens*); Vosnesensky's isopod (*Pentidotea wosnesenskii*); and white-spotted rose anemone (*Cribrinopris albopunctata*).

The detailed imagery splits the difference between cartoony and nature illustration; in fact, Bak has described his comics as a continuation of Steller's work in another medium, and as the "cartoon version of an Audubon" (presentation). The effect is to decenter the human in ways that to some extent recall Ed Dodd's *Mark Trail*.

And despite the stagey, even clinical approach to the subject matter, made up of far-away views with very few close-ups (of people, anyway), Bak's work paradoxically holds a rare affective power. Sometimes the emotion is conveyed by his angry text ("*symbol* of *contrived nostalgia*"), sometimes by the felt tenderness of the animal portraits (I am enchanted by his sea otters). The strategy, it seems to me, could pay dividends in kindling readers' active responses to the Anthropocene's many ongoing disasters. This seems to be what Bak had in mind in his answer to a question about the ecological crisis during a 2023 podcast interview:

> I think there's the great example of Rachel Carson, her impact and how that affected policy, even, eventually. So there's a vital role that art plays, as far as raising public awareness and creating awareness among people in power, who can affect legislation and affect not just policy but action in everyone.
>
> It's a tricky situation. There's so many crises, like habitat crises. There's so many things to be concerned about. There's also ecology that's recovering on its own. There's also habitat restoration. There's also the question of is stewardship ecologically ethical? And how much? . . .
>
> [T]o me the real vital thing is paying attention to what's happening, but I also really try to avoid alarmist perspectives in my work. I'm more interested in the ecology itself. I'm not oblivious to things that seem to me to not be working. . . . My perspective is: focus on what these relationships are, what's happening in the ecosystem, what's the ecology, what's really happening over the long term. . . .
>
> [I] think it's kind of tricky to minimize what's happening, but it's also tricky to oversimplify it. ("Episode 179")

MITA MAHATO: THERE ONCE WAS . . .

I don't know if I would call Seattle artist Mita Mahato's poetry comics "alarmist" in Bak's terms, though they definitely deal with things going seriously wrong; they are a sort of wake-up call. Mahato grew up in the Midwest before moving to Southern California and eventually the PNW. Her works, often constructed through a meticulous cut-paper collage technique, center on grief and loss—both personal and ecological; they are beautiful and harrowing at once—Morton's dark ecology brought to fruitful, colorful life.[22]

"Especially in the context of the ongoing climate crisis," she explains, "I think it's important to acknowledge that we're always in a situation of loss and consider, then, how we live with it. Collage allows me to conceptualize grief as something expansive and transformative rather than limiting or powerless—something that can move us to joy as well as sadness" (E. Harris). The foregoing often makes Mahato's comics shocking in generative ways; they mash together disparate media, styles, and moods for unpredictable emotional payoffs. In her pages, tears and laughter are both expressed in full measure, yet they coexist, intermingle, contaminate each other. To me, her work represents a new type of hybrid Anthropocene literature/art, overspilling with the messy affective baggage that comes with living in this era.

In "The Extinction Limericks" (2017), for example, Mahato crafts a visual-verbal language that covers the full spectrum of feelings from jokey to mournful. As she told an interviewer: "The limerick tends to be a bawdy, funny poetic form—but what kept repeating in my head was that line that often starts these poems: 'There once was . . .' And it occurred to me that the limerick could be approached as an elegy" (E. Harris). We wind up with full-page cut-out silhouettes of different animals, with variations on that familiar refrain: "There once was a crow from Hawaii"; "There once was a tiger from Java"; "There once was a Western black rhino," etc. (*In Between*) The art appears simple, even naïve, something that might look good as a logo. But look closer. Each of the blank animal silhouettes is impaled by something: the crow by two of the feathers that seem to swirl about; the tiger by some "stripes" that also surround it; the dolphin by drops that carve into its back. The rhino balances on a large horn—the very part of its body that dooms it to extinction by poaching. These are images of violent penetration and death—paired with the most whimsical of poetic icebreakers. The repeated "There once was . . ." comes off as both blackly humorous and incantatory, commemorative and playful. This is Nicole Seymour's irreverent "bad environmentalism" along multiple tracks.

Mahato has related the kind of media-mixing and emotional curry she often cooks up in her work both to notions of environmental contamination and transcorporeality, as well as to the inherent multimodality of comics itself. Her reference to Anna Lowenhaupt Tsing's *The Mushroom at the End of the World* on symbiosis, commensalism, and collaboration among life forms[23] mirrors my discussion of comics as Mortonian ecological objects in part I of this study: "It's an entangled way of working and being in the world, which I see echoed in the way the comics medium works.... [I]n comics, word and image are in collaboration even when they're sharply defined against each other" (E. Harris).

Mahato sees further evidence for this outlook in the environmental diversity of the Pacific Northwest, at the intersection of ocean, mountains, and forest. As she told me:

> We have so many different ecosystems in this area, entangled and colliding with each other. It makes me think of all these histories, like when the Duwamish River was moved. And it does make me think that, in facing climate change, it's not about individual species or animals but the ecosystems in which they live. We might think about these resident orca whales on the one hand, but it's not just the marine environment that's at risk. Those threats are being caused by what's happening on land and resource extraction. That's one of the things that I'm really drawn to here: how the threats of climate change are so visible because of the multiple ecosystems that surround us. (personal interview)

Another word-image clash/collaboration manifests with a startling cumulative power in "IT'SALLOVER and Other Poems on Animals" (2020). If poetry is a constant fostering of unexpected encounters, a twisting of language into unfamiliar forms precisely to make weird connections that wouldn't come up in "normal" speech, then this piece disarms and devastates with its simple plea for humans to, basically, when it comes to mass extinctions, shut the fuck up. Well, of course, that's not all it's saying, but a burning rage about language and its obfuscations clearly fuels the thing.

Once more we see silhouettes of recognizable animals, these in odd colors (red dolphin, yellow elephant).[24] Overlaying these portraits, in harsh all-caps, Mahato writes the sort of empty platitudes that cling like barnacles to occasions for grieving: "THELASTIMETHELASTIMETHELASTIME..." over the dolphin, "THERETHERETHERE THERETHERE" over the elephant. Once more, the effect is paradoxical, dissonant. The wall of "SORRYSORRYSORRYSORRY SORRYSORRY..." over the picture of a deer expresses a deep sorrow, an admission of guilt and their opposite: hollow cliché. They are both a sincere acceptance of responsibility and the comics version of an air kiss.

Above all, "IT'SALLOVER..." is traumatic—but whose trauma do we mean? I might go so far as to say that the text overwhelms, obscures the animal pictures the way that banal phrases elide engagement. Note too that Mahato

> IT'SALLOVERIT'SALLOVERIT'SALLOVE SALLOVER
> RIT'SALLOVERIT'SALLOVERIT'SALLOVER ALLOV
> ERIT'SALLOVERIT'SALLOVERIT'SALLOVERIT'SALLOVE
> RIT'SALLOVERIT'SALLOVERIT'SALLOVERIT'SALLOVERIT
> 'SALLOVERIT'SALLOVERIT'SALLOVERIT'SALLOVERIT'SA
> LLOVERIT'SALLOVERIT'SALLOVERIT'SALLOVERIT'SALLO
> VERIT'SALLOVERIT'SALLOVERIT'SALLOVERIT'SALLOVERI
> T'SALLOVERIT'SALLOVERIT'SALLOVERIT'SALLOVERIT'
> SALLOVERIT'SALLOVERIT'SALLOVERIT'SALLOVERIT'SALL
> OVERIT'SALLOVERIT'SALLOVERIT'SALLOVERIT'SALLOVE
> RIT'SALLOVERIT'SALLOVERIT'SALLOVERIT'SALLOVERIT'
> SALLOVERIT'SALLOVERIT'SALLOVERIT'SALLOVERIT'SA
> LLOVERIT'S VERIT'SALLOVERIT'SALLOVERIT'SAL
> LOVERIT'SALLOVERIT'SALLOVERIT'SALLOVERIT'SALLOV
> ERIT'SALLOVERIT'SALLOVERIT'SALLOVERIT'SALLOVERIT'SA
> LLOVERIT'SALLOVERIT'SALLOVERIT'SALLOVE IT'SALL
> OVERIT'SALLOVERIT'SALLOVERIT'SALLOVERIT'SALLOV
> ERIT'SALLOVERIT'SALLOVERIT'SALLOVERIT'SALLOVERI

From Mita Mahato's "IT'SALLOVER and Other Poems on Animals" (2020). © Mita Mahato.

highlights some of the words or parts of them, once more drawing attention away from the deer, dolphin, elephant, etc. in question. The piece becomes less about mass extinction or fake people and more about the (futile) struggle to come up with an adequate response to the Anthropocene. (And what would "adequate" mean, anyway?) In this regard, I would relate the work to Andy Warhol's *Death in America* series (1964), made up of repeated duplicate photographs of US car accidents and other graphic carnage, colored and otherwise processed by Warhol such that the design elements start to take over from the grisly content. And also, paradoxically, not. In his Lacanian reading of *Death in America*, art historian Hal Foster maintains that "repetition serves to screen the real understood as traumatic. But this very need also *points* to the real, and at this point the real ruptures the screen of repetition" (132).

When I asked her about the role repetition plays in her work, Mahato replied:

> There is an element of the ritualistic through the repetition, but there's also a call to make your rituals meaningful. Repetition can empty things of meaning—they become habit, there's a loss of spirituality, and so on. How do you keep the ritual going in a way that remains meaningful? The repetition is a self-reflective moment for me, where I'm just repeating these trite words of compassion, [but] do they really do anything? And I'm hoping that in the process what will emerge is this animal above me,

atop of me, saying, "You are inadequate. And here I am." So I work in that ambiguity between joy and grief . . .

Sometimes I do question the value of art in addressing this huge crisis, species extinction, the end of the world as we know it, who it reaches, what it does. It satisfies a very individual need. (personal interview)

Works like "The Extinction Limericks" and "IT'SALLOVER . . ." embrace like few other contemporary comics Timothy Morton's formulation by way of the Talking Heads: "You *may* find yourself living in a mass extinction" (my emphasis). No coincidence that Mahato titled her 2017 collection *In Between*; she labors, in her words, betwixt joy and grief, but also between panels, in the gutters, in the hazy, shifting space between acceptance and denial. Precisely for its defiance of conventional comics design, for its ambiguity and self-reflexivity, Mahato's art embraces the vagueness, the here-and-not-here, the "subjunctive" quality of the Anthropocenic present.

ROGER FERNANDES: THERE IS NO DEATH

A conversation with Roger Fernandes cemented the notion for me that, as historian Coll Thrush puts it, "all environmental history is native history, because it has all happened on Indian land" (15). Fernandes, a member of the Lower Elwha S'Klallam Tribe on the Olympic Peninsula, works as an artist, storyteller, and educator devoted to preserving the cultural memory of western Washington's Coast Salish peoples. He has taught all over the Puget Sound region, including at the University of Washington and the Northwest Indian College.

Early in our talk, Fernandes underscored words attributed to Chief Seeathl, which he takes as his personal mantra. During negotiations for the 1855 Treaty of Point Elliott, which handed large swathes of land to the white settlers, the Native leader famously said: "Let the white man deal kindly with my people, for the dead are not powerless. Dead, did I say dead? There is no death, only a change of worlds" (quoted in Thrush 6).

"That always stayed with me," Fernandes told me. "Death is just transformation" (personal interview).[25] Though can we maintain that sort of equanimity in an era of disastrous human-induced pollution, mass extinction, and ecosystem collapse?[26] His comics story "Homecoming 2" (2021)[27] makes for a relevant test case, given its curious blend of Native metaphysics and fatalism.

In the six-pager, an unidentified balding man jumps from Seattle's Aurora Bridge, a large span over the Lake Washington Ship Canal notorious for suicides. (Since its construction in 1932, over two hundred people have jumped from the bridge, which reaches almost 170 feet above the frigid waters.) Over the next four impressionistic pages, the man's body floats in the murk (seen from below), where it seems to rejoin the elements and the ancestors (symbolized by salmon with Native markings), among other Native iconography. We follow the salmon and the river as they move on to the mountains. The man has "come home"—absorbed into the spirit world, the land, the environment.

"Homecoming 2" comes off as equal parts disturbing and reassuring. Why does the sad-looking man jump off the bridge? "I don't tell you," Fernandes said. "You have to fill in the blanks. That's Native storytelling. Everyone derives their own meaning. I didn't key the reader in, though to me the man's agency is powerful." He elaborates:

> My frame of death is not the Western frame, that it's the end, or that you have to wait to go to some place up in the sky. Instead, in this frame you enter the spirit world right away and your new life has begun in the spirit world. I didn't think in terms of the finality of someone committing suicide, the darkness of the person jumping off the bridge, ending their life. I thought of it in a Native way, that a person is moving on to another world, the spirit realm. He joins the salmon spirit. (personal interview)

A more feel-good, dare I say Disneyesque approach is employed in *Salmon Boy* (2013), a graphic novel that reworks a Northwest coast legend about the close relationship between humans and salmon,[28] giving it a contemporary twist worthy of the sci-fi TV series *Man from Atlantis* (1977). In the story, a group of Native kids in the 1960s is net-fishing a river, despite the fact that only a local fishery has the legal right to those waters. They unexpectedly catch a Native boy, who calls himself Swimmer, a representative of the Fish People below. He explains his fact-finding mission:

> The water is filled with poison! The water becomes warmer! There are stone walls blocking the way. Our journey has become harder every year . . .
> The Old Ones say the above people have forgotten the promise. We do not hear the prayers. . . .
> The Old Ones say if you have forgotten we will stop returning to the rivers.

The girl Maureen replies, "Swimmer, there are new people who do not believe the promises. They do not want us to believe. They say the earth belongs to them. They can do whatever they want. We have been fighting them. We will not forget."

Swimmer approaches the city in Roger Fernandes's *Salmon Boy* (2013). © Roger Fernandes.

Unfortunately, at this point two white men, one of them with a badge, violently arrest the kids, except for Swimmer, who manages to escape into the river. The authorities throw the book at Maureen: illegal fishing, resisting arrest, assaulting a police officer. Her testimony about Salmon Boy prompts a judge to cast doubt on her mental health. The court decides to keep her in custody, away from her parents, "while we determine if foster care is a preferable option." Here Fernandes alludes to the state's horrendous early twentieth-century history of removal of Native children from their families and placement in boarding schools for purposes of assimilation/wiping out of Native language and culture.

Salmon Boy part 1 ends on a cliffhanger, with a splash page in which Swimmer emerges from the waters of Puget Sound, his back to the reader, and strides toward the modern-day structures of Seattle. He has returned on a new mission: to gain more knowledge about the surface world to help the Old Ones decide the right path. How will the denizens of that great city receive the supernatural stranger? Better, let us hope, than this region has historically treated indigenous folk. The image powerfully recalls Thrush's contention about how modernity wipes Native lives out of the here and now, as if "Native history and urban history—and, indeed, Indians and cities—cannot coexist, and one must necessarily be eclipsed by the other" (Thrush 7–8). Part 1's ending poses a real challenge to that dichotomous way of thinking.[29]

Several times during our talk, Fernandes said he was "on a backwards journey" to unlearn the ways he was taught when growing up in Seattle, living away from the peninsula, the sacred Elwha River, and his tribe. To return as best he could to the understanding and beliefs of his ancestors. Some of this finds an echo in *Salmon Boy*, as when Swimmer repeatedly refers to himself in the first person plural ("They fought to protect us. . . . We trust them."), erasing distinctions between the individual and the collective.

Fernandes also made frequent references to another Chief Seeathl utterance: "The Earth does not belong to man, man belongs to the Earth."[30] He explained:

> My people, we belong to that river, the Elwha River. We are given life by that river, we do not own that river. The animals and plants there are equal nations. We need to make sure our lives are not built on their suffering.
>
> If you go back and look at the history, at past discussions of it, white people were always talking about "taming" the river. "Hey, if we tame the river, dam it up, we can get some power." It was always "We must tame the river, tame the wilderness, tame the Indian." What is it about Western culture that just can't let things be?
>
> In all my work I'm confronting that Western materialist, reductive "It" culture that turns living creatures into objects. I feel desperate to try to change that as fast and in whatever way I can. I have children. I have grandchildren. I don't want to leave this world with them on the edge of a cliff. So, "the Earth does not belong to man, man belongs to the Earth": that's my foundation. (personal interview)

Sadly, as the PNW's experience in summer 2021 would confirm, man has indeed taken the Earth and remade it—catastrophically.

JON STRONGBOW: A PERSON IS A LANGUAGE

As a child, Jon Strongbow (1954–2022) was riding with his father along a forested Pacific Northwest highway. "I remember thinking, 'Well, at least we're protecting the trees,'" he told me. "But my dad, who was a real advocate for the environment, said, 'Don't believe what you see.' I said, 'What do you mean?' And he stops the car. And he takes me into the tree line. He walks me through the trees about twenty feet in and—clear-cut. You just don't see it from the road. They just keep that pretty little picture by the road" (personal interview).

Recalling a similar scene in Powers's *The Overstory*, this "Potemkin forest" episode affected Strongbow deeply. *The trees are not what they seem.*

Along with Megan Kelso, the late Strongbow inspired this chapter on the PNW in a book about comics and the Anthropocene. To a considerable extent, he inspired the book itself. One of Seattle's true originals, an eccentric, clown, gonzo shaman, artist, musician, street seller beloved among the Pike Place Market community, Strongbow migrated here in childhood with his family from, as he put it, "the flatlands of Nebraska."

His multimedia arts practice came about through a combination of recovery from personal trauma, a love of US popular culture (especially comics, psychedelia, rock, and psychotronic cult cinema) and exposure to the spiritual teachings of the Red Cedar Circle (a community of Northwest coast First Peoples), the Tulalip tribe cultural ambassador Johnny Moses, and Tibetan Buddhism. As he explained in 2022: "Art comes from necessity. When you go insane, you need a cure for it. Graphic storytelling is a great way to heal your own madness, in a way. You start drawing and you don't know what's going to happen, you don't make an outline, you keep looking at the drawings and you keep doing drawings and pretty soon there's a story. Then you start wondering what the hell that story is" ("Nature and Climate Change").

Inspired in particular by "The Words of Chief Seattle,"[31] a 1988 short comics piece by French master Moebius (Jean Giraud)—which uncritically reproduces the historically dubious speech discussed earlier—Strongbow set about blurring the borders between the modern city and uncounted millennia of Indigenous history/culture. "[I wanted] to bring indigenous people, so-called primitives, into the urban environment, because we're starving for that here," he said. "I thought, 'Hey, I can do that here because this is Chief Seattle's city" ("Nature"). Indeed, as one journalist put it, "Much of Strongbow's art is specifically about the city he lived in, as both a commentary on and chronicle of how Seattle has changed over time" (Wilde).

Mostly self-published, Strongbow thrived on the fringes of the Seattle comics scene, exhibiting in taverns, galleries, and other nontraditional comics spaces. He also occasionally took part in events like the city's mainstays the

Short Run Comix & Arts Festival and Emerald City Comic Con. As recently as late 2022, you could find him on Mondays and Thursdays, hawking his prints, music, and comics in downtown Seattle's tourist-saturated Pike Place Market, where he had held court in a jester's hat since the late 1990s.

His work is not so much narrative driven, but rather composed of an ecosystem of images, archetypes, historical/mythological strata, collage, mélange (a word Strongbow liked throwing into conversations, e.g., "As the French say, it's a mélange")—a kind of dreamtime PNW. As discussed, this region seems to predispose artists toward the weird and eerie; Strongbow tapped into that vein more deeply than most through psychedelic, hallucinatory, and haunting images of extinct animals and Indigenous specters from around the world, all inhabiting the cityscape, walking its streets. He sold some of this imagery as black light posters, as well as in comics collections with multiple amended editions like *The Ocean of Time* (2008), *Mystic City* (2017), *The Hidden World* (1996/2017), *City of Spirits* (2017), and *A Walkabout Seattle* (2000/2013). *All One Life*, a posthumous collection of 3D versions of Strongbow's work, was released by Fantagraphics in 2023.[32]

"The land, the trees, they're like a nature park, with so many stories embedded in it, so many layers," Strongbow told me (personal interview). His experimental comics involve stripping those layers, palimpsest-like, so that they intermingle, bringing hidden things back to light. Furthermore, by "the land, the trees," he also means Seattle itself. This work is not about taking the viewer/reader out into the wilds of a forest or ocean, but keeping them in the city and showing how ancestors, dinosaurs, and mythological figures are already embedded there. The city is not separate from some pristine "natural" world.

Strongbow called his ongoing project—spread over several books, posters, and other media—*The Secret City*. He labored over it from 1992 until his death thirty years later. It brings together different temporalities against the "hyperframe" of recognizable Seattle locations (many of which no longer exist in this fast-changing city), to demonstrate that nothing is ever "gone." Those stories, those layers were always there, are still there, will forever remain. Hence, we see Native shamans, Wandjina spirits from Australia, Hopi Kachinas, etc. wandering the metropolis along with velociraptors, pterodactyls—and ordinary, living Seattlites.[33]

Indigenous peoples from around the globe ply the crowded avenues on their boats and canoes. Masai warriors levitate above the floor of the long-gone Broadway market. Tibetan monks worship a giant statue of Buddha perched atop the ruins of the old Music Hall (1929–1991) on Olive and Seventh. A herd of dinosaurs strides along the railroad tracks in the south of the city, near the baseball stadium. Disorienting by design, these potentially morbid black-and-white drawings, rife with stippling, still preserve a sense of play. They never take themselves too seriously. A picture of colossal Olmec heads cascading down onto Seattle's downtown is accompanied by the text: "If it ever starts raining Olmec heads, my advice would be to run for cover" (*The Ocean of Time*). A scene at the corner of John and Broadway, in the bustling Capitol Hill neighborhood, shows ancient spirits crossing the thoroughfare, among them a Sumerian bird-headed genius and the Egyptian god of the underworld Anubis.[34] The Rite-Aid Pharmacy's marquee, a remnant of the Society Theater (1911–1990), advises, "Don't forget to remember" (*The Hidden World*).[35]

In short, we may draw a direct line between *The Secret City*'s gothic visions and Chief Seeathl's speech, which Seattle journalist Eric Scigliano called "a ghost story like no other" (quoted in Thrush 6):

> And when the last red man shall have perished from the earth and his memory among the white men shall have become a myth, these shores will swarm with the invisible dead of my tribe; and when your children's children shall think themselves alone in the fields, the store, the shop, upon the highway, or in the silence of the pathless woods, they will not be alone. In all the earth there is no place dedicated to solitude. (5)

The chief's words find their echo today in the mouth of his descendant Ken Workman, a living member of the Duwamish:

> [I] say, well, an entire city, there are people all over the place, the bones, ten thousand years they're underneath the sidewalks, they're underneath the streets, they're underneath your houses, the buildings—they're everywhere. And so, if you want to help, just be respectful and know they're here. Don't think this land is yours. I know you have the deed to it and all that stuff. These people have been here for ten thousand years longer. And they're still there." (Garbacik xxxi)

And as Fernandes, too, took away from this discourse: There is no death, only transformation.

In our interview Strongbow discussed his process and approach, which he saw as an extension of his similarly freeform jazz-influenced music (or vice versa: the music was an extension of his artwork).[36] He chuckled when I suggested maybe the best way to read his comics is to have one of his albums playing at the same time:

> There's power in words and pictures. I wasn't setting out to draw a specific strip. I wanted the work to be touching on the narrative that exists in each person, without engaging them in a story. It's like walking down the street, the lost art of walking . . .

The idea is that without the spiritual presences, the energy of those ancestors in the city, we'd have to prop it up ourselves. Otherwise it's just a bunch of concrete.

A 2004 *Secret City* panel, "The Mask of Beauty," concretizes Strongbow's humanist vision. It shows Seattle's world-famous Space Needle close by in the distance, with Rangda, evil demon queen of Balinese mythology, staring at the viewer and dancing in what we might read as a menacing manner. To her right, dwarfed by her, stands a diminutive girl in a traditional Thai dancer's costume. She has just removed her mask, which resembles the face of a tusked Thai mythological giant. Beaming, she grins, seemingly on the verge of laughter. Though a single image (or mega-image), the piece implies a sequence, a before and after, as Strongbow himself confirmed. "You don't know what's underneath that scary mask," he told me. "Then she takes it off and—a little girl!" "It's like when you take off Darth Vader's mask and find a sick old man," I said. "Exactly!" Strongbow laughed. "Like that" (personal interview).

Photorealist cityscape, surrealism, and natural history come together in another *Secret City* drawing, "The Cosmic Sea."[37] Here a North African man[38] stands before a panoramic overlook of Seattle's skyscraper-strewn downtown and Interstate 5, which cuts through the center. The man holds a stick of some kind, with a cord attached to a jellyfish floating above, like a balloon. More than two dozen jellyfish and similar life forms fill the dark sky, luminous as if generating their own light, etched with a naturalist's eye for detail. (They would not look out of a place in a T Edward Bak comic.) As in so much of Strongbow's work, the juxtaposition of disparate temporospatial elements attains an ethical dimension. "We are connected to Everything! We just don't believe it!" the artist said of this piece on his website. This is a depiction of deep time coupled with dreamtime; for one thing, jellyfish are an unfathomably ancient species, with some estimated to be as much as 700 million years old.

But as the title "Cosmic Sea" also implies, we see here a reminder that the entire Pacific Northwest region was once underwater[39]—and given the accelerated pace of climate change, may be again, sooner than would otherwise have been the case. The piece, too, makes us grapple with our own complicity in these processes as moderns who consume fossil fuels. The many cars speeding down the highway, as well as the steel and glass city itself, are spewing greenhouse gases that only spur the planet's ecosystem to greater and greater instability. The jellyfish ghosts, though, will be fine. The spirit realm will always remain—but material, physical life on Earth will suffer greatly. Ultimately, this will include even the most privileged among us, likely up to the point of our own aided and abetted extinction. As Strongbow puts it, in words that disquiet as much as they stir: "The ocean of time knows no boundaries" (*The Ocean of Time*).

From Jon Strongbow's "Autobiography of a Tree" (2008). © The estate of Jon Strongbow.

Strongbow's work is heavy, macabre. Tragic, even, if you want to read it that way. But as noted, that weightiness is balanced out by a ludic, exuberant lightness of touch. He was as much jester as shaman—and never a mere scold. His "Autobiography of a Tree" (2008) bears out that characterization. While unconventional in form, this piece much more closely resembles a standard comics story than do the various *Secret City* publications. For one thing, sequentiality plays a crucial part in its design.

"Autobiography" unfolds through the conceit that one is reading an illustrated, machine-printed booklet handed out by a stranger on the street. The booklet's cover, a portrait of a tree, sports the title of the story and says it was written by "Connie Fir & Dee Sidyous." The rest of the work is mostly told in two-page spreads that show two hands, one at bottom left, the other at bottom right, holding up said booklet against a black background; we thus consume the piece through an unseen reader's point of view. Over some fourteen pages, the tree tells its tale in words and pictures, drawing on history, nature studies, and occult iconography to make an impassioned plea for kindness toward our leafy friends:

> Trees, like humans, enjoy being loved and touched,
> and hugged and appreciated. Trees, like humans,
> dislike being burned, gouged, ripped to shreds or
> turned into ticket stubs or bus transfers. Man likes
> to think that his suffering is unique and somehow
> important. His vision of God is a man nailed to a cross,
> but he fails to remember that the cross was made of wood,
> and the wood was once a tree. (*The Ocean of Time*)

In the course of reading, the booklet weaves its spell, as from one page to the next the "reader's" hands steadily transform into branches and leaves; skin dissolves into whorled bark. "I've gone to great lengths to get this message to you," the pamphlet says near the end. "In fact [...] I got pulped!" The "reader" finishes the pamphlet, holding it closed with his now-Groot-like hands. "I feel an urgent need to put down roots!" he concludes.

"Autobiography of a Tree" is a story about transformation, both of trees into paper and readers into trees. *We are connected to Everything! We just don't believe it!* It both evokes myths like that of Apollo and Daphne (minus the sexual violence) and anticipates a major theme of Powers's *The Overstory*, along with research into tree cognition, communication, and sentience pioneered by ecologist Suzanne Simard and forester Peter Wohlleben.[40] Strongbow told me about some of what inspired the piece: "I had a friend who decided to go out and cut trees, to make money. But he was too sensitive. When the tree started to fall, he would hear it screaming. So he stopped doing that" (personal interview).

Such a sentiment writ large informs much of Strongbow's big-hearted multimedia arts practice. While hardly a propagandist, he saw his work as a means to wake people up about the ecological crisis and other modern ills. As expressed on his website, he felt "a sort of urgency, in relation to what he saw as the wiping out of natural resources, not only in the form of trees and land and minerals, but of people and traditions." Or as he put it in our interview:

> Johnny Moses always told me: We kill things, we wipe out a species or humans, and each time we make something extinct we lose a part of ourselves. That goes for humans, flora, fauna, everything. A person is a language, they know things, they have a way of talking, a whole ecological system that's fragile. It's very sad. We can't afford to lose the creation, the people, the animal-people.

Sadly, Strongbow passed away in December 2022 after a long illness. His memorial celebration the next spring, held just steps away from his Pike Place Market haunts, was the most joyous and fun such event I've ever attended.

2021

> "You will not know whether the temperature is what it's 'supposed' to be."
> —MCKIBBEN, *THE END OF NATURE* 50

As noted, the comics of Megan Kelso, T Edward Bak, Mita Mahato, Roger Fernandes, and Jon Strongbow, grounded as they are in the Pacific Northwest, made me want to speak with them about the role of place in their work. But to tell the truth, there was one topic in particular that I wanted to ask them about: how they experienced the deadliest weather-related disaster in the history of the region.

From June 26 to July 2, 2021, a tall ridge of high-pressure air settled over the PNW, forming a barrier to the cooler wind from the Pacific Ocean, trapping and compressing heat. This heat dome brought appallingly high temperatures to a Northern people who routinely refer to the sixth month as "Junuary." Portland and Salem hit 112 degrees Fahrenheit, both new records. Eugene, Oregon, hit 108. Seattle reached 108, another all-time record. Lytton, British Columbia, saw 121. Then a wildfire destroyed the town. The Seattle light rail had to slow down due to the excessive heat on the tracks (Associated Press, "All-Time Records"). Just in Washington State, over 128 all-time high temperature records were shattered.[41] What made the event so deadly was not just the unheard-of heat, but the fact that it persisted over several days, with little relief at night. It was more than some could take.

More than 100 people in Washington died from the direct effects of the heat, with another 400 who died soon after listed as excessive deaths (Vogel et al. 1). In all, estimates put the heat dome's mortality rate from Oregon to British Columbia at 1,200 (Ryan, "Can Seattle Take the Heat?"). And that was just the humans. As many as a *billion* shellfish caught along the coast at low tide were baked to death (Ryan, "Extreme Heat"). Trees were scorched, some succumbed. Micaela Petrini of the Great Peninsula Conservancy (based in Bremerton, Washington) told me, for example, that she's observed the western red cedar experiencing a significant dieback in the area: "A lot of the research being done on it has ruled out fungus, pathogens, pests, disease, and other factors, leaving only climate change: It's just drought and heat that's killing them" (personal interview).[42]

And while we cannot directly attribute any one particular weather event to human-induced climate change, it's also true that year-on-year temperatures have been rising globally due to human-induced climate change. Those generally warmer conditions make events like the 2021 heat dome more severe when they do occur (Pulkkinen). In addition, those conditions, according to the climate models, will make such dramatic events more common (Vogel et al. 5).[43]

Still, I repeat, this region was not ready, and had long thought itself as not *needing* to be ready—even with all the headlines about climate change.[44] That had partly to do, I think, with the affluence and remoteness of the PNW.

So, the toll was also psychological. Solastalgic. Traumatically so.

"There was a naivety that this wouldn't affect us in the north-west," said one Seattlite. "People have recognized that this might happen in theory," noted a Seattle doctor, "but I don't think they expected it to happen. . . . They certainly didn't expect it to happen now, and they didn't expect it to be this bad" (Pulkkinen).[45]

I'd venture to say that most people here were like me. Atmospheric river? Sure, I know what that means; as mentioned above, I experienced my first less than a month after moving to Seattle. Heat dome? Someone had to explain it to me.

When it hit, Fernandes found himself with his family at the Columbia River gorge, along the border with Oregon:

> Where we were at, half the trees were red, burnt to a crisp, and the other half, in the shade, were green. So you have this witness of the trees. One of the stories that came out was that it was so hot that little baby birds—herons, eagles—were jumping out of the nests. They just could not take the heat. That, to me, is a powerful statement as to where we are right now. Life cannot maintain itself. The changes we've brought to the

environment, to the climate, they've reduced little baby birds to jumping out of their nests. It's almost like people jumping out of the Twin Towers as they were burning. They had decided, "I will not burn alive. I'm going to leave. I'll die another way." Like the man in my "Homecoming 2." (personal interview)

When our conversation turned to climate change and the heat wave, the class clown Strongbow came the closest in his interview to being glum, even angry:

The forest fires you get every year now, with all that smoke, it's so bad, oh, well, we're doomed. Unless we open up as individuals and start asserting the rights of the planet. We were meant to caretake the animals and the planet, not devour everything in sight. But we're all under the delusion of the almighty buck, chasing our tails, as we say. Chasing the almighty dollar. And that's the main problem. The whole system is set up as a death system, to destroy. And it starts to destroy people, people who are aware of the need for a change, who know that change has to happen, if there's going to be anything for humanity outside of a bleak, dreary, futuristic dystopic world....

Once you're made aware how your mind is being controlled by so many different aspects of modern life, not only media but the people who are holding the purse strings, the people that could easily change their ways of harvesting trees, easily change from gasoline to clean energy. It's going to happen eventually. If it doesn't, we'll all just fucking fuck off and die. (personal interview)

Mahato happened to be moving during the heat dome of all times. Hauling her stuff, driving by, she saw people on the street in the triple-digit temperatures. They seemed completely unmoved by what was happening:

I'm thinking: Why is everyone out on the street so happy? Why are they laughing? We're so miserable! It was funny....

Those people, I don't know what they were laughing about. I don't have the context. I don't want to be judgmental. But in my brain, what that was linked to was a certain obliviousness. When I think of joy, I don't think of oblivion. I don't think of denial. I don't think of repression.

When I think of the joy that comes out of grief, it's more about seeing differently. Because I think there is a side to grief that can be very disarming and very much about feeling stuck. And then there's that turn where you just can't see the same anymore. Your perspective has shifted. And I think of that as a space where—I still make art about this, though I have doubts about it now and again—this is a space where art can come in and say, "What can we do creatively about this crisis?" And then you start to find community. And then you start to find some answers.

I have severe doubts that our government will do anything about climate change. So then, where do I turn? What can shift policy? And, so finding those answers, I think, brings up—I don't even want to say a lightness to it, because I think joy can be heavy—so when I say joy I'm really talking about play and experimentation and the ability to see things new that sparks that "Oh!" That exuberance of seeing your way out of a place that feels stuck. . . .

[But] that joy and connection in my work is hard-won. (personal interview)

Kelso, who pondered my questions the longest before answering, told me about trying to cool off in her backyard during the heat dome, splashing water on herself, and how the water evaporated disturbingly fast. Then she too took a reflective turn:

I don't know how comics can address this. I know that comics do have a capacity for education . . .

I'll be honest: In terms of the work I do, I've always exempted myself from doing overt polemic. I like telling stories. I definitely have a political perspective, and I usually bring that into my work, but I wouldn't really describe my work as polemical. And I don't really want it to be, truth be told. But I also can't help having the feeling—that I think a lot of us are having—that's more like, "Well, when does it get so bad that we just all have to drop everything and work on the problem?" I think Mita has already decided that we're there, from looking at her recent work. I think she's already made that decision: "We're there. That's what we're working on now." And I don't think I'm there yet. And I do wonder, am I gonna get to that point where it seems pointless to do anything except try to put my shoulder to the wheel for climate change? (personal interview)

She added that, given all that's happened apart from climate change since the Trump administration, like the Supreme Court's 2022 Dobbs decision overturning *Roe v. Wade*, other matters felt to her, if not more urgent, certainly more in her lane as an artist: "Right now I'm more taken with the struggle for reproductive rights. That's in my face, I feel that's a problem at a scale that I feel more equipped to address through my comics" (personal interview).

Over breakfast in Portland, Bak answered to the effect that (as he argues in the passage from his podcast appearance, which I quoted above) we need to look at the system as a whole, not only at individual events, no matter how dramatic. Yes, the 2021 heat dome was horrific for the region's flora and fauna, but almost immediately, he maintained, they started to recover and continue to show resilience, as ecosystems tend to do. (Until they don't, of course, due to overwhelming stresses.)

None of this is to make Bak sound dismissive of climate change. Interestingly, it was both Bak, who has studied biology, and Fernandes, a Native tribe member with a close connection to the land, who tended to see these matters over a longer term, beyond human lifetimes. *There is no death.* A needed perspective. Maybe someday (sooner than we think?) that quip from the Seattle band the Postal Service's song "Sleeping In," about swimming any day in November, will come true. We'll be able to swim in Lake Washington any day in November. And to those people living in that future, it will likely seem normal. Natural.

In October 2019, my wife and I took advantage of my sabbatical year to move from Seattle to rural Washington. We resettled in unincorporated Longbranch, about ninety minutes south of the Emerald City, on the Key Peninsula in Pierce County. From now on, to get to work, I would need to take a ferry or cross the famous Tacoma Narrows Bridge, a.k.a. Galloping Gertie. We got a lot more animals, including goats and ducks.

The mere act of relocating from a city to a house on ten acres in the countryside, of course, changes your understanding of the world and especially of its environment. Cities are brilliant curations; they displace ecological rhythms in favor of their own. In our new home, we live with those rhythms intimately, every day. You feel them more, incorporate them into your being, learn the names of trees, plants, natives, and invasives. You see how the forest inhales and exhales, season after season. You can tell when it's stressed.

Stephanie LeMenager has written that climate change "represents, among other things, an assault on the everyday" ("Climate Change" 221).[46] Relatedly, Alexa Weik von Mossner argues, "When we try to envision climate change, most of us rather swiftly reach the limits of our imaginary abilities" (Weik von Mossner 139). Even in the middle of the sort of extreme weather event climate change models have long predicted, a sort of mental short circuit kicks in. Living it day by day, you're denying and not denying at the same time. *You may find yourself living in a mass extinction.*

So, what was my 2021 heat dome experience like?

Since I come from South Texas, the heat itself was not unfamiliar to me. But to have it here, in Longbranch, so far from where I grew up, felt like some kind of weird invasion. It was indeed like a war for my wife Kristin and me, because we just kept running around the whole time, trying to keep our animals alive, cooling, hydrating, shading, watering down. Taking fire. *Incoming.*

"We Live Here: Heat Wave" by José Alaniz. *The Key Peninsula News* (October, 2021). © José Alaniz.

We thought we had taken the right precautions—and we had, for a regular heat wave. But this was not that, and *it wouldn't stop*. A lingering, oppressive heat like I'd never known. The nights brought only minimal relief. Our animals were suffering. We thought we were going to lose them all. We thought, you know, we need to move them inside. We can't keep them alive out here.

I vividly recall one morning on day two or three. I hadn't slept well, my thoughts were consumed with our animals' welfare—*how will they make it through another day?*—when I saw the sun rising, peeking through the leaves, and already I felt it getting warmer again. I experienced a strong sense of dread.⁴⁷ *Incoming.* Later that day I was taking one of our ducks to a vet about forty minutes away. My car's thermometer registered the outside temperature: 113. *An assault on the everyday. You will not know whether the temperature is what it's "supposed" to be.*

The heat didn't just feel "unnatural." There was something eerily agentic and intentional seeming about it, like it had a mind of its own. A living presence. A predator, a dragon with flaming breath, too large to see, like in John Boorman's *Excalibur* (1981). More than that: It was like humans were pulling its strings. The heat dome was us (to differing degrees, as already discussed). And *us* definitely, meaning middle-class North Americans, living in the most wasteful, energy-bloated, fossil fuel–burning nation in history. Definitely us. That was the most uncanny aspect of the heat, that it was somehow ourselves refracted and reflected and magnified back, raining terror from the sky, from the sun, from everywhere. Take a deep, hot, stifling breath of us. *We* were what made most of the snow on Mount Rainier vanish virtually overnight.

If there's one phrase I'd use to describe my experience of the 2021 heat dome, I would say that the whole time it felt like the future. The future no longer as something you read about. The future as the Lacanian Real. Here and now.

The heat wave took two of our silkie chickens, Jean Grey on June 27 and Ororo Munroe on July 3. It would be more accurate to say that the heat wave exacerbated their underlying health conditions, especially for the elderly Jean Grey, and finished them off. I made a comic strip about what happened, which appeared in a local newspaper, *The Key Peninsula News.*

CODA: AN OBLIGATORY NOTE OF HOPE

In June 2023, I visited the Bellevue Arts Museum to see *Strange Weather*, a show of contemporary works that "explore the relationships and boundaries between bodies and the environment," as the literature put it. Despite the show's heavy hitters like Kehinde Wiley, it was actually a small painting in an adjoining exhibit in the museum's lobby that most caught my eye. This was part of a "20 Under 20" show, featuring works by youngsters who had responded to the prompt "Daydreaming."

A work in acrylic by Lora Kwon of Redmond High School, *Oddity* (2023), shows a young woman in a formal red dress and sunglasses, eating what look like McDonald's french fries as fast-rising waters flood the light rail train car in which she sits. The other passengers seem similarly nonchalant about the torrent; one's looking at her phone.

On the accompanying label, the artist reflects, "I painted a surrealist alternative universe in which I am the girl in red—boldly dressing as I please without a care of my surroundings." Though of course it was hard for me to not see this as a prophetic work, rather than a fantasy about an alternate life. Young Ms. Kwon, this is your future, I thought. Read another way, *Oddity* brilliantly captures the early twenty-first-century's persistent lack of engagement with climate change, especially in a country whose citizens, despite all the mounting evidence (mounting like those waters), "see[m] to have particular difficulties in registering the urgency of the issue" (Weik von Mossner 139).

UN Secretary General António Guterres seemed to have no such trouble when, at the twenty-seventh Climate Change Conference of the Parties (COP27) in November 2022, he declared, "We are on a highway to climate hell with our foot on the accelerator" (Carrington). Despite some middling progress, post-pandemic greenhouse gas emissions that year hit record highs, as did global temperatures. We're going in the wrong direction. The industrialized countries had already blown through any realistic hopes of keeping planetary warming to under 1.5 degrees centigrade above preindustrial levels, as called for under the 2015 Paris Agreement. With greater warming, our world would more and more resemble that greenhouse planet Venus.

Guterres still seemed pretty sure of himself the following month, when he told the United Nations Convention on Biological Diversity (CBD) summit in Montreal: "With our bottomless appetite for unchecked and unequal economic growth, humanity has become a weapon of mass extinction" (Einhorn and Leatherby). The (unenforceable) agreement that emerged from that international conference, dubbed "30 × 30," set an ambitious goal of protecting 30 percent of the world's land and water by 2030. Good luck with that.

My own temperament is such that, when mired in the most pessimistic doldrums while contemplating the Anthropocene, I seek not amelioration and comfort but affirmation. I turn to a writer like Mary Gaitskill, who says it like it is: "Perhaps—let's face it, probably—literature has moved on. We don't look at the physical world as we once did, and so we don't write about it as we once did. And that is just one way it is being taken for granted and abused to the point of destruction."

But if my reader still craves an obligatory note of hope, as Jenny Offill wryly calls it, then here's one. At the 2023 International Comic Arts Forum (ICAF) in Vancouver, Haida manga artist and environmental activist Michael Nicoll Yahgulanaas of the Haida nation devoted part of his keynote speech to what has come to be known as the Hummingbird Parable, a tale of the Quechua people of Peru. During a huge forest fire, a fearless hummingbird races back and forth, picking up water from a pond, carrying it in its beak, and dropping it on the fire. The other animals berate the hummingbird, "You're too small!

What good will your tiny drops of water do against that raging fire?" The hummingbird replies, "I'm doing what I can."

There's a middle ground, too, beyond despair and hope, where most of us actually live. Art helps us see it more clearly. LeMenager describes the matter well when she writes that "Cli-fi ... marks another way of living in the world—a world remade profoundly by climate change" ("Climate Change" 222). She adds: "It is at best a project of reinventing the everyday as a means of paying attention and preparing, collectively, a project of staying home and, in a sense distant from settler-colonialist mentalities, *making* home in a broken world" (225–26).

Washington poet Derek Sheffield's "What Will Keep Us" articulates well that moment of suspension, uncertainty, and threat of decline: "We trudge our miles, stepping over oscillating anemones in sunlit pools to pause at Hole-in-the-Wall and let their tentacles tongue our dipped fingers. And what's this holographic sheen? Not the oil we would keep from this shore, and not plastic, we see, just a rainbow's iridescence beaming from a plant" (60).

Is it oil or plastic they see, or a wild plant's healthy luminescence? It feels like a reprieve—if only a temporary one—when it turns out to be the latter. Given that Sheffield wrote that poem to commemorate the 2018 "Save Our Coast" hike to protest a Trump administration proposal to open the Olympic Peninsula coastline to offshore drilling, it too charts a moment of defiance, action, getting involved. Making home and protecting home, if you can. Increasingly, that is our Anthropocene zeitgeist.

We see further evidence for this "staying/making home" ethic in the comics representation of postapocalyptic settings in Sarah Welch's series *Holdouts* (2017), James Romberger's *Post-York* (2021), and Jonathan Case's *Little Monarchs* (2022), to name a few. Sarnath Banerjee's *All Quiet in Vikaspuri* (2015), on the water crisis in India, takes it as a given that we are living in a new world, too, while Pablo Fajardo, Sophie Tardy-Joubert, and Damien Roudeau's *Crude: A Memoir* (2021) reminds us to keep resisting even against hopeless odds.

Perhaps more striking are works in which climate change and mass extinction set the tone for more personal material that is at most tangentially related to the Anthropocene. I'm thinking of Kate Beaton's award-winning memoir *Ducks* (2022), as much about misogyny and sexual violence as it is about resource extraction. Alison Bechdel's navel-gazy *The Secret to Superhuman Strength* (2021) is mostly about how sports and fitness trends have affected the author's development, but it too occasionally breaks away from the mirror to acknowledge the environmental crisis and climate change, because again, that's just the world we live in now.

Leave it to the most well-known and highly lauded Pacific Northwest comics artist, Joe Sacco of Portland, to remind us that to stay/make a home, we first have to find it. Late in Sacco's nonfiction *Paying the Land* (2020), the young

Eugene Boulanger pauses to reflect in Joe Sacco's *Paying the Land* (2020). © Joe Sacco.

subject Eugene Boulanger, a Dene of the Canadian Northwest Territories, recounts a hunting trip in which he found himself alone in the mountains, gutting a downed caribou by a rushing river. In solitude, in the wilderness with his kill, Boulanger feels an intense sense of connection:

> I could hear the river beside me rushing down, and I thought the river sounds so beautiful.
> And I realized that sound had been happening here every year for thousands and thousands of years.
> ... I looked at the big rocks that I was standing on and realized how many countless thousands of moccasins have touched these rocks over the years. Big ones, small ones.
> How many hooves had clambered over these rocks over the years?
> I looked up behind me. There was this big mountain there.
> And I was like, Grandpa!
> It had this energy.
> Grandpa! (256–57)

As he does throughout *Paying the Land*, Sacco uses borderless, gutterless pages, with individual moments spilling onto each other, to depict his subjects' reveries and reported memories. Boulanger's story unfurls over three pages, in the course of which the hazy-edged panels diminish in number and get bigger. The scene culminates with a splash page mega-image of the tiny Boulanger, a mere speck in the lower left, as part of a vast landscape with mountains, river, pines. A place filled with his ancestors, in a sense made up of them. Reciprocity is key here. He gazes at—is part of—home/the ancestors, and home/the ancestors gaze(s) back at him: "I kind of felt like they were looking at me" (257). In more ways than one he is home.

Will he stay there? Will he make home in a broken world? We don't know; Boulanger finishes his story by saying, "And I just kind of thought, Huh, that's cool, and kept working" (259). Some readers might feel deflated, but that very ambiguity about the outcome, I believe, opens up some important opportunities.

In July 2024, I attended the inaugural Bloomberg Green Festival in Seattle. Among the many speakers, cutting-edge PowerPoints, the good and bad news about our climate situation that I heard at the event, the words of Washington's governor, Jay Inslee, stood out to me. Inslee's pronouncements on this matter carry considerable weight, since he has been at the forefront of this issue for years, even running in the 2020 Democratic presidential primaries as the "climate candidate." Among other things, the Inslee administration instituted the nation's toughest cap-and-trade program (called "cap and invest") in 2023.[48] During his stage interview the governor said:

> We live in a very special moment. . . . If you look at the whole scope of human history, there is no group of people that are more consequential for the whole species through time. There's been world wars, there's been bubonic plague, all these other things, but we live in the most consequential moment of human history because our ability to tame climate change is the one [factor] that will set the course for millennia, and we have to win.[49]

A crucial insight, but at the end of the day the climate issue is too important to be left entirely to politicians, even good ones. We're all in this.

One of the people I admire most in the world is my friend Leonard Rifas, an educator, activist, curator, publisher, and cartoonist. A long-ago transplant from the Bay Area, Rifas is one of Seattle's direct links to the underground comix scene of the 1960s/1970s. He has used comics to advocate for green causes and food justice, and against nuclear energy and fossil fuels. In 1980, his company Educomics published the first translated full-length manga in the West, Keiji Nakazawa's *Gen of Hiroshima* (better known as *Barefoot Gen*). He recently retired from Seattle Central College, but he keeps fighting the fight.

Along with Strongbow, Kelso, and Bak, I invited Rifas to take part in "Nature and Climate Change in PNW Comics," a panel I organized for the 2022 Emerald

City Comic Con. His talk that day proceeded from concepts outlined in Joanna Macy and Chris Johnstone's *Active Hope: How to Face the Mess We're in Without Going Crazy* (2012). Drawing on deep ecology, Buddhism, and general systems theory, Active Hope "is about becoming active participants in bringing about what we hope for," they write, adding, "Since Active Hope doesn't require our optimism, we can apply it even in areas where we feel hopeless" (3).

No obligatory hope? He had my attention. But it was the central role Rifas gave to both comics and uncertainty—how it makes Active Hope possible, in a sense how it makes effective resistance in our current era of horrors possible—that leads me to give him, in this book about comics in the Anthropocene, the last word.

He said:

One of the things that I think has been very demobilizing for people is living in a world where people do not treat crises as if they are crises. It's hard to believe in a global climate change crisis if we don't know anyone who acts like that's really the case. And so, in my classes I've brought in as guest speakers people who have sat down on railroad tracks to block oil trains, people who have turned the dial to shut off the flow of tar sands crude oil into the United States to refine. . . .

As with past activism in the 1970s that shut down nuclear power reactors scheduled for Washington state, in the last 15 years people have shut down the facilities that would have shipped fossil fuel to Asia. That's a kind of heroism, and if the media doesn't tell us these stories, it slows things way down. . . .

I still believe in comics. I still believe that if you want to convey information about what our situation is, what our options are in a way that is accessible to people, if you want to talk about visions and what we might be hoping for and what might still be possible, and if you want to talk about adventure and heroism, comics are there.

And it's the uncertainty that makes them worth doing, the not knowing whether it's going to do any good or not. ("Nature and Climate Change")

NOTES

INTRODUCTION: "WE ARE THE ASTEROID": COMICS AND THE "END OF NATURE"

1. This chapter's references to yearly global temperature averages are derived from https://earthobservatory.nasa.gov/world-of-change/global temperatures.

2. The moon's "Blue Area" first appeared in *Fantastic Four* vol. 1 #13 (Apr. 1963). Attilan was previously re-sited in *What If?* vol. 1 #30 (Dec. 1981).

3. Throughout this study, all comics emphases and ellipses are in original except where noted otherwise.

4. Supreme Headquarters International Espionage Law-Enforcement Division.

5. Putting it in the company of the TV series *Battlestar Galactica* (1979) and Chris Adrian's *The Children's Hospital* (2006), a novel in which a pediatric hospital transforms into a de facto ark to survive a latter-day biblical flood.

6. It happened in *Fantastic Four* vol. 1 #105 (Dec. 1970)—"Whole Earth José."

7. Morton defines hyperobjects as "massive entities distributed in time and space, in such a way that we can only point to tiny slices of them at a time" (*All Art* 34–35).

8. For more on multiscalar approaches to comic art, see the work of Susan M. Squier: https://www.graphicmedicine.org/scaling-up-graphic-medicine-susan-squiers-2018-conference-keynote-address//.

9. These include Erin James, David Herman, Sidney Dobrin, and others cited in this book.

10. The numerous industry figures who contributed just to the ongoing Attilan narrative include Byrne, Kirby, Lee, Ron Wilson, Joe Sinnott and Peter Gillis.

11. The booklet was created by April Anson et al., with support from the Association for the Study of Literature and Environment and others.

12. As she puts it, "There are plenty of troubling things about the Anthropocene. But to my mind, one of its most troubling dimensions is the sheer number of people it fails to trouble." Many of us who can relate feel stuck in Jennifer Lawrence's role in *Don't Look Up* (d. Adam McKay, 2021).

13. Stoermer coined the term in the 1980s. Crutzen and Stoermer popularized it at the turn of the century. On the term's prehistory and development, see Kolbert 183; Parham 1; and Lewis and Maslin.

14. A phrase that often appears in our media; for example, journalist Elizabeth Kolbert noted in 2014: "The fifth extinction, the one that did in the dinosaurs, was caused by an asteroid. Interestingly, today, you hear knowledgeable scientists say, '*We* are the asteroid'" (Dreifus).

15. On the disputes over the inapplicability of the term *Anthropocene* to geological classification schemes, namely stratigraphy, see Brannen. On the opposing side, Stephanie LeMenager argues that "the Anthropocene arises not as a geological epoch so much as a lived experience" ("Climate Change" 226).

16. More recent work has turned to plutonium signatures in the ocean for a precise determination of the start of the Anthropocene in its nuclear/Great Acceleration aspect (Yokoyama et al.).

17. In May 2024, the Anthropocene Working Group's proposal to designate a new geologic era was rejected by a vote of the Subcommission on Quaternary Stratigraphy. It must wait ten years to try again (Kaplan).

18. John Parham calls Romanticism a "calamity form" response to industrialization (13).

19. See Gottlieb and the selections in Stradling for useful historical treatments.

20. In 2018, Swedish teenager Greta Thunberg (b. 2003) declared a school strike and sat outside the national Parliament to protest government inaction on climate change. Others joined her. The country's leadership eventually agreed to more robust climate policies in keeping with the 2015 Paris Climate Accords. She went on to found the international climate strike movement Fridays for Future. Thunberg has become the face of climate activism, giving fiery speeches on the world stage, decrying public and government apathy and foot-dragging on the climate crisis. Other prominent figures in the movement include Ugandan climate activist Vanessa Nakate (b. 1996). She was a Fridays for Future representative in Uganda and founded the Rise Up Climate Movement, a major social justice movement in Africa. She has also actively campaigned against deforestation in the Congo.

21. Extinction Rebellion (XR) formed in London in 2018 and has since gained thousands of adherents and supporters worldwide. The nonhierarchical group has conducted mass street actions (including dressing up as polar bears to protest fossil fuels) and disrupted public transport, extracting some concessions on climate policy from the UK government. But some criticize its tactics and class/racial makeup (Shackle).

22. On groups that have further divided public opinion, such as Insulate Britain and Just Stop Oil (whose members have thrown soup at classic paintings), see Shackle.

23. Some details: "Two major reports released this month paint a grim portrait of the future for our planet's wildlife. First, the Living Planet Report from the World Wildlife Fund (WWF), published last week, found that in half a century, human activity has decimated global wildlife populations by an average of 68 percent. . . . All told, the drastic species decline tracked in this study 'signal a fundamentally broken relationship between humans and the natural world,' the WWF notes in a release" (McGreevey).

24. See Chauhan.

25. Ronald Reagan, the governor in question, actually said something else, but his words during his 1966 gubernatorial campaign were really no different in spirit from the famous misquote (see Mikkelson).

26. See Whitney.

27. See Nixon, "The Great Acceleration."

28. Where responsibility lies: a variant of Lenin's *Who Is to Blame?* As Malm puts it, "After denialism, this is emerging as the great divide in the debate on global warming" (390).

29. "Plantationocene is a historical 'de-soilization' of the Earth," according to Bruno Latour (591–92).

30. On these and other proposed terms, see Peterson and Uhlin 145; Parham 2; and Opperman and Iovino 11. Mark Bould proffers some parodic terms (7–8). See also Laura Marris's 2024 essay collection *The Age of Loneliness*, whose title is the literal meaning of E. O. Wilson's coinage, "Eremocene."

31. Dipesh Chakrabarty in his seminal 2009 essay "The Climate of History: Four Theses" most famously advanced the idea of humans as agential actors on the species level effecting global environmental change—to much blowback. See for example Vergès.

32. Stephanie LeMenager: "To know oneself as embodied in a deep, evolutionary sense may bring about both a profound remembering of ecological enmeshment and an invitation to forget one's specific history or relationship to power" ("Climate Change" 230).

33. In this it recalls the scene from Sergei Eisenstein's *The General Line* (1929) in which a grasshopper's call "becomes" the rumble of a tractor's engine; it's precisely because the film (like comics) is silent that it can make such evocative associations.

34. See also the comments on the utility of the term *Anthropocene* by Finney and Edwards, quoted in Wolford 1663fn1.

35. In November 2017, Pyron, a herpetologist and associate professor in the Department of Biological Sciences at George Washington University, published an op-ed, "We Don't Need To Save Endangered Species. Extinction Is Part of Evolution" in *The Washington Post*. After intense online backlash, Pyron posted a partial retraction on Facebook.

36. On the blowback Franzen received from the National Audubon Society and other environmentalist organizations for his critique, see Franzen 20–21. Yet Franzen was only anticipating a line of reasoning that has become more prominent since (see Wallace-Wells, "Has Climate Change Blinded Us").

37. Alaimo sheds a crucial light on the interactions among biological, climatic, economic, and political forces, writing, "Potent ethical and political possibilities emerge from the literal contact zone between human corporeality and more-than-human nature. Imagining human corporeality as trans-corporeality, in which the human is always intermeshed with the more-than-human world, underlines the extent to which the substance of the human is ultimately inseparable from 'the environment'" (2).

1. ART, AFFECT, AND THE ANTHROPOCENE

1. In a concurring opinion, Erin James writes: "An Anthropocene narrative theory argues that all novels have built into their foundations the attitudes and ideologies that produced the Anthropocene and climate change and thus, in this sense, are all representative of the epoch in their form" ("Narrative" 189).

2. Bracke discusses what goes into a definition of cli-fi in "Worldmaking Environmental Crisis" (169–72).

3. The Anthropocene thereby provokes what Lauren Berlant calls "genre flailing" (in short, experimentation); see Parham 4. We may in fact read, say, *The Puma Blues* as an example of

a "flailing genre": It has an unconventional antihero who does nothing throughout the narrative (as opposed to a more conventional comics depiction like Captain America) and an experimental, hard-to-follow anti-narrative structure.

4. On the intersections of colonialism, whiteness, and the Anthropocene, see LeMenager, "Climate Change" 227; Coates, *Between the World and Me* 152; and Yusoff.

5. See Emperor Wen's lament from 163 BCE. Another highlight: Titania's soliloquy on the "progeny of evils" wrought on nature by her quarrel with Oberon in Act II, Scene 1 of Shakespeare's *A Midsummer Night's Dream* (1605).

6. Noheden sees von Trier's work as evocative of Morton's dark ecology (137).

7. Though nature shows are problematic for their profound constructedness. See Burt 47–48.

8. Modern art too has explored the affectual relation to the Anthropocene, as seen in the video art of Cecilia Condit (Woodward, "The Feeling of Freedom") and Marina Zurkow. See also the indigenous representations examined by Monani.

9. Much of Carson's work carried a powerful affective charge. See Lockwood.

10. Notable figures in the development of affect theory include Sara Ahmed and the late Lauren Berlant (see Berlant, *Cruel Optimism*). According to Patricia Clough, "the turn to affect . . . returned critical theory and cultural criticism to bodily matter, which had been treated in terms of various constructionisms under the influence of poststructuralism and deconstruction. The turn to affect points instead to a dynamism immanent to bodily matter and matter generally" (206–7). Mel Chen argues that "affect is something not necessarily corporeal and that it potentially engages many bodies at once, rather than (only) being contained as an emotion within a single body. Affect inheres in the capacity to affect and be affected" (11). For a useful discussion of affect and the Anthropocene, see Bladow and Ladino 4.

11. I deal with this and similar notions of new materialist "vibrant matter" in this study's chapter devoted to the Black Panther's Wakanda.

12. Listen to a dreary example of rage involving an osprey cam at https://www.thisamericanlife.org/545/if-you-dont-have-anything-nice-to-say-say-it-in-all-caps/act-three-0.

13. See also Sarah Ensor's concept of "spinster ecology." For a good primer on queer studies' intervention in the environmental humanities, see Bladow and Ladino 9.

14. Such norms hold sway even among scientists with a front seat view of the Anthropocene. At a 2016 American Geophysical Union meeting in San Francisco, paleoclimatologist Kim Cobb spoke candidly: "It has been a very tough year for me personally, having scuba dived on a reef in the far reaches of the tropical Pacific, and watching 85 percent of that reef die between one of my trips and the next in six months . . . We have for too long, as scientists, rested on the assumption that by providing indisputable facts and great data that we are providing enough, . . . and obviously that strategy has failed miserably. . . . But the public and policymakers simply don't speak our language, and this is why we need to know when to shed the mantle of scientific authority and speak from the heart. We need to let our emotions shine through; we need to become storytellers" (Kalmus: "To My").

15. Among the memorable 1970s TV PSAs I grew up with, I would also count a highly disturbing one that showed a shooting gallery with targets in the shape of trees, which were blown up by gunfire.

16. It starred Iron Eyes Cody, an actor of Sicilian, not Native American, heritage and was produced by America the Beautiful, an anti-littering nonprofit funded by, among others, soft drink companies Pepsi and Coca-Cola.

17. Such critics have in mind statements like those delivered at the United Nations Climate Action Summit in New York in September 2019: "You have stolen my dreams and my childhood with your empty words." Thunberg even drew commentary from the tweeter-in-chief himself, who concluded with "Chill Greta, Chill!" See it if you must at https://twitter.com/realdonaldtrump/status/1205100602025545730?lang=en.

18. See also Lockwood and Keen—the latter addressing graphic narrative.

19. "Over the top" has its virtues when talking about the Anthropocene, argues Michael Mann.

20. Relatedly, John Raymond's cli-fi novel *Denial* (2022) leans into the trend to depict Anthropocenic change in a matter-of-fact, *fait accompli* key. According to Frederick Buell, the ecological crisis has become "part of people's daily, domestic experience . . . problems that people now cope with daily, not just nightmares the future will bring more fully out" (280).

21. Other such reports include one released in 2012 by the National Wildlife Federation on the psychological effects of climate change, which predicted that over 200 million Americans would be affected. A 2018 Yale survey partly validated that claim (Scher).

22. Oklahoma Senator James Inhofe's speech delivered in Congress during a 2015 polar vortex event in Washington, DC, during which he displayed a snowball in a Ziploc bag to "disprove" the global warming thesis, has become a classic of such denialist discourse.

23. See Pihkala for a useful summary. In a previous era, some of these terms penetrated into the wider culture, as attested by conservative columnist David Brooks, who in 1987 addressed "earthgrief, a term used . . . to describe the sadness we should feel about the coming destruction of our planet" (91).

24. At the inaugural Cody Summer Institute in the Environmental Humanities in 2019, Stephanie LeMenager likened humans' relationship to the planetary commons to palliative care for the terminally ill.

25. Drawing on my own off-topic reading for moments of Anthropocenic horror/regret, I offer Francisco Cantú's 2018 memoir *The Line Becomes a River: Dispatches from the Border*, in which a retired New Mexico contractor describes a guilt that "visit[ed] him even in his sleep. It's overwhelming sometimes, he said, to think of all the trees I've killed, all the scars I've left on the land" (128). Russian comics artist Olga Lavrenteva channels not regret but outrage to document the destruction of her beloved Karelian Isthmus, near St. Petersburg, to industrial interests in *My Own Atlantis* (2023), portions of which she posted online.

26. See also Gardner. "Trace" language risks obscuring that fact that, as Hatfield usefully reminds, we are still dealing here with a convention of publishing, encountered in reproduction, after several layers of processing and assembly by diverse hands: "To speak of his *presence* or touch on the page, or on the board, is *ipso facto* to indulge in metaphor" (*Hand of Fire* 47).

27. See Williams. For "body genre" tropes in comics, see Alaniz, "'Rutting in Free Fall'" and "Speaking the 'Truth.'"

28. A term originally coined by Beth Dempster; see Haraway chapter 3.

29. Clare's thought strongly resonates with Morton's dark ecology, which compels us to love the partial and impure, "to love the disgusting, inert, and meaningless. Ecological politics

must constantly and ruthlessly reframe our view of the ecological: the monstrous thing.... The most ethical act is to love the other precisely in their artificiality, rather than seeking to prove their naturalness and authenticity" (*Ecology Without Nature* 195). They go further: "We choose this poisoned ground. We will be equal to this senseless actuality. Ecology may be without nature. But it is not without us" (*Ecology Without Nature* 205). Kristoffer Noheden describes dark ecology as "conceiv[ing] of the world as a dense mesh in which everything is interconnected, but this is not cosy holism. The mesh twists and turns, generating riddles and distorting perspectives like a maze filled with so many funhouse mirrors. The world as seen through the mesh is more a Gothic mansion than an emerald-green meadow" (137).

30. See also Kafer. On the related matter of racial/ethnic others likened to invasive species, see Hook.

2. NATURE, COMICS, AND THE MEGA-IMAGE

1. See S. Lee, *Son of Origins* 206 and Hatfield, *Hand of Fire* 133, 135.

2. I derive annual estimates on atmospheric carbon from the National Oceanic and Atmospheric Administration's Global Monitoring Laboratory, at https://gml.noaa.gov/ccgg/trends/.

3. Wright wrote more sedately, declaring it "prone to existential musings and outraged moralizing on such human maladies as war, environmental destruction and famine" (*Comic*: 233).

4. For a brief history of atmospheric ozone depletion due to man-made CFCs, which entered public consciousness in the 1970s, see Kolbert 184–85.

5. See Dunaway, "Gas Masks" 71–73 for a discussion of the ubiquitous presence of people in gas masks and similar gear in 1970s US representations of the ecological crisis after the first Earth Day. One famous example appeared in *Life* magazine in January 1970, of a woman pushing a child in a stroller, with a look of "ready equanimity."

6. Lawrence Buell coined the term "environmental imagination" in his 1995 book of the same name.

7. I'm thinking of what Hatfield calls the undivided polyptych "suggesting a character's timeless immersion in a rich, diverting space" (*Alternative Comics* 53). See also Loss, "Profluent Lingering" and "Poetry Comics" on "profluent lingering" in graphic narrative.

8. I am, by the way, far from wedded to this term; few things would depress me more than to give a talk where someone mishears me as saying, "MAGA-image."

9. Similarly, Andrei Molotiu defines "splash page" as "a single-panel page. Often the title page (for which, indeed, the terms was originally reserved), in which case it may be used for the depiction of a crucial story moment out of narrative continuity, for a montage panel symbolic of the story's themes, etc." ("List of Terms").

10. See Andrei Molotiu's concept of iconostasis or the "perception of the layout of a comics page as a unified composition" ("Abstract Form" 91). This section's various cited modes of addressing narrative arrest in comics both owe something to and contend with Gotthold Ephraim Lessing's notion of the "pregnant moment" in visual art (thanks to Charles Hatfield for that insight). See Karin Kukkonen's discussion of same in "Comics as a Test Case."

11. Relatedly, see Timothy Morton's comments on ekphrasis as time/narrative suspension: "Vivid description slows down or suspends narrative time" (*Ecology Without Nature* 44), which they relate to the subjective experiencing of the Anthropocene.

12. Kirby's collages take this a step further into abstraction, to evoke worlds beyond conventional human perception (Bukatman, *Hellboy's World* 67–68). For more on Kirby's collages, see Bukatman, "Kirby."

13. See James, *Narrative* 110–11 for a discussion of narration "vs." description.

14. Pericolo elaborates: "In adopting, combining, and adjusting these pictorial conventions, Caravaggio above all planned to steer the beholder's attention toward a three-pronged, virtually contradictory approach to the picture. More concretely, the viewer, who is spontaneously induced to experience the scene in its closeness, immediacy, and intelligibility, winds up enticed into a process of comprehension that instead triggers distance, duration, and ambivalence. By manipulating the perception of space and time as interplaying factors in the reading of a pictorial narrative, Caravaggio succeeded in involving the beholder in the mechanism of recognition, or anagnorisis, potentially inherent in *The Supper at Emmaus*: like the apostles, though on a different level, viewers may hesitate to recognize or decipher the acting figure of Jesus" (528–29).

15. Though I don't relish making too many fast and loose comparisons between cinema and comics, we might to an extent also liken what I call the "mega-image" to *Matrix*-style "bullet time" and freeze-frames in the movies. Those too split the difference between pure spectacle and narrative flow. Tom Gunning's "cinema of attractions" concept (derived from Eisenstein) also has some relevance here. As noted, it was Peterson and Uhlin's Anthropocenic reading of the Hitchcockian "vertigo zoom" that first launched me on this train of thought.

16. In ways that resonate with Morton's "subjunctive mode" and the "weird," Ghosh advances the uncanny as a primary mode for artists to represent the Anthropocene, to engage with imagery and themes of a fundamentally altered world. As he told an interviewer: "As soon as you conceive of your object as something called 'climate change,' your work dissolves. What you have to be writing about is actually your changed reality" (Paulson). The Anthropocenic mega-image, a manifestation of the uncanny in comics form, does just that.

17. Jeet Heer notes that "the inevitable and unstoppable passage of time was something King often thought about, as was the idea that the family was part of the larger cycle of life" (iii).

18. Ware's comments in this paragraph come from his exhibit description to "Chicago: Where Comics Came to Life" (2021), which he cocurated. Seeing some of these Sunday pages as mammoth, wall-size reproductions definitely made an impact on me. The exhibit's unique format enhanced the sense of immersion, as the work came to swallow up one's entire field of vision (see Alaniz, "A Review Essay").

19. This 1940 specimen precedes even Jack Kirby's first use of the double-page spread in Captain America, which debuted the following year.

20. Dodd's series was even honored with a wilderness trail (Dobrin, "EcoComix" 4).

21. Post-Dodd artist Jack Elrod took such moments to new comedic heights. See for example the *Mark Trail* for August 6, 1996, in which odd speech balloon placement seems to indicate that a goose wandering the grounds outside our hero's cabin is the one speaking, instead of Trail.

22. That said, Vold rightly points out that the series did nothing to challenge the heteronormativity and white-centeredness of the conservation movements of the time (71–72).

23. Kelly remains in high regard as one of the masters of twentieth-century comic art. In 2021, Ohio State University's Billy Ireland Cartoon Library & Museum organized the exhibit "Into the Swamp: The Social and Political Satire of Walt Kelly's *Pogo*." *Pogo* also got a postage stamp (Dobrin, "EcoComix" 4).

24. Cremins elaborates: "While Lovecraft and later comic book writers including Steve Gerber and Alan Moore depicted the swamp as a trapdoor to other dimensions and unspeakable evil, Kelly invented an 'imagined geography' in which complex social problems including racism, segregation, war, political strife, and environmental blight could be contained and resolved with humor, compassion, and often surreal wordplay" (30).

25. As noted by Dunaway, "the one quotation repeated most frequently to explain the origins of the crisis was first uttered not by a leading ecologist or political activist, but rather by a comic strip character: Pogo the Possum" ("Gas Masks" 78). The *Saturday Review* reported in March 1970 that a "White House Council on Environmental Quality—an advisory body appointed by President Richard Nixon—had quoted the cartoon character at a recent meeting" (Dunaway, "Gas Masks" 80). Pogo's famous phrase appeared on lapel buttons, flyers, and banners and as part of a major exhibition, "Can Man Survive?" at the Museum of Natural History, which ran from 1969 to 1971 (80–81).

26. Kelly wrote in 1972: "The big polluter did not start out with smokestacks. He didn't start pumping gunk into the waters of our world when he was six years old. He started small. Throwing papers underfoot in the streets, heaving old bottles into vacant lots, leaving the remnants of a picnic in the fields and woodlands. Just like the rest of us. At last the stuff is catching up to us. Man has turned out to be his own worst enemy" (W. Kelly).

27. See Dunaway, "Gas Masks" for a discussion of the visual culture around the first Earth Day and how media discourses of the era tended to elide or obfuscate systemic factors that disproportionately affected the poor and people of color.

28. See an account of their enactment in Gottlieb 175–85.

29. See Wright chapter 8.

30. Two other comics works from this era stand out for me in terms of their treatment of environmental themes: the Steve Englehart/Marshall Rogers series *Coyote* (first appearance 1981) from Eclipse and Marvel; and the heartstrings-tugging Bradburyan story "Ride the Blue Bus" by Bruce Jones and George Pérez in *Alien Worlds* #7 (Apr. 1984) from Pacific Comics. In the latter, a young boy living in a postapocalyptic zone glimpses a green Edenic space through virtual-reality technology. "Oh, it's *wonderful!*" he exclaims. "The *trees!* The *trees!*" Devastating.

31. "Dying in Paradise" by Don McGregor and Jim Lee in *Marvel Comics Presents* #33 (Nov. 1989) again utilizes Namor to treat an environmental theme, here in response to the March 1989 Exxon Valdez oil spill.

32. See Richard Reynolds's comments on the traditional passivity of the superhero, who "is not called upon to act unless the status quo is threatened by the villain's plans" (50–51).

33. The vexed issue of poor and working-class people from developing nations, mostly BIPOC, participating in the destruction of ecosystems out of need but also greed animates much discussion in the environmental humanities. As Timothy Clark argues, "One cannot polarise into good and bad what is really a grey and uncertain gradation between victimhood and complicity, passive acquiesence and active cooperation in unsustainable forms of exploitation" (*The Value of Ecocriticism* 140).

34. Interesing phrasing. What's this "your world"? The Brazilian worker's dialogue underscores the perception that those in the developing and developed worlds live on different planets (they don't). It also anticipates the words of Tosi Mpanu Mpanu, the Democratic Republic of Congo's lead representative on climate issues, when he announced in 2022 that

his country would auction off vast tracts of old-growth rainforest to oil and gas interests (Maclean and Searcey).

35. To in a sense reassure the reader that they are still reading a bona fide Superman story, the comic references the character's long history: He lifts a car overhead (evoking the cover of *Action Comics* #1, the figure's 1938 debut); bystanders exlaim, "Look! Up in sky!," a phrase whose origins date to the 1940 Superman radio serial; he patrols Earth from orbit as in the 1978 film *Superman*; also recalling that film, he holds up Pa Kent's truck during a repair job.

36. *Superman for Earth* belongs to a trend of post-*Watchmen* comics that explored the limits of the superhero genre in the modern world. Representative works include Dini and Ross's *Wonder Woman: Spirit of Truth* (2002), in which the heroine is attacked for her revealing attire by the conservative Muslims she's trying to help; Dematteis and Sharp's *Superman: Death Where Is Thy Sting* (2001); and Ellis and Nielsen's *Avengers: Ruins* (1995). The high/low point of this literature is Alan Moore and Rick Veitch's satirical "The Story of the Year" in *Supreme: The New Adventures* #44 (Jan. 1997).

37. The inside cover proudly states, "Printed on American Eagle 61 lbs, 50% recycled paper from Westvaco, cover printed on Cornwall CIS 10 pts, 50% recycled paper from Domtar."

38. This also applies to Grant Morrison and Richard Case's genderqueer Danny the Street, introduced in *Doom Patrol* vol. 2 #35 (Aug. 1990), which figures as an urban counterpart to "natural" characters like Krakoa.

39. As Sean Parson writes, "the Green represents a 'town hall' or public agora for the chlorphillic [sic] world."

40. Swamp Thing himself becomes a "mega-monster" like the original Krakoa and attacks Gotham City in a winking metatextual storyline that culminates in *Swamp Thing* vol. 2 #53 (Oct. 1986). Talk about plant sentience.

41. On sexuality and Swamp Thing, see also Alaniz, "'Rutting in Free Fall"; B. Johnson; and Costello.

42. Ghosh told an interviewer: "What I really look for in writing that interests me is a recognition of this—that we are in a completely different world—and that we can no longer write about the world as if it were the world from 30 years ago" (Sinha).

43. As Adele Haverty Bealer puts it, "*Concrete* is best read as a hybrid of material memoir and ecobiography" (181).

44. Leopold titled one of the sections in *A Sand County Almanac* "Thinking Like a Mountain." The phrase has been taken up as a mantra by many in the environmentalist movement.

45. Porcellino's *King-Cat* (launched 1989) and Jenny Zervakis's *Strange Growths* (1991–1997), two preeminent minicomix series that often explore ecological themes, deserve more scrutiny from Environmental Humanities scholars.

46. Charles Hatfield coined the term "technological sublime" for Jack Kirby's depiction of near-psychedelic machinery (*Hand of Fire* chapter 4). Oddly, Porcellino's descriptions of the plant echo Lee and Kirby's Wakandan "mechanical jungle" in the *Fantastic Four* series. See my discussion of same in chapter 6.

47. In the book's introduction, Porcellino explains: "[I'm] certainly not proud of what I did as a mosquito man; in fact, I feel downright ashamed." He produced "Chemical Plant/Another World" especially for this collection (in summer 2004), as if it took several years for the author to fully process the ethical consequences of what he was doing before committing

to paper. Porcellino dedicates the book "with love, to mosquitoes, men, women, and all beings; grasses, rocks, fences and sky."

48. The original version of "Here" appeared in *Raw*, vol. 2 #1 (1989). Chris Ware among others have cited it as catalyzing for their own work.

49. Kuper mounted an exhibit of another nature-related work, "INterSECTS: Where Arthropods and Humans Meet," at the New York Public Library in 2022.

50. See also James's longer discussion of *Here* (*Narrative* 135–38). Michael Chaney presents a balanced view of the graphic novel's purported posthumanism: "McGuire's premise enables a departure from the tyranny of the human altogether," but at the same time, "the possibilities the book suggests for rethinking the primacy of the humans in terms of place are likewise biased, eventually giving way to a decidedly human preference, not to mention a specific regional affiliation—New England and colonial history" (*Reading Lessons in Seeing* 177–78). On posthumanism and the graphic novel in Latin America, with Alexis Figueroa and Claudio Romo's graphic novel *Informe Tunguska* (Chile, 2009) as case study, see King and Page chapter 6.

51. Kuper has worked in comics since the 1970s, on such series as *Mad*, *World War 3 Illustrated*, and his own graphic novels. His work represents a link between the underground comix era and modern graphic narrative. *Ruins* won a 2016 Eisner Award, the industry's highest honor.

52. Or butterflies; a nonhuman, insect subject introduces a degree of ambiguity.

53. He's referring to a foldout section in Kevin Huizenga's *Gloriana* 2001.

54. See Bracke 175–79 for an analysis of comparable strategies from Barbara Kingsolver in her 2012 novel *Flight Behavior*.

55. Perhaps a relative of Warren Worthington III, filthy rich alter ego of the X-Men's Angel.

56. The ocean's largest pacific gyre (massive circular currents), the Great Pacific Patch, lies halfway between Hawaii and California. It contains at least 79,000 tons of plastic, claims the Ocean Cleanup Foundation (Roth).

57. To say nothing of the use of *Peanuts* figures for a 1970s environmentalist campaign (see Vold 74).

58. With the rise of newspaper strips at the turn of the twentieth century, especially in the US, animals appeared as sidekicks or companions, e.g., the pit bull terrier Tige in Richard Outcault's *Buster Brown* (1902–ca. 1921). Often these animals (dogs, cats, rabbits) figure as "out of control" elements of chaos, as seen in James Swinnerton's *Jimmy* (a.k.a. *Little Jimmy*, 1904–1958) and Winsor McCay's *Little Nemo in Slumberland* (1905–1926).

Avoiding the obvious examples everyone knows, among the notable and more obscure animal protagonists or supporting cast members in comics I would name Edwina Dumm's pit bull terrier Tippie; the trained seal Battler from Steve Broder's Kinks Mason stories; Bingo the intelligent kangaroo in S. M. Iger and Jerry Winters's *Kangaroo Man*; Superman's pet Krypto the Superdog, created by Otto Binder and Curt Swan. For much fuller surveys and treatments of animals in comics, see Alaniz, "Animals" and Yezbick, "Lions."

59. Similarly, commenting on Art Spiegelman's celebrated Holocaust graphic memoir *Maus* (1986–1991), which employs a "hybrid bodies" trope of mouse heads to represent Jews, Katalin Orbán argues "the empty gaze—and the animal head that serves the same purpose in Spiegelman's work—evokes not only a *connection* but also a *disconnection*. Besides the connection of blindness and understanding, it also evokes that dissociation of sight and comprehension that is central to trauma and a recurring element in the Holocaust survivors' accounts" (63).

60. Elsewhere, Burt adds on this vexed issue of representation: "It is usually argued that the exploitation of visual imagery for the purposes of animal rights is due to the fact that animals cannot speak up for themselves, so the message is in greater need of visual reinforcement than, presumably, for issues of human rights. In fact, the actual power of this imagery derives from a much longer term concern over public codes concerning what should and should not be seen" (168).

61. See my discussion, after Elisabeth Bronfen and Sarah Godwin, of death's resistance to representation leading to the corpse's polysemic potential in comics (Alaniz, *Death, Disability, and the Superhero* 162–63 and chapter 9).

62. Though Bezan calls it into question as corrosive of agency and on other grounds; she advances a different approach, proceeding in part from vitalist philosophy. See especially 191–94.

63. As noted, the introduction of an animal into a civilized human setting often sets off scenes of chaos. To cite a non-comics example: "Never Name a Duck," an episode from season 2 of *The Dick Van Dyke* show, which aired on September 26, 1962.

64. Visions as varied as the suffering, Christlike animal from Grant Morrison and Chas Truog's "Coyote Gospel" in *Animal Man* #5 (Dec. 1988), Jay Hosler's *Clan Apis* (1998), and Gerry Alanguilan's *Elmer* (2010) seem descended from this line.

65. The foregoing makes works that challenge conventional anthropocentric comics form all the more critical. I'm thinking of examples like Ilan Manouach's *Les lieux et les choses qui entouraient les gens désormais* (2003) and Pedro Franz's "Dead Horses Remains on Highway" (2016). See also Alaniz, "In the Empire."

66. Alternatively, Nikkilä and Vuorrine argue that we could read these "tears" as emanata indicating an inner state in turmoil, though to me they seem too naturalistically drawn for that purpose.

67. In fact, *The Isthmus* bears comparison to recent documentary cinema centering animal mothers, such as the pig in *Gunda* (d. Viktor Kossakovsky, Russia, 2020) and the cow in *Cow* (d. Andrea Arnold, USA, 2021).

3. COMICS AS ECOLOGICAL OBJECTS

1. Other media scholars have come to this fork in the road as well. For example, in their introduction to *Cinema and the Environment in Eastern Europe*, Masha Shpolberg and Lukas Brasiskis work through what they and others see as a crucial distinction between "ecocinema" and "environmental cinema," arguing for the former as deeply involved with questions of form rather than narrative, theme, genre—in short, content. Their "inclusive, process-oriented vision of ecocinema" means they are "far less interested in adjudicating what 'counts' as ecocinema than in learning to see films—all films—eco-critically" (8).

2. Morton tends to define these as objects "massively distributed in time and space in ways that baffle humans and make interacting with them fascinating, disturbing, problematic, and wondrous" (*Hyperobjects* 58; on the page preceding, Morton uses a Tom Gauld comic to advance the concept).

3. See Roux; Noheden; and Meis for useful, concise summaries.

4. They elaborate: "Ecology shows us that all things are connected. *The ecological thought is the thinking of interconnectedness. The ecological thought is a thought about ecology, but

it's also a thinking that is ecological. Thinking the ecological thought is part of an ecological project. The ecological thought doesn't just occur 'in the mind.' It's a practice and a process of becoming fully aware of how human beings are connected with other beings—animal, vegetable or mineral" (*The Ecological Thought* 7).

5. Cronon adds: "The dream of an unworked natural landscape is very much the fantasy of people who have never themselves had to work the land to make a living—urban folk for whom food comes from a supermarket or a restaurant instead of a field, and for whom the wooden houses in which they live and work apparently have no meaningful connection to the forests in which trees grow and die" ("The Trouble with Wilderness" 16–17) and "The removal of Indians to create an 'uninhabited wilderness'—uninhabited as never before in the human history of the place—reminds us just how invented, just how constructed, the American wilderness really is" (15–16).

6. We might reductively see Morton's thought, a sort of hypertrophied negative capability, as a mishmash of agnosticism and animism. They themself muse, "Perhaps I'm aiming for an upgraded version of animism" (*The Ecological Thought* 8).

7. They further complain: "The dreamlike quality is precisely what is most real about ecological reality, so in effect, throwing out factoids and statistics in information dump mode is making ecological experience, ecological politics and ecological philosophy utterly impossible" (*All Art* 23).

8. They laud Denise Levertov's poem "'To the Reader,'" which "achieves a sense of the surrounding environment, not by being less artful, but by being more so. This conscious, reflexive, postmodern version is all the *more* ecomimetic for that" (*Ecology Without Nature* 31).

9. Tiya Miles provides a beautifully evocative example: "[1]977 and 1978 were two years among the 14 times, out of 126 winters on record (since scientific recording began in 1874), that the Ohio River froze. I still recall my trepidation and exhilaration at stepping onto the mighty Ohio, transformed into a crystal sheet beneath my boots."

10. See also Morton's holding forth on timbre in music, how—they point out—"the violin-ness of the sound" "undermines the normal distinction we make between medium as atmosphere or environment—as a background or 'field'—and medium as a material thing—something in the foreground" (*Ecology Without Nature* 38). Such blurrings of background and foreground matter a great deal for Morton's ecological thought.

11. In fact, one could draw parallels between comics' irreducible irony (see for example Hatfield's notion of the "ironic authentication" of autobiographical comics discussed in *Alternative Comics* 125–26) to sociologist Bronislaw Szerszynski's "ecological irony." This he sees as intimately bound up with modernist modes of contradiction, uncertainty, and an undermining of modernity's cult of instrumental reason, with a "generalized irony [as] the master trope" (Szerszynski 340).

12. See Spiegelman 61.

13. These are the translator's own descriptions.

14. In *Hand of Fire*, Hatfield goes so far as to say that "all comic art is semiotically ambiguous . . . organically and inconsistently straddling presumed divisions between sign 'types.' Cartooning derives much of its power from this very indeterminacy. . . . Suffice it to say that comic art is rife with contradiction" (49).

15. See also Casper's discussion of comics' "ecomorphic form" (10).

16. In this regard, see also Dobrin's argument for Paul Chadwick's *Concrete* as itself a kind of ecocritical text ("Follow the Concrete Submersible" 81).

17. Morton's arguments for how ambient poetics "encode the literal space of their inscription—if there is such a thing—the spaces between the words, the margins of the page, the physical and social environment of the reader" (*Ecology Without Nature* 3) map remarkably well onto Szép's vulnerability/haptic reading model.

18. Casper here references Frahm, "Weird Signs."

19. See also Morton's discussion of the "weird weirdness" of ecological awareness in *Dark Ecology* 5–7.

20. Here I mean comics' physical assemblage by machines from raw materials such as wood pulp and ink or their digital creation and storage as files on vast servers accessed via various devices, all of which requires emissions-spewing electricity and concomitant environmental destruction. (To paraphrase Robert Crumb, how many trees had to be cut down to print this book?) See Worden, *Petrochemical Fantasies*.

21. The Montreal-based Thomas produces *Birdstrips*, a nature-focused webcomic.

22. A reminder of Morton's insistence that, rather than maintaining the gap between us and the environment, "ambient poetics seeks to undermine the normal distinction between background and foreground" (*Ecology Without Nature* 38).

23. On comics treatments of the Zone and "Stalkerverse," see Alaniz, "([Post-]Soviet) Zone of Dystopia."

24. French publisher Actes Sud-L'An 2 released the first volume of Harder's trilogy on the history of the known universe in 2009. The German version appeared in 2010 from Carlsen Comics. Knockabout published an English translation for the UK market in 2015. Follow-up volumes in the trilogy take the story up to the (human) present and future.

25. Robinson's antihero Frank May puts it even more bluntly: "You're killing the world and you want me to remember what words you used to cover your ass?" (*Ministry* 98).

26. You'll find them in Shakespeare's *Hamlet* (1601), act 2, scene 2.

27. *Mr. Smith Goes to Washington*, directed by Frank Capra (1939).

28. Everybody and everything alive that we love will die, is dying. No hope for anything else. That doesn't stop us from serving them/it, fighting for them/it, if nothing else just being with them/it. On this and related matters, see Johnston; and Jensen.

29. This edifying tidbit popped up on my Facebook feed on December 4, 2021.

30. I.e., capitalism, a modern idea that "evolved from the violence of colonization and the forceful transformation of land into wealth" (L. Johnson 46).

31. The original character was created by Bob Byrd in 1936 at Timely. Its rights passed on to Marvel. Lee and Kirby reintroduced Ka-Zar with a new identity into the Silver Age Marvel universe in *The X-Men* #10 (March 1965).

32. For a lot more on death in superhero comics, see Alaniz, *Death, Disability, and the Superhero* chapters 7–9.

33. It seems Stern and Buscema may have taken inspiration from the nuclear holocaust TV movie *The Day After* (d. Nicholas Meyer, 1983).

34. The story spells it "Shalan" rather than "Shalahn" as in *Ka-Zar the Savage* #2, in which the race first appears. Whether an oversight or an editorial decision (the current Marvel comics spelling is "Shalan"), the change marks another, subtle means of

decentering Jones and Anderson's original vision and Ka-Zar's whole milieu—which in this story is wiped out in toto.

35. On sacrifice zones, see Lerner; and Nixon, *Slow Violence*. Chris Hedges and Joe Sacco's *Days of Destruction, Days of Revolt* (2012) presents an account of several US sacrifice zones, some in the form of comics.

36. See also the discussion of "supe time" in Smith and Alaniz, *Uncanny Bodies* 19–20.

37. This being mainstream serialized superhero comics, before too long, the Savage Land is restored, rebooted for more adventures thanks to the High Evolutionary and some interdimensional beings, blah blah blah I don't care.

38. In 2019, Thunberg tweeted: "I have Asperger's and that means I'm sometimes a bit different from the norm. And—given the right circumstances—being different is a superpower" (see https://twitter.com/GretaThunberg/status/1167916944520908800 and Farmer).

4. HOW MANY TREES HAD TO BE *CUT DOWN* FOR THIS CHAPTER? R. CRUMB AS IRONIC ECO-ELEGIST

1. *CoEvolutionary Quarterly* (1974–1985) descended from Stewart Brand's *Whole Earth Catalog*. "A Short History of America" was soon reprinted in *Snoid Comics* #1 (1979).

2. Emerson here reflects a nineteenth-century transcendentalist strain in US environmentalist thought that recognized nature as resource.

3. Compare such discourse to that of Emerson and of early conservationist George Perkins Marsh, who wrote in *Man and Nature* (1864): "But man is everywhere a disturbing agent. Wherever he plants his foot, the harmonies of nature are turned to discords. The proportions and accommodations which insured the stability of existing arrangements are overthrown. Indigenous vegetable and animal species are extirpated, and supplanted by others of foreign origin" (36).

4. For more on age-old descriptions of nature as feminine and "virgin," see Merchant, "Reinvinting Eden."

5. Publisher Denis Kitchen's online store bills it as "arguably Robert Crumb's most popular and most timeless image" and Kitchen Sink Press's best-selling poster: http://www.deniskitchen.com/mms/merchant.mvc?Screen=PROD&Store_Code=SK&Category_Code=PO&Product_Code=P_SHOA&Search=&Per_Page=9&Sort_By=newest.

6. The poster, with all twelve original panels and an additional three I discuss at the end of this essay, was designed by Peter Poplaski in 1981, according to the same Kitchen Sink Press online store site noted above.

7. See for example this version, to the accompaniment of Joni Mitchell's "Big Yellow Taxi" (1970): https://www.youtube.com/watch?v=mRkq595NhD0&app=desktop.

8. Many—perhaps most—post-hippie generation Crumb fans discovered the piece in semi-animated form, as a minute-long sequence in Terry Zwigoff's documentary *Crumb* (1994). Here, "A Short History of America" unfolds in slow dissolves from panel to panel, to the accompaniment of "A Real Slow Drag" from Scott Joplin's 1911 opera *Treemonisha*, played by Crumb himself. At least, we first see Crumb playing the overture before switching to "Short History" as the music continues.

9. Crumb's message is perhaps not so "unimpeachable." After all, the "edenic" initial panel erases the presence of Indigenous people, who of course lived in North America long

before the arrival of European settlers. "A Short History" thus functions as an example of problematic "white eco-male-ancholia," a theme I return to in chapter 7.

10. In this regard, "A Short History of America" mirrors the three-pager "Mr. Natural's 719th Meditation," published in *Mr. Natural* #1 (1970), which preceded it by nine years.

11. As Crumb writes in his "Litany of Hate," "For me, to be human is, for the most part, to hate what I am. When I suddenly realize that I am one of them, I want to scream in horror" (Crumb and Poplaski, *The R. Crumb Handbook* 387).

12. Later *Slow Death*.

13. For more on *Slow Death*, see Witek 54–55; and Rifas.

14. The wording references Stephanie Mills's 1969 valedictory address at Mills College, in which she declared, "Mankind has spread across the face of the earth like a great, unthinking, unfeeling cancer" (470).

15. On the role played by nuclear anxiety in forming the counterculture, see Rifas. Cold War environmentalists used the ecological consequences of nuclear war as an argument for denuclearization (see Hamblin 241)

16. In addition to being a major philosopher, Russell actively worked for nuclear disarmament and cofounded the Campaign for Nuclear Disarmament.

17. Off the comics page, Crumb gave voice to his nuclear dread in more "straight" ways, in interviews and letters such this one, from 1961: "I don't want to be around when the bombs start falling. All my life I've had a sort of terror in me" (I. Thompson 152).

18. A notoriously difficult term to precisely define, "irony" (from Greek *eironeia*, denoting an artful double meaning since around the fourth century BCE) "produces and implies aesthetic *distance*: we imagine some authorial point of judgment that is other than the voice expressed" (Colebrook 160).

19. Hatfield adds: "Underground comix ironized the comic book medium itself: the package was inherently at odds with the sort of material the artists wanted to handle, and this tension gave the comix books their unique edge" (*Alternative Comics* 7–8) and "the central irony of that most ironic of packages, the underground comix book, was the way it mimicked the very format of the corporatized comic books of yore" (11).

20. Rifas's useful overview in "The Politics" identifies such environmentally themed underground comix works as Larry Welz's cover to *Yellow Dog* #17 (March 1970, a month before the first Earth Day) and Denis Kitchen's "Terry the Turgid Toad and His Sidekick Cosmic Dog" (*Snarf* #2, 1972).

21. In 1972, President Nixon also signed the Coastal Zone Management Act; the Ocean Dumping Act; the Marine Mammal Protection Act; the Federal Insecticide, Fungicide, and Rodenticide Act; and the Toxic Substances Control Act. President Ford signed the Safe Drinking Water Act in 1974. See Scheffer.

22. See also I. Thompson 112 for Crumb's opinion on the link between having children and the declining fertility of soil tenant farmers, in a 1960 letter.

23. See "Litany of Hate": "I hate the modern world. For one thing there are just too Goddamn many people. I hate the hordes, the crowds in their vast cities, with all their hateful vehicles, their noise and their constant meaningless comings and goings. I hate cars" (Crumb and Poplaski, *The R. Crumb Handbook* 386).

24. This recalls the scene in Zwigoff's *Crumb* in which Aline Kominsky-Crumb complains about surveyors and "dream homes" surrounding their property.

25. See Crumb's two mid-1990s sketches of the French "Mer des Rochers," one of which he titles, "Getting Away from People . . . Must Be Back by Aperitif Time . . ." (Crumb and Poplaski, *The R. Crumb Coffee Table Art Book* 216–17).

26. Norwegian philosopher Arne Naess coined the term "deep ecology" in 1973. See Stark 260–61. Bill Devall and William Sessions published a central text of the movement, *Deep Ecology*, in 1985.

27. See McCarthy 44–48 for a brief history of US views on and key figures in the wilderness debates.

28. For discussions of radical environmentalists as "ecofascist" and misanthropic, see Ellis 265; and Woodhouse 184 and passim.

29. Other midcareer Crumb works in this vein include the one-pager "Let's Talk About This Here Modern America" (*Hipster Times*, 1976) and the back cover to *Carload o' Comics* (1976), which depicts Crumb sitting before a blank sheet of paper, poised to draw, while through a series of panels above we see a tree transformed first into raw material for a paper factory, then a commodity to deliver, argue over, and sell (reproduced in Crumb and Poplaski, *The R. Crumb Handbook* 161).

30. A gentler, better-received illustration for *Winds of Change*, of Mr. Natural watering the "caring tree" from 1983, would go on to adorn posters and T-shirts.

31. As Crumb told the *PM Magazine* television show in 1985, "[I'm] in total agreement with the politics of it." See https://www.youtube.com/watch?v=wldzZEUFEeA. On its frontispiece, the book bears a 1985 picture of Crumb and Abbey together in Arches National Park, Utah.

32. In his book *Where Bigfoot Walks: Crossing the Dark Divide*, on the legend and its rootedness in the US Pacific Northwest, Robert Michael Pyle writes that among the Bigfoot enthusiast community ("Bigfooters") in the region, "no question enthralled and confused them as much as the animal's possible humanity" (308).

33. See Crumb and Poplaski, *The R. Crumb Handbook* 91–92. Crumb also addressed his childhood fetish in the first part of "My Troubles with Women" (1980).

34. Ecofeminism as a philosophy links the oppression of women to that of the Earth (Laplante 166). Coined by Françoise Deaubonne in the 1970s and further popularized in March 1980 at Amherst's "Women and Life on Earth: A Conference on Eco-Feminism in the 1980s" (Mies and Shiva 14), ecofeminism "re-examine[s] the formation of a world-view and a science that, reconceptualizing reality as a machine, rather than a living organism, sanctioned the domination of both nature and women" (Merchant, *The Death of Nature* xxi).

35. The Black Angelfood McSpade, whom Roy Cook calls "Crumb's most controversial creation" (37), had appeared on the arm of a figure strongly resembling Whiteman in "Angelfood McSpade" (*Zap* #2, 1968). Here called Angelfood McDevilsfood, she appears in *Homegrown Funnies* #1 in "Backwater Blues," in which a flood washes her out of her home while she sleeps. Floating flat on her back, she makes for an eerie precursor to Beyoncé's Hurricane Katrina–themed *Formation* video (2016). The feminine figure lying prone on her back, sexually available, reappears in the form of Sheena in "My Troubles with Women" (1980) and at the conclusion of "Whiteman Meets Bigfoot," as I discuss.

36. Nelson goes on to critique the story on feminist grounds: "The fact that 'Big Foot gives his daughter to Whiteman as mate,' or that Whiteman's first sexual act towards the female Yeti begins when she is asleep, is rendered apolitical and uncritically amoral, allowed to exist in

what, in this comic at least, seems to be the only utopia Crumb will advocate in his work: the natural realm and the uninhibited sexual impulse that is presumed to accompany it" (144).

37. Indeed, the fetishization of Yetti bears some striking parallels to that of Angelfood McSpade. See Wanzo's discussion of the latter in *The Content of Our Caricature* 180–82.

38. Crumb tells "Whiteman Meets Bigfoot's" story almost entirely in standard three tier panel arrangements, ranging from six to eight panels per page. These two large panels really stand out.

39. See Merchant's discussion of John Gast's 1872 painting *American Progress* ("Reinventing Eden" 147–48), showing a spectral white woman towering over pioneers and settlers in covered wagons on their journey west (figured as right to left on the canvas).

40. Of course, such a "right-to-left = freedom" depiction also reinscribes colonialist discourses, even if Yetti herself here represents the Indigenous population.

41. As Crumb himself did when he moved to California from Ohio in 1967.

42. As Denis Kitchen's website explains, "After the popular but depressing 12-panel poster went out of print, Crumb added three panels to answer the 'What next?' question posed in his original final 12th panel." The three new panels were printed on the back cover of *Whole Earth Review* #61 (1988) and added to subsequent printings of the "Short History" poster.

43. DiPaolo writes, rather unconvincingly, "The tone of a given work by Crumb is notoriously difficult to pin down, but one gets the feeling that he not only prefers the final panel, but believes it is the only way we really can proceed from here" (274).

44. Seymour adds: "It's not just that an ecocritical turn to the absurd, perverse or otherwise 'unserious' texts *is itself* absurd and perverse, but that such a turn can force us to critically reexamine our own investments and strategies, in addition to those of the texts we read" ("Toward an Irreverent Ecocriticism" 65).

5. "WINNER TAKE ALL!": CHILDREN, ANIMALS, AND MOURNING IN KIRBY'S *KAMANDI*

1. A seminal figure in superhero comics, Jack Kirby (1917–1994) cocreated Captain America, the Fantastic Four, and many other characters, and along with Stan Lee and others inaugurated the so-called Marvel Silver Age of comics in the early 1960s.

2. The cage bars parallel the comics grid itself (left uncolored, they have the same hue as gutters, or the conventionally white space between panels), foreshadowing the modular page compositions Kirby uses at the end of the story, when the humanimals make good their escape.

3. According to Ronin Ro, DC Comics editor Carmine Infantino suggested the concept to Kirby, given the films' popularity in the early 1970s (167). *Kamandi* debuted between the fourth and fifth films in the *Apes* series, though Kirby may never have seen any of them before launching his own work about a world where animals have displaced humans (Hatfield, "Kirby's Post-Apocalyptic Child").

4. Kirby's longest-running series at DC, he wrote and drew it from 1972 to 1976 (other writers/artists took it over afterward). *Kamandi* formed part of Kirby's unprecedented auteurist slate of titles for Marvel's rival publisher (he had left Marvel in some acrimony in 1970, after decades there). By the mid-1970s, Kirby would return to Marvel.

5. Some critiqued Kirby's flipping of the human-animal hierarchy and other details as too derivative of *The Planet of the Apes*, a 1963 novel by French author Pierre Boulle

adapted into a US film in 1968. We can trace Kirby's human-animal reversal trope further, though, at least to Jonathan Swift's satirical 1726 novel *Gulliver's Travels*, in which the hero visits the land of the Houyhnhnms, a race of intelligent horses who have domesticated the brutish, humanoid Yahoos.

6. Such an Aryan youth figure had preoccupied Kirby's imagination for decades. Hatfield ("Kirby's Post-Apocalyptic Child") compares the golden-tressed Kamandi to the artist's similar Serifan of *The Forever People* (DC, 1971–1972); Angel of *Boys' Ranch* (Harvey, 1950–1951); and *Tuk, Caveboy* (Timely, 1941), as well to his long list of rambunctious boy heroes, including the Newsboy Legion, Boy Commandoes, and, from the period when Kirby had returned to Marvel, *Moon Boy and Devil Dinosaur* (1978). Also deserving mention: Kirby's sole autobiographical comics work, "Street Code," about his brutal working-class upbringing in New York's prewar Lower East Side (first published in 1990). Kirby seems to have recycled ideas from previous works (published and unpublished) for the series, such as the comic strip proposal *Kamandi of the Animals* from the 1950s (Ro 165) and "The Last Enemy!" (*Alarming Tales* #1, Sept. 1957). Kirby's original pitch art shows an older, shorter-haired adventurer and the possible title *Kamandi of Earth: Planet of the Future Beasts* (Morrow 28).

7. Blogger Alex Cox, for example, opines that "[the series] looks a little childish and exceedingly violent," with the boy hero presenting as "a pretty blank slate. Even visually, there's not much going on there; he wears cutoffs and boots, and his only accessories are a gun and a holster" (Cronin).

8. Stratemeyer describes Bomba as having the "body of a boy and the heart of a hero!" (quoted in Kidd, *Making American Boys* 107), a tagline that would suit Kamandi. He too has an athletic physique and battles savage headhunters and cannibals as volcanoes erupt and rivers flood. DC published a *Bomba the Jungle Boy* comics series, in part based on the novels, from 1967 to 1968, written by George Kashdan and Dennis O'Neil, with art by Leo Sommers and others. Other near-immediate precursors to Kamandi include the DC prehistoric series *Anthro* ("the first boy," 1968–1969) and Marvel's golden-tressed Ka-Zar (a.k.a. Kevin Plunder, debuted in *X-Men* #10, March 1965), a reiteration of a Golden Age jungle hero. I discuss the latter in the conclusion to part I.

9. The name recalls the Hindu monkey god Hanuman, a hero of the Indian epic *The Ramayana*.

10. While often traced to Mark Twain, the quote is of unknown origin. See https://quoteinvestigator.com/2014/01/12/history-rhymes/.

11. For an elaboration of that thesis, and an attentive analysis of focalization between human and human-animal hybrid perspectives in *Kamandi*, see Fischer.

12. See Alaniz, "'The Most Famous *Dog*.'"

13. See for example reader Karl G. Heinemann's critique in the letters page to *Kamandi* #12 (Dec. 1973), in which he calls out Kirby's precluding of intelligent horses from the milieu.

14. He facetiously cites as his reason for penning the column: "Continuous drumbeating by maudlin partisans of specific species, such as horses, cows, chickens and wombats . . ."

15. The scene comes off as so raw and brutal, in fact, that it nearly gives the lie to Kirby's remarks in a 2002 interview: "Speaking for myself, I know there's violence, but I like to show violence in a graceful way, a dramatic way, but never in its true way. I just don't like to look at it that way. There is something stupid in violence as violence" (Hebert 13).

16. Worth compares Kirby to William de Kooning, Steve Wheeler, and Frank Stella, though as Hatfield notes, the artist's eccentricities and deviations from both major publishers' house styles came to repel many comics fans (Worth 76). Jonathan Lethem goes so far as to call late Kirby "a kind of autistic primitivist genius" (8), not the only critic to label the cartoonist a sort of outsider artist. Lethem further describes his childhood friend Karl's incensed reaction to 1970s Kirby: "[He] sucked because he didn't draw the human body right. Karl was embarrassed by the clunkiness, the raw and ragged dynamism, the lack of fingernails or other fine detail" (15). Here seems as good a place as any to admit that I myself, growing up in the 1970s, shared Karl's opinion on late Kirby. Not anymore.

17. Kirby explains his reasons for this mutation and Kliklak's more "horse-like" herd behavior in the aforementioned column from *Kamandi* #17.

18. Of all Kirby's animal characters, only the Inhumans' Lockjaw has greater charm.

19. In shifting the gaze from one tier to another, our eyes traverse nearly the width of a page, from right to left, what we might term the "hyper-tier." Artists can capitalize on that momentary interruption and resuturing back into narrative to introduce changes, contrasts, shifts in tone or action, as Kirby does here. I have elsewhere commented on a more severe break from the action, the page-turn (or "hyper-gutter") along similar principles. See Alaniz, "In the Empire."

20. The image recalls a scene from the cult film *Harold and Maude* (directed by Hal Ashby, USA, 1971), in which a funeral procession bears the coffin out of a church in full view of a roaring parade.

21. The comic book's facing page contains a gaudily illustrated full-page ad for "Karate Judo Jiu Jitsu Savate: The *Total* Defense System," which only adds to the absurdity.

22. Not the only point in the series in which Kamandi is explicitly likened to an animal. At the end of the contest, he sarcastically asks, "What do I win?—A box of *dog biscuits?*" (13).

23. Other precursors to Kliklak's killing in children's literature include the slaying of a deer in Marjorie Kinnan Rawlings's *The Yearling* (1938) and Charles Alexander Eastman's *Indian Boyhood* (1902), in which the hero relinquishes his beloved dog to the Great Mystery.

24. Wells associates the "moral trauma associated with the kill" with "acceptance of the Darwinian order" (76).

25. See F. Butler for a catalogue of death in children's literature through the early 1970s. L. Gibson notes that the first books addressed specifically to the young, such as James Janeway's *A Token for Children* (1671), dealt with death (232). Indeed, the trope of death has a long pedigree in children's literature and even played a central role in defining the genre. So, incidentally, have animals: http://publicdomainreview.org/2014/05/14/in-the-image-of-god-john-comenius-and-the-first-childrens-picture-book/.

26. Both Kirby's wartime experience and Kliklak's death eerily serve as variations on the Russian Jewish author Isaak Babel's short story "The Death of Dolgushov," part of his 1926 *Red Cavalry* collection (based on his own reportage of the Polish-Soviet conflict in the wake of the 1917 revolution). In the piece, the Cossack soldier Afonka berates—and almost kills—the intellectual (and Babel stand-in) Lyutov for his failure to put a mortally injured comrade to death, to spare him from torture by the enemy. I have no idea if Kirby ever read this story.

27. "The Watergate Secrets!" (*Kamandi* #15, Mar. 1974, 1). Many of Kirby's *Kamandi* stories set the stage with some variant of this language.

28. For a brief history of the term, see Chakrabarty, "The Climate of History" 209–10.

29. For a discussion of cli-fi narratives in comics, see P. Smith.

30. In this case partly lifted from the famous image of the Statue of Liberty protruding from a beach in the future world of the 1968 *Planet of the Apes* film adaptation (see Hatfield, "Kirby's Post-Apocalyptic Child").

31. As discussed in part I, McCarthy invokes the disappearance of moths in massive numbers from the English night as a sign of nature's decline over the last fifty years: "It had been the most powerful of all the manifestations of abundance, this blizzard of insects in the headlights of cars, this curious side effect of technology, this revelatory view of the natural world which was only made possible with the invention of the motor vehicle. It was extraordinary; yet even more extraordinary was the fact that it had ceased to exist" (105).

32. See Alaniz, "'In the Empire'" for a discussion of Jon Burt's actor network theory model of animal agency, a contrast to Ioannides's affect-driven approach.

33. In the catalogue preface to *Remembering Animals: Rituals, Artifacts and Narratives*, a 2018 photography exhibit she curated, Schlosser writes: "From overwhelmingly large issues like factory farming, animal experimentation and species extinction to the closer-at-home deaths of pets and road-killed animals, we're all faced with difficult choices regarding our relationships with non-human animals every day" (v). As in the case of Kliklak, Anthropocene animal death blurs personal/global distinctions.

34. Such a linkage returns us to Kidd's feral child and to Heimermann's "conceptualization of children as grotesque, as creatures belonging to multiple worlds but fully belonging to none" (234).

6. WAKANDA SPEAKS: ANIMALS AND ANIMACY IN "PANTHER'S RAGE"

1. According to A. E. Keir Nash et al.: "Within five days after the Santa Barbara spill, tidal pools and beaches were covered with sheets of oil. Hundreds of birds became covered with the sticky mess and began to die unpleasant deaths. Almost immediately, three treatment centers were set up by the local residents to care for oil-soaked birds. During the first month after the spill 1,575 birds were brought in for treatment. Initial estimates were that 80 percent of these birds died, and that the total number of birds killed, those treated and untreated, was as high as 8,000" (25). Later estimates brought the total of dead birds down to below 4,000, with survival rates for those treated below 11 percent. We will never know the exact death toll, since "Countless birds that died were unaccounted for because many responders and residents discarded them without bringing them to the centers" (Spezio 138).

2. Popular books continued to fan public interest in the years after the event, including Lee Dye's *Blowout at Platform A: The Crisis That Awakened a Nation* (1971); Robert Easton's *Black Tide: The Santa Barbara Oil Spill and Its Consequences* (1972); and Carol and John Steinhart's *Blowout: A Case Study of the Santa Barbara Oil Spill* (1972).

3. The British supertanker *Torrey Canyon* had spilled much more, up to 36 million gallons, off the coast of the UK in 1967 (Nash et al. 25).

4. Such coverage also made those with a perceived lack of sensitivity on the environment stand out all the more. President of Union Oil Fred Hartley struck the wrong chord with the public when he expressed in a 1969 congressional hearing that he was "always tremendously

impressed at the publicity that death of birds receives versus the loss of people in our country in this day and age" (Spezio 136–37).

5. Along with other high-profile environmental debacles like Ohio's thoroughly polluted Cuyahoga River infamously catching fire on June 22, 1969.

6. For more on the federal leases negotiated by the previous Johnson administration with the oil industry and the initial ham-handed response to the spill, see Spezio chapter 5.

7. In Spezio's words: "The lack of federal leadership in pollution control and prevention would be the defining lesson of the spill" (140).

8. By the time he took office, the new president had built a reputation on foreign policy expertise and political ruthlessness. As Rinde put it: "In retrospect Nixon is hardly thought of as a nature lover. Reviewing his crucial role in the establishment of the nation's environmental-protection apparatus induces not admiration but cognitive dissonance."

9. Through the technological sublime, Hatfield argues, Kirby combined the "retrograde . . . gosh-wow effusiveness and social naïveté of the seminal SF pulps" with his own "graphic mythopoesis" and will to worldbuilding (*Hand of Fire* 153). For more on Kirby's technological sublime, see Hatfield, *Hand of Fire* chapter 4.

10. On the Marvel Method, see Hatfield, *Hand of Fire* 90–95; and Howe 50.

11. The term built in part on such pop culture precursors marking the harsh realities of city life as the noir heist film *The Asphalt Jungle* (d. John Huston, 1950); the inner-city drama *Blackboard Jungle* (d. Richard Brooks, 1955); and *The Concrete Jungle* (a.k.a. *The Criminal*, directed by Joseph Losey, 1960). Bob Marley released his urban alienation song "Concrete Jungle" in 1973.

12. On Negative Capability, John Keats's quality of "being in uncertainties, Mysteries, doubts, without any irritable reaching after fact and reason," see Bate 331.

13. Other critics see reflected in the "man-made jungle's" instability the ideological contradictions of T'Challa himself. Martin Lund, reading these stories through their original Cold War framework, argues that "Wakanda's progress is limited to a hi-tech 'man-made jungle,' created by Black Panther 'just for a lark,' and to a partial modernization of the tribal warriors' arsenal. Moreover, as the site where Black Panther chooses to attack the FF, the techno-jungle is not only an irresponsible use of technology, but one that signifies African development as a potential threat to the West."

14. This iteration anticipates the 1990s restaurant/retail chain Rainforest Café, with its animatronic animals, talking banyan trees, hanging vines, and a sky of fiber-optic stars, along with jungle noises and "a simulated thunder and lightning storm that sweeps through the restaurant every 18 minutes" (Heimlich). See also Price, "Looking for Nature" on the Nature Company stores. Both profit-driven ventures exemplify a middle-class urban (dis)engagement with nature in late capitalism.

15. It first appears in chapter 3.

16. Up until issue 5, which reprints "The Monarch and the Man-Ape" from *Avengers* #62, *Jungle Action* was an embarrassing anachronism, "devoted to reprints of white imperialist fantasies from the 1950s" (Howe 132).

17. McGregor (b. 1945) had worked primarily as a proofreader and editor for Marvel starting in 1972. When offered the *Jungle Action* gig, the writer had as his only stipulation that he had to set the Black Panther stories in Africa. The second-tier title had minimal editorial input and oversight, which contributed to its creators' experimental ethos

(Howe 132). McGregor came to earn a reputation for "gravitas," "extreme wordiness," and purple prose (133).

18. See *Jungle Action* #6 (Sedlmeier 60). Howe claims that McGregor intended these paratextual materials to fill out the back of the book so that they wouldn't be taken up by old jungle comics reprints (133), though this issue of *Jungle Action* features a backup story, "Double Danger," starring Lorna the Jungle Girl, which originally appeared in *Lorna the Jungle Girl* #13 (May 1955).

19. Killmonger's cronies Tayete and Kazibe sit on the ground and eat matoke, mashed and steamed bananas (Sedlmeier 133). Other "ordinary" Wakandans come off as stereotypically uneducated and superstitious, like the xenophobic village woman Karota (173).

20. Kirby's own *Kamandi: The Last Boy on Earth* comes close; see Hatfield, "Kirby's Post-Apocalyptic Child" and chapter 5 in this volume.

21. In a key passage, Mitchell writes, "Landscape *painting* is best understood . . . not as the uniquely central medium that gives us access to ways of seeing landscape, but as a representation of something that is already a representation in its own right. . . . Landscape is already artifice in the moment of its beholding, long before it becomes the subject of pictorial representation" ("Imperial Landscape" 14). Art historian Simon Schama, too, reminds that the Germanic root *landschaft*, from which the English word is derived, originally meant a unit of human occupation (10).

22. Such mediation has important potential for ethics. As historian William Cronon puts it, "The autonomy of nonhuman nature seems to me an indispensable corrective to human arrogance. Any way of looking at nature that helps us remember—as wilderness tends to do—that the interests of people are not necessarily identical to those of every other creature or of the earth itself is likely to foster *responsible* behavior" ("The Trouble with Wilderness" 87).

23. On Leonardo's *La Gioconda* (a.k.a. Mona Lisa, ca. 1510) as the first modern portrait subject "estranged from the landscape," see Van den Berg 60. See also Mimei Ito's discussion of imagery in J. B. Callicott's apprehension of landscape as an "articulate unity" (130).

24. As critic Tom Speelman put it, "He gets put through hell. Death by waterfall, extreme heat and cold, wolf attack, and being bashed into a rock by leopards are just some of the traumas Panther endures. And he doesn't get away cleanly. His costume gets torn to shreds, he's battered and torn and bloody. At some points, he can't even speak because of how exhausted he is."

25. Throughout his career, McGregor has displayed a fetish for loving descriptions of bloody torture and violence, as when T'Challa contends with the T-rex: "His blood flows again. . . . The panther's torn costume has become a dark cloth sponge that absorbs the *warmth* of his blood. . . . Saliva, the consistency of *membranous tissue*, falls upon his chest . . . mixing with the red fluid that *rushes* from *new* wounds" (Sedlmeier 194, my ellipses). McGregor famously subjected T'Challa to crucifixion on a burning cross in a later storyline featuring the Ku Klux Klan (*Jungle Action* #20 and 21 [March and May 1976]). In that storyline, an older white woman opens a gash on his forehead with a can of cat food. The text box says, "The scar will be *slight*, hardly noticeable, but he will *carry* it for the *rest* of his life" (302).

26. In their words: "There's limitations on how far the comic could've gone with the violence—I couldn't begin to specify what they are, but it was 1973 and we know that there were lines McGregor wouldn't have tried to cross—but if you examine the language and

results of the battles that do occur, it's obvious how much more graphic all of the Panther's fights are against these non-human opponents."

27. McGregor describes the rhinoceros as "unaccountably infuriated," with "no conscious thought process here, only blind unreasoning *fury*" (Sedlmeier 98). But wouldn't mere territoriality account for its behavior?

28. McGregor's much-mocked writing often comes off as verbose and over the top—even by 1970s superhero comics standards. In the words of Stone and Brothers: "He plays it like some bastard version of Shakespeare, predating the soap-dripping mouth of Chris Claremont's Phoenix love poems completely, choosing instead to channel Robert E. Howard's barbarian violence through a Jack Kirby view of the world." Yet in many cases, his text is not merely restating what the art already shows, opening up productive avenues for visual-verbal tension and complexity, as seen here. For more on McGregor's writing and its representation of character interiority, see Borenstein chapter 5.

29. William Boyd played Hopalong Cassidy in dozens of Western films in the 1930s and 1940s. For Lund, episodes like this typify T'Challa's Cold War ideological allegiance to the West: "Black Panther is made to embrace and express values and tastes thought to be central to the culture and society of the United States and thus become 'American.'" In a self-reflective moment courtesy of McGregor, when the Panther references Hitchcock's MacGuffin, he reprimands himself: "Must all of his reference points be so foreign to his native land?" (Sedlmeier 139).

30. The rhinoceros scene has taken on iconic status in Black Panther continuity, generating homages in *Black Panther* vol. 2 (1988), *Black Panther* vol. 3 (1998); *Black Panther* vol. 4 (2005), and in the 2018 Ryan Coogler film adaptation.

31. As McGregor's text informs us, two major religions developed in Wakanda, one based on the Panther cult and the other on "*the awe-inspiring White Gorillas!*" (Sedlmeier 171). "The Monarch and the Man-Ape" in *Avengers* #62 (1969), featuring the gorilla-worshipping villain M'Baku, had earlier established this piece of continuity.

32. As argued by, among others, Jean Baudrillard: "Whatever it may be, animals have always had, until our era, a divine or sacrificial nobility that all mythologies recount.... The trajectory animals have followed, from divine sacrifice to dog cemeteries with atmospheric music, from sacred defiance to ecological sentimentality, speaks loudly enough of the vulgarization of the status of man himself—it once again describes an unexpected reciprocity between the two" (134).

33. The term, coined by Estonian semiotician Ivar Puura, denotes "a situation in which signs and stories that are significant for someone are destroyed because of someone else's malevolence or carelessness, thereby stealing a part of the former's identity" (quoted in Maran 147). Ecocritics and environmentalists have applied the concept to conditions in the Anthropocene; see Wheeler.

34. Pieces of the thick frame "bleed" into the next borderless panel, showing T'Chaka and his son enjoying themselves on a body of water. These black fragments appear viscous in the water, subtly recalling the oil slick in Serpent Valley—a marker of the present "contaminating" a precious memory.

35. The bizarre blend of bathos and wonder recalls Emily Dickinson's "I Heard a Buzz Fly When I Died" ("With Blue—uncertain—stumbling buzz—between the light—and me") (before 1887).

36. For more on the "relevance movement" in US superhero comics, see Wright chapter 8.

37. Félix Guirand confirms these details, adding that a neighboring tribe of the Bomitaba, the Kakar, had a "'man-panther' or fetish-doctor. He is especially consulted to detect the committer of a crime or misdemeanor" (482).

38. Irreverently, Mokadi also recalls John Keats's "Ode to Autumn" (1819), in which a manifestation of the season "watches the last oozings hours by hours" (Perkins 1271).

39. Bennett relates vibrant matter to Henry David Thoreau's attitude to wildness: "not-quite-human force that addled and altered human and other bodies. It named an irreducibly strange dimension of matter, an *out-side*" (2–3).

40. Note how Bennett to some extent reinscribes Aldo Leopold's "land ethic," which "changes the role of *Homo sapiens* from conqueror of the land community to plain member and citizen of it. It implies respect for his fellow-members, and also respect for the community as such" (*A Sand County Almanac* 204).

41. See also Leopold's comments on extirpating wolves (*A Sand County Almanac* 130–32).

42. Doubts remain about whether creators Lee and Kirby knew about this connection. Kirby's granddaughter, Jilian Kirby, tweeted in March 2018: "My grandfather, Jack Kirby, self taught [sic], well versed in religion and philosophy, researching his Western comics in the 50's & 60's, predating Black Panther, no doubt would have encountered and understood the significance of Wakanda" (quoted in Manseau). A to me more relevant and direct source for the word "Wakanda" comes from *The Man-Eater*, a 1915 novel by *Tarzan* creator Edgar Rice Burroughs. (Kirby was an avid reader of sci-fi and adventure tales.) In it, a native tribe in Belgian Congo, the Wakandas, murder some white hunters and missionaries.

43. See Thomas and Buscema, "Look Homeward"; and Hudlin and Lashley.

7. "DEATH DRIVE" TO LOS ALAMOS: *PUMA BLUES* AS ECO-MALE-ANCHOLIA

1. I wish to thank Amanda Boetzkes, Kyle Whyte, Anthony Lioi, and the organizers of the inaugural Colby Summer Institute in the Environmental Humanities in August, 2019, whose input greatly improved this chapter.

2. Henceforth *TPB*.

3. Having previously written at length on *The Puma Blues* (see Alaniz, "'Rutting in Free-Fall'" and "'In the Empire'"), in this chapter I restrict myself to a fairly cursory introduction.

4. On December 3, 1984, a Union Carbide pesticide plant released toxic gas that killed and injured several thousand people in Bhopal, India. On April 26, 1986, Chernobyl Nuclear Reactor No. 4 (in Ukraine) exploded in the worst nuclear disaster in history. On March 29, 1989, the tanker *Exxon Valdez* spilled over 10.8 million gallons of crude oil into Prince William Sound, Alaska.

5. Among the copious pop culture references: Walt Kelly's 1948–1975 comic strip *Pogo* (Kelly championed the environmentalist movement late in his career) and Philip K. Dick's 1976 dystopian novel *Radio Free Albemuth*, about an alternate USA in which a corrupt president, Ferris F. Fremont, sparks a resistance movement.

6. Immer rocks out to Pop's "Cry for Love" (1986). *The Puma Blues* incorporates several popular songs, including David Bowie's "Watch That Man" (1973); Bill Nelson's "Empire of the Senses" (1982); "White Rabbit" (1967) by Jefferson Airplane; and *Wild Thing* (1966) by the Troggs, the latter discussed further on.

7. See Dueben, "Interview."

8. Pliers, "deracinated" from the urban milieu, appear in a nature still life by Zulli (*TPB* 1). Immer attacks his victim's left ear at the precise spot where he himself sported an earring on his own ear, and where Ganz coincidentally(?) zooms in during his video antics (182).

9. The term dates to Freud's early writings. Such superficial references to psychoanalysis pepper the series, as when Ganz quotes Freud, complete with portrait (164), and discusses Jung's archetypes (231–33).

10. "Runnin' Blue" (1969) by the Doors.

11. The word has specifically been used to mean a coming to terms with Germany's twentieth-century history of fascism and communism.

12. In our world, Jack Kemp (1935–2009), Republican congressman from New York, served as housing secretary under President George H. W. Bush.

13. See Lifton 6–7 for a discussion of the *hibakusha*.

14. Dave Sim, creator of Cerebus the Aardvark, was the original publisher of *The Puma Blues*.

15. The fear of nuclear war, radiation, and environmental collapse also pervades the supporting character Jack's dreams (*TPB* 54). See also Searles's comments on mushroom clouds as "infantilizing" the subject (364).

16. Though fewer in number than those who attack the death drive concept, as we shall see, Freud's "Mourning and Melancholia" essay has its critics. Nonetheless, Freud's ideas in the essay deeply influenced the pioneers of grief studies in the mid-twentieth century (Bradbury 218).

17. The series teases us with moments of near-connections, or connections at deeper levels, between father and son, as when a child Immer shows a UFO-themed comic book he's made to Ganz, which may play a role in the latter's obsession with UFOs, alien abductions, and conspiracy theories (*TPB* 216).

18. See Murphy's blog *Contains Traces of* (September 16, 2010): http://containstracesof.blogspot.com/search?updated-max=2010-10-05T07:43:00-04:00&max-results=20&reverse-paginate=true. As explained in the blog, Murphy's legal father Joe was not his biological father, a fact Murphy feels must have contributed to the two's estrangement: "My mother wanted a child so badly. Just look at what she undertook in order to have me. But look at the wreckage it caused! . . . Some days I just can't live with it" (July 27, 2012). http://containstracesof.blogspot.com/search?updated-max=2012-08-08T07:58:00-04:00&max-results=20&reverse-paginate=true. See also July 24, 2012. Lest any doubt remain, elsewhere in the blog Murphy explicitly identifies with Immer, saying, "He is me" (June 19, 2012). http://containstracesof.blogspot.com/search?updated-max=2012-07-12T06:38:00-04:00&max-results=20&reverse-paginate=true.

19. The blog, illustrated in a faux-*Peanuts* minimalist style, was drawn by Murphy himself.

20. *Contains Traces of* (June 18, 2012). http://containstracesof.blogspot.com/search?updated-max=2012-07-12T06:38:00-04:00&max-results=20&reverse-paginate=true.

21. *Contains Traces of* (June 13, 2012). http://containstracesof.blogspot.com/search?updated-max=2012-06-14T06:09:00-04:00&max-results=20&start=120&by-date=false. He adds: "I don't think I ever fully recovered from it" (June 26, 2012). http://containstracesof.blogspot.com/search?updated-max=2012-07-12T06:38:00-04:00&max-results=20&reverse-paginate=true.

22. *Contains Traces of* (August 14, 2012). http://containstracesof.blogspot.com/search?updated-max=2012-09-05T09:26:00-04:00&max-results=20&reverse-paginate=true.

23. *Contains Traces of* (August 21, 2012). Murphy did not break the fever until he started working in the Mirage Studios and socialized more. Hanging out with people in studio, he became more like a boy, "like my id overcame my *superego*. In the *Freudian* sense, you know?" "Yes, I know," answers his off-panel therapist (August 17, 2012). http://containstracesof.blogspot.com/search?updated-max=2012-09-05T09:26:00-04:00&max-results=20&reverse-paginate=true. Murphy structures the blog primarily as a series of sessions with an unseen therapist, who periodically informs him, "time's up."

24. *Contains Traces of* (June 22, 2012). http://containstracesof.blogspot.com/search?updated-max=2012-07-12T06:38:00-04:00&max-results=20&reverse-paginate=true.

25. See also Martin Jordan's discussion of Theodore Roczak's ecopsychology, whereby "the core of the mind is the ecological unconscious, a place where our inherent reciprocity and connection to the natural world exists as the center of our being," which through industrialization has been "repressed[,] resulting in madness and rampant ecological destruction" (134). See also DeLay's more recent *Future of Denial*.

26. These were not included in Dover's *The Puma Blues* complete edition. See Alaniz, "'In the Empire.'"

27. This sequence, of course, was produced in 2015 for the Dover edition, after the end of the series' twenty-six-year hiatus.

28. Immer's verdict on the Occupy movement, too, for all its acuity and twenty-first-century recapitulation of ecomelancholic tropes, sounds like the sullen diatribe of a scold: "The social media that helped the occupiers spread their message ultimately only helped them occupy one another's Facebook pages and Twitter accounts. / No one was willing to take down much less confront the industrial infrastructure that was systematically dismembering the planet. To do so would be to face *the complicity of want*" (*TPB* 494).

29. As he lectures the insensate Immer: "Real heroism lies not in conformity nor in the meek acceptance of 'fate' but in acts of moral courage. / Aw, kid, you ain't even listening!" (326). The series presents much more evidence of Immer's "failure as a man," including his portrayal as a cowardly superhero in the dream chapter "Amidst Wings" (394).

30. Compare this passage to Searles's diagnosis, quoted earlier. The mention of "thin or permeable boundaries" strongly recalls Freud's comments on overwhelming stimuli "break[ing] through the protective shield" of the psyche in *Beyond the Pleasure Principle* (30).

31. Murphy misquotes here, as he does with most of the songs that appear in *The Puma Blues*. The actual lyrics read "I, I wish you could swim / Like the dolphins, like dolphins can swim."

32. These include the patrician Mrs. Malcomson; the US government agent and Immer's supervisor Lieutenant Europa Buckley; Jennifer, the student who needles Jack over his dream in class; Jack's partner Ruth; and, as discussed further, the Chinese agent Suki and Immer's mother Theodora Fein.

33. The name Kate, with its links to powerful women such the eighteenth-century Russian empress Catherine the Great, bears scrutiny. See my discussion of women's names in "Act of Faith," a short story set in the *Puma Blues* universe (Alaniz, "'Rutting in Free-Fall'").

34. Ronda develops these ideas further in her book *Remainders: American Poetry at Nature's End* (2018).

35. See Crutzen.

36. The theory seemingly stepped back from Freud's earlier conviction as to the insuperability of the Pleasure Principle, as Zilboorg notes. On Freud's own ambivalence about the theory, the arduous process of its development, and the politics of its reception within the psychoanalytic community, see Dufresne.

37. Anthony Storr reads the preorganic as "the final regression beyond infancy and conception to that earliest state of all, before life itself made its appearance" (8). On the allure of the preorganic, the repetition compulsion, and Freud's understanding of the Nirvana principle (i.e., homeostasis or theory of constancy), see Dufresne 52–53.

38. Detractors or partial detractors include Storr ("this theory is one of the stranger byways of thought and the majority of psychologists have never accepted it" [6]); Kristeva ("conjectures that most analysts since Freud do not endorse" [17]); and Dufresne, who sees it chiefly as a rhetorical strategy to defend against criticism ("The death drive became for Freud a repository into which he could dump everything that didn't fit well in the categories of sexuality and libido" [34]). Razinsky also includes Otto Rank, Ernest Becker, Lifton, and Searles, among others, in the legion of naysayers (146–47). We should note that Freud struggled with the death drive theory, even within the pages of *Beyond the Pleasure Principle* itself. If asked about the validity of its tenets, he concedes, "My answer would be that I am not convinced myself and that I do not seek to persuade other people to believe in them. Or, more precisely, I do not know how far I believe in them" (71). Reassuring!

39. Brown also gets positively snippy in his defense: "Psychoanalysts after Freud, who have not accepted the life-and-death duality, have not been able to produce any alternative. They content themselves with rejecting the death instinct, and thus drift into instinctual monism, as Jung did, or into that general theoretical skepticism or indifference which is so congenial to the practitioner-technician" (81). He does, however, concede that the theory "results in complete therapeutic pessimism" (81). The death drive, which "links psychoanalysis to existential thought" (Razinsky 133), was taken up by Melanie Klein, Jacques Lacan, and other notable psychoanalysts. More recent thinkers make free use of the concept: Teresa Heffernan defines it as "the traumatized cultural imaginary" (67), while Lee Edelman finds its Lacanian formulation useful for resisting a much-maligned "reproductive futurism" (2).

40. See Razinsky's comparison of the death drive with Heidegger's being-toward-death (149), relevant particularly in light of Immer's suicide in the new, 2015 ending to *TPB*.

41. Zulli's use of Duoshade in "Under a Deep Blue Sun" makes for a more "stark" and desolate look, and strongly contrasts the desert death panels with the life panels (which don't incorporate Duoshade). Zulli, over his three years on the original series, went through several changes in art style.

42. Szasz also mentions Georgia Green, a blind girl from Socorro, New Mexico, who perceived the flash (85), as do Murphy and Zulli (430). Murphy may have used Szasz's book as a reference, given the similar anecdotes about nuclear bomb testing he utilizes in *The Puma Blues*.

43. Murphy and Zulli also sell short the profoundly mixed emotions with which the "fathers" approached their task. *The Puma Blues* mentions that Fermi, as the flash erupted, "took bets that New Mexico would be incinerated" (427) but ignore testimony like that of explosions expert George Kistiakowsky, who said, "I am sure . . . that at the end of the world—in the last millisecond of the Earth's existence—the last men will see what we saw" (quoted in Szasz 89).

44. On the "return to origins," see also Razinsky's discussion of James Grotstein's "black hole" concept, a psychotic state of entropy and meaninglessness, which he links to the death drive (152fn); Dufresne on Sándor Ferenczi's claims that all life is driven to return to the womb (59); and Peter Walton's analysis of the "monstrous maternal" in Charles Burns's *Black Hole*.

45. Of the copious psychoanalytic literature on (bad) motherhood, see especially Baker's discussion of the Kleinian "paranoid schizoid position" vis-à-vis nature (J. Baker 58); Searles's casting of nature as the bad mother and technology as the good mother in modernity (368); and Slavoj Žižek's disconcerting portrait of a sadistic "'maternal' superego" (103).

46. Kate's word balloons have no tails, further "devoicing" her and rendering her a mere body or sexual being.

47. Not the only time women in *The Puma Blues* are likened to animals. See my discussion of Ruth and Donna Fein in Alaniz, "'Rutting in Free-Fall' and "'In the Empire.'"

48. "Mother," lyrics by Andy Summers, from the Police album *Synchronicity* (1983), may well have been playing on Murphy and Zulli's radio while they were creating *The Puma Blues*.

49. "Gift from God."

50. She has the same family name as Donna Fein, a seemingly unrelated character from "Act of Faith," a short story written by Alan Moore and set in the *Puma Blues* universe.

51. Of the living supporting characters, her number of appearances come in second only to the puma. Like Jack, Mrs. Malcolmson, and a few others, Fein's life activities go beyond Immer. At one point, alone, she reflects on her estranged friend Blanche, to whom she'd "complain about Gav" (148–49). In another episode she mistakes a man on the street for Ganz, then berates herself: "Ohhh. How foolish. Goddamn hope of hopes" (160). But, like all of *The Puma Blues*' subplots, Fein's is dropped once Immer leaves the Quabbin.

52. Interacting with parents (one of them dead) through a video monitor functions as a parody of Superman's "talks" with his deceased Kryptonian parents in Richard Donner's *Superman* (1978) and Donner and Richard Lester's *Superman II* (1981).

53. The French and Russian are erroneous.

54. In any case, Murphy reports having had an at times strained relationship with his mother. See for example *Contains Traces of* (September 29, 2010). http://containstracesof.blogspot.com/search?updated-max=2010-10-05T07:43:00-04:00&max-results=20&reverse-paginate=true.

55. The irony here pertains to the fact that these are "children" in more than one sense; in his video Ganz consorts with people dressed like this, radical eco-activists (Ganz calls them "clear-eyed seers" [177]). They appear unfurling a banner that says, "Zoodisc" (243). These young people represent hope for the future.

56. For example, as Robert Rowland Smith notes: "Whereas suicide entails 'destruction,' the death instincts fixate on preservation—on preserving the psyche at zero level, composing 'death' as an atavistic and ultimately simple state" (71).

57. Yet another example of language's ambiguity in relation to (m)other. Recall also how, during their first dialogue in the story, Immer tells his parent that he's doing "Fine, Fein." She comes back with, "Very punny" (21).

58. Significant also that the only other characters who speak Spanish are either women (Ruth, who is Latina); of indeterminate gender (the person of color who sings *Piel Canela* [434]); or nonhuman (the saucy male-presenting robot). With the exception of the dead, German-speaking Ganz, white males in the story speak only English. It also strikes me as

odd and unfortunate that no one corrected this and other foreign language errors for the later Dover edition of *The Puma Blues*. Symptoms of something extra-textual.

59. To Ganz's paranoid rants about UFOs, Immer merely opines, "I hate flying saucer shit" (190). At the end of the videotape, he insolently declares, "Rosebud" (247), in sneering reference to Orson Welles's *Citizen Kane* (1941), and fixes himself a sandwich he ends up not eating (but the puma does [251]). As we have seen, however, Ganz's posthumous fatherly message cuts him deep.

60. Freud, who wrote *The Interpretation of Dreams* (1900) in reaction to his own father's death, would later claim that the death of a father was "the most important event, the most poignant loss, in a man's life" (quoted in Woodward: "Late Theory" 86). Immer's denial of Ganz's legacy thus constitutes a major transgression but also fulfills a major theme in the work, that "rebellion is where faith begins" (*TPB* 181, 211). In a dream, for example, Ganz reads to a child-Immer the opening lines from Milton's *Paradise Lost* (1667) on "man's first disobedience" (159). Freud famously addressed a similar theme in *Totem and Taboo* (1913).

61. In the new final chapter for the 2015 Dover edition, titled "Poor Little Greenie," Murphy and Zulli set forth Immer's final fate: Now an old man ravaged by disease, he commits suicide in 2037 as the world itself seems to die in a nuclear holocaust (*TPB* 517–19). Though as previously noted, even this is not necessarily the end for Immer.

62. See Linthicum for a useful summary.

63. Whiteness in graphic narrative remains understudied as well, though see Guynes and Lund's collection *Unstable Masks* and the work of Chris Gavaler, like "The Ku Klux Klan and the Birth of the Superhero," for the sort of scholarship that may prove catalyzing.

64. The flag-wrapped puma appears on the covers of *The Puma Blues* #3; the first collection, reprinting the story arc "Watch that Man" (1988); and the 2015 Dover edition.

65. In what might seem a minor point (but actually not, given how deeply the series is invested in music): The songs quoted and referenced are all by white singers, with the notable exception of *Piel Canela*, discussed below.

66. Not only does this sequence flirt with red-facing (a white performance of indigeneity), but the Native American depicted bears a resemblance to the famously red-facing Iron Eyes Cody (born Espera Oscar de Corti, to Sicilian immigrant parents), who appeared in Norman C. McCleod's *The Paleface* (1948) and most lugubriously in "Keep America Beautiful," a 1971 anti-littering public service announcement on US television.

67. On Shoshone land converted to nuclear test ranges, see also T. N. Johnson.

68. *Piel Canela*, written by Bobby Capó (1953). The misquoted, grammatically garbled refrain should actually read "Me importas tú, y tú, y tú / Y solamente tú, y tú, y tú / Me importas tú, y tú, y tú / Y nadie más que tú."

CONCLUSION: THE PACIFIC NORTHWEST IN WORDS AND PICTURES

1. Seattle has about a 28 percent citywide tree canopy, though it's been declining for years (K. Brown).

2. See this National Weather Service report: https://www.weather.gov/media/sew/events_page/Oct%2020%202003%20wet.pdf.

3. Except where otherwise listed, the historical sketch in this chapter was drawn primarily from Workman, et al., *We Are Puget Sound*.

4. You can see the human toll of those economic changes on the local logging community in Daniel Hoffman and Lynn M. Thomas's remarkable 2023 documentary *The Maple Cutter*, about a tree poacher in rural Mason county: https://www.youtube.com/watch?v=eWUpja-CJak.

5. See also Godwin; and Cummings. *A Tale of Two Waters*, a 2021 short film from Crosscut, explores the history and environmental justice issues surrounding Seattle's Duwamish River, in part through an interview with B. J. Cummings, manager of community engagement for the University of Washington Superfund Research Program.

6. See Riddle; and Gallup.

7. See Kohl-Welles; and Ryan, "Grief-Stricken Orca."

8. See the anthology *Evergreen: Grim Tales & Verses from the Gloomy Northwest* (2021) for a recent addition to the list of "weird PNW" artifacts.

9. Comics-adjacent figures from the PNW worth mentioning include Ronald Debs Ginther (1907–1969), who produced documentary series on ink and watercolor bearing witness to the labor movement and the lives of the dispossessed in the early twentieth century (see "R. D. Ginther") and Jacob Lawrence, the noted African American painter who took up residence in Seattle in 1970, and who created several multipanel series such as "The Life of Harriet Tubman" (1940) and "The Migration Series" (1941).

10. See also Woodring's PNW nature-focused 1990 minicomic *Big Red's Last Hurrah*.

11. As John Kelly notes, "Dougan anticipates the future of environmental degradation and eventual climate change."

12. Kelso describes the attributes of the PNW physical environment: "There's the sky. Especially how low the clouds are here. Like the low-hanging dark clouds we have this June. The way the green of the evergreen trees is so dark that if you see them from a distance, they tend to read as black. Also how they are almost always poking up in the horizon" (Personal interview).

13. Kelso lived in New York from 2001 to 2007. She told me in our interview that she felt homesick. Since then she has remained in Seattle.

14. Writer Jeff Jensen and artist Jonathan Case, in their nonfiction graphic novel *Green River Killer: A True Detective Story* (2011), also make a strong link between the Pacific Northwest environment and sexual violence. During his police interrogation, serial killer Ridgway describes his methods for killing women, as the background shifts from an office to deep woods over several panels. The sequence climaxes with a chilling mega-image of Ridgway demonstrating a choke hold, fully "transported" to the forest in his memory (41–43).

15. Indeed, in the oft-quoted words of Potawatomi botanist and scholar Robin Wall Kimmerer: "Knowing that you love the earth changes you, activates you to defend and protect and celebrate. But when you feel that the earth loves you in return, that feeling transforms the relationship from a one-way street into a sacred bond" (124–25).

16. Kelso also alluded to uncomfortable and/or stressful experiences (mild hypothermia, sunburn) while out camping as a child with her outdoor enthusiast parents; she put some of this into "The Golden Lasso," from the 2022 collection *Who Will Make the Pancakes*.

17. Kelso credits a paid gig, *Lost Valley: A Trashy Story of Excess* (1999), with sparking her interest in doing stories set—even if only metaphorically—in PNW outdoor spaces. The educational comic was spearheaded by writers Daniel Snyder and Bryn Houghton and funded by the Washington State Parks and Recreation Commission and a grant from the Washington State Department of Ecology.

18. "Comics and Climate Change in the Pacific Northwest," which I organized as part of the 2022 Emerald City Comic Con in Seattle.

19. In the autobiographical story "The Golden Lasso," Kelso expresses similarly complex feelings about the outdoors, in a story about being molested as a child by a rock-climbing instructor. Toward the end, the narrator says, "I still go into the mountains to experience the sacred" (*Who Will Make the Pancakes* 196).

20. Charles Hatfield puts it similarly: "No one else is doing quite what Bak is doing at the intersection of comics, history, and the natural sciences" (The Editors, "The Best Comics").

21. The collection's title comes from Gary Snyder's essay "The Etiquette of Freedom": "Nature is not a place to visit. It is *home*—and within that home territory there are more familiar and less familiar places" (*The Practice of the Wild* 7).

22. Mahato's *Sea* (2015) received the award for "Best Comic Book of 2017" from Cartoonists Northwest, an association of professionals and amateurs. She turned to environmental themes in 2015 partly due to a fascination with orca echolocation; see "Keynote Address."

23. Mahato's "We Are Contaminated by Our Encounters," a 2021 exhibit at Seattle's Common Area Maintenance gallery, quotes Tsing's *The Mushroom at the End of the World* in its title.

24. As in Fauvism, the odd coloring sparks unexpected associations and meanings, just as word-image tension can bring about cognitive dissonance, "this magical third thing." As Mahato explained, "It's part of the surprise. I want to push that as much as I can. So part of that is: 'I'm going to make the whale orange'" (personal interview).

25. Fernandes produced a similarly themed mural, *Changing of Worlds* (2022) for the Chief Seattle Club's ʔálʔal Café in downtown Seattle, part of a center that serves Native people. He felt compelled to help them, he told me, because "sometimes it seems that cities are meant to destroy Native cultures."

26. More importantly, should we? In his plenary speech at the 2023 Association for the Study of Literature and the Environment (ASLE) conference held in Portland, JoDe Goudy, former chairman of the Yakama Nation in eastern Washington, brought the room to a hush when he asked, "What is the point of all the fisheries, all the ameliorative policies, if fifty years from now the salmon won't manage to survive?" He was referencing the projected impacts of climate change on salmon populations, which are central to his people's sustenance and culture.

27. Full disclosure: Fernandes received funding for this piece from the city of Seattle, as part of its Arts & Culture Bridge Residencies program, on whose 2020 award committee I served.

28. Fernandes uses the story in his teaching; see for example the video "Traditional Native Storytelling with Roger Fernandes: 'Salmon Boy,'" in which he recounts the tale: https://www.youtube.com/watch?v=g2FTrPUpXNQ/.

29. Fernandes did have some kind words for what he called Seattle's "nice racism": "It's educated, it's cultured, it's really nice to you. It's not so bad, compared to other places' racism. 'Oh, just bear with us here, we're not really racist.' They can keep it masked for a long time" (personal interview). Way to go, Emerald City.

30. Thrush provides an important reminder: "The authenticity of [Seeathl's] speech cannot be proven. It first appeared in print more than three decades after Seeathl put his mark on the Treaty of Point Elliott, and it bears a suspicious resemblance to Victorian prose lamenting the passing of the 'red man.' There is no question that Seeathl spoke eloquently at the treaty proceedings—he carried Thunder, which gave skills of oratory, as one of his

many spirit powers—but his exact words are lost. What we do know, however, is that the speech has become a key text of both indigenous rights and environmentalist thinking, with some of its adherents going so far as to call it a 'fifth Gospel'" (7). See also https://www.snopes.com/fact-check/chief-seattle/.

31. Found in Moebius's *Made in LA* (Casterman, 1988).

32. Strongbow also produced a graphic novel, *The Fury of Four Corners* (1988), influenced in art style and narrative approach by the underground comix of the 1960s/'70s. Late in life he planned to publish an expanded version.

33. Strongbow's website describes *The Secret City* thus: "It takes you on a shamanic journey through the streets of Seattle. You will meet vanishing peoples from many different worlds: Aboriginal Australians, New Guinea tribesmen; Tibetans; Native Americans: Kwakiutl, Nootka, Makuna, Lakota, Hopi, Makaw, Zuni; Chinese Ghosts, Balinesian dancers, African dancers and drummers, the Dogons of Mali, the Masai, and many more. In a modern milieu, these colorful dancers, priests, mythological beings, and shamans are healers of contemporary man, who, through his own lack of spiritual insight, has been reduced to a walking ghost. This series also embraces extinct species, as well as endangered species. This series, which began in 1992, also reveals the changing face of the city of Seattle, and shows many of the lost and forgotten people and shops and scenes of the 80's and 90's." See https://www.jonstrongbow.com/.

34. Some have responded to Strongbow's art with charges of cultural appropriation, including the Native comics artist Cole Pauls. I spoke with Pauls about his reaction to Strongbow's work at the 2023 International Comics Art Forum in Vancouver. Even if Strongbow ran in Native circles and respected the various traditions he depicted, at the end of the day, Pauls told me, he was a non-Native white man trafficking in the imagery of historically oppressed and colonized peoples.

35. Strongbow repurposed many of the same images for different books, cropping or uncropping them, adding or removing text boxes. Compare for example "Gone but Not Forgotten," his contribution to the *Ghosts of Seattle Past* project, to *A Walkabout Seattle*.

36. Strongbow produced over twelve albums of music, on his own and with the band Mystery School.

37. Undated, though it adorns the cover of *The Ocean of Time* (2008).

38. Strongbow's website refers to this figure as "a North African man who is a member of a secret Muslim sect where men wear masks in public," possibly pointing to the Tuareg, a subset of the Berbers.

39. Very recently in geological terms—a mere seventeen thousand years ago—what would become Seattle and its surrounding area were buried under a massive glacier, the Cordilleran ice sheet.

40. "Autobiography's" didactic tone also recalls for me Hermann Hesse's short essay "Trees": "When we are stricken and cannot bear our lives any longer, then a tree has something to say to us: Be still! Look at me! Life is not easy, life is not difficult. Those are childish thoughts. Let God speak within you, and your thoughts will grow silent. You are anxious because your path leads away from mother and home. But every step and every day lead you back again to mother. Home is neither here nor there. Home is within you, or home is nowhere at all. . . . Every path leads homeward, every step is birth, every step is death, every grave is mother" (*Wandering* 58–59).

41. The 2021 heat dome, in fact, was a once-in-a-ten-thousand-year event. No kidding (Mulkern and E&E News Service).

42. Micaela, a friend, gave me valuable insights on the 2021 heat dome and its effects, based on her conservation work in the field, much of which involves planting trees: "Our forests were relatively resilient. I didn't see too many impacts, apart from young trees and newly planted trees. The heat was not kind to our seedlings. We have a limited capacity to care for new tree seedlings. If the summers continue like this and we can't get summer genotypes that are more adapted to heat, then, if we want to do any reforestation, we'll have to just plant a lot and hope that some survive, or we'll have to plant and baby them and water them and put shade panels up on the south side. So, we need to think about the management implications for forest, shoreline, and stream land during these heat waves. A lot of the water still flows underground, but that summer we were really surprised at how low the streams got on our properties. That impacts things like salmon runs."

43. How much more common? According to a 2023 study coauthored by the University of Washington's Climate Impacts Group: "Climate model projections indicate summer temperatures in the Pacific Northwest in the 2050s warming by about 4 to 6 degrees F relative to the last half of the 20th century. . . . Between 1971 and 2021, Washington experienced an average of three extreme heat days per year. By the 2050s, there will be between 17 and 27 extreme heat days on average for western Washington and between 20 and 30 for eastern Washington. By the 2080s, the upper end of that range nearly doubles with an average of 20 to 48 extreme heat days for western Washington and 23 to 47 days for eastern Washington" (Vogel et al. 5). Needless to say, most of the flora and fauna in this region did not evolve to handle such conditions. It is doomed.

44. Seattle remains the least-air-conditioned metropolitan center in the nation, with only 33.7 percent of the population covered (Balk). Since 2021, that has creeped up to more like 40 percent in some quarters, though class/racial disparities persist, with only 34 percent of households that earn $50,000 or less in surrounding counties having AC at home. For rental domiciles, that goes down to 29 percent (Vogel et al. 14). And of course, in the Anthropocene, fossil fuel–driven AC only exacerbates the problem.

45. A two-panel meme circulated during and after the event. It shows Bart Simpson complaining, "This is the *hottest* summer of my life." In the second panel Homer Simpson consoles his son as only Homer can: "This is the *coldest* summer of the rest of your life." The meme, attributed to @QueerSatanic, included an image of a PNW heat dome map: https://starecat.com/this-is-the-hottest-summer-of-my-life-this-is-the-coolest-summer-of-the-rest-of-your-life-the-simpsons/.

46. She elaborates: "Habit, the subjective practice of reality, frays in this unique moment of global ecology, and such fraying indicates a potential shift in human understandings of the everyday" ("Climate Change" 220).

47. On the Gothic and Anthropocenic anxiety, see Weinstock.

48. And yes, cap-and-trade programs have a lot of problems. See H. Blake. In 2024, Inslee's program, which had raised over $1 billion, was under threat of repeal by a statewide voter initiative. It survived.

49. See the interview here: https://www.youtube.com/watch?v=cwtPhQD8hHw.

BIBLIOGRAPHY

Abadzis, Nick. *Laika*. First Second, 2007.
Abbey, Edward. *The Monkey Wrench Gang*. Roaming the West, 1991.
Ahmed, Maheen. "Child-Animal Relationships in Comics: A First Mapping." *Strong Bonds: Child-Animal Relationships in Comics*, edited by Maheen Ahmed, Presses Universitaires de Liège, 2020, pp. 9–25.
Ahmed, Sara. *The Promise of Happiness*. Duke UP, 2010.
Alaimo, Stacy. *Bodily Natures: Science, Environment, and the Material Self*. Indiana UP, 2010.
Alaniz, José. "Animals in Graphic Narrative." *The Oxford Handbook of Comic Book Studies*, edited by Frederick Luis Aldama. Oxford, 2019, pp. 326–34.
Alaniz, José. "Death and Mourning in Graphic Narrative." *The Routledge Companion to Death and Literature*, edited by W. Michelle Wang et al., Routledge, 2021, pp. 117–22.
Alaniz, José. *Death, Disability, and the Superhero: The Silver Age and Beyond*. UP of Mississippi, 2014.
Alaniz, José. "'In the Empire of the Senses' and the Narrative Horizons of Comics." *Humanities: Special Issue on Animal Narratology*, vol. 6, no. 2, 2017, http://www.mdpi.com/2076-0787/6/2/31.
Alaniz, José. "'The Most Famous *Dog* in History': Mourning the Animot in Abadzis' *Laika*." *Seeing Animals: Visuality, Derrida, and the Exposure of the Human*, edited by Sarah Bezan and James Tink, Lexington Books, 2017, pp. 39–64.
Alaniz, José. "*Okraina* and 'Oil Ontology' in Post-Soviet Russian Cinema." *Cinema and the Environment in Eastern Europe: From Communism to Capitalism*, edited by Lukas Brasiskis and Masha Shpolberg, Berghan, 2023, pp. 177–95.
Alaniz, José. "([Post-] Soviet) Zone of Dystopia: Voronovich/Tkalenko's 'Sterva.'" *Slavic and East European Journal*, vol. 57, no. 2, 2013, pp. 203–28.
Alaniz, José. "A Review Essay: Chicago: Center of the Comics Universe." *The International Journal of Comic Art*, vol. 24, no. 1 spring/summer 2022, pp. 691–708.
Alaniz, José. "'Rutting in Free-Fall': Moore and Bissette/Zulli's 'Act of Faith.'" *The International Journal of Comic Art*, vol. 10, no. 1, spring/summer 2008, pp. 407–19.
Alaniz, José. "Speaking the 'Truth' of Sex: Moore & Gebbie's *Lost Girls*." *The International Journal of Comic Art*, vol. 8, no. 2, fall 2006, pp. 307–18.
Alaniz, José. "'We Are All Scream! Woodgod and the 'Animal Superhero.'" *Superheroes and Critical Animal Studies: The Heroic Beasts of Total Liberation*, edited by Joe Leeson-Schatz and Sean Parson, Lexington Books, 2017, pp. 33–48.

Alaniz, José. "We Live Here: Heat Wave." *Key Peninsula [WA] News*, 29 Sept. 2021, https://keypennews.org/stories/we-live-here,4882.

Alaniz, José. "'Where Is My Soil?': Ms. Mystic in the Anthropocene." *The Other 80s: Reframing Comics' Crucial Decade*, edited by Brannon Costello and Brian Cremins, Louisiana State UP, 2021, pp. 222–38.

Albrecht, Glenn. "Solastalgia and the New Mourning." *Mourning Nature: Hope at the Heart of Ecological Loss and Grief*, edited by Ashlee Cunsolo and Karen Landman, McGill-Queen's UP, 2017, pp. 292–315.

Andreoni, Manuela. "Nature Lawyers Up." *The New York Times*, 5 May 2023, https://www.nytimes.com/2023/05/05/climate/legal-rights-of-nature.html.

Associated Press. "All-Time Records Fall as a Heat Wave Roasts the Northwest US." *NPR*, 28 June 2021, https://www.npr.org/2021/06/28/1010836214/all-time-records-fall-as-a-heat-wave-roasts-the-northwest-u-s.

Associated Press. "Elephants Have Evolved to Be Tuskless Because of Ivory Poaching, a Study Finds." *NPR*, 22 Oct. 2021, https://www.npr.org/2021/10/22/1048336907/elephants-tuskless-ivory-poaching-africa.

Atkinson, Jennifer. "Addressing Climate Grief Makes You a Badass, Not a Snowflake: Students Studying the Emotional Toll of Environmental Loss Faced a Wave of Vitriol." *High Country News*, 29 May 2018, https://www.hcn.org/articles/opinion-addressing-climate-grief-makes-you-a-badass-not-a-snowflake.

Atkinson, Jennifer. "Episode 5: Is Hope Overrated?" *Facing It*, 2020–21, https://podcasts.apple.com/us/podcast/episode-5-is-hope-overrated/id1509537727?i=1000485544117.

Bak, T Edward. *Not a Place to Visit*. Floating World Comics, 2020.

Bak, T Edward. Presentation on *Not a Place to Visit*. Seattle Public Library, 10 Nov. 2019.

Bak, T Edward. *Sea of Time Chapter 1*. Floating World Comics, 2022.

Baker, Jan. "What Have We Done to Mother Earth? Psychodynamic Thinking Applied to Our Current World Crisis." *Psychodynamic Practice*, vol. 19, no. 1, 2013, pp. 55–67.

Baker, Russell. "The Great Paver." *American Earth: Environmental Writing Since Thoreau*, edited by Bill McKibben, Penguin Putnam, 2008, pp. 377–79.

Baker, Steve. *Picturing the Beast: Animals, Identity, and Representation*. U of Illinois P, 2001.

Balk, Gene. "Seattle Is Least Air-Conditioned Metro Area in the U.S. So How Do Locals Keep Cool?" *Seattle Times*, 23 July 2018, https://www.seattletimes.com/seattle-news/data/seattle-is-least-air-conditioned-metro-area-in-the-u-s-census-data-show-so-how-do-locals-keep-cool/.

Banerjee, Bidisha. "Kinship Between 'Companion Species': A Posthuman Refiguration of the Immigrant Condition in Shaun Tan's *The Arrival*." *Journal of Postcolonial Writing*, vol. 52, no. 4, 2016, pp. 399–414.

Barber, Tiffany. "25 Years of Afrofuturism and Black Speculative Thought: Roundtable with Tiffany E. Barber, Reynaldo Anderson, Mark Dery, and Sheree Renée Thomas." *Topia: Canadian Journal of Cultural Studies*, vol. 39, 2018, pp. 136–42.

Bares, Annie. "'Each Unbearable Day': Narrative Ruthlessness and Environmental and Reproductive Injustice in Jesmyn Ward's *Salvage the Bones*." *MELUS: Multi-Ethnic Literature of the U.S.*, vol. 44, no. 3, fall 2019, pp. 21–40.

Barr, Jessica Marion. "Auguries of Elegy: The Art and Ethics of Ecological Grieving." *Mourning Nature: Hope at the Heart of Ecological Loss and Grief*, edited by Ashlee Cunsolo and Karen Landman, McGill-Queen's UP, 2017, pp. 190–226.

Bate, Walter Jackson. "Negative Capability." *Romanticism and Consciousness: Essays in Criticism*, edited by Harold Bloom, W. W. Norton, 1970, pp. 326–43.
Battistoni, Alyssa. "How Not to Talk About Climate Change." *Jacobin*, 3 Aug. 2018, https://www.jacobinmag.com/2018/08/new-york-times-losing-earth-response-climate-change.
Baudrillard, Jean. *Simulacra and Simulation*. U of Michigan P, 1994.
Bauer, Andrew M., and Mona Bahn. *Climate Without Nature: A Critical Anthropology of the Anthropocene*. Cambridge UP, 2018.
Bealer, Adele Haverty. *Graphic Environments: Performing Ecocriticism at the Confluence of Image and Text*. 2014. University of Utah, PhD dissertation.
Bean, Jennifer. "Affect: The Alchemy of the Contingent." *Feminist Media Histories*, vol. 7, no. 2, spring 2021, pp. 1–20.
Beineke, Colin. "'Her Guardian': Alan Moore's *Swamp Thing* as Green Man." *ImageTexT*, vol. 5, no. 4, 2010, https://imagetextjournal.com/her-guardiner-alan-moores-swamp-thing-as-the-green-man/.
Beineke, Colin. "On Comicity." *Inks: The Journal of the Comics Studies Society*, vol. 1, no. 2, 2017, pp. 226–53.
Bennett, Jane. *Vibrant Matter: A Political Ecology of Things*. Duke UP, 2010.
Berger, John. *About Looking*. Vintage International, 1991.
Berger, Knute. "Mossback's Northwest: Before Woodstock, There Were the 'Nature Men.'" *Crosscut*, 12 May 2023, https://crosscut.com/mossback/2023/05/mossbacks-northwest-woodstock-there-were-nature-men.
Berlant, Lauren. *Cruel Optimism*. Duke UP, 2011.
Bezan, Sarah. "Necro-Eco: The Ecology of Death in Jim Crace's *Being Dead*." *Mosaic: A Journal for the Interdisciplinary Study of Literature*, vol. 48, no. 3, Sept. 2015, pp. 191–207.
Bissette, Steve. "Acts of Faith: A Coda." *The Puma Blues: The Complete Saga in One Volume*, edited by Stephen Murphy and Michael Zulli, Dover, 2015, pp. 527–40.
Bladow, Kyle A., and Jennifer K. Ladino. "Toward an Affective Ecocriticism: Placing Feeling in the Anthropocene." *Affective Ecocriticism: Emotion, Embodiment, Environment*, edited by Kyle A. Bladow and Jennifer K. Ladino, U of Nebraska P, 2018, pp. 1–22.
Blake, Heidi. "The Great Cash-for-Carbon Hustle." *The New Yorker*, 16 Oct. 2023, https://www.newyorker.com/magazine/2023/10/23/the-great-cash-for-carbon-hustle.
Blake, William. "The Sick Rose." *English Romantic Writers*, edited by David Perkins, Harcourt Brace, 1995, p. 96.
Blasdel, Alex. "'A Reckoning for Our Species': The Philosopher Prophet of the Anthropocene." *The Guardian*, 15 June 2017, https://www.theguardian.com/world/2017/jun/15/timothy-morton-anthropocene-philosopher.
Blecha, Peter. "Hale, Robert 'Bob' (1918–1983)." *HistoryLink.org*, 18 July 2021, https://www.historylink.org/File/21274.
Blecha, Peter. "Robert W. Patten, the Iconic Seattle Street Character Known as the Umbrella Man, Suffers a Stroke That the *Seattle Times* Reports Two Days Later on April 17, 1910." *HistoryLink.org*, 23 Oct. 2018, https://www.historylink.org/File/20653.
Blin-Rolland, Armelle. "Towards an Ecographics: Ecological Storylines in *Bande Dessinée*." *European Comic Art*, vol. 15, no. 2, autumn 2022, pp. 107–31.
Boggs, Colleen Glenney. *Animalia Americana: Animal Representations and Biopolitical Subjectivity*. Columbia UP, 2013.
Borenstein, Eliot. *Marvel Comics in the 1970s: The World Inside Your Head*. Cornell UP, 2023.

Bould, Mark. *The Anthropocene Unconscious*. Verso, 2021.
Bracke, Astrid. "Worldmaking Environmental Crisis: Climate Fiction, Econarratology, and Genre." *Environment and Narrative: New Directions in Econarratology*, edited by Erin James and Eric Morel, Ohio State UP, 2020, pp. 165–82.
Bradbury, Mary. "Freud's Mourning and Melancholia." *Mortality*, vol. 6, no. 2, 2001, pp. 212–19.
Brannen, Peter. 'The Anthropocene Is a Joke." *The Atlantic*, 13 Aug. 2019, https://www.theatlantic.com/science/archive/2019/08/arrogance-anthropocene/595795/.
Bronfen, Elisabeth. *Over Her Dead Body: Death, Femininity, and the Aesthetic*. Routledge, 1992.
Brooks, David. "Good Vibrations." *The Eighties: A Reader*, edited by Gilbert Sewall, Addison-Wesley, 1997, pp. 88–95.
Brown, Kristin. "Seattle Releases 2021 Tree Canopy Assessment Showing Slow Decline in Canopy Cover Between 2016 and 2021." *Greenspace Blog*, 1 Mar. 2023, https://greenspace.seattle.gov/2023/03/seattle-releases-2021-tree-canopy-assessment-showing-slow-decline-in-canopy-cover-between-2016-and-2021/#sthash.bNL5Ifod.83d98z7C.dpbs.
Brown, Lisa. "A Graphic Novel Raises Ethical Issues." *Society and Animals*, no. 16, 2008, pp. 293–96.
Brown, Lisa. "An Introduction to the Illustrated Animal." *Antennae*, no. 16, spring, 2011, pp. 3–6.
Brown, Norman O. *Life Against Death: The Psychoanalytic Meaning of History*. 2nd ed. Wesleyan UP, 1985.
Buell, Frederick. *From Apocalypse to Way of Life*. Routledge, 2003.
Buhs, Joshua. "Tracking Bigfoot Through 1970s North American Children's Culture: How Mass Media, Consumerism, and the Culture of Preadolescence Shaped Wildman Lore." *Western Folklore*, vol. 70, no. 2, 2011, pp. 195–218.
Bukatman, Scott. "Comics and the Critique of Chronophotography, or 'He Never Knew When It Was Coming!'" *Animation*, vol. 1, no. 1, 2006, pp. 83–103.
Bukatman, Scott. *Hellboy's World: Comics and Monsters on the Margins*. U of California P, 2016.
Bukatman, Scott. "Kirby, Collage and Kaleidoscopes." *Comic Book Apocalypse: The Graphic World of Jack Kirby*, edited by Charles Hatfield and Ben Saunders, IDW, 2015, pp. 89–104.
Bukatman, Scott. *Matters of Gravity: Special Effects and Supermen in the 20th Century*. Duke UP, 2003.
Burroughs, John. "The Grist of the Gods." *American Earth: Environmental Writing Since Thoreau*, edited by Bill McKibben, Penguin Putnam, 2008, pp. 159–68.
Burt, Jonathan. *Animals in Film*. Reaktion, 2002.
Butler, Francelia. "Death in Children's Literature." *Children's Literature*, vol. 1, 1972, pp. 104–24.
Butler, Judith. *Frames of War: When Is Life Grievable?* Verso, 2009.
Butler, Judith. *Precarious Life: The Powers of Mourning and Violence*. Verso, 2006.
Byrne, John. "Exodus!" *Fantastic Four*, vol. 1, no. 240, Mar. 1982.
Byrne, John. "Purpose!" *Namor the Sub-Mariner*, vol. 1, no. 1, Apr. 1990, pp. 1–30.
Byrne, John. ". . . That I Be Shunned By All . . ." *Namor the Sub-Mariner*, vol. 1, no. 7, Oct. 1990, pp. 1–31.
Calma, Justine. "Texas' Fragile Grid Isn't Ready for Crypto Mining's Explosive Growth." *The Verge*, 14 July 2022, https://www.theverge.com/2022/7/14/23206795/bitcoin-crypto-mining-electricity-texas-grid-energy-bills-emissions.
Cameron, Chris. "Climate Activist Dies After Setting Himself on Fire at Supreme Court." *The New York Times*, 24 Apr. 2022, https://www.nytimes.com/2022/04/24/us/politics/climate-activist-self-immolation-supreme-court.html.

Camus, Albert. *The Plague*. Translated by Stuart Gilbert. Vintage, 1972.
Cantú, Francisco. *The Line Becomes a River: Dispatches from the Border*. Riverhead, 2018.
Capp, Al. *The Short Life and the Happy Times of the Shmoo*. Overlook Press, 2003.
Carrington, Damian. "Environmental Review of 2022: Another Mile on the 'Highway to Climate Hell.'" *The Guardian*, 30 Dec. 2022, https://amp.theguardian.com/environment/2022/dec/30/environmental-review-of-2022-another-mile-on-the-highway-to-climate-hell.
Carson, Rachel. *Silent Spring*. Houghton Mifflin Harcourt, 2001.
Casper, Cord-Christian. "What Grows in the Gutter? Eco-Comics." *Closure*, no. 7, 2020, pp. 1–17.
Cavazos, Elsa. "Thousands of Cold-Stunned Turtles Rescued in Texas." *Valley Morning Star* [Harlingen, TX], 23 Mar. 2021, https://journalstar.com/news/national/thousands-of-cold-stunned-turtles-rescued-in-texas/article_8bf9ec41-4bba-5e4e-b071-7fc3c8486ccb.html?mode=nowapp.
Cech, John. "The Violent Shadows of Children's Culture." *Handbook of Children, Culture, and Violence*, edited by Nancy E. Dowd et al., Sage Publications, 2006, pp. 135–47.
Chadwick, Paul. *Concrete: Think Like a Mountain*. Dark Horse, 1997.
Chakrabarty, Dipesh. "Anthropocene Time." *History and Theory*, vol. 57, no. 1, March 2018, pp. 5–32.
Chakrabarty, Dipesh. "Climate and Capital: On Conjoined Histories." *Critical Inquiry*, vol. 41, no. 1, autumn 2014, pp. 1–23.
Chakrabarty, Dipesh. "The Climate of History: Four Theses." *Critical Inquiry*, vol. 35, no. 2, winter 2009, pp. 197–222.
Chaney, Michael A. "Animal Subjects of the Graphic Novel." *Drawing from Life: Memory and Subjectivity in Comic Art*, edited by Jane Tolmie, UP of Mississippi, 2013, pp. 44–66.
Chaney, Michael A. "The Animal Witness of the Rwandan Genocide." *Graphic Subjects: Critical Essays on Autobiography and Graphic Novels*, edited by Michael A. Chaney, U of Wisconsin P, 2011, pp. 93–100.
Chaney, Michael A. *Reading Lessons in Seeing: Mirrors, Masks, and Mazes in the Autobiographical Graphic Novel*. UP of Mississippi, 2016.
Chauhan, Shreya. "Shame On Humans: Starving Pregnant Orangutan Clings to Last Tree in Jungle Razed by Authorities." *India Times*, 9 Oct. 2019, https://www.indiatimes.com/trending/environment/indonesia-starving-pregnant-orangutan-extinction-palm-oil-boon-mee-377439.html.
Chen, Mel Y. *Animacies: Biopolitics, Racial Mattering, and Queer Affect*. Duke UP, 2012.
Chute, Hillary L. *Disaster Drawn: Visual Witness, Comics, and Documentary Form*. Belknap Press, 2016.
Chute, Hillary L. *Graphic Women: Life Narrative and Contemporary Comics*. Columbia UP, 2010.
Chute, Hillary L. "'The Shadow of a Past Time': History and Graphic Representation in *Maus*." *A Comics Studies Reader*, edited by Jeet Heer and Kent Worcester, UP of Mississippi, 2009, pp. 340–62.
Clare, Eli. *Brilliant Imperfection: Grappling with Cure*. Duke UP, 2017.
Clare, Eli. *Exile and Pride: Disability, Queerness, and Liberation*. Duke UP, 2015.
Clare, Eli. "Notes on Natural Worlds, Disabled Bodies and a Politics of Cure." *Disability Studies and the Environmental Humanities: Toward an Eco-Crip Theory*, edited by Sarah Jaquette Ray and Jay Sibara, U of Nebraska P, 2017, pp. 242–65.

Clark, Timothy. "Some Climate Change Ironies: Deconstruction, Environmental Politics and the Closure of Ecocriticism." *Oxford Literary Review*, vol. 32, no. 1, 2010, pp. 131–49.

Clark, Timothy. *The Value of Ecocriticism*. Cambridge UP, 2019.

Clarke, K. C., and Jeffrey J. Hemphill. "The Santa Barbara Oil Spill, A Retrospective." *Yearbook of the Association of Pacific Coast Geographers*, vol. 64, 2002, pp. 157–62.

Clayton, Susan, et al. *Mental Health and Our Changing Climate: Impacts, Implications, and Guidance*. American Psychological Association and ecoAmerica, 2017.

Clough, Patricia T. "The Affective Turn: Political Economy, Biomedia, and Bodies." *The Affect Theory Reader*, edited by Melissa Gregg and Gregory J. Seigworth, Duke UP, 2010, pp. 206–25.

Cloyd, Aaron A. "Voices from the Margins: The Place of Wilderness in *Watchmen*." *The International Journal of Comic Art*, vol. 16, no. 1, spring 2014, pp. 223–43.

Coates, Ta-Nehisi. *Between the World and Me*. Spiegel & Grau, 2015.

Coates, Ta-Nehisi, and Brian Stelfreeze. *Black Panther: A Nation Under Our Feet*. Marvel Comics, 2017.

Coetzee, J. M., and Amy Gutmann. *The Lives of Animals*. Princeton UP, 1999.

Cohen, Jeffrey Jerome. "Posthuman Environs." *Environmental Humanities: Voices from the Anthropocene*, edited by Serpil Oppermann and Serenella Iovino, Rowman & Littlefield International, 2017, pp. 25–44.

Cole, Teju. "On The Blackness of the Panther." *Medium*, 6 Mar. 2018, https://medium.com/s/story/on-the-blackness-of-the-panther-f76d771b0e80.

Colebrook, Claire. *Irony*. Routledge, 2004.

Coogan, Peter. *Superhero: The Secret Origin of a Genre*. Monkey Brain Books, 2006.

Cook, Roy. "Underground/Alternative Comics." *The Routledge Companion to Comics*, edited by Frank Bramlett et al., Routledge, 2017, pp. 34–43.

Cooke, Jon B. "Welcome to the End!" *Slow Death Zero: The Comix Anthology of Ecological Horror*, edited by Jon B. Cooke and Ronald E. Turner, Last Gasp, 2020.

Costello, Brannon. "Strange Daddy: Uprooting the Environmentalist Family Romance in Nancy A. Collins' *Swamp Thing*." *Inks: The Journal of the Comics Studies Society*, vol. 6, no. 1, 2022, pp. 1–25.

Craps, Stef, and Ida Marie Olsen. "Grief as a Doorway to Love: An Interview with Chris Jordan." *American Imago*, vol. 77, no. 1, April 2020, pp. 109–35.

Cremins, Brian. "Bumbazine, Blackness, and the Myth of the Redemptive South in Walt Kelly's *Pogo*." *Comics and the U.S. South*, edited by Brannon Costello and Qiana J. Whitted, UP of Mississippi, 2011, pp. 29–61.

Cronin, Brian. "Kamandi Is Awesome." *Comics Beat*, 14 Apr. 2008, https://www.cbr.com/kamandi-is-awesome/.

Cronon, William. "Foreword to the Paperback Edition." *Uncommon Ground: Rethinking the Human Place in Nature*, edited by William Cronon, W. W. Norton, 1996, pp. 19–22.

Cronon, William. "Introduction: In Search of Nature." *Uncommon Ground: Toward Reinventing Nature*, edited by Williams Cronon, W. W. Norton, 1996, pp. 23–68.

Cronon, William. "The Trouble with Wilderness, or Getting Back to the Wrong Nature." *Uncommon Ground: Rethinking the Human Place in Nature*, edited by William Cronon, W. W. Norton, 1996, pp. 69–90.

Crumb, Robert. "The Desperate Character Writhes Again." *Home Grown Funnies No. 1*. Kitchen Sink, 1971, back cover.

Crumb, Robert. "King of Motor City?" *Motor City Comics*. Last Gasp, 1969.
Crumb, Robert. "Mr. Sketchum" *Hydrogen Bomb and Biochemical Warfare Funnies*. Rip Off, 1970.
Crumb, Robert. *My Troubles with Women*. Last Gasp, 1992.
Crumb, Robert. "Smogville Blues." *Slow Death Funnies*, no. 1. Last Gasp, 1970.
Crumb, Robert. "Whiteman." *Zap Comix*, no. 1. Apex Novelties, 1967.
Crumb, Robert. "Whiteman Meets Bigfoot." *Home Grown Funnies No. 1*. Kitchen Sink, 1971.
Crumb, Robert, and Peter Poplaski. *The R. Crumb Coffee Table Art Book*. Back Bay Books, 1998.
Crumb, Robert, and Peter Poplaski. *The R. Crumb Handbook*. MQ Publications Limited, 2005.
Crumb, Robert, et al. *The Comics Journal Library, Volume Three: Crumb*. Fantagraphics, 2004.
Crutzen, Paul J. "Geology of Mankind." *Nature*, vol. 415, no. 6867, 2002, p. 23.
Cummings, B. J. *The River That Made Seattle: A Human and Natural History of the Duwamish*. U of Washington P, 2020.
Cunsolo, Ashlee, and Karen Landman. "Introduction: To Mourn Beyond the Human." *Mourning Nature: Hope at the Heart of Ecological Loss and Grief*, edited by Ashlee Cunsolo and Karen Landman, McGill-Queen's UP, 2017, pp. 3–26.
Dalton, Jane. "Coronavirus: Exterminating Bats Blamed for Spreading Covid-19 Would Increase Risk of Further Diseases, Warn Experts." *The Independent*, 24 Apr. 2020, https://www.independent.co.uk/climate-change/news/coronavirus-bats-china-pangolin-colony-wildlife-kill-pandemic-covid-19-a9469551.html.
Daniels, Les. *Comix: A History of Comic Books in America*. Bonanza Books, 1971.
Davies, Jeremy. *The Birth of the Anthropocene*. U of California P, 2016.
Davis, Brangien. "ArtSEA: New ʔálʔal Cafe Brings Native Food, Art to Pioneer Square." *Crosscut*, 17 Nov. 2022, https://crosscut.com/culture/2022/11/artsea-new-alal-cafe-brings-native-food-art-pioneer-square.
Dean, Sam. "Mike Davis Is Still a Damn Good Storyteller." *The Los Angeles Times*, 25 July 2022, https://www.latimes.com/lifestyle/image/story/2022-07-25/mike-davis-reflects-on-life-activism-climate-change-bernie-sanders-aoc-los-angeles-politics.
de Beauvoir, Simone. "Must We Burn Sade?" Translated by Kim Allen Gleed et al. *Simone De Beauvoir: Political Writings*, edited by Margaret A. Simons and Marybeth Timmermann, U of Illinois P, 2012, pp. 44–101.
DeLay, Tad. *Future of Denial: The Ideologies of Climate Change*. Verso, 2024.
Derrida, Jacques. *The Animal That Therefore I Am*. Translated by David Wills. Edited Marie-Louise Mallet. Fordham UP, 2008.
DiPaolo, Marc. *Fire and Snow: Climate Fiction from the Inklings to Game of Thrones*. State U of New York P, 2018.
Di Placido, Dani. "Kylie Jenner's 'Climate Criminal' Controversy, Explained." *Forbes*, 19 July 2022, https://www.forbes.com/sites/danidiplacido/2022/07/19/kylie-jenners-climate-criminal-controversy-explained/?sh=5022ab8126a4.
Dobrin, Sidney I. "EcoComix: An Introduction." *EcoComix: Essays on the Environmental in Comics and Graphic Novels*, edited by Sidney I. Dobrin, McFarland, 2020, pp. 1–9.
Dobrin, Sidney I. "Follow the Concrete Submersible." *EcoComix: Essays on the Environmental in Comics and Graphic Novels*, edited by Sidney I. Dobrin, McFarland, 2020, pp. 80–96.
Dodds, Joseph. *Psychoanalysis and Ecology at the Edge of Chaos: Complexity Theory, Deleuze, Guattari and Psychoanalysis for a Climate in Crisis*. Taylor & Francis, 2011.
Dougan, Michael. "Piggly Wiggly." *Bumberhead Comics*, no. 2, 1988, p. 5.

Dreifus, Claudia. "Chasing the Biggest Story on Earth." *The New York Times*, 10 Feb. 2014, https://www.nytimes.com/2014/02/11/science/the-sixth-extinction-looks-at-human-impact-on-the-environment.html.

Dueben, Alex. "Interview: Stephen Murphy Opens Up About Fear and Slivers of Hope in *The Puma Blues* and *Umbra*." *The Beat*, 21 Sept. 2016, http://www.comicsbeat.com/interview-stephen-murphy-opens-up-about-fear-and-slivers-of-hope-in-the-puma-blues-and-umbra/.

Dueben, Alex. "The Michael Zulli Interview." *The Comics Journal*, 25 July 2016, http://www.tcj.com/the-michael-zulli-interview/.

Dufresne, Todd. *Tales from the Freudian Crypt: The Death Drive in Text and Context*. Stanford UP, 2000.

Dunaway, Finis. "The 'Crying Indian' Ad That Fooled the Environmental Movement." *Chicago Tribune*, 21 Nov. 2017, http://www.chicagotribune.com/news/opinion/commentary/ct-perspec-indian-crying-environment-ads-pollution-1123-20171113-story.html#.

Dunaway, Finis. "Gas Masks, Pogo, and the Ecological Indian: Earth Day and the Visual Politics of American Environmentalism." *American Quarterly*, vol. 60, no. 1, March 2008, pp. 67–99.

Duncan, B. N. "A Joint Interview with R. Crumb and Aline Kaminsky-Crumb." *Crumb: Conversations*, edited by D. K. Holm, UP of Mississippi, 2004, pp. 117–32.

Dyer, Richard. *White*. Routledge, 1997.

Edelman, Lee. *No Future: Queer Theory and the Death Drive*. Duke UP, 2004.

The Editors. "The Best Comics of 2022." *The Comics Journal*, 31 Dec. 2022, https://www.tcj.com/the-best-comics-of-2022/?fbclid=PAAaZTdISYrXDNKP3MJlYt6jTo_l-qMcVoGt4VDxnIeMgVfxrik1D51DuoCCU.

Einhorn, Catrin, and Lauren Leatherby. "Animals Are Running Out of Places to Live." *The New York Times*, 9 Dec. 2022, https://www.nytimes.com/interactive/2022/12/09/climate/biodiversity-habitat-loss-climate.html?action=click&module=RelatedLinks&pgtype=Article.

Ellis, Jeffrey C. "On the Search for a Root Cause: Essentialist Tendencies in Environmentalist Discourse." *Uncommon Ground: Toward Reinventing Nature*, edited by William Cronon, W. W. Norton, 1995, pp. 256–68.

Emerson, Ralph Waldo. "Nature (1936)." *Ralph Waldo Emerson: The Major Prose*. Edited by Ronald A. Bosco and Joel Myerson. Harvard UP, 2015, pp. 34–73.

Emperor Wen. "Where Does the Blame Lie?" *Lapham's Quarterly*, fall 2019, p. 175.

Englehart, Steve, and Keith Pollard. "I Want to Die!" *Fantastic Four*, vol. 1, no. 311, Feb. 1988, pp. 1–22.

"Episode 179: T Edward Bak." *Something (Rather than Nothing) Podcast*, no. 179, Mar. 2023, https://zencastr.com/z/iLSd9sxo.

Evanier, Mark. *Kirby: King of Comics*. Abrams, 2008.

"Exxon Valdez Oil Spill." Office of Response and Restoration, National Oceanic and Atmospheric Administration. n.d., https://response.restoration.noaa.gov/oil-and-chemical-spills/significant-incidents/exxon-valdez-oil-spill.

Farmer, Sam. "How Greta Thunberg's Autism Helped Make Her the World's Most Important Person for 2020." *The Hill*, 12 Dec. 2019, https://thehill.com/changing-america/well-being/468091-opinion-activist-greta-thunbergs-autism-doesnt-hold-her-back/.

Fawaz, Ramzi. "Legions of Superheroes: Diversity, Multiplicity and Collective Action Against Genocide in the Superhero Comic Book." *Social Text*, vol. 36, no. 4, 2018, pp. 21–55.

Federalist Editors. "A Roundtable On 'Laudato Si.'" *The Federalist*, 25 June 2015, https://thefederalist.com/2015/06/25/a-roundtable-on-laudato-si/.

Fernandes, Roger. *Change of Worlds: The Fremont Bridge Cycle*. Seattle Office of Arts & Culture, 2021.

Fernandes, Roger. Personal interview. Summer 2023.

Fernandes, Roger. *Salmon Boy*. Red Soaring Eagle/4Culture, 2013.

Fernández L'Hoeste, Héctor. "A Matter of Affect: Illustrated Responses to the Immigration Debacle." *The International Journal of Comic Art*, vol. 21, no. 1, spring/summer, 2019, pp. 551–66.

The Fight to Save America's Waters: A Mark Trail Adventure in Public Health and Conservation. Federal Security Agency. Public Health Service, 1950.

Fischer, Craig. "'For an Animal': Kamandi and Focalization." *The Kirby Effect: The Journal of the Jack Kirby Museum & Research Center*, 9 Aug. 2012, http://kirbymuseum.org/blogs/effect/author/craigf/.

Fisher, Clare. "The Centrality of the Trivial: Reading Jenny Offill's *Weather*." *Alluvium*, 13 July 2020, https://alluvium.bacls.org/2020/07/13/the-centrality-of-the-trivial/.

Flippen, J. Brooks. *Nixon and the Environment*. U of New Mexico P, 2012.

Foster, Hal. *The Return of the Real: The Avant Garde at the End of the Century*. MIT Press, 1996.

Frahm, Ole. "Too Much Is Too Much. The Never Innocent Laughter of the Comics." *ImageTexT*, Oct. 2003, https://www.imageandnarrative.be/inarchive/graphicnovel/olefrahm.htm.

Frahm, Ole. "Weird Signs: Comics as Means of Parody." *Comics & Culture: Analytical and Theoretical Approaches to Comics*, edited by Anne Magnussen and Hans-Christian Christiansen, U of Copenhagen P, 2000, pp. 177–91.

Franklin, Eroyn. "The Cabin." *Now: The New Comics Anthology*, no. 5, 2018, pp. 62–75.

Franzen, Jonathan. *The End of the End of the Earth: Essays*. Farrar, Straus & Giroux, 2018.

Freud, Sigmund. *Beyond the Pleasure Principle*. Translated James Strachey. W. W. Norton, 1961.

Freud, Sigmund. *Civilization and Its Discontents*. Translated by J. Riviere. Hogarth Press, 1930.

Freud, Sigmund. "Mourning and Melancholia." *The Standard Edition of the Complete Psychological Works of Sigmund Freud*. Vol. XIV. Translated by James Strachey. Hogarth Press, 1953–1974, pp. 237–58.

Gabilliet, Jean-Paul. *Of Comics and Men: A Cultural History of American Comic Books*. Translated by Bart Beaty and Nick Nguyen. UP of Mississippi, 2010.

Gaitskill, Mary. "The Deracination of Literature." *Unherd*, 17 June 2022, https://unherd.com/2022/06/the-death-of-literature/.

Gallup, Lauren. "A Park from Pollution: 30 Years After the ASARCO Smokestack Demolition, Tacoma's Waterfront Transforms." *Northwest Public Broadcasting*, 20 Jan. 2023, https://www.nwpb.org/2023/01/20/a-park-from-pollution-30-years-after-the-asarco-smokestack-demolition-tacomas-waterfront-transforms/.

Garbacik, Jaimee. "Introduction. Harbor Island and the Duwamish: An Interview with Ken Workman, Great-great-great-great-grandson of Si'Ahl, Chief Seattle." *Ghosts of Seattle Past: An Anthology of Lost Seattle Places*, edited by Jaimee Garbacik, Chin Music Press, 2017, pp. xxi–xxxvi.

Gardner, Jared. "Autobiography's Biography, 1972–2007." *Biography*, vol. 31, no. 1, 2008, pp. 1–26.

Garrard, Greg. "Ecocriticism as Narrative Ethics: Triangulating Environmental Virtue in Richard Powers' *Gain*." *Environment and Narrative: New Directions in Econarratology*, edited by Erin James and Eric Morel, Ohio State UP, 2020, pp. 107–26.

Gavaler, Chris. "The Ku Klux Klan and the Birth of the Superhero." *Journal of Graphic Novels and Comics*, vol. 4, no. 2, 2013, pp. 191–208.

Gerber, Steve, and Sal Buscema. "Savage Time!" *Defenders*, no. 26, Aug. 1975, pp. 1–31.

Gibson, L. "Death in Children's Literature: Taboo or Not Taboo?" *Children's Literature Association Quarterly*, vol. 16, no. 4, 1991, pp. 232–34.

Ginsberg, Allen. "Howl." *The Poetry Foundation*. 1955–1956. https://www.poetryfoundation.org/poems/49303/howl.

Gipson, Fred. *Old Yeller*. Harper & Row, 1956.

Godwin, Mandy. "How the Duwamish River Defined Seattle—and Could Again." *Crosscut*, 30 June 2020, https://crosscut.com/2020/06/how-duwamish-river-defined-seattle-and-could-again.

Gold, Glen David. "The Red Sheet." *Comic Book Apocalypse: The Graphic World of Jack Kirby*, edited by Charles Hatfield and Ben Saunders, IDW, 2015, pp. 67–75.

Gomes, Mario, and Jan Peuckert. "Memento Mori: A Portuguese Style of Melancholy." *Comics as a Nexus of Cultures: Essays on the Interplay of Media, Disciplines and International Perspectives*, edited by Mark Berninger et al., McFarland, 2010, pp. 116–26.

Gottlieb, Robert. *Forcing the Spring: The Transformation of the American Environmental Movement*. Island Press, 1993.

Goulart, Ron. *The Great Comic Book Artists*. St. Martin's Press, 1986.

Grad, Shelby. "The Environmental Disaster That Changed California—and Started the Movement Against Offshore Oil Drilling." *Los Angeles Times*, 28 Apr. 2017, https://www.latimes.com/local/lanow/la-me-santa-barbara-spill-20170428-htmlstory.html.

Green, Keith. "What's a Nice Counter-Culture Visionary Like Robert Crumb Doing on a Secluded Farm in California?" *Crumb: Conversations*, edited by D. K. Holm, UP of Mississippi, 2004, pp. 92–104.

Groensteen, Thierry. *Animaux En Cases: Une Histoire Critique De La Bande Dessinée Animalière*. Futuropolis, 1987.

Groensteen, Thierry. *Comics and Narration*. Translated by Ann Miller. UP of Mississippi, 2013.

Groensteen, Thierry. *The System of Comics*. Translated by Bart Beaty and Nick Nguyen. UP of Mississippi, 2007.

Groth, Gary. "Introduction." *Your Vigor for Life Appalls Me: Robert Crumb Letters, 1968–1977*, edited by Ilse Thompson, Fantagraphics, 2012, pp. vi–xii.

Groth, Gary. "A Marathon Interview with Legendary Underground Cartoonist Robert Crumb." *The Comics Journal Library*, vol. 9, edited by Michael Dean, Fantagraphics, 2015, pp. 11–45.

Gruen, Lori. "Facing Death and Practicing Grief." *Ecofeminism: Feminist Intersections with Other Animals and the Earth*, edited by Carol J. Adams and Lori Gruen, Bloomsbury, 2014, pp. 127–41.

Guirand, Félix. *New Larousse Encyclopedia of Mythology*. Prometheus, 1968.

Gustines, George. "*Mark Trail* Jumps Into an Adventure with a New Cartoonist." *The New York Times*, 25 Sept. 2020, https://www.nytimes.com/2020/09/25/arts/mark-trail-new-cartoonist.html.

Guynes, Sean, and Martin Lund, eds. *Unstable Masks: Whiteness and American Superhero Comics*. Ohio State UP, 2019.

Hamblin, Jacob Darwin. *Arming Mother Nature: The Birth of Catastrophic Environmentalism*. Oxford UP, 2013.

Haraway, Donna Jeanne. *Staying with the Trouble: Making Kin in the Chthulucene*. Duke UP, 2016.

Harder, Jens. *Alpha: Directions*. Knockabout Press, 2015.

Harpold, Terry. "The Middle Voice of EcoComix: Reading Philippe Squarzoni's *Climate Changed*." *Essays on the Environmental in Comics and Graphic Novels*, edited by Sidney I. Dobrin, McFarland, 2020, pp. 29–51.

Harris, Eliza. "The Poetry of Comics: A Conversation with Collage Artist Mita Mahato." *Catapult*, 8 Feb. 2022, https://catapult.co/dont-write-alone/stories/the-poetry-of-comics-a-conversation-with-collage-artist-mita-mahato-by-eliza-harris-cut-paper-underground-comix-processing-grief-ecosystem-loss.

Harris, Joe, and Martín Morazzo. *Great Pacific: Trashed!* Image, 2013.

Hartman, Geoffrey H. "The Romance of Nature and the Negative Way." *Romanticism and Consciousness: Essays in Criticism*, edited by Harold Bloom, W. W. Norton, 1970, pp. 280–305.

Harvey, Robert C. *The Art of the Funnies: An Aesthetic History*. UP of Mississippi, 1994.

Harvey, Robert C. "Death in the Funnies." *The Comics Journal Blog*, 30 July 2010, http://classic.tcj.com/strips/death-in-the-funnies/.

Hatfield, Charles. *Alternative Comics: An Emerging Literature*. UP of Mississippi, 2005.

Hatfield, Charles. *Hand of Fire: The Comics Art of Jack Kirby*. UP of Mississippi, 2012.

Hatfield, Charles. "Introduction." *ImageTexT*, vol. 3, no. 3, spring 2007, http://www.english.ufl.edu/imagetext/archives/v3_3/introduction.shtml.

Hatfield, Charles. "Kirby's Post-Apocalyptic Child." *Hand of Fire: The Comics Art of Jack Kirby* blog, 28 Jan. 2017, https://handoffire.wordpress.com/2017/01/28/kirbys-post-apocalyptic-child/.

Hatfield, Charles, et al., eds. *The Superhero Reader*. UP of Mississippi, 2013.

Head, Lesley. *Hope and Grief in the Anthropocene: Re-Conceptualising Human-Nature Relations*. Routledge, 2016.

Hebert, Mark. "Interview I: There Is Something Stupid in Violence as Violence." *The Comics Journal Library Volume 1: Jack Kirby*, edited by Milo George, Fantagraphics, 2002 pp. 2–13.

Heer, Jeet. "Introduction." King, Frank O. *Sundays with Walt and Skeezix*, edited by Peter Maresca, Sunday Press, 2007, pp. iii–v.

Heffernan, Teresa. "The Post-Apocalyptic Imaginary: Science, Fiction, and the Death Drive." *English Studies in Africa*, vol. 58, no. 2, 2015, pp. 66–79.

Heimermann, Mark. "The Grotesque Child: Animal-Human Hybridity in *Sweet Tooth*." *Picturing Childhood: Youth in Transnational Comics*, edited by Mark Heimermann and Brittany Tullis, U of Texas P, 2017, pp. 234–50.

Heimlich, Cheryl Kane. "Rainforest Café Becoming the 'Disney World' of Eateries." *South Florida Business Journal*, vol. 17, no. 3, Nov. 1996, pp. 1+, http://link.galegroup.com/apps/doc/A19064311/ITOF?u=wash_main&sid=ITOF&xid=0214d055.

Herman, David. "Introduction: More-Than-Human Worlds in Graphic Storytelling." *Animal Comics: Multispecies Storyworlds in Graphic Narratives*, edited by David Herman, Bloomsbury Academic, 2018, pp. 1–25.

Herman, David. *Narratology Beyond the Human: Storytelling and Animal Life.* Oxford UP, 2018.

Herman, David. "Storyworld/Umwelt: Nonhuman Experiences in Graphic Narratives." *SubStance*, vol. 40, no. 1, 2011, pp. 156–81.

Hesse, Hermann. *Wandering: Notes and Sketches.* Translated by James Wright. Farrar, Straus & Giroux, 1972.

Hirsch, Marianne. "Mourning and Postmemory." *Graphic Subjects Critical Essays on Autobiography and Graphic Novels*, edited by Michael Chaney, U of Wisconsin P, 2011, pp. 17–44.

Holm, D. K., ed. *R. Crumb: Conversations.* UP of Mississippi, 2004.

Hook, Leise. "The Vine and the Fish." *The Believer: The Survival Issue*, May 2020, pp. 81–93.

Howe, Sean. *Marvel Comics: The Untold Story.* Harper, 2012.

Hudlin, Reginald, and Ken Lashley. *Black Panther: Shuri—Deadliest of the Species.* Marvel, 2018.

Huebert, David. "Scenting Wild: Olfactory Panic and Jack London's Ocular Dogs." *Seeing Animals After Derrida*, edited by Sarah Bezan and James Tink, Lexington Books, 2018, pp. 127–44.

Husband, Timothy, and Gloria Gilmore-House. *The Wild Man: Medieval Myth and Symbolism.* Metropolitan Museum of Art, 1980.

Inge, M. Thomas. *Comics as Culture.* UP of Mississippi, 1990.

Ioannides, George. "Re-membering Sirius: Animal Death, Rites of Mourning, and the (Material) Cinema of Spectrality." *Animal Death*, edited by Jay Johnston and Fiona Probyn-Rapsey, Sydney UP, 2013, pp. 103–18.

Irons, Greg. "It Grows." *Slow Death Funnies*, no. 1, 1970.

Ito, Mimei. "Seeing Animals, Speaking of Nature: Visual Culture and the Question of the Animal." *Theory, Culture & Society*, vol. 25, no. 4, 2008, pp. 119–37.

James, Erin. "Narrative in the Anthropocene." *Environment and Narrative: New Directions in Econarratology*, edited by Erin James and Eric Morel, Ohio State UP, 2020, pp. 183–202.

James, Erin. *Narrative in the Anthropocene.* Ohio State UP, 2022.

James, Erin, and Birgit Spengler. "(Life) Narrative in the Posthuman Anthropocene: Erin James in Conversation with Birgit Spengler." *Life Writing in the Posthuman Anthropocene*, edited by Ina Batzke et al., Palgrave Macmillan, 2021, pp. 225–55.

Jaques, Zoe. *Children's Literature and the Posthuman: Animal, Environment, Cyborg.* Routledge, 2015.

Jensen, Derrick. "Beyond Hope." *Orion*, 2 May 2006, https://orionmagazine.org/article/beyond-hope/.

Jensen, Jeff, and Jonathan Case. *Green River Killer: A True Detective Story.* Dark Horse, 2011.

Johnson, Brian. "Libidinal Ecologies: Eroticism and Environmentalism in *Swamp Thing*." *Sexual Ideology in the Works of Alan Moore: Critical Essays on the Graphic Novels*, edited by Todd A. Comer and Joseph Michael Sommers, McFarland, 2012, pp. 16–27.

Johnson, Lacey M. "Sanctuary." *Orion*, autumn 2022, pp. 39–47.

Johnson, Taylor N. "'The Most Bombed Nation on Earth': Western Shoshone Resistance to the Nevada National Security Site." *Atlantic Journal of Communication*, vol. 26, no. 4, 2018, 224–39.

Johnston, Emily. "Loving a Vanishing World." *Medium*, 9 May 2019, https://medium.com/@enjohnston/loving-a-vanishing-world-ace33c11feo.

Jones, Bruce, and Brent Anderson. "A New Dawn . . . A New World!" *Ka-Zar the Savage*, vol. 1, no. 1, Apr. 1981, pp. 1–31.

Jones, Bruce, and Brent Anderson. "To Air Is Human." *Ka-Zar the Savage*, vol. 1, no. 2, May 1981, pp. 1–31.

Jones, Gerard. *Killing Monsters: Why Children Need Fantasy, Super Heroes, and Make-Believe Violence*. Basic Books, 2002.

Jones, Ryan Tucker. *Empire of Extinction: Russians and the North Pacific's Strange Beasts of the Sea, 1741–1867*. Oxford, 2014.

Jordan, Martin. "Did Lacan Go Camping? Psychotherapy in Search of an Ecological Self." *Vital Signs: Psychological Responses to the Ecological Crisis*, edited by M. Rust and N. K. Totton, 2012, pp. 133–45.

Kafer, Alison. "Bodies of Nature: The Environmental Politics of Disability." *Disability Studies and the Environmental Humanities: Toward an Eco-Crip Theory*, edited by Sarah Jaquette Ray et al., U of Nebraska P, 2017, pp. 201–41.

Kalmus, Peter. "To My Fellow Climate Scientists: Be Human, Be Brave, Speak Truth." *Yes!*, 7 Feb. 2017, https://www.yesmagazine.org/issue/science/2017/02/07/to-my-fellow-climate-scientists-be-human-be-brave-tell-the-truth.

Kaplan, Sarah. "Are We Living in an 'Age of Humans'? Geologists Say No." *Washington Post*, 5 May 5 2024, https://www.washingtonpost.com/climate-environment/2024/03/05/anthropocene-epoch-meaning-crawford-lake/.

Karliner, Joshua. *The Corporate Planet: Ecology and Politics in the Age of Globalization*. Sierra Club Books, 1997.

Kastenbaum, Robert, and Ruth Aisenberg. *The Psychology of Death*. Springer, 1976.

Keats, John. "Ode to a Nightingale." *English Romantic Writers*. Edited by David Perkins. Harcourt Brace, 1995, p. 1252.

Keen, Suzanne. "Fast Tracks to Narrative Empathy: Anthropomorphism and Dehumanization in Graphic Novels." *SubStance* #124, vol. 40, no. 1, 2011, pp. 135–55.

Kelly, John. "Searching for Michael Dougan." *The Comics Journal*, 14 Feb. 2023, https://www.tcj.com/searching-for-michael-dougan/.

Kelly, Walt. *Pogo: We Have Met the Enemy and He Is Us*. Simon & Schuster, 1972.

Kelso, Megan. *Artichoke Tales*. Fantagraphics, 2010.

Kelso, Megan. Personal interview. Summer 2022.

Kelso, Megan. *The Squirrel Mother: Stories*. Fantagraphics, 2006.

Kelso, Megan. *Who Will Make the Pancakes*. Fantagraphics, 2022.

Kerridge, Richard. "Foreword." *Environmental Humanities: Voices from the Anthropocene*, edited by Serpil Oppermann and Serenella Iovino, Rowman & Littlefield, 2016, pp. xiii–xvii.

Kidd, Kenneth. "'A' Is for Auschwitz: Psychoanalysis, Trauma Theory, and the 'Children's Literature of Atrocity.'" *Children's Literature*, vol. 33, 2005, pp. 120–49.

Kidd, Kenneth. *Making American Boys: Boyology and the Feral Tale*. U of Minnesota P, 2004.

Kimmerer, Robin Wall. *Braiding Sweetgrass: Indigenous Wisdom, Scientific Knowledge, and the Teachings of Plants*. Milkweed Editions, 2013.

"Kim Stanley Robinson on 'Utopian' Science Fiction." *The New Yorker Politics and More Podcast*, 30 Aug. 2021, https://www.newyorker.com/podcast/political-scene/kim-stanley-robinson-on-utopian-science-fiction.

Kindlon, Patrick, and Marco Ferrari. *Frontiersman: Volume 1*. Image, 2022.

King, Edward, and Joanna Page. *Posthumanism and the Graphic Novel in Latin America*. UCL Press, 2017, pp.163–81.

King, Frank O. *Sundays with Walt and Skeezix*. Edited by Peter Maresca. Sunday Press, 2007.

Kirby, Jack. "The Devil and Mr. Sacker." *Kamandi: The Last Boy on Earth*, vol. 1, no. 12, Dec. 1973, pp. 1–20.

Kirby, Jack. "The Gift!" *Kamandi: The Last Boy on Earth*, vol. 1, no. 16, Apr. 1974, pp. 1–20.

Kirby, Jack. "The Last Boy on Earth!" *Kamandi: The Last Boy on Earth*, vol. 1, no. 1, Oct. 1972, pp. 1–22.

Kirby, Jack. "Subject: Animals That Stand Erect . . ." *Kamandi: The Last Boy on Earth*, vol. 1, no. 17, May 1974, pp. 1–20.

Kirby, Jack. "Winner Take All!" *Kamandi: The Last Boy on Earth*, vol. 1, no. 14, Feb. 1974, pp. 1–20.

Kleege, Georgina. *More Than Meets the Eye: What Blindness Brings to Art*. Oxford UP, 2018.

Klingle, Matthew W. *Emerald City: An Environmental History of Seattle*. Yale UP, 2007.

Kohl-Welles, Jeanne. "Let's Make Sure Orcas Get What They Need from Us." *Crosscut*, 12 Dec. 2018, https://crosscut.com/2018/12/lets-make-sure-orcas-get-what-they-need-us.

Kohn, Eduardo. *How Forests Think: Toward an Anthropology Beyond the Human*. U of California P, 2013.

Kolbert, Elizabeth. *Field Notes on a Catastrophe: Man, Nature and Climate Change*. Bloomsbury, 2015.

Krauthammer, Charles. "Saving Nature, But Only for Man." *Time*, 17 June 1991, https://content.time.com/time/subscriber/article/0,33009,973199,00.html.

Kristeva, Julia. *Black Sun: Depression and Melancholia*. Columbia UP, 1989.

Kudlow, Larry. "Stop the G20 Assault on Growth and Prosperity." *Fox Business*, 1 Nov. 2021, https://www.foxbusiness.com/media/kudlow-stop-g20-assault-growth-prosperity.

Kukkonen, Karin. "Comics as a Test Case for Transmedial Narratology." *SubStance*, vol. 40, no. 1, 2011, pp. 34–52.

Kunert-Graf, Rachel. "Dehumanized Victims: Analogies and Animal Avatars for Palestinian Suffering in *Waltz with Bashir* and *War Rabbit*." *Humanities*, vol. 7, no. 3, 2018, https://www.mdpi.com/2076-0787/7/3/79/pdf-vor.

Kunzle, David. *The History of the Comic Strip*. U of California P, 1990.

Kuper, Peter. *Ruins*. SelfMadeHero, 2015.

LaDuke, Winona. "The Militarization of Indian Country." *Peace and Freedom*, vol. 72, no. 2, 2012, pp. 11–27.

Lamb, Jonathan. *The Things Things Say*. Princeton UP, 2011.

Lapham, Lewis. "Paying the Piper." *Lapham's Quarterly*, fall 2019, 13–21, https://www.laphamsquarterly.org/climate/paying-piper.

Laplanche, Jean, and J.-B. Pontalis. *The Language of Psycho-Analysis*. Norton, 1974.

Laplante, Kevin de. "Making the Abstract Concrete: How a Comic Can Bring to Life the Central Problems of Environmental Philosophy." *Comics as Philosophy*, edited by Jeff McLaughlin, UP of Mississippi, 2005, pp. 153–72.

Latour, Bruno, et al. "Anthropologists Are Talking—About Capitalism, Ecology, and Apocalypse." *Ethnos*, vol. 83, no. 3, 2018, pp. 587–606.

Lee, Russell. "1947: Year of the Flying Saucer." Smithsonian National Air and Space Museum, 24 June 2022, https://airandspace.si.edu/stories/editorial/1947-year-flying-saucer.

Lee, Stan. *Son of Origins of Marvel Comics*. Simon & Schuster, 1975.

Lee, Stan, and John Buscema. "The Origin of the Silver Surfer!" *Silver Surfer*, vol. 1, no. 1, Aug. 1968, pp. 1–38.

Lehrer, Eli. "Reagan, the Environmentalist." *Weekly Standard*, 17 June 2013, https://www.weeklystandard.com/eli-lehrer/reagan-the-environmentalist.

LeMenager, Stephanie. "Climate Change and the Struggle for Genre." *Anthropocene Reading: Literary History in Geologic Times*, edited by Tobias Menely and Jesse Oak Taylor, Pennsylvania State UP, 2017, pp. 220–38.

LeMenager, Stephanie. *Living Oil: Petroleum Culture in the American Century*. Oxford UP, 2014.

Leopold, Aldo. *Round River: From the Journals of Aldo Leopold*. Oxford UP, 1972.

Leopold, Aldo. *A Sand County Almanac: And Sketches Here and There*. Oxford UP, 1987.

Lerner, Steve. *Sacrifice Zones: The Front Lines of Toxic Chemical Exposure in the United States*. MIT Press, 2012.

Lertzman, Renee. *Environmental Melancholia: Psychoanalytic Dimensions of Engagement*. Routledge, 2015.

Lethem, Jonathan. "The Return of the King, or, Identifying with Your Parents." *Give Our Regards to the Atomsmashers! Writers on Comics*, edited by Sean Howe, Pantheon, 2004, pp. 2–22.

Levin, Bob. *The Pirates and the Mouse: Disney's War Against the Counterculture*. Fantagraphics, 2003.

Lewis, Simon L., and Mark A. Maslin. "Defining the Anthropocene." *Nature*, no. 519, Mar. 2015, pp. 171–80.

Lifton, Robert Jay. *Death in Life: Survivors of Hiroshima*. U of North Carolina P, 1991.

Limnios, Michael. "Interview with American Illustrator/Artist Robert Crumb, Widely Considered to Be the 'Father of Underground Comics.'" *Blues.gr*, 6 Nov. 2015, http://blues.gr/profiles/blogs/interview-with-american-illustrator-artist-robert-crumb-widely.

Linthicum, Kent. "Learning to Teach in the Anthropocene." *Tech Style*, 26 Aug. 2019, http://techstyle.lmc.gatech.edu/learning-to-teach-in-the-anthropocene/.

Llana, Sarah Miller. "Grieving for the Environment, Without Saying 'Climate Change.'" *Christian Science Monitor*, 21 Aug. 2019, https://www.csmonitor.com/World/Americas/2019/0821/Grieving-for-the-environment-without-saying-climate-change.

Lockwood, Alex. "The Affective Legacy of *Silent Spring*." *Environmental Humanities*, vol. 1, 2012, pp. 123–40.

Loh, Waiyee. "Supernatural Monsters and Neo-Victorian Detectives: Capitalism, Rationality and Affect in Japanese Girls' Comics." *Journal of Postcolonial Writing*, vol. 52, no. 4, 2016, pp. 464–80.

Lopez, Barry. *About This Life: Journeys on the Threshold of Memory*. Alfred A. Knopf, 1998.

Lorah, Michael C. "Jens Harder Charts the Universe from Its Alpha . . . Directions." *CBR*, 31 Aug. 2015, https://www.cbr.com/jens-harder-charts-the-universe-from-its-alpha-directions/.

Loss, Robert. "Poetry Comics, Profluent Lingering, and Two Works by Bianca Stone." *The Comics Journal*, 9 Mar. 2015, https://www.tcj.com/poetry-comics-profluent-lingering-and-two-works-by-bianca-stone/.

Loss, Robert. "Profluent Lingering, Trauma and Subjectivity in *Incognegro*." *The International Journal of Comic Art*, vol. 15, no. 2, fall 2013, pp. 528–45.

Luedecke, Patti. "Affect and the Body in Melville's *Bartleby* and Jillian Tamaki and Mariko Tamaki's *Skim*." *The International Journal of Comic Art*, vol. 11, no. 2, fall 2009, pp. 299–321.

Lund, Martin. "'Introducing the Sensational Black Panther!' *Fantastic Four* #52–53, the Cold War, and Marvel's Imagined Africa." *The Comics Grid: Journal of Comics Scholarship*, no. 6, 23 May 2016, https://www.comicsgrid.com/articles/10.16995/cg.80/.

Macdonald, Helen. *H Is for Hawk*. Jonathan Cape, 2014.

Macdonald, Helen. "What Animals Taught Me About Being Human." *The New York Times Magazine*, 16 May 2017, https://www.nytimes.com/2017/05/16/magazine/what-animals-taught-me-about-being-human.html.

Maclean, Ruth, and Dionne Searcey. "Congo to Auction Land to Oil Companies: 'Our Priority Is Not to Save the Planet.'" *The New York Times*, 24 July 2022, https://www.nytimes.com/2022/07/24/world/africa/congo-oil-gas-auction.html?smid=url-share.

Macy, Joanna, and Chris Johnstone. *Active Hope: How to Face the Mess We're in Without Going Crazy*. New World Library, 2012.

Mahato, Mita. *In Between: Poetry Comics by Mita Mahato*. Pleiades Press, 2017.

Mahato, Mita. "*IT'SALLOVER* and Other Poems on Animals." *Anomaly*, no. 30, Apr. 2020, https://anmly.org/ap30/mita-mahato/.

Mahato, Mita. "Keynote Address—Material Comics." Summarized by Madeline Gangnes. *ImageTexT*, vol. 11, no. 3, 2020, https://imagetextjournal.com/keynote-address-material-comics/.

Mahato, Mita. Personal interview. Summer, 2022.

Malm, Andreas. *Fossil Capital: The Rise of Steam Power and the Roots of Global Warming*. Verso, 2016.

Mann, Charles C. *1493: Uncovering the New World Columbus Created*. Knopf, 2011.

Mann, Michael E. "Global Destruction Isn't Funny, but When It Comes to the Climate Crisis, It Might Have to Be." *The Boston Globe*, 21 Dec. 2021, https://www.bostonglobe.com/2021/12/21/opinion/global-destruction-isnt-funny-when-it-comes-climate-crisis-it-might-have-be/.

Manseau, Peter. "The Surprising Religious Backstory of 'Black Panther's' Wakanda." *The Washington Post*, 7 Mar. 2018, https://www.washingtonpost.com/news/acts-of-faith/wp/2018/03/07/the-surprising-religious-backstory-of-black-panthers-wakanda/?noredirect=on&utm_term=.91d290c8582d.

Maran, Timo. "Enchantment of the Past and Semiocide. Remembering Ivar Puura." *Sign Systems Studies*, vol. 41, no. 1, 2013, pp. 146–49.

Marran, Christine L. *Ecology Without Culture: Aesthetics for a Toxic World*. U of Minnesota P, 2017.

Marsh, George Perkins. *Man and Nature*. Edited by David Lowenthal. U of Washington P, 2003.

McCarthy, Michael. *The Moth Snowstorm: Nature and Joy*. New York Review of Books, 2015.

McCloud, Scott. *Making Comics: Storytelling Secrets of Comics, Manga and Graphic Novels*. Harper, 2006.

McCloud, Scott. *Understanding Comics: The Invisible Art*. HarperPerennial, 1994.

McCulloch, Joe. "This Week in Comics! (10/8/14—the Cat Returns)." *The Comics Journal*, 7 Oct. 2014, http://www.tcj.com/this-week-in-comics-10814-the-cat-returns/.

McGreevey, Nora. "Humans Wiped Out Two-Thirds of the World's Wildlife in 50 Years." *Smithsonian*, 16 Sept. 2020, https://www.smithsonianmag.com/smart-news/humans-wiped-out-two-thirds-worlds-wildlife-50-years-180975824/.

McGregor, Don, Billy Graham, et al. "Panther's Rage." *The Black Panther Epic Collection: Panther's Rage*, edited by Cory Sedlmeier, Marvel, 2016, pp. 46–275.

McGuire, Richard. *Here*. Pantheon, 2014.

McKenna, Christine. "Moving Day: A Visit with R. Crumb." *Crumb: Conversations*, edited by D. K. Holm, UP of Mississippi, 2004, pp. 158–63.

McKibben, Bill, ed. *American Earth: Environmental Writing Since Thoreau*. Penguin Putnam, 2008.

McKibben, Bill, ed. *The End of Nature*. Random House, 2006.

Meis, Morgan. "Timothy Morton's Hyper-Pandemic." *The New Yorker*, 8 June 2021, https://www.newyorker.com/culture/persons-of-interest/timothy-mortons-hyper-pandemic.

Menning, Nancy. "Environmental Mourning and the Religious Imagination." *Mourning Nature: Hope at the Heart of Ecological Loss and Grief*, edited by Ashlee Cunsolo and Karen Landman, McGill-Queen's UP, 2017, pp. 39–63.

Merchant, Carolyn. *The Death of Nature: Women, Ecology, and the Scientific Revolution*. Harper & Row, 1980.

Merchant, Carolyn. "Reinventing Eden: Western Culture as a Recovery Narrative." *Uncommon Ground: Toward Reinventing Nature*, edited by William Cronon, W. W. Norton, 1995, pp. 132–70.

Mercier, Jean-Paul. "Who's Afraid of Crumb?" *Crumb: Conversations*, edited by D. K. Holm, UP of Mississippi, 2004, pp. 191–222.

Mies, Maria, and Vandana Shiva. *Ecofeminism*. Fernwood, 1993.

Mikkelson, David. "Ronald Reagan 'If You've Seen One Tree . . .'" *Snopes*, 20 May 2008, https://www.snopes.com/fact-check/if-youve-seen-one-tree/.

Mikkonen, Kai. "Focalization in Comics. From the Specificities of the Medium to Conceptual Reformulation." *Scandinavian Journal of Comic Art*, vol. 1, no. 1, spring 2012, pp. 71–95.

Miles, Tiya. "Everything Has a History: The Ohio River." *Perspectives on History*, 21 Jan. 2022, https://www.historians.org/publications-and-directories/perspectives-on-history/february-2022/the-ohio-river.

Miller, Frank. *The Dark Knight Returns: Tenth Anniversary Edition*. DC, 1996.

Miller, Frank, and Dave Gibbons. *Give Me Liberty*, no. 2, Sept. 1990.

Mills, Stephanie. "Mills College Valedictory Address." *American Earth: Environmental Writing Since Thoreau*, edited by Bill McKibben, Penguin Putnam, 2008, pp. 469–72.

Mitchell, Stephen. *Gilgamesh: A New English Version*. Free Press, 2004.

Mitchell, W. J. T. *Iconology: Image, Text, Ideology*. U of Chicago P, 1986.

Mitchell, W. J. T. "Imperial Landscape." *Landscape and Power*, edited by W. J. T. Mitchell, U of Chicago P, 1994, pp. 5–34.

Moisseinen, Hanneriina. *Kannas*. Kreegah Bundolo, 2016.

Molotiu, Andrei. "Abstract Form: Sequential Dynamism and Iconostasis in Abstract Comics and in Steve Ditko's *Amazing Spider-Man*." *Critical Approaches to Comics: Theories and Methods*, edited by Matthew J. Smith and Randy Duncan, Taylor & Francis, 2012, pp. 84–100.

Molotiu, Andrei. "List of Terms for Comics Studies." *Comics Forum*, 26 July 2013, https://comicsforum.org/2013/07/26/list-of-terms-for-comics-studies-by-andrei-molotiu/.

Monani, Salma. "Evoking Sympathy and Empathy: The Ecological Indian and Indigenous Eco-Activism." *Moving Environments: Affect, Emotion, Ecology and Film*, edited by Alexa Wiek von Mossner, Wilfrid Laurier UP, 2014, pp. 225–47.

Monastersky, Richard, and Nick Sousanis. "The Fragile Framework." *Nature*, no. 527, 24 Nov. 2015, pp. 427–35, https://www.nature.com/articles/527427a.

Monbiot, George. "After the Failure of Cop26, There's Only One Last Hope for Our Survival." *The Guardian*, 14 Nov. 2021, https://www.theguardian.com/commentisfree/2021/nov/14/cop26-last-hope-survival-climate-civil-disobedience.

Mooallem, Jon. "Our Climate Future Is Actually Our Climate Present." *The New York Times Sunday Magazine*, 19 Apr. 2017, https://www.nytimes.com/2017/04/19/magazine/our-climate-future-is-actually-our-climate-present.html.

Moore, Alan, and Stephen Bissette. "Rite of Spring." *Swamp Thing: Love and Death*, edited by Dale Crain, DC Comics, 1990, pp. 185–206.

Moore, Alan, and Rick Veitch. "All Flesh Is Grass." *The Saga of the Swamp Thing: Book Six*, edited by Scott Nybakken, DC Comics, 2014, pp. 105–28.

Morales, Christina, and Allyson Waller. "A Gender-Reveal Celebration Is Blamed for a Wildfire. It Isn't the First Time." *The New York Times*, 7 Sept. 2020; updated 21 July 2021, https://www.nytimes.com/2020/09/07/us/gender-reveal-party-wildfire.html.

Morrow, John. "Kirby at DC." *Jack Kirby 100*. Comic Con International, 2017, pp. 27–30.

Morse, Kathryn. "There Will Be Birds: Images of Oil Disasters in the Nineteenth and Twentieth Centuries." *Journal of American History*, vol. 99, no. 1, 2012, pp. 124–34.

Morton, Timothy. *All Art Is Ecological*. Penguin, 2021.

Morton, Timothy. *Dark Ecology: For a Logic of Future Coexistence*. Columbia UP, 2016.

Morton, Timothy. *The Ecological Thought*. Harvard UP, 2010.

Morton, Timothy. *Ecology Without Nature: Rethinking Environmental Aesthetics*. Harvard UP, 2007.

Morton, Timothy. *Hyperobjects: Philosophy and Ecology After the End of the World*. U of Minnesota P, 2013.

Morton, Timothy. "Queer Ecology." *PMLA*, vol. 125, no. 2, Mar. 2010, pp. 273–82.

Mulkern, Anne C., and E&E News Service. "Deadly Heat Dome Was a 1-in-10,000-Year Event." *Scientific American*, 3 Oct. 2022, https://www.scientificamerican.com/article/deadly-heat-dome-was-a-1-in-10-000-year-event/.

Murphy, Stephen, and Michael Zulli. *The Puma Blues: The Complete Saga in One Volume*. Dover, 2015.

Nagel, Thomas. "What Is It Like to Be a Bat?" *Philosophical Review*, vol. 83, no. 4, Oct. 1974, pp. 435–50.

Nama, Adilifu. *Super Black: American Pop Culture and Black Superheroes*. U of Texas P, 2011.

Nash, A. E. Keir, et al. *Oil Pollution and the Public Interest: A Study of the Santa Barbara Oil Spill*. Institute of Governmental Studies, Berkeley. U of California P, 1972.

"Nature and Climate Change in PNW Comics." Panel organized by José Alaniz. Emerald City Comic Con 2022, 19 Aug. 2022.

Nelson, Brandon. "'Sick Humor Which Serves No Purpose': Whiteman, Angelfood and the Aesthetics of Obscenity in the Comix of R. Crumb." *Journal of Graphic Novels and Comics*, vol. 8, no. 2, 2017, pp. 139–55.

Nikkilä, Aura, and Anna Vuorinne. "Encountering Others Through Graphic Narrative: Layers of Empathy in Hanneriina Moisseinen's *The Isthmus*." *View: Theories and Practices of Visual Culture*, no. 26, 2020, https://www.pismowidok.org/en/archive/empathetic-images#toc.

Nixon, Rob. "The Great Acceleration and the Great Divergence: Vulnerability in the Anthropocene." *MLA Profession*, 2014, https://profession.mla.org/the-great-acceleration-and-the-great-divergence-vulnerability-in-the-anthropocene/.

Nixon, Rob. *Slow Violence and the Environmentalism of the Poor*. Harvard UP, 2013.

Noheden, Kristoffer. "Hypnotic Ecology: Environmental Melancholia in Lars Von Trier's Films." *Journal of Scandinavian Cinema*, vol. 8, no. 2, 2018, pp. 135–48.

Offill, Jenny. *Weather*. Alfred A. Knopf, 2020.

O'Keefe, Derrick. "Imagining the End of Capitalism with Kim Stanley Robinson." *Jacobin*, 10 Oct. 2020, https://jacobin.com/2020/10/kim-stanley-robinson-ministry-future-science-fiction.

Oppermann, Serpil, and Serenella Iovino. "Introduction: The Environmental Humanities and the Challenges of the Anthropocene." *Environmental Humanities: Voices from the Anthropocene*, edited by Serpil Oppermann and Serenella Iovino. Rowman & Littlefield, 2016, pp. 1–21.

Orbán, Katalin. "Trauma and Visuality: Art Spiegelman's *Maus* and *In the Shadow of No Towers*." *Representations*, vol. 97, no. 1, winter 2007, pp. 57–89.

Outka, Paul. *Race and Nature from Transcendentalism to the Harlem Renaissance*. Palgrave Macmillan, 2008.

Parham, John. "Introduction—With or Without Us: Literature and the Anthropocene." *The Cambridge Companion to Literature and the Anthropocene*, edited by John Parham, Cambridge UP, 2021, pp. 1–33.

Parson, Sean. "Thinking Like a Swamp Thing? Developing a Plant Politics and Ethics (Part 2)." *Reading Superheroes Politically*, 29 Apr. 2015, https://readingsuperheroespolitically.wordpress.com/2015/04/29/thinking-like-a-swamp-thing-developing-a-plant-politics-and-ethics-part-2/.

Paulson, Steve. "Where's the Great Climate Change Novel? A Conversation with Amitav Ghosh." *Los Angeles Review of Books*, 22 Sept. 2017, https://lareviewofbooks.org/article/wheres-the-great-climate-change-novel-a-conversation-with-amitav-ghosh/.

Peeters, Benoît. "Four Conceptions of the Page." Translated by Jesse Cohn. *ImageTexT*, vol. 3, no. 3, 2006–2007, https://imagetextjournal.com/four-conceptions-of-the-page/.

Pericolo, Lorenzo. "Visualizing Appearance and Disappearance: On Caravaggio's London *Supper at Emmaus*." *Art Bulletin*, vol. 89, no. 3, Sept. 2007, pp. 519–39.

Perkins, David, ed. *English Romantic Writers*. Harcourt Brace, 1995.

Peterson, Jennifer, and Graig Uhlin. "Introduction: In Focus: Film and Media Studies in the Anthropocene." *Journal of Cinema and Media Studies*, vol. 58, no. 2, winter 2019, pp. 142–46.

Petrini, Micaela. Personal interview. Summer 2023.

Pick, Anat. *Creaturely Poetics: Animality and Vulnerability in Literature and Film*. Columbia UP, 2011.

Pihkala, Panu. "Climate Grief: How We Mourn a Changing Planet." *BBC*, 2 Apr. 2020, https://www.bbc.com/future/article/20200402-climate-grief-mourning-loss-due-to-climate-change.

Poll, Ryan. *Aquaman and the War Against the Oceans: Comics Activism and Allegory in the Anthropocene*. U of Nebraska P, 2022.

Pollan, Michael. "The Intelligent Plant." *The New Yorker*, 15 Dec. 2013, https://www.newyorker.com/magazine/2013/12/23/the-intelligent-plant.

Porcellino, John. *Diary of a Mosquito Abatement Man*. La Mano, 2005.
Powers, Richard. *The Overstory*. W. W. Norton, 2018.
Price, Jennifer. "Looking for Nature at the Mall: A Field Guide to the Nature Company." *Uncommon Ground: Rethinking the Human Place in Nature*, edited by William Cronon, W. W. Norton, 1996, pp. 186–203.
Price, Jenny. *Stop Saving the Planet! An Environmentalist Manifesto*. W. W. Norton, 2021.
Pulkkinen, Levi. "'We Thought It Wouldn't Affect Us': Heatwave Forces Climate Reckoning in Pacific North-West." *The Guardian*, 3 July 2021, https://www.theguardian.com/us-news/2021/jul/03/pacific-northwest-heat-dome-climate-change.
Pyle, Robert Michael. *Where Bigfoot Walks: Crossing the Dark Divide*. Houghton Mifflin, 1995.
Pyle, Robert Michael. *Wintergreen: Rambles in a Ravaged Land*. Charles Scribner's Sons, 1986.
Pyron, Alexander. "We Don't Need to Save Endangered Species. Extinction Is Part of Evolution." *The Washington Post*, 22 Nov. 2017, https://www.washingtonpost.com/outlook/we-dont-need-to-save-endangered-species-extinction-is-part-of-evolution/2017/11/21/57fc5658-cdb4-11e7-a1a3-0d1e45a6de3d_story.html.
Rabiroff, Zach. "The Strange Second Life of Legacy Comic Strips or: I Want Wilbur Weston Dead." *The Comics Journal* 21 March 2022, https://www.tcj.com/the-strange-second-life-of-legacy-comic-strips-or-i-want-wilbur-weston-dead/.
Ragland, Ellie. "Lacan, the Death Drive, and the Dream of the Burning Child." *Death and Representation*, edited by Sarah McKim Webster Goodwin and Elisabeth Bronfen. Johns Hopkins UP, 1993, pp. 80–102.
Ray, Sarah Jaquette, and Jay Sibara. *Disability Studies and the Environmental Humanities: Toward an Eco-Crip Theory*. U of Nebraska P, 2017.
Razinsky, Liran. *Freud, Psychoanalysis and Death*. Cambridge UP, 2013.
"R. D. Ginther, Workingman Artist and Historian of Skid Row." *California Historical Quarterly*, vol. 54, no. 3, 1975, pp. 263–71.
Reagan, Ronald. "Address Before a Joint Session of Congress on the State of the Union. January 25, 1984." Reagan Library Archives, 25 Jan. 1984, https://www.reaganlibrary.gov/archives/speech/address-joint-session-congress-state-union-january-1984.
Reagan, Ronald. "Remarks at Dedication Ceremonies for the New Building of the National Geographic Society." Reagan Library Archives, 19 June 1984, https://www.reaganlibrary.gov/archives/speech/remarks-dedication-ceremonies-new-building-national-geographic-society.
Reichelt, Herb, and Jack Elrod. *Mark Trail Tells the Story of a Fish in Trouble*. US Fish and Wildlife Service. Department of the Interior, 1992.
Revkin, Andrew. "Confronting the 'Anthropocene.'" *The New York Times Blog*, 11 May 2011, https://dotearth.blogs.nytimes.com/2011/05/11/confronting-the-anthropocene/.
Reynolds, Richard. *Super Heroes: A Modern Mythology*. UP of Mississippi, 1992.
Rich, Nathaniel. "Losing Earth: The Decade We Almost Stopped Climate Change." *The New York Times Sunday Magazine*, 1 Aug. 2018, pp. 8–70. https://www.nytimes.com/interactive/2018/08/01/magazine/climate-change-losing-earth.html.
Rich, Nathaniel. *Second Nature: Scenes from a World Remade*. Farrar, Straus & Giroux, 2021.
Richardson, Sarah. "A Very Dirty Word: Cuteness as Affective Strategy in the Comics of Julie Doucet." *The Comics of Julie Doucet and Gabrielle Bell*, edited by Tahneer Oksman and Seamus O'Malley, UP of Mississippi, 2019, pp. 97–121.

Riddle, Margaret. "The ASARCO Smokestack—Once the World's Largest—Is Demolished at the Company's Old Copper Smelter in Ruston, North of Tacoma, on January 17, 1993." *HistoryLink.org*, 26 Aug. 2008, https://www.historylink.org/File/8744.

Rifas, Leonard. "The Politics of Underground Comix and the Environmental Crisis." *The International Journal of Comic Art*, vol. 20, no. 2, fall/winter 2018, pp. 128–50.

Rinde, Meir. "Richard Nixon and the Rise of American Environmentalism." *Distillations*, 2 June 2017, https://www.sciencehistory.org/distillations/richard-nixon-and-the-rise-of-american-environmentalism.

Riney-Kehrberg, Pamela. *The Nature of Childhood: An Environmental History of Growing Up in America Since 1865*. UP of Kansas, 2014.

Ro, Ronin. *Tales to Astonish: Jack Kirby, Stan Lee, and the American Comic Book Revolution*. Bloomsbury, 2004.

Robinson, Kim Stanley. *The Ministry for the Future*. Orbit, 2020.

Ronda, Margaret. "Mourning and Melancholia in the Anthropocene." *Post45*, 10 June 2013, http://post45.research.yale.edu/2013/06/mourning-and-melancholia-in-the-anthropocene/.

Rosenfeld, Jordan. "Facing Down 'Environmental Grief': Is a Traumatic Sense of Loss Freezing Action Against Climate Change?" *Scientific American*, 21 July 2016, https://www.scientificamerican.com/article/facing-down-environmental-grief/.

Rosenkranz, Patrick. *Rebel Visions: The Underground Comix Revolution, 1963–1975*. Fantagraphics, 2002.

Roth, Annie. "The Ocean's Biggest Garbage Pile Is Full of Floating Life." *The New York Times*, 6 May 2022, https://www.nytimes.com/2022/05/06/science/great-pacific-garbage-patch-pollution.html.

Roux, Alwyn. "A Mesh of Strange Strangers in Juliana Spahr's *Well Then There Now* (2011): An Exploration of Timothy Morton's Ecological Thought." *Journal of Literary Studies*, vol. 37, no. 1, 2021, pp. 53–69.

Rovnak, John. "Panel to Panel Classics #2: Steve Murphy Comes Out of His Shell." *Panel to Panel: Exploring Words and Pictures*, 17 Feb. 2013, http://paneltopanel.net/?tag=steve-murphy.

Russell, Adrienne. *The Mediated Climate: How Journalists, Big Tech, and Activists Are Vying for Our Future*. Columbia UP, 2023.

Ryan, John. "Can Seattle Take the Heat? Officials Say Area Is Better Prepared This Summer." 22 June 2023, https://www.kuow.org/stories/officials-say-seattle-is-better-prepared-now-for-extreme-temps-than-in-2021.

Ryan, John. "Extreme Heat Cooks Shellfish Alive on Puget Sound Beaches." *KUOW*, 7 July 2021, https://www.kuow.org/stories/extreme-heat-cooks-shellfish-alive-on-puget-sound-beaches.

Ryan, John. "Grief-Stricken Orca Has a New Baby in Salish Sea." *KUOW*, 6 Sept. 2020, https://www.kuow.org/stories/grief-stricken-orca-has-a-new-baby.

Sacco, Joe. *Paying the Land*. Metropolitan Books, 2020.

Scammell, Rosie. "Cardinal Pell on Environmental Encyclical: Church Has 'No Particular Expertise in Science.'" *America: The Jesuit Review*, 17 July 2015, https://www.americamagazine.org/issue/cardinal-pell-church-has-no-particular-expertise-science.

Scarry, Elaine. *The Body in Pain: The Making and Unmaking of the World*. Oxford UP, 1985.

Schama, Simon. *Landscape and Memory*. A. A. Knopf, 1995.

Scheffer, Victor B. *The Shaping of Environmentalism in America*. U of Washington P, 1991.

Scher, Avichai. "'Climate Grief': The Growing Emotional Toll of Climate Change." *NBC*, 24 Dec. 2018, https://www.nbcnews.com/health/mental-health/climate-grief-growing-emotional-toll-climate-change-n946751.

Schlosser, Julia. *Remembering Animals: Rituals, Artifacts and Narratives*. California State University Northridge, 2018.

Scranton, Roy. *Learning to Die in the Anthropocene: Reflections on the End of a Civilization*. City Lights, 2015.

Sealts, Merton M., et al. *Emerson's Nature: Origin, Growth, Meaning*. 2nd ed. Southern Illinois UP, 1979.

Searles, Harold F. "Unconscious Processes in Relation to the Environmental Crisis." *Psychoanalytic Review*, no. 59, 1972, pp. 361–74.

Sedlmeier, Cory, ed. *Black Panther Epic Collection: Panther's Rage*. Marvel, 2016.

Seymour, Nicole. *Bad Environmentalism: Irony and Irreverence in the Ecological Age*. U of Minnesota P, 2018.

Seymour, Nicole. "Toward an Irreverent Ecocriticism." *Journal of Ecocriticism*, vol. 4, no. 2, July 2012, pp. 56–71.

Shackle, Samira. "'We'll Be Hated, but It Will Stir Things Up': Insulate Britain on What Happened Next—and Being Right All Along." *The Guardian*, 17 Dec. 2022, https://www.theguardian.com/environment/2022/dec/17/insulate-britain-on-what-happened-next-energy-crisis.

Shakespeare, William. *Hamlet*. Edited by Harold Jenkins. Methuen, 1982.

Sharp, Patrick B. "Questing for an Indigenous Future: Leslie Marmon Silko's *Ceremony* as Indigenous Science Fiction." *Black and Brown Planets*, edited by Isiah Lavendar III, UP of Mississippi, 2014, pp. 117–30.

Sheffield, Derek. "What Will Keep Us." *Dear America: Letters of Hope, Habitat, Defiance and Democracy*, edited by Simmons Buntin et al., Trinity UP, 2020, pp. 60–61.

Shepard, Paul. *Man in the Landscape: A Historic View of the Esthetics of Nature*. Texas A&M UP, 1991.

Shneidman, Edwin S. *Deaths of Man*. Quadrangle, 1973.

Shpolberg, Masha, and Lukas Brasiskis. "Introduction." *Cinema and the Environment in Eastern Europe*, edited by Masha Shpolberg and Lukas Brasiskis, Berghan, 2023, pp. 1–18.

Silko, Leslie Marmon. "Landscape, History and the Pueblo Imagination." *At Home on the Earth: Becoming Native to Our Place: A Multicultural Anthology*, edited by David Landis Barnhill, U of California P, 1999, pp. 30–42.

Sinha, Arushi. "'All I'm Trying to Do Is Write About the World as I See It': Amitav Ghosh on His New Book, His Inspirations and His Hopes for the Future of Literature." *Vogue*, 25 Oct. 2021, https://www.vogue.in/culture-and-living/content/amitav-ghosh-on-his-new-book-the-nutmegs-curse-parables-for-a-planet-in-crisis.

Smith, Katharine Capshaw. "Forum: Trauma and Children's Literature." *Children's Literature*, vol. 33, 2005, pp. 115–19.

Smith, Philip. "Rhyming Events: Contested Narratives and 'Cli-Fi' in Richard McGuire's *Here*." *Inks: The Journal of the Comics Studies Society*, vol. 2, no. 1, spring 2018, pp. 38–48.

Smith, Robert Rowland. *Death-Drive: Freudian Hauntings in Literature and Art*. Edinburgh UP, 2010.

Smith, Scott T., and José Alaniz. *Uncanny Bodies: Superhero Comics and Disability*. Penn State University Press, 2019.

Smolderen, Thierry. "Of Labels, Loops and Bubbles: Solving the Historical Puzzle of the Speech Balloon." *Comic Art*, no. 8, summer 2006, pp. 90–112.

Snyder, Gary. *The Practice of the Wild: Essays by Gary Snyder*. North Point Press, 1990.

Soles, Carter. "Mad Max: Beyond Petroleum?" *Gender and Environment in Science Fiction*, edited by Christy Tidwell and Bridgitte Barclay, Lexington Books, 2019, pp. 185–201.

Solnit, Rebecca. "The Thoreau Problem." *American Earth: Environmental Writing Since Thoreau*, edited by Bill McKibben, Penguin Putnam, 2008, pp. 971–74.

Sommer, Lauren. "Here's What World Leaders Agreed to—and What They Didn't—at the U.N. Climate Summit." *NPR*, 13 Nov. 2021, https://www.npr.org/2021/11/13/1055542738/cop26-climate-summit-final-decision.

Speelman, Tom. "How Black Panther Pioneered Modern Comics with 'Panther's Rage.'" *Comics Alliance*, 16 May 2016, https://comicsalliance.com/black-panther-panthers-rage-don-mcgregor/.

Spezio, Teresa Sabol. *Slick Policy: Environmental and Science Policy in the Aftermath of the Santa Barbara Oil Spill*. U of Pittsburgh P, 2018.

Spiegelman, Art. "Commix: An Idiosyncratic Historical and Aesthetic Overview." *Print*, no. 42, Nov.–Dec. 1988, pp. 61–73, 195–96.

Stanescu, James. "Species Trouble: Judith Butler, Mourning, and the Precarious Lives of Animals." *Hypatia*, vol. 27, no. 3, 2012, pp. 567–82.

Stark, Jeffrey A. "Postmodern Environmentalism: A Critique of Deep Ecology." *Ecological Resistance Movements: The Global Emergence of Radical and Popular Environmentalism*, edited by Bron Raymond Taylor, State U of New York P, 1995, pp. 259–81.

Stein, Daniel. *Authorizing Superhero Comics: On the Evolution of a Popular Serial Genre*. Ohio State UP, 2021.

Stern, Roger, and John Buscema. "Holocaust in a Hidden Land!" *The Avengers*, vol. 1, no. 257, July 1985, pp. 1–22.

Stern, Roger, and John Buscema. "Pyrrhic Victory!" *The Avengers*, vol. 1, no. 258, Aug. 1985, pp. 1–22.

Stern, Roger, and John Buscema. "This Power Unleashed!" *The Avengers*, vol. 1, no. 256, June 1985, pp. 1–22.

Stern, Roger, and Kerry Gammill. *Superman for Earth*. DC Comics, 1991.

Stone, Tucker, and David Brothers. "Fear of a Black Panther." *The Comics Journal*, 16 Feb. 2018, http://www.tcj.com/fear-of-a-black-panther/.

Storr, Anthony. *Human Aggression*. Bantam, 1970.

Stradling, David, ed. *The Environmental Moment: 1968–1972*. U of Washington P, 2012.

Strongbow, Jon. "Gone but Not Forgotten." *Ghosts of Seattle Past: An Anthology of Lost Seattle Places*, edited by Jaimee Garbacik, Chin Music Press, 2017.

Strongbow, Jon. *The Hidden World*. Starhead Comix, 1996.

Strongbow, Jon. *The Ocean of Time*. Strangebeau Productions & Mystery School Press, 2008.

Strongbow, Jon. Personal interview. Summer 2022.

Strycker, Noah. "To Save Birds, Should We Kill Off Cats?" *National Geographic*, Oct. 2019, https://www.nationalgeographic.com/animals/article/essay-to-save-birds-should-we-kill-off-cats.

Swanson, Heather Anne. "The Banality of the Anthropocene." *Fieldsights*, 22 Feb. 2017, https://culanth.org/fieldsights/the-banality-of-the-anthropocene.

Szasz, Ferenc Morton. *The Day the Sun Rose Twice: The Story of the Trinity Site Nuclear Explosion, July 16, 1945*. U of New Mexico P, 1984.

Szép, Eszter. *Comics and the Body: Drawing, Reading, and Vulnerability*. Ohio State UP, 2020.

Szerszynski, Bronislaw. "The Post-Ecologist Condition: Irony as Symptom and Cure." *Environmental Politics*, vol. 16, no. 2, Apr. 2007, pp. 337–55.

Taylor, Jesse Oak. "Anthropocene." *Victorian Literature and Culture*, vol. 46, nos. 3–4, 2018, pp. 573–77.

Taylor, Sunaura. "Beasts of Burden: Disability Studies and Animal Rights." *Qui Parle: Critical Humanities and Social Sciences*, vol. 19, no. 2, 2011, pp. 191–222.

Thielman, Sam. "The Cute and Horrifying World of Jim Woodring." *The New Yorker*, 9 Aug. 2022, https://www.newyorker.com/books/page-turner/the-cute-and-horrifying-world-of-jim-woodring.

Thomas, Cathy. "'Black' Comics as Cultural Archive of Black Life in America." *Feminist Media Histories*, vol. 4, no. 3 2018, pp. 49–95.

Thomas, Roy, and John Buscema. "The Monarch and the Man-Ape!" *The Avengers*, vol. 1, no. 62, Mar. 1969, pp. 1–18.

Thomas, Roy, and Sal Buscema. "Look Homeward, Avenger!" *The Avengers*, vol. 1, no. 87, Apr. 1971, pp. 1–20.

Thompson, Ben. "Adventures of Ka-Zar the Great." *Marvel Mystery Comics* #11, Sept. 1940, n.p.

Thompson, Ilse, ed. *Your Vigor for Life Appalls Me: Robert Crumb Letters, 1968–1977*. Fantagraphics, 2012.

Thrush, Coll. *Native Seattle: Histories from the Crossing-Over Place*. U of Washington P, 2009.

Tidwell, Christy. "Spiraling Inward and Outward: Junji Ito's *Uzumaki* and the Scope of Ecohorror." *Fear and Nature: Ecohorror Studies in the Anthropocene*, edited by Carter Soles and Christy Tidwell, Penn State UP, 2021, pp. 42–67.

Tribunella, Eric L. *Melancholia and Maturation: The Use of Trauma in American Children's Literature*. U of Tennessee P, 2010.

Tumey, Paul C. "The Seattle Underground Comics Scene Is Alive and Oozing." *The Comics Journal*, 25 Apr. 2014, https://www.tcj.com/the-seattle-undergound-comics-scene-is-alive-and-oozing/.

Tumey, Paul C. *The Umbrella Man: Dok Hager—Seattle's First Great Cartoonist*. Unpublished.

Van den Berg, J. H. "The Subject and his Landscape." *Romanticism and Consciousness: Essays in Criticism*, edited by Harold Bloom, W. W. Norton, 1970, pp. 57–65.

Van Syckle, Edwin. *They Tried to Cut It All*. Pacific Search Press, 1980.

Vaughan, Adam. "Greta Thunberg: You Have Stolen My Childhood with Your Empty Words." *New Scientist*, 23 Sept. 2019, https://www.newscientist.com/article/2217418-greta-thunberg-you-have-stolen-my-childhood-with-your-empty-words.

Veitch, Rick. "Tiny Dancer." *Slow Death Zero: The Comix Anthology of Ecological Horror* edited by Jon B. Cooke and Ron Turner, Last Gasp, 2020, pp. 73–80.

Verdery, Katherine. *The Political Lives of Dead Bodies: Reburial and Postsocialist Change*. Columbia UP, 1999.

Vergès, Françoise. "Racial Capitalocene." *Futures of Black Radicalism*, edited by Gaye Theresa Johnson and Alex Lubin, Verso, 2017, pp. 72–82.

Vogel, J., et al. *In the Hot Seat: Saving Lives from Extreme Heat in Washington State.* University of Washington Climate Impacts Group et al., 2023.

Vold, Veronica. "The Aesthetics of Environmental Equity in American Newspaper Strips." *Ecomedia: Key Issues*, edited by Stephen Rust et al., Routledge, 2016, pp. 72–82.

Wald, Chelsea. "Archaeageddon: How Gas-Belching Microbes Could Have Caused Mass Extinction." *Nature*, 2014, https://www.nature.com/articles/nature.2014.14958#citeas.

Walker, Alice. "Everything Is a Human Being." *American Earth: Environmental Writing Since Thoreau*, edited by Bill McKibben, Penguin Putnam, 2008, pp. 659–70.

Wallace-Wells, David. "Beyond Catastrophe: A New Climate Reality Is Coming Into View." *The New York Times*, 26 Oct. 2022, https://www.nytimes.com/interactive/2022/10/26/magazine/climate-change-warming-world.html.

Wallace-Wells, David. "Has Climate Change Blinded Us to the Biodiversity Crisis?" *The New York Times*, 21 Dec, 2022, https://www.nytimes.com/2022/12/21/opinion/climate-change-biodiversity-crisis-cop15.html.

Walton, Peter: "The 'Archaic Mother' in Charles Burns' *Black Hole*: A Psychoanalytic Reading." *The International Journal of Comic Art*, vol. 10, no. 1, 2008, pp. 522–34.

Wandtke, Terrence. "Frank Miller Strikes Again and Batman Becomes a Postmodern Anti-Hero: The Tragi(Comic) Reformulation of the Dark Knight." *The Amazing Tansforming Superhero: Essays on the Revision of Characters in Comic Books, Film and Television*, edited by Terrence Wandtke, McFarland, 2007, pp. 87–111.

Wanzo, Rebecca Ann. "And All Our Past Decades Have Seen Revolutions: The Decolonization of Black Panther." *The Black Scholar*, 19 Feb. 2018, https://www.theblackscholar.org/past-decades-seen-revolutions-long-decolonization-black-panther-rebecca-wanzo/.

Wanzo, Rebecca Ann. *The Content of Our Caricature: African American Comic Art and Political Belonging*. New York UP, 2020.

Watson, Richard B., and Dennis D. Muraoka. "The Northern Spotted Owl Controversy." *Society & Natural Resources*, vol. 5, no. 1, 1992, pp. 85–90.

Wegner, Gesine. "Reflections on the Boom of Graphic Pathography: The Effects and Affects of Narrating Disability and Illness in Comics." *Journal of Literary and Cultural Disability Studies*, vol. 14, no.1, 2020, pp. 57–74.

Weik von Mossner, Alexa. *Affective Ecologies: Empathy, Emotion, and Environmental Narrative*. Ohio State UP, 2017.

Weil, Kari. *Thinking Animals: Why Animal Studies Now?* Columbia UP, 2012.

Wein, Len, and Dave Cockrum. "Second Genesis." *Giant Size X-Men* #1, May 1975, pp. 1–68.

Weinstock, Jeffrey Andrew. *Gothic Things: Dark Enchantment and Anthropocene Anxiety*. Fordham Press, 2023.

Wells, Paul. *The Animated Bestiary: Animals, Cartoons, and Culture*. Rutgers UP, 2009.

Weston, Phoebe. "Half of World's Bird Species in Decline as Destruction of Avian Life Intensifies." *The Guardian*, 28 Sept. 2022, https://www.theguardian.com/environment/2022/sep/28/nearly-half-worlds-bird-species-in-decline-as-destruction-of-avian-life-intensifies-aoe.

Wicker, Alden. "Don't Let Consumerism Co-opt the Zero-Waste Concept." *Yes! The Solving Plastic Issue*, summer 2021, pp. 30–34.

Wheeler, Wendy. "Ecologies of Meaning and Loss." *The Dark Mountain Project*, 25 Aug. 2017, https://dark-mountain.net/in-other-tongues-ecologies-of-meaning-and-loss/.

White, Curtis. "The Ecology of Work." *Orion*, May/June 2007, https://orionmagazine.org/article/the-ecology-of-work/?fbclid=IwAR2H5Omio_dOtbeUo4fMFMy1fNomXniGu8WR9zSvG6lV6lCC5SvvTZjOhI.

White, Curtis. "The Idols of Environmentalism." *Orion*, Mar./Apr. 2007, https://orionmagazine.org/article/the-idols-of-environmentalis/.

White, Lynn, Jr. "The Historical Roots of Our Ecological Crisis." *American Earth: Environmental Writing Since Thoreau*, edited by Bill McKibben, Penguin Putnam, 2008, pp. 405–12.

White, Richard. "'Are You an Environmentalist, or Do You Work for a Living?': Work and Nature." *Uncommon Ground: Toward Reinventing Nature*, edited by William Cronon, W. W. Norton, 1995, pp. 171–85.

Whitney, Elspeth. "Lynn White Jr.'s 'The Historical Roots of Our Ecologic Crisis' After 50 Years." *History Compass*, vol. 13, no. 8, 2015, pp. 396–410.

Whyte, Kyle. "Settler Colonialism, Ecology, and Environmental Injustice." *Environment and Society*, vol. 9, no. 1, 2018, pp. 125–44.

Wilde, Thomas. "Remembering Jon Strongbow, a Mainstay of Seattle's Art Scene." *GeekWire*, 24 Mar. 2023, https://www.geekwire.com/2023/remembering-jon-strongbow-a-mainstay-of-seattles-art-scene/.

Williams, Linda. *Hard Core: Power, Pleasure and the Frenzy of the Visible*. U of California P, 1989.

Wimsatt, W. K. "The Structure of Romantic Nature Imagery." *Romanticism and Consciousness: Essays in Criticism*, edited by Harold Bloom, W. W. Norton, 1970, pp. 77–88.

Witek, Joseph. *Comic Books as History: The Narrative Art of Jack Jackson, Art Spiegelman, and Harvey Pekar*. UP of Mississippi, 1989.

Wolfe, Cary. *Animal Rites: American Culture, the Discourse of Species, and Posthumanist Theory*. U of Chicago Press, 2003.

Wolford, Wendy. "The Plantationocene: A Lusotropical Contribution to the Theory." *Annals of the American Association of Geographers*, vol. 111, no. 6, Feb. 2021, pp. 1622–39.

Wolk, Douglas. *Reading Comics: How Graphic Novels Work and What They Mean*. Da Capo, 2007.

Woodhouse, Keith Mako. *The Ecocentrists: A History of Radical Environmentalism*. Columbia UP, 2018.

Woodward, Kathleen. "The Feeling of Freedom, Planetary Affect, and Feminist Emotion: Recent Work by Video Artist Cecelia Condit." *Feminist Media Histories*, vol. 7, no. 2, 2021, pp. 65–91.

Woodward, Kathleen. "Late Theory, Late Style: Loss and Renewal in Freud and Barthes." *Aging and Gender in Literature: Studies in Creativity*, edited by Anne Wyatt-Brown and Janice Rossen, U of Virginia P, 1993, pp. 82–101.

Woodyat, Amy. "A Baby Zebra Died in a Zoo in England After Being Startled by Fireworks." *CNN*, 11 Nov. 2020, https://www.cnn.com/travel/article/zebra-firework-intl-scli-gbr/index.html.

Woolf, Virginia. "The Death of the Moth." *The Norton Book of Nature Writing*, edited by Robert Finch and John Elder, W. W. Norton, 1990, pp. 374–77.

Worden, Daniel. *Petrochemical Fantasies: The Art and Energy of American Comics*. Ohio State UP, 2024.

Worden, Daniel. "The Shameful Art: *McSweeney's Quarterly Concern*, Comics and the Politics of Affect." *Modern Fiction Studies*, vol. 52, no. 4, winter 2006), pp. 891–917.

Workman, David et al. *We Are Puget Sound: Discovering and Recovering the Salish Sea.* Braided River, 2019.

Worth, Alexi. "Genius in a Box." *Art in America*, vol. 104, no. 1, Jan. 2016, pp. 68–75.

Wright, Bradford W. *Comic Book Nation: The Transformation of Youth Culture in America.* Johns Hopkins UP, 2001.

Yezbick, Daniel F. "Lions and Tigers and Fears: A Natural History of the Sequential Animal." *Animal Comics: Multispecies Storyworlds in Graphic Narratives*, edited by David Herman, Bloomsbury, 2018, pp. 29–51.

Yokoyama, Yusuke, et al. "Plutonium Isotopes in the North Western Pacific Sediments Coupled with Radiocarbon in Corals Recording Precise Timing of the Anthropocene." *Scientific Reports*, vol. 12, no. 1, 2022, n.p.

Yusoff, Kathryn. *A Billion Black Anthropocenes or None.* U of Minnesota P, 2018.

Zhong, Raymond. "For Planet Earth, This Might Be the Start of a New Age." *The New York Times*, 17 Dec. 2022, https://www.nytimes.com/2022/12/17/climate/anthropocene-age-geology.html.

Zilboorg, Gregory. "Introduction." Freud, Sigmund. *Beyond the Pleasure Principle*. Translated by James Strachey. W. W. Norton, 1961, pp. xxv–xxxv.

Žižek, Slavoj. *Looking Awry: An Introduction to Jacques Lacan Through Popular Culture.* MIT Press, 1991.

INDEX

Active Hope, 255
affect, 9, 26–40, 54, 76, 137, 157, 182, 187, 260nn8–10; and comics, 33–38, 43, 45, 47–48, 61, 78, 147, 230–31, 276n32
Alaimo, Stacy, 18, 36–37, 198, 259n37
Anderson, Brent, 100–102, 269n34
animal death, 60, 78–80, 140, 148–50, 152–58, 160–63, 172–77, 219, 249–50, 270n3, 276n33, 276n1
animals, 9, 12, 17, 34, 45, 51–53, 57, 73–80, 87–88, 94, 96–97, 101–2, 113, 128–30, 133, 139–58, 159–84, 203, 209, 211–12, 228, 229–33, 237, 239, 244, 246, 248, 249–51, 253, 266nn58–59, 267n60, 267nn62–64, 267n67, 268n4, 272n32, 273n3, 273n5, 274n6, 274n11, 275n18, 275n22, 275n25, 276n32, 277n14, 279n32, 284n47
Anthropocene: alternate names for, 14, 213; defined, 5; origins of term, 10; resistance to the term, 10–11
anthropocentrism, 15, 18, 28, 53, 88, 156, 160, 267n65
Association for the Study of Literature and the Environment (ASLE), 8, 257n11, 287n26
atomic bomb, 11, 23, 54, 66, 73, 106, 116, 120, 185–88, 192, 199, 202, 204–5, 283n42
Avengers, 8, 23, 103–8, 168, 174, 265n35, 277n16, 279n31

"Bad Environmentalism," 26, 137, 232. *See also* Seymour, Nicole
Bak, T Edward, 227–30, 241, 244, 247, 254, 287n20

Baudrillard, Jean, 279n32
Biden, Joe, 99
Bigfoot, 127–35, 220–21, 272n32
Black Bolt, 4–7
Black Panther (T'Challa), 80, 102, 159–84
Black Panther Party, 226
Brown, Norman O., 185, 199, 209, 283n39
Bukatman, Scott, 46–48, 73, 108, 263n12
Buscema, John, 55, 103–8, 168, 269n33
Buscema, Sal, 45–46, 280n43
Butler, Judith, 36, 153, 188
Byrne, John, 3–7, 9, 44–43, 46, 55–56, 61–62, 64, 257n10

"Cancer Alley," 24, 108
capitalism, 14–15, 31, 43, 48, 56, 68, 78, 107, 196, 210, 228, 246, 269n30, 277n14
Capp, Al, 77–78
Captain America (Steve Rogers), 103, 106, 108, 259n3, 263n19, 273n1
Carson, Rachel, 11, 25, 45, 122, 155, 164, 209, 230, 260n9
Casper, Cord-Christian, 84–85, 87–88, 109, 269n18
Chadwick, Paul, 70–72, 85, 269n16
Chakrabarty, Dipesh, 18, 90, 259n31, 276n28
Chen, Mel, 4, 36, 39, 181–82, 260n10
Chernobyl, 185, 187, 280n4
Christianity, 13–14, 127
Chute, Hillary, 33–35, 37, 106, 120
Clare, Eli, 38–39, 88
Clean Air Act (1970), 11, 98, 121, 164
cli-fi, 22, 25, 32, 156, 252, 259n2, 261n20, 276n29

319

climate change, 5, 7, 9–12, 14, 18, 21–22, 24–25, 27–28, 30–33, 37, 45, 48, 81–82, 85, 89–90, 94–100, 108, 115–16, 154–55, 185, 189, 218–19, 225, 228, 231–32, 238, 241, 245–48, 251–52, 254–55, 258n20, 259n1, 263n16, 264n34, 286n11, 287n26, 289n43; and activism, 97, 109, 258n20, 261n25; and climate denialism, 11, 261n22, 18; and mental health, 30–31, 261n21. *See also* eco-anxiety

climate change refugees, 3, 8, 58, 96

Cold War, 23, 25, 54, 116, 120, 187, 189, 192, 199, 271n15, 277n13, 279n29. *See also* atomic bomb

consumerism, 11, 21, 22–23, 129, 135

COVID-19 pandemic, 96, 99, 215

Crumb, Robert, 26, 34, 113–38

Crutzen, Paul J., 10, 257n13, 282n35

Crystal (Inhuman), 4, 7

dark ecology, 14–15, 95, 102, 231, 260n6, 261n29, 269n19. *See also* Morton, Timothy

Dark Mountain Project, 25, 64

Darwin, Charles, 13, 153, 275n24

Death Drive, 199, 201, 203, 208–10, 283n39

de Beauvoir, Simone, 138

deep ecology, 31, 88, 116, 121–26, 136, 191, 255, 272n26

deep time, 22–23, 73, 81, 90–93, 241

Deepwater Horizon disaster, 24, 182

Defenders, The, 44

deforestation, 5, 11, 21, 24, 56–58, 197, 217–18, 258n20

Derrida, Jacques, 76, 156–57

Dobrin, Sidney, 22, 45, 81, 257n9, 263n20, 263n23

Dodd, Ed, 52–53, 160, 230, 263nn20–21

Don't Look Up (McKay), 27, 257n12

Dr. Doom (Victor Von Doom), 167

Earth Day, 9, 27, 43, 45, 54–55, 60, 99, 109, 115–16, 140, 155, 164, 262n5, 264n27, 271n20

eco-anxiety, 31, 97

ecocriticism, 22, 27, 38, 81, 136–37, 181, 210, 264n33

eco-grief, 29–33, 44, 88, 96, 189, 261n25. *See also* eco-anxiety

Edinburg, TX, 9, 45

Eisner, Will, 76, 78

Endangered Species Act (1973), 11, 54, 121, 164

Environmental Protection Agency, 11, 45, 54, 56, 121, 164, 218–19

Extinction Rebellion, 12, 258n21

Fantastic Four, 3–9, 41, 61, 105, 165–68, 257n2, 257n6, 265n46, 273n1

Fernandes, Roger, 234–37, 240, 244–46, 248, 287n25, 287nn27–29

Floyd, George, 220

fossil fuels, 10, 12, 21, 98, 241, 250, 254–55, 258n21, 289n44

Frahm, Ole, 84, 269n18

Franzen, Jonathan, 18, 259n35

Freud, Sigmund, 129–30, 153, 187–88, 190, 197–99, 201, 207, 281n9, 281n16, 282n30, 283nn36–39, 285n60

Friedrich, Caspar David, 43, 206

Fury, Nick, 4, 7

gender reveal, 10–11, 24, 97

Gerber, Steve, 44–46, 264n24

Ghosh, Amitav, 8, 18, 48, 263n16, 265n42

Gibbons, Dave, 47, 68–69

Godzilla, 23, 29, 64, 98

Great Acceleration, 11, 25, 258n16

Groensteen, Thierry, 47

Hager, John Ross "Dok," 221–22

Hansen, James, 22

Haraway, Donna, 14, 18, 31, 36–37, 210, 261n28

Harder, Jens, 90–93, 269n24

Hatfield, Charles, ix, 41, 47–48, 84–85, 120, 141, 146–47, 154, 165, 167, 261n26, 262n1, 262n7, 262n10, 265n46, 268n11, 268n14, 271n19, 273n3, 274n6, 275n16, 276n30, 277nn9–10, 278n20, 287n20

Hawkeye (Clint Barton), 97

Homo destructor, 21

hyperobjects, 7, 14–15, 81, 103, 167, 257n7, 267n2. *See also* Morton, Timothy

Indigeneity, 4, 17, 24, 28, 37, 57, 107, 136, 211, 225, 227–28, 237–39, 260n8, 285n66, 270n3, 270n9, 273n40, 287n25, 287n30. *See also* Fernandes, Roger; Native Americans
Industrial Revolution, 11
Inhumans, 3–9, 96, 105
Inslee, Jay, 219, 254, 289n48

Jones, Bruce, 100–102, 264n30, 269n34

Kamandi, the Last Boy on Earth, 139–58
Ka-Zar (David Rand), 51–52, 269n31
Ka-Zar (Kevin Plunder), 100–103, 106–8, 269n31, 269n34, 274n8
Kelly, Walt, 53–54, 263n23, 264nn24–26, 280n5
Kelso, Megan, 223–27, 238, 244, 247, 286nn12–13, 286nn16–17, 287n19
Key Peninsula News, 249–50
King, Frank, 49–51, 85, 263n17
Kirby, Jack, 47, 61, 85, 139–58, 165–68, 257n10, 263n12, 263n19, 265n46, 269n31, 273nn1–5, 274n6, 274n15, 275nn16–19, 275nn26–27, 277n9, 278n20, 280n42
Kirby Krackle, 105
Kuper, Peter, 73–75, 266n49, 266n51

Lee, Stan, 41–43, 61, 165–68, 257n10, 262n1, 265n46, 269n31, 273n1, 280n42
LeMenager, Stephanie, ix, 18, 21–22, 24, 32–33, 164, 248, 252, 258n15, 259n31, 260n4, 261n24
Leopold, Aldo, 25, 33, 71, 122, 179, 265n44, 280nn40–41

Mahato, Mita, 231–34, 244, 246–47, 287n24
McCloud, Scott, 85
McGuire, Richard, 33, 72–73, 76, 266n50
McKibben, Bill, 5, 115, 244
"mega-image," 41, 46–55, 60–61, 63–74, 83, 92, 105, 241, 254, 263nn15–16, 286n14
Miller, Frank, 66–69
Ministry for the Future, The (Robinson), 25, 95, 269n25
Moisseinen, Hanneriina, 78–80

Moore, Alan, 47, 64–66, 264n24, 265n36, 284n50
Morton, Timothy, 7, 9, 14–15, 17, 22, 28, 33, 81–83, 85–89, 93–96, 102, 107, 109, 167, 181, 231–32, 234, 257n7, 260n6, 261n29, 262n11, 263n16, 267n2, 268n6, 268n10, 269n17, 269n19, 269n22
Muir, John, 25, 27, 122, 210
Murphy, Stephen, 16–17, 38, 76, 88–89, 185–213, 281nn18–22, 282nn23–24, 283nn42–43, 284n48, 284n54. See also *Puma Blues, The*

Nakate, Vanessa, 258n20
Namor the Submariner, 62
Native Americans, 27, 55, 66, 211–12, 214–15, 218, 220, 228, 234–37, 239–40, 248, 261, 287n25, 288nn33–34. *See also* Fernandes, Roger; Indigeneity
Nelson, Brandon, 115, 129, 133, 135, 137, 272n36
Nelson, Gaylord, 54
Nixon, Richard, 11, 45, 121, 164, 264n25, 272n21, 277n8
nuclear weapons. *See* atomic bomb

Oppenheimer, J. Robert, 203
Ormes, Jackie, 35
overpopulation, 10, 55
Overstory, The (Powers), 25, 27, 71, 218, 238, 243

Pacific Northwest, 24, 71, 109, 214–55, 272n32
Paris Agreement (2015), 11, 99, 251
"People Start Pollution, People Can Stop It" (PSA, a.k.a. "Crying Indian"), 27, 261n16
Peeters, Benoît, 46, 84
plastic pollution, 23, 28, 32, 219, 223, 252, 266n56
Pope Francis (Jorge Mario Bergoglio), 12
Porcellino, John, 71–72, 265n47
posthumanism, 73, 156, 159, 181, 266n50
Puma Blues, The, 13, 16–17, 37–38, 43, 55, 57, 76, 88–89, 95, 185–213, 259n3, 280nn3–6, 281nn14–15, 281n17, 282nn26–29,

282nn31–33, 283nn42–43, 284nn47–53, 284n55, 284nn57–58, 285nn59–61, 285nn64–66. *See also* Murphy, Stephen; Zulli, Michael
Pyle, Robert Michael, 217, 221, 272n32

Quicksilver (Pietro Maximoff), 3–4, 8

Reagan, Ronald, 4, 196, 198, 258n25
Rifas, Leonard, 55, 121, 254–55
Robinson, Kim Stanley, 12, 25, 95, 269n25
Romanticism, 11, 38, 43, 45, 87–88, 141, 168, 170, 190, 208, 258n18

Sacco, Joe, 36, 252–54, 270n35
sacrifice zones, 108, 270n35
Sagan, Carl, 23
Santa Barbara oil spill (1969), 162–64, 180, 276nn1–2, 276n4, 277n7
sasquatch. *See* Bigfoot
Seattle, WA, 214–20, 222–24, 226–27, 234, 237–40, 241, 244–45, 248, 254, 285n1, 286n5, 287n29, 288n33, 288n39, 289n44
Seeathl (a.k.a. Si'ahl, Duwamish/Suquamish chief), 216, 234, 237, 240, 287n30
Seymour, Nicole, 26, 136–37, 273n44
Shanna the She Devil (Shanna O'Hara), 100, 102–3, 107–8
Silver Surfer (Norrin Radd), 41–43, 54–55
sixth mass extinction, 9–10, 12, 33, 60, 80, 116, 156
slow violence, 7, 108
solastalgia, 31, 56, 73, 88, 106, 189, 245
Soprano, Tony, 29, 99
Soviet Union, 66, 78, 275n26. *See also* Cold War
Spahr, Juliana, 27, 197–98
Stern, Roger, 56, 58–60, 103–8, 168, 269n33
Stoermer, Eugene, 10, 257n13
Strongbow, Jon, 238–44, 246, 254, 288nn32–38
sublime, 23–24, 64, 72, 82, 146, 165, 175–76, 210, 265n46, 277n9
superhero, 3–9, 39, 41–46, 55–68, 76, 96–109, 159–84, 262n32, 265nn35–36, 265n38, 265n46, 266n55, 267n61, 267n64, 269nn31–32, 270nn37–38, 273n1, 274n8, 282n29, 285n63
Superman (Kal-El/Clark Kent), 56–60, 66–68, 98, 265nn35–36, 266n58, 284n52
Szép, Eszter, 35–39, 85–86, 269n17

Thunberg, Greta, 12, 27, 109, 258n20, 261n17, 270n38
Tolstoy, Leo, 25
transcorporealism, 18, 26, 36–39, 66, 71
Trump, Donald, 99, 247, 252
Turner, Ron, 99–100, 116, 118
2021 heat dome, 219, 237, 244–50, 289nn41–45
Twin Peaks, 185, 214, 221–22

Ukraine, 99, 280n4
Uncanny X-Men, 3, 63–64, 103, 266n55, 269n31, 274n8

vibrant matter, 36, 181–83, 260n11, 280n39
von Trier, Lars, 23, 260n6

Wanzo, Rebecca, 137–38, 168, 273n37
Ware, Chris, 34, 49, 263n18, 266n48
Watcher (Uatu), 4
Weather (Offill), 27–29, 95, 99
Whyte, Kyle, 18, 210, 280n1
wildfire, 10, 24, 30, 44–46, 244, 246, 251–52

Zabu, 100, 102–3, 108
Zulli, Michael, 16–17, 38, 76, 88–89, 185–213, 281n8, 283nn41–43, 284n48, 285n61. *See also Puma Blues, The*

ABOUT THE AUTHOR

Photo by José Alaniz

JOSÉ ALANIZ, professor in the Department of Slavic Languages and Literatures and the Department of Cinema and Media Studies (adjunct) at the University of Washington, Seattle, has published three books: *Komiks: Comic Art in Russia* (University Press of Mississippi, 2010); *Death, Disability, and the Superhero: The Silver Age and Beyond* (University Press of Mississippi, 2014); and *Resurrection: Comics in Post-Soviet Russia* (Ohio State University Press, 2022). He has also coedited two essay collections, *Comics of the New Europe: Reflections and Intersections* (with Martha Kuhlman, Leuven University Press, 2020) and *Uncanny Bodies: Superhero Comics and Disability* (with Scott T. Smith, Penn State University Press, 2019). He formerly chaired the executive committee of the International Comic Arts Forum and was a founding board member of the Comics Studies Society. His comics/prose collections and other creative work include *The Phantom Zone and Other Stories* (Amatl Comix, 2020), *The Compleat Moscow Calling* (Amatl Comix, 2023), *Puro Pinche True Fictions* (FlowerSong Press, 2023), and *Tales of Bart: A Novel in Three Acts* (FlowerSong Press, 2025).

www.ingramcontent.com/pod-product-compliance
Lightning Source LLC
Chambersburg PA
CBHW021832220426

43663CB00005B/218